LARGE LANGUAGE MODELS:
From Fundamentals to Future Frontiers

SANJIV KUMAR JHA

ISBN
Paperback 979-8-89632-805-6
Hardcase 979-8-89744-604-9

TABLE OF CONTENTS

PREFACE

In the rapidly evolving landscape of artificial intelligence, Large Language Models (LLMs) stand as one of the most transformative technologies of our time. My journey into this fascinating field began with a desire to deeply understand these systems - not just their surface-level capabilities, but the foundational principles that drive their remarkable performance. This book is the culmination of that journey, where I've combined countless hours of research, hands-on experimentation, and real-world implementation with various clients to build a comprehensive understanding of LLMs from the ground up.

ORIGINS AND MOTIVATION

The inspiration for this book emerged from my own learning path, where I realised that while there is abundant information about LLMs scattered across academic papers, blog posts, and documentation, there was a need for a resource that bridges the gap between theory and practice. Working with numerous customers on LLM projects, I encountered recurring questions and challenges that demanded clear, intuitive explanations grounded in a deep understanding of the underlying principles.

What sets this book apart is its focus on building a strong intuitive foundation. While mathematical and technical depth is important, I believe that developing a solid grasp of the fundamental concepts is crucial for anyone working with these systems. Each chapter is structured around the questions I faced and the answers I discovered through a combination of research and practical experience, taking the reader on a journey from understanding the core principles to building and extending LLMs using advanced techniques like fine-tuning and Retrieval-Augmented Generation (RAG).

WHO THIS BOOK IS FOR

This book is written for a diverse readership:
- Students seeking to understand LLMs from first principles
- Practitioners looking to implement LLM-based solutions
- Professionals wanting to grasp the potential and limitations of this technology
- Anyone curious about how these powerful AI systems work

Importantly, I've designed this book to be accessible. While prior exposure to deep learning and machine learning is helpful, it's not essential. I've included a primer chapter that covers necessary background concepts. Similarly, while the book contains Python code examples to reinforce concepts, coding expertise is not a prerequisite for understanding the material.

WHAT YOU'LL LEARN

By reading this book, you will:
- Develop a deep understanding of the mathematical foundations and algorithmic principles that underpin LLMs
- Learn how to build and train LLMs from scratch, using techniques like embedding, attention, and neural network optimization
- Master practical skills for fine-tuning and extending LLMs for specific tasks and applications
- Explore advanced concepts like Retrieval-Augmented Generation and autonomous LLM Agents
- Gain insights into the ethical considerations and best practices for responsible LLM development
- Develop an intuitive grasp of how these systems work and how to effectively leverage them

BOOK ORGANIZATION AND FEATURES

The book progresses logically from foundations to advanced applications, with each chapter building upon the previous ones. However, the chapters are also designed to be somewhat self-contained, allowing readers to focus on specific areas of interest.

Throughout the book, you'll find several key features to enhance your learning experience:
- **Discussion**: At the end of each chapter, you'll find a discussion section that summarizes the key takeaways and links them to the broader themes of the book. These discussions are designed to deepen your understanding and help you connect the concepts across different chapters.
- **Key Takeaways**: Each chapter concludes with a concise list of the most important lessons learned, providing you with a quick reference to the core ideas.
- **Reflective Prompts**: Scattered throughout the book, you'll encounter thought-provoking prompts that encourage you to reflect on the material and apply it to real-world scenarios. These prompts are aimed at helping you develop a more intuitive and practical grasp of the concepts.

By leveraging these features, you can maximise your learning and effectively transition from understanding the underlying principles to building and extending your own LLM-powered solutions.

For feedback or comments, please contact the author directly at sanjiv_jha@yahoo.com

ACKNOWLEDGMENTS

This book would not have been possible without the support and contributions of many individuals. I am deeply grateful to my data science colleagues who have been constant sources of knowledge and inspiration. Special thanks to the many interns who, through their questions and enthusiasm, helped me develop clearer ways of explaining complex concepts.

I owe a debt of gratitude to my customers, whose real-world challenges and applications have been invaluable sources of learning and insight. Their practical needs and feedback have significantly shaped the content and approach of this book.

My sincere appreciation goes to the technical reviewers who provided invaluable feedback and helped ensure the accuracy and clarity of the content.

I am particularly thankful to my longtime friend Sanjay Jha and my brothers Rajeev and Ranjeev, whose long hours of philosophical conversations and guidance sparked and nurtured my curiosity to deep dive into this fascinating field. Our discussions have profoundly influenced my approach to understanding and explaining complex technological concepts.

I want to express my gratitude to my management team at AWS Public Sector for supporting my curiosity and giving me the freedom to explore areas of interest and work at my own pace. Special thanks to my colleagues and managers who have been instrumental in my professional journey.

I wish to express my sincere gratitude to my father-in-law, Dr. Yogendra Pathak Viyogi, a retired scientist of the Department of Atomic Energy, Government of India, for being an inspiration in my journey of writing this book. His constant encouragement, valuable suggestions, detailed feedback, and diligent proofreading were instrumental in bringing this book to completion. Without his unwavering support, this book would not have been possible.

On a personal note, I want to express my deepest gratitude to my wife, Madhulika, and son, Pratulya, for their unwavering support and understanding during the long hours of writing and research. To my parents, Hit Narayan Jha and Premlata Jha, thank you for instilling in me the curiosity to explore and learn.

The views and opinions expressed in this book are my own and based on my personal experience and research. They do not reflect the official policy or position of any agency or organization I have worked with.

It is my sincere hope that this book serves as both a comprehensive guide and a practical reference for anyone interested in understanding and working with Large Language Models. The field is evolving rapidly, but the fundamental principles and intuitions presented here will remain valuable as the technology continues to advance.

I would like to express my heartfelt gratitude to everyone who played a role in bringing this book to life.

A special thanks to my Publishing Manager, Ms. Manvi Sharma, for her invaluable guidance and support throughout this journey. Her expertise and encouragement made the publishing process smooth and enjoyable.

I extend my sincere appreciation to Mr. Francis Bomban, whose brilliant cover design perfectly captures the the essence of this book, and to Satish Kumar, whose meticulous typesetting ensured a polished and professional presentation.

A big thank you to the entire Notion Press Team for their dedication and hard work in making this book a reality. Your efforts behind the scenes have been instrumental in turning my vision into a finished product, and I am truly grateful.

Finally, my deepest gratitude goes to my readers – your support and love for stories fuel my passionfor writing. This book is for you.

Sanjiv Kumar Jha
14 January 2025

THE MATHEMATICS AND ALGORITHMS BEHIND LARGE LANGUAGE MODELS

Reflective Prompt: The quick brown fox jumps over the lazy dog. What mathematical concept allows computers to process and understand human language in ways that traditional rule-based systems cannot?

INTRODUCTION

Rather than jumping directly into the concepts of Large Language Models (LLM), let's first understand the core mathematical principles and key algorithms that make these models possible.

As we explore these concepts, we'll start with fundamental representations in vector spaces, move to probabilistic frameworks, then build up to the transformations and optimization techniques that enable learning. Finally, we'll see how these mathematical foundations combine in modern language model algorithms.

After studying this chapter, you should be able to:

- Understand how words are represented in high-dimensional spaces
- Explain the role of probability in language modelling
- Describe how optimization enables learning in neural networks
- Connect mathematical principles to practical algorithms

VECTOR SPACES AND DIMENSIONALITY

Understanding Vector Spaces

A vector space is a mathematical structure where objects (vectors) can be added together and multiplied by numbers (scalars). Think of it as a space where every point has both magnitude and direction. In two dimensions, we can easily visualize this on a graph. In three dimensions, we can still visualize it in physical space, but the real magic happens when we move beyond three dimensions. While we can no longer visualize these spaces, their mathematical properties remain consistent. A 100-dimensional vector space follows the same rules as a 2D space - we can still add vectors, multiply by scalars, and measure distances. The only difference is that each point needs 100 coordinates to be specified.

The behaviour of high-dimensional spaces often defies our intuition:
- Most points tend to be far apart from each other
- Random vectors are likely to be almost perpendicular
- The volume of a sphere relative to its circumscribing cube becomes vanishingly small

In language models, words are represented as vectors in high-dimensional spaces (often 256 to 1024 dimensions). This allows:
- Similar words to be "close" to each other
- Relationships between words to be captured as vector operations
- Complex meaning to be encoded across many dimensions

Having established how we represent words in high-dimensional spaces, we now turn to the question of how to manipulate these representations in meaningful ways.

These vector operations form the basis for both the probability distributions we'll explore next and the transformations we'll use to manipulate them.

PROBABILITY AND INFORMATION THEORY

Understanding Probability Distributions

Building upon our exploration of vector spaces, we now turn to probability theory, which provides the mathematical framework for understanding uncertainty and making predictions in language models. Just as words exist in high-dimensional vector spaces, their relationships and occurrences follow probabilistic patterns that we can model mathematically.

Probability distributions are mathematical functions that describe the likelihood of different outcomes in a random process. In the context of language models, they are used to represent the probability of a particular word or sequence of words occurring. These distributions can be thought of as existing in the same high-dimensional space as our word vectors, where each dimension contributes to the overall probability of a sequence.

Maximum Likelihood Estimation

At its core, language modelling is an exercise in probability estimation. Given a sequence of words $(w_1, w_2, ..., w_n)$, we aim to model the probability:

$P(w_n \mid w_1, w_2, ..., w_{n-1})$

This conditional probability represents the likelihood of the next word given all previous words. Maximum Likelihood Estimation (MLE) provides a principled approach to learning these probabilities from data. The objective is to find model parameters θ that maximise:

$$L(\theta) = \prod P(w_i \mid w_1, ..., w_{i-1}, \theta)$$

In practice, we work with the log-likelihood to avoid numerical underflow and to convert the product into a sum:

$$\log L(\theta) = \sum \log P(w_i \mid w_1, ..., w_{i-1}\}; \theta)$$

Entropy and Cross-Entropy

Information theory provides crucial metrics for measuring the uncertainty and predictive power of our models. The entropy H of a probability distribution P is defined as:

$$H(P) = -\sum P(x) \log P(x)$$

This measures the average uncertainty in the distribution. For language models, lower entropy indicates more confident predictions. Cross-entropy, which we'll explore more deeply in the optimization section, measures the difference between our model's predictions and the true distribution:

$$H(P,Q) = -\sum P(x) \log Q(x)$$

where P is the true distribution and Q is our model's distribution. This forms the basis for our loss function during training.

Temperature Sampling

When generating text, we can control the randomness of our model's outputs through temperature sampling. The temperature, T, modifies the probability distribution:

$$P(w_i \mid \text{context}, T) = \text{softmax}(\text{logits}/T)$$

where:
- $T > 1$ increases randomness and diversity
- $T < 1$ makes the distribution more peaked and deterministic
- $T = 1$ uses the raw model probabilities

This connects directly to the attention mechanisms we'll explore later, where similar scaling factors play a crucial role.

Autoregressive Models and Conditional Probability

Modern language models are fundamentally autoregressive, meaning they generate text one token at a time, conditioning each prediction on all previous tokens. This builds on the chain rule of probability:

$$P(w_1, w_2, ..., w_n) = P(w_1) \times P(w_2|w_1) \times ... \times P(w_n|w_1, ..., w_{n-1})$$

This decomposition enables models to capture complex dependencies while maintaining a tractable optimization problem. The autoregressive nature of these models influences both their architecture and training methodology, which we'll explore in the subsequent sections on linear transformations and optimization.

Connection to Neural Architectures

The probabilistic framework directly influences how we structure neural networks for language modelling. The output layer typically uses a softmax function to convert network activations into a proper probability distribution:

$$P(w_i|\text{context}) = \text{softmax}(z)_i = \exp(z_i)/\textstyle\sum \exp(z_j)$$

where z represents the pre-softmax logits produced by the network. This connects our probabilistic framework with the linear transformations and optimization techniques we'll explore next.

Practical Considerations

Several practical challenges arise when implementing probabilistic language models:
- Vocabulary size affects the dimensionality of the probability distribution
- Rare words can lead to sparse probability estimates
- Long-range dependencies make probability estimation challenging
- The trade-off between model confidence and generation diversity

These challenges motivate many of the architectural innovations we'll discuss in subsequent sections, particularly attention mechanisms and sophisticated sampling strategies.

As we move forward to explore linear transformations and optimization techniques, keep in mind that all these operations ultimately serve to model and manipulate these probability distributions. The transformations we'll study provide the tools to map between vector spaces while preserving probabilistic interpretations, and our optimization objectives will be grounded in probabilistic principles.

LINEAR TRANSFORMATIONS AND MATRICES

The Mathematics of Transformations

Linear transformations are functions that preserve vector addition and scalar multiplication. They can be represented by matrices, which are rectangular arrays of numbers. When we multiply a matrix by a vector, we transform that vector in a predictable way.

Key properties of linear transformations:
1. They preserve straight lines
2. The origin stays fixed
3. Parallel lines remain parallel
4. Scaling is proportional

These properties make linear transformations particularly useful because they are:
- Computationally efficient
- Mathematically well-understood
- Composable (can be chained together)

The efficiency and composability of linear transformations underpin modern language processing architectures. Their ability to preserve important geometric relationships while transforming data has proven invaluable in developing scalable attention mechanisms and deep neural architectures. The mathematical elegance of these transformations enables the processing of vast amounts of text while maintaining computational feasibility. The composability of these transformations is particularly crucial for deep neural networks, where we stack multiple layers of transformations to learn increasingly complex patterns.

While static transformations are powerful, language models need to learn from data. This is where calculus and optimization enter the picture.

CALCULUS IN MULTIPLE DIMENSIONS

Understanding Gradients and Optimization

The gradient is a vector that points in the direction of the steepest increase of a function. In multiple dimensions, it is composed of partial derivatives with respect to each variable:

Consider a function $f(x_1, x_2,..., x_n)$. Its gradient is: $\nabla f = (\partial f/\partial x_1, \partial f/\partial x_2,..., \partial f/\partial x_n)$

This vector has remarkable properties:
- It's perpendicular to level sets of the function
- Its magnitude indicates how steep the function is
- Following it in the negative direction leads to local minima

These properties make gradients incredibly useful for optimization. In the context of machine learning, we often have a cost function that we want to minimise. This could be a measure of how much our model's predictions differ from the true values. By computing the gradient of this cost function with respect to the model's parameters, we can determine the direction in which we should adjust these parameters to reduce the cost.

This is where gradient descent comes in. It's an iterative optimization algorithm that uses the gradient to update the model's parameters in the direction that minimizes the cost function. At each step, the parameters are updated by taking a step in the negative direction of the gradient, scaled by a learning rate hyperparameter.

Mathematically, if θ represents our model's parameters and $J(\theta)$ is our cost function, the update rule for gradient descent is:

$$\theta := \theta - \alpha \, \nabla J(\theta);$$

where α is the learning rate.

The learning rate determines the size of the steps we take in the negative gradient direction. If it's too small, learning will be slow. If it's too large, we might overshoot the minimum and even diverge.

By repeatedly taking these gradient steps, our model's parameters gradually converge towards values that minimise the cost function. This is how neural networks learn: by starting with random parameters and iteratively adjusting them based on the gradients of the prediction error with respect to these parameters.

The elegance of this approach lies in how it translates the abstract mathematical concept of a gradient into a practical tool for learning. By providing a principled way to adjust complex models with millions or billions of parameters, gradient descent and backpropagation have become the workhorses of modern deep learning.

KEY ALGORITHMS IN LANGUAGE MODELS

Backpropagation and Gradient Descent

Backpropagation is the fundamental algorithm that enables neural networks to learn. It works by computing the gradient of the loss function with respect to each weight in the network and then updating the weights in the direction that minimises the loss.

Gradient descent is the optimization algorithm that uses these gradients to update the weights. There are several variants:

- Batch gradient descent: Computes gradients for the entire dataset before each update
- Stochastic gradient descent (SGD): Updates weights based on gradients from individual examples
- Mini-batch gradient descent: A compromise between batch and SGD, using small subsets of data for each update

Attention Mechanisms

Attention is a key innovation that allows language models to selectively focus on different parts of the input when making predictions. The basic idea is to compute a weighted sum of the input representations, where the weights are determined by a learned attention function.

The most common form of attention is the scaled dot product attention used in the Transformer architecture:

$$\text{Attention}(Q, K, V) = \text{softmax}(QK^T / \sqrt{d\_k})V$$

Where Q, K, and V are learned matrices that map the input to a query, key, and value representation.

Attention mechanisms combine the linear transformations we discussed earlier with the probabilistic weighting schemes to create a powerful architecture for processing sequences.

Beam Search and Sampling Methods

For generating text from a trained model, we need algorithms to select the most likely or most appropriate next word based on the model's predictions. Two common approaches are:

- Beam search: Keeps track of the k most likely sequences at each step, and expands them to generate the next word
- Sampling methods (e.g., top-k sampling, nucleus sampling): Randomly select the next word based on the model's predicted probabilities, often with some constraints to promote diversity or coherence

These algorithms form the computational backbone of modern language models. Backpropagation and gradient descent enable these models to learn from vast amounts of data. Attention mechanisms allow them to handle long-range dependencies and focus on relevant information, while search and sampling methods provide ways to generate coherent and diverse text.

As the field progresses, we can expect to see continued innovation in these core algorithms, leading to more efficient training, more powerful architectures, and more capable language models.

DISCUSSION

The mathematics and algorithms we've explored aren't merely theoretical constructs - they represent the fundamental language through which modern AI systems understand and process information. When we observe a language model making surprisingly accurate predictions or exhibiting unexpected capabilities, we can often trace these behaviours back to the **mathematical** properties we've discussed. Some limitations we encounter are practical - computational resources, training data availability, or implementation challenges. But others are fundamental, arising from the mathematical properties themselves. Understanding this distinction is crucial because it guides where we should focus our innovation efforts.

The elegance of these systems lies not just in their mathematical foundations, but in how these foundations enable emergence - the appearance of capabilities that weren't explicitly programmed but arise from the interaction of simpler principles. This emergence hints at deeper patterns in how information can be represented and manipulated, a theme that will become particularly apparent as we explore embeddings in a subsequent chapter. As we'll see, embeddings represent not just a practical technique for processing language, but a profound insight into how meaning itself can be represented and manipulated in computational systems.

As the field of natural language processing continues its rapid evolution, maintaining this connection between fundamental principles and practical applications becomes increasingly crucial. Each new architecture or technique isn't just an engineering solution - it's an expression of these underlying mathematical principles in a new form. By understanding both the mathematics and its manifestation in real systems, we position ourselves to contribute meaningfully to the next generation of advances in language modelling and artificial intelligence.

KEY TAKEAWAYS:

1. Vector spaces and embeddings provide the foundation for representing words and meanings in high-dimensional spaces.
2. Probability distributions and maximum likelihood estimation are crucial for language modelling.
3. Backpropagation and gradient descent form the core optimisation algorithms for training LLMs.

REFLECTIVE PROMPTS:

1. How do the mathematical representations explored in this chapter enable LLMs to process and understand human language in ways that traditional rule-based systems cannot?

2. What are the potential limitations of modelling language purely through statistical patterns and probability distributions? How might these limitations be addressed in future developments?
3. What ethical considerations arise from the heavy reliance on optimization techniques like gradient descent when training large-scale AI systems?

After a brief exposition of the biological neural network of the human brain in Chapter 2, we move forward to Chapter 3, where we'll explore how these mathematical foundations enable the creation of rich, dense vector representations that capture semantic meaning in language data.

THE BRAIN AND THE MACHINE: UNDERSTANDING LARGE LANGUAGE MODELS THROUGH BIOLOGY

Reflective Prompt: A human brain analyses language using billions of neurons yet consumes less power than a light bulb, while Large Language Models require massive computing resources to achieve similar capabilities. What can the elegant design of biological neural networks teach us about building more efficient and capable artificial intelligence systems?

BACKGROUND

The remarkable efficiency of the human brain stands as both an inspiration and a challenge to artificial intelligence. Each of us carries within our skulls a neural network of staggering complexity – approximately 86 billion neurons interconnected by trillions of synapses – that processes language with an elegance and efficiency that our most advanced artificial systems can only aspire to match. This biological supercomputer, consuming mere watts of power, performs feats of language understanding and generation that require massive data centres when replicated by Large Language Models.

Understanding this biological blueprint isn't just an academic exercise. As we strive to develop more sophisticated artificial intelligence, the brain's architecture offers crucial insights into how nature solved the fundamental challenges of language processing. How does a collection of neurons, communicating through both electrical and chemical signals, give rise to understanding? What principles of neural organization enable such remarkable efficiency? And perhaps most importantly, what lessons can we extract from this biological machinery to inform the next generation of artificial intelligence?

In this chapter, we'll explore the fundamental building blocks of biological intelligence, from individual neurons to complex neural networks, drawing parallels with their artificial counterparts. By understanding how nature accomplishes so much with so little, we can better appreciate both the achievements and limitations of current Large Language Models while illuminating paths towards more efficient and capable artificial systems.

THE BASIC BUILDING BLOCK: A SINGLE NEURON'S STORY

Before we can understand how billions of neurons work together to process language, we need to appreciate the sophistication of a single neuron. Imagine a neuron as a tiny but incredibly sophisticated information processing unit. Unlike the simple on-off switches in your computer, a biological neuron is more like a miniature chemical computer, making complex decisions about when and how to transmit information.

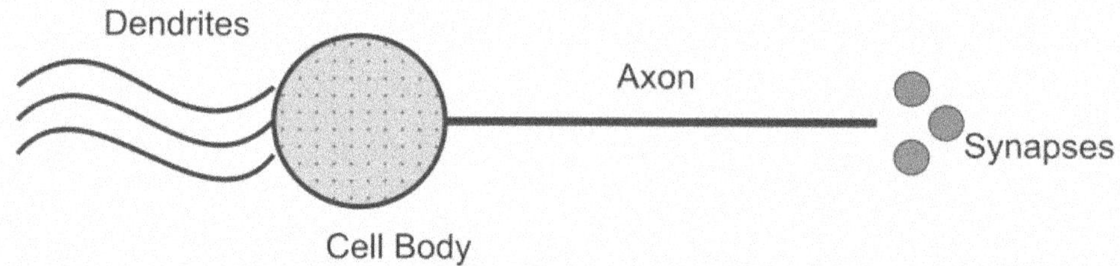

Fig. 2.1: A branching network of dendrites receives signals that travel to the cell body, then down a long axon to synaptic terminals connecting to other neurons.

Each neuron has three main parts that work together in a carefully choreographed dance, as illustrated in Fig.2.1. First are the dendrites - branching structures that act like cellular antennas, collecting signals from thousands of other neurons. These signals travel to the cell body, or soma, where they're integrated and processed in ways we're still working to fully understand. If the combined signals reach a certain threshold, the neuron fires, sending an electrical pulse racing down its axon - a long, cable-like extension that can stretch for remarkable distances.

But the real magic happens at the synapses - specialized junctions where neurons communicate with their neighbours. When an electrical signal reaches a synapse, it triggers the release of chemical messengers called neurotransmitters. These molecules cross a tiny gap to influence the receiving neuron, creating a form of communication that's both electrical and chemical. This hybrid signalling system allows for remarkable flexibility and efficiency in information processing.

Understanding how a single neuron operates helps us appreciate both the similarities and differences with artificial neural networks. While artificial neurons in our Large Language Models perform a rough approximation of this biological process - taking inputs, weighing them, and producing an output - they're vastly simplified versions of their biological counterparts. A biological neuron might receive input from thousands of other neurons, release different types of neurotransmitters that have varying effects, and adapt its behaviour based on past activity - capabilities we're only beginning to incorporate into artificial systems.

The sophistication of a single neuron raises an intriguing question: if one neuron is this complex, what emerges when billions of them work together? This brings us to our next exploration - how neurons organise themselves into the networks that make language understanding possible.

BUILDING NEURAL NETWORKS: FROM ONE TO MANY

When neurons come together in networks, something remarkable happens. Just as a single musician can play a melody, but an orchestra can create a symphony, networks of neurons can process information in ways far more sophisticated than any single neuron could manage. In your brain, these networks form through trillions of connections, each refined through experience and learning.

Consider what happens when you read the word "apple." Instantly, your brain activates patterns of neurons that encode not just the word itself, but its meaning, memories of apples you've eaten, their taste, smell, and even associated concepts like pies or computers. This rich web of meaning emerges from the coordinated activity of neural networks distributed throughout your brain.

LANGUAGE IN THE BRAIN: A NETWORK OF NETWORKS

When it comes to language processing, your brain employs multiple specialised networks working in concert. The most famous of these are Broca's area, primarily involved in speech production, and Wernicke's area, crucial for language comprehension. But these are just part of a much larger language network that includes regions for visual word recognition, sound processing, and meaning integration.

What's particularly fascinating is how these networks achieve their results. Unlike a computer processing words one at a time, your brain processes language in parallel, with multiple possible interpretations and meanings being evaluated simultaneously. When you hear an ambiguous word like "bank," your brain activates networks associated with both financial institutions and river edges, quickly using context to determine the relevant meaning.

MEMORY AND LEARNING: THE PLASTIC BRAIN

Perhaps the most remarkable feature of biological neural networks is their ability to learn and adapt. When you learn something new, the physical structure of your brain actually changes. Connections between neurons can strengthen or weaken, and entirely new connections can form. Scientists call this capability "neuroplasticity," and it's fundamental to how our brains adapt to new information and experiences.

This biological learning process differs significantly from how Large Language Models learn. While LLMs typically learn through massive one time training sessions, your brain learns continuously, constantly adjusting its neural connections based on experience. Every conversation you have, every book you read, slightly modifies your brain's neural networks.

THE EFFICIENCY PUZZLE: NATURE'S SOLUTIONS

The human brain's efficiency in processing language presents one of the most intriguing puzzles in neuroscience and AI development. How does a network of relatively slow components (neurons fire hundreds of times per second, while computer processors operate at billions of cycles per second) achieve such remarkable performance? The answer lies in several key principles:

1. Massive Parallelism: Your brain processes information through millions of parallel pathways simultaneously.
2. Sparse Activation: At any given moment, only a small percentage of neurons are actively firing, conserving energy while maintaining processing capacity.
3. Local Learning Rules: Neurons adjust their connections based on local information, without needing centralised control.
4. Chemical Signalling: The brain's use of neurotransmitters allows for rich, nuanced communication between neurons that goes beyond simple binary signalling.

BRIDGING BIOLOGY AND TECHNOLOGY

Understanding how biological neural networks process language has profoundly influenced the development of artificial neural networks and Large Language Models. Many key innovations in AI, from parallel processing to attention mechanisms, draw inspiration from biological principles. However, significant differences remain:

While artificial neural networks typically use uniform, simplified neurons, biological networks employ diverse types of neurons with varying properties. Biological networks also integrate information across multiple timescales and modalities in ways we're still working to replicate in artificial systems.

LOOKING FORWARD: BIO-INSPIRED INNOVATION

As we continue to develop more sophisticated AI systems, the brain's architecture offers valuable insights for future innovations. Emerging technologies like neuromorphic computing attempt to more closely mimic biological neural networks, while new training approaches seek to incorporate more brain-like learning mechanisms.

DISCUSSION

The intersection between biological neural networks and artificial intelligence reveals fascinating insights about how we process and understand language. Throughout this chapter, we've seen how nature's solution to intelligence - the human brain - both inspires and humbles our artificial approaches. While LLMs can process language with remarkable capability, the biological efficiency of neural networks showcases the vast potential for improvement in our artificial systems.

What makes biological neural networks particularly intriguing is their position at the crossroads of efficiency and complexity. While previous chapters focused on mathematical foundations and subsequent chapters will explore sophisticated architectures, this biological perspective demonstrates how nature achieves remarkable results through an elegant combination of parallel processing, chemical signalling, and local learning rules. Expert neuroscientists and AI researchers consistently emphasise studying biological systems not just for inspiration but for fundamental insights into efficient computation and adaptation.

Looking ahead to embedding techniques and architectural choices, the principles we've observed in biological systems - from parallel processing to hierarchical organization - provide crucial context for understanding why certain approaches work well in artificial systems. The brain's ability to seamlessly integrate multiple levels of meaning while maintaining energy efficiency points toward promising directions for future AI development. Success in this domain will ultimately depend not just on scaling our current approaches but on incorporating more of the sophisticated mechanisms that make biological intelligence so remarkably effective.

KEY TAKEAWAYS:

1. The human brain's neural architecture provides crucial insights for artificial neural networks while highlighting significant differences in implementation and efficiency.
2. Biological neural networks achieve sophisticated language processing through a combination of parallel computation, chemical signalling, and continuous adaptation.
3. The efficiency gap between biological and artificial systems suggests important directions for improving LLM architectures and training approaches.

REFLECTIVE PROMPTS:

1. The brain processes language with remarkable efficiency using mechanisms fundamentally different from those in LLMs. How might understanding these differences influence the development of more efficient AI architectures?
2. As LLMs continue to scale, what lessons from biological neural networks might become increasingly relevant for addressing challenges of efficiency and adaptability?
3. The brain's ability to learn continuously and adapt from limited examples stands in stark contrast to current LLM training approaches. How might these biological insights inform the development of more flexible and efficient learning systems?

This biological perspective sets the stage for our exploration of embeddings and representations in the next chapter, where we'll see how artificial systems attempt to capture the sophisticated meaning representations that come so naturally to biological neural networks.

THE ART AND SCIENCE OF EMBEDDINGS: FROM SYMBOLS TO MEANING

Reflective Prompt: Imagine a book with pages of geometric shapes. How do the properties of these shapes reflect the way humans understand and reason about language?

INTRODUCTION: THE QUEST TO REPRESENT KNOWLEDGE

The challenge of representing knowledge has been at the heart of artificial intelligence since its inception. How do we take the rich, nuanced understanding that humans possess and encode it in a way that machines can process? This fundamental question has driven decades of research, leading us from early symbolic approaches to the sophisticated embedding techniques that power today's Large Language Models.

Consider how humans understand the concept of a "cup." We know it's a container that holds liquid, typically has a handle, comes in various materials, and serves multiple purposes. We understand its relationship to other objects like mugs, glasses, and bowls. We grasp both its physical attributes and its social context - from formal tea ceremonies to casual coffee breaks. This rich, multifaceted understanding poses a formidable challenge for artificial intelligence: how do we represent such knowledge computationally?

Early AI researchers approached this challenge through symbolic representation, creating explicit rules and relationships. A cup might be defined through predicates and attributes in a formal logic system:

$$Cup(x) \rightarrow Container(x) \wedge HasHandle(x) \wedge HoldsLiquid(x)$$

While elegant in their precision, these symbolic approaches faced fundamental limitations. They struggled with ambiguity, required extensive manual encoding of knowledge, and couldn't easily capture the fluid, contextual nature of meaning. The symbol grounding problem, articulated by Stevan Harnad, highlighted a crucial issue: how do we connect abstract symbols to their real-world meanings?

Embeddings emerged as a revolutionary solution to these challenges. Instead of explicitly encoding relationships through rules and symbols, embeddings represent concepts as points in a continuous vector space, where relationships emerge from patterns in data. This approach bridges the gap between symbolic and sub-symbolic processing, offering a powerful framework for representing knowledge that scales to the demands of modern AI systems.

Consider how current Large Language Models like GPT-4 process and understand text. At their core, these models don't manipulate explicit symbols or rules. Instead, they operate on dense vector representations - embeddings - that capture meaning through geometric relationships in high-dimensional spaces. A simple word like "cup" isn't represented by a set of logical predicates, but by a vector whose position and relationships to other vectors encode its various meanings, associations, and uses.

The impact of this shift cannot be overstated. Embeddings have enabled:

- Efficient processing of massive text corpora
- Capture of nuanced semantic relationships
- Emergence of zero-shot and few-shot learning capabilities
- Scalable architecture for billion-parameter models
- Natural handling of ambiguity and context.

This transition from symbolic to embedding-based representations wasn't sudden – it emerged through decades of research and experimentation. Let's trace this evolution to understand how we arrived at today's sophisticated embedding approaches.

The Evolution of Knowledge Representation

Symbolic Approaches and Their Limitations

The journey of knowledge representation in AI begins with symbolic approaches. In the 1960s and 1970s, researchers developed sophisticated frameworks for encoding knowledge:

```
Expert Systems relied on explicit rules and facts.
IF (IsContainer(x) AND HasHandle(x) AND Volume(x) < 500ml)
THEN IsCup(x)
```

Semantic networks represent knowledge as graphs of concepts and relationships:

```
Cup --ISA--> Container
Cup --HAS--> Handle
Cup --USED_FOR--> Drinking
```

Frames and Scripts provided structured templates for common situations and objects:

```
Frame: Cup
Slots:
Material: [ceramic, glass, plastic]
Function: [drinking, measuring]
Parts: [base, body, handle]
```

These approaches excelled at encoding explicit, rule-based knowledge but struggled with:

- Scalability: Manual encoding of knowledge became impractical
- Flexibility: Rigid structures couldn't handle novel situations
- Learning: Systems couldn't easily acquire new knowledge
- Uncertainty: Binary logic poorly represented real-world ambiguity

While symbolic approaches provided a clear framework for representing knowledge, their limitations prompted researchers to explore statistical methods that could learn from data directly.

The Statistical Revolution

The limitations of symbolic approaches led to a fundamental shift toward statistical methods. This transition began with simple but powerful ideas:

One-hot encoding represented words as sparse vectors where each dimension corresponded to a vocabulary entry. For a vocabulary of size V, each word was a vector of length V with a single 1 and (V-1) zeros. While simple, this approach highlighted a crucial insight: words could be represented as vectors, enabling mathematical operations on language.

Distributional semantics, embodied in Firth's famous quote "You shall know a word by the company it keeps," suggested that meaning could be derived from statistical patterns of word co-occurrence. This led to more sophisticated approaches like TF-IDF (Term Frequency-Inverse Document Frequency):

TF-IDF(w,d) = frequency(w,d) × log(N/document_frequency(w))
Where:
frequency(w,d) counts word occurrences in a document
N is the total number of documents
document_frequency(w) counts documents containing the word

The Neural Revolution: Distributed Representations

The transition from statistical counting to neural approaches marked a fundamental shift in how we represent meaning. Rather than explicitly tracking co-occurrences or defining symbolic relationships, neural approaches learn representations through exposure to data. This shift embodies a profound insight: meaning emerges from patterns of usage rather than explicit definition.

The concept of distributed representations, pioneered by researchers like Hinton and Bengio, suggests that information should be encoded across multiple neurons, with each concept represented by a pattern of activations rather than a single unit. This approach offers several key advantages:

1. Efficiency: n binary neurons can represent 2^n different concepts
2. Generalisation: Similar concepts naturally share components of their representations
3. Robustness: Degradation is graceful rather than catastrophic
4. Discovery: The system can learn optimal representations from data

This theoretical foundation set the stage for modern embedding techniques, where meaning is distributed across hundreds or thousands of dimensions.

Modern Embedding Approaches

While statistical approaches marked a significant advance, the real breakthrough came with neural embedding methods. These approaches, starting with Word2Vec, would fundamentally change how we represent and process language revolution.

Word2Vec: The Prediction Paradigm

The neural revolution in embeddings began with a deceptively simple insight: we could learn word representations by predicting word contexts. This idea found its most influential expression in Word2Vec.

Word2Vec's elegance lies in how it transforms the challenge of learning word meanings into a prediction task. The model comes in two architectural variants: Skip-gram and Continuous Bag of

Words (CBOW). While these approaches might appear different at first glance, they're actually two sides of the same coin, each offering distinct advantages.

Skip-gram: Predicting Context from Target

The Skip-gram architecture takes a target word and tries to predict its surrounding context words. Imagine reading a text where we occasionally cover up all words except one and ask the model to guess what words might appear nearby.

Consider the sentence: "The quick brown fox jumps over the lazy dog."

If we focus on the word "fox", the Skip-gram model would try to predict nearby words within a certain window size (typically 5-10 words). For a window size of 2, it would learn to predict:

- Previous words: "quick", "brown"
- Following words: "jumps", "over"

CBOW: Predicting Target from Context

CBOW (Continuous Bag of Words) inverts this relationship. Instead of predicting context from a target word, it predicts a target word from its context. Using the same sentence, if "fox" is our target, CBOW would take "quick", "brown", "jumps", and "over" as input and try to predict "fox".

The beauty of this approach lies in its simplicity and effectiveness. The learned embeddings exhibit remarkable properties:

1. Semantic Relationships: Similar words cluster together
2. Analogical Relationships: Vector arithmetic works meaningfully
   - king - man + woman $\approx$ queen
   - paris - france + italy $\approx$ rome
3. Semantic Composition: Meanings combine naturally
   - "computer" + "science" captures the meaning of the compound

Global Statistical Information: GloVe

While Word2Vec learns from local context windows, GloVe (Global Vectors for Word Representation) combines the insights of prediction-based methods with global matrix factorisation approaches. GloVe starts with the observation that ratios of co-occurrence probabilities can encode meaning:

For words i, j, and k, the ratio $P(k|i)/P(k|j)$ captures how relevant word k is to the relationship between words i and j. For example, when considering the words "ice" and "steam", the ratio will be high for context words like "solid" (associated with ice) and low for words like "gas" (associated with steam).

The Mathematics of Meaning

Modern embedding approaches reveal something profound: meaning can be encoded in the geometry of a continuous vector space. This geometric nature of embeddings enables several powerful operations:

1. Similarity Measurement: The cosine similarity between vectors captures semantic similarity:
   $$sim(a,b) = (a \cdot b)/(\|a\| \cdot \|b\|)$$

2. Analogical Reasoning: Vector arithmetic enables analogical reasoning: v("king") - v("man") + v("woman") ≈ v("queen")

3. Compositionality: Phrase meanings can be approximated by combining word vectors: v("artificial") + v("intelligence") ≈ v("AI")

The dimensionality of embedding spaces typically ranges from 100 to 1000, providing a rich space for encoding semantic relationships while remaining computationally tractable. This represents a sweet spot between expressiveness and efficiency:

- Too few dimensions: Unable to capture complex relationships
- Too many dimensions: Computational overhead and potential overfitting

Yet, despite these advances, static embeddings faced a fundamental limitation: they couldn't capture how word meanings shift with context. This challenge would spark the next major revolution in representation learning.

THE CONTEXTUAL REVOLUTION

The move from static to contextual embeddings represents one of the most significant paradigm shifts in Natural Language Processing (NLP), comparable to the earlier transition from symbolic to distributed representations.

From Static to Dynamic Representations

The transition from static to contextual embeddings represents one of the most significant advances in natural language processing. While Word2Vec and GloVe made tremendous strides in capturing word meanings, they faced a fundamental limitation: each word had exactly one embedding regardless of context. Consider the word "bank":

"I deposited money in the bank." "The river bank was muddy."

In Word2Vec or GloVe, "bank" would have a single embedding that attempts to capture both meanings simultaneously. This limitation becomes particularly apparent in technical or domain-specific language, where words often carry precise meanings based on context.

The Birth of Contextual Embeddings

The first major breakthrough in contextual embeddings came with ELMo (Embeddings from Language Models) in 2018. ELMo introduced a crucial insight: word representations should be a function of the entire input sentence. Rather than learning a single static embedding for each word, ELMo learns a model that generates embeddings based on the context in which a word appears.

ELMo accomplishes this through a two-layer bidirectional LSTM architecture:

1. Lower layer: Captures syntax and basic context
2. Higher layer: Captures semantic roles and meaning
3. Final embedding: Weighted combination of all layer representations

The result is that the same word can have different representations in different contexts.

The Transformer Revolution: BERT and Beyond

BERT (Bidirectional Encoder Representations from Transformers) took contextual embeddings to the next level by leveraging the transformer architecture's self-attention mechanism. Unlike ELMo's sequential processing, BERT processes entire sequences in parallel, allowing for richer contextual understanding.

BERT introduced several key innovations:
1. **Masked Language Modelling (MLM)**
    o Randomly mask 15% of tokens in the input
    o Train the model to predict masked tokens
    o Forces model to use bidirectional context
Input: "The [MASK] fox jumps over the [MASK] dog"
Task: Predict "quick" and "lazy"
2. **Next Sentence Prediction (NSP).**
    o Predict if two sentences follow each other
    o Helps models understand discourse relationships
    o Enables document-level understanding
3. **Subword Tokenization**
    o Uses WordPiece tokenization
    o Balances vocabulary size with coverage
    o Handles out-of-vocabulary words effectively

The attention mechanism in transformers enables each token to directly interact with every other token in the sequence. The attention weights at each layer reveal how the model combines contextual information.

Modern Contextual Architectures
The evolution of contextual embeddings has led to several powerful architectures:
1. **BERT Family**
    o RoBERTa: Optimised training process
    o DistilBERT: Compressed version for efficiency
    o ALBERT: Parameter-efficient variation
2. **GPT Series**
    o Unidirectional context (left-to-right)
    o Autoregressive language modelling
    o Increasingly large model scales
3. **T5 and Unified Approaches**
    o Text-to-text framework
    o Consistent pre-training objective
    o Flexible task adaptation

Each architecture brings unique innovations in how context is processed and represented:

```
BERT-style bidirectional context:
Position: The bank [MASK] my money
Context: ← "The bank" + "my money" →
Task: Predict "held"
GPT-style unidirectional context:
Position: The bank held
Context: ← "The bank held"
Task: Predict next word
```

BERT can look at both the words before the [MASK] ("The bank") AND after it ("my money") to understand that this is a financial context and predict that [MASK] should be "held" - unlike GPT which can only look at words that came before. This ability to use both left and right context is what makes BERT bidirectional, leading to better understanding of word meaning in context.

The power of these contextual architectures lies in their ability to:
1.   Disambiguate word meanings based on context
2.   Capture long-range dependencies
3.   Generate context-appropriate representations
4.   Transfer knowledge across tasks and domains

EMBEDDINGS IN LARGE LANGUAGE MODELS

Modern LLMs represent the culmination of embedding technology's evolution, synthesizing insights from static embeddings, contextual representations, and deep neural architectures. Their sophisticated processing pipeline demonstrates how theoretical advances in representation learning have been transformed into practical, powerful systems. Understanding this pipeline not only reveals how LLMs work, but also illuminates why they're so effective at processing language.

How Modern LLMs Process Words

When you input a sentence into a large language model like GPT-3 or BERT, the model needs to convert your words into a format it can understand. This process is more sophisticated than simple word embeddings, involving several crucial steps.

Step 1: Breaking Down Words

Let's examine how LLMs process language, moving from raw text to rich, contextual representations through three crucial steps.

```
First, the model breaks down words into smaller pieces. Take a simple example:
Input: "unbelievable"
Breaks down to: ["un", "believe", "able"]
```

This approach is clever because:
- Instead of needing to know every possible word, the model learns parts of words
- New or rare words can be understood from their pieces.
- Common patterns in language are captured efficiently

Consider another example:
Input: "I love machine learning"
Tokenized: ["I", "love", "machine", "learn", "ing"]

Each of these pieces then gets converted into a number (its token ID) that the model can process.

This tokenization process reflects a key insight from earlier embedding approaches: meaning can be constructed from smaller, compositional pieces.

Step 2: Creating Rich Representations

With tokens identified, the model must then transform these discrete symbols into rich, continuous representations that capture their meaning and relationships.

Once words are broken into pieces, each piece needs to be converted into a format that captures its meaning. Modern LLMs do this through multiple types of embeddings working together:

1. **Basic Meaning Embedding**
   o   Each token piece gets converted into a vector that represents its basic meaning
   o   For example, "cat" and "kitten" would have similar vectors because they're related concepts
2. **Position Information**
   o   The model needs to know where each word appears in the sentence
   o   Example: "Dog bites man" means something very different from "Man bites dog"
   o   This information gets added to the basic meaning embedding
3. **Combined Understanding**
   Final Understanding = Word Meaning + Position Information

This multifaceted representation approach combines the geometric intuitions of word embeddings with the contextual awareness of transformer architectures.

Step 3: Processing in Layers

The true power of LLM embeddings emerges in how they are processed through the model's layers, each adding depth to the model's understanding.

What makes LLMs special is how they process these embeddings through multiple layers:
1. **First Layer**
   o   Looks at basic word meanings
   o   Like understanding individual words in isolation
2. **Middle Layers**
   o   Start combining words to understand phrases
   o   Begin to grasp context and relationships
3. **Deep Layers**
   o   Develop a sophisticated understanding of the whole text
   o   Can handle complex meanings and subtle implications

This layered processing hierarchy mirrors our understanding of how language comprehension builds from basic word meanings to sophisticated contextual understanding.

THE FUTURE OF EMBEDDINGS

As powerful as current embedding approaches are, they point towards even more intriguing possibilities and challenges. Understanding these is crucial for grasping where the field is headed.

Current Challenges

The remarkable success of embeddings in modern AI systems has brought us to a fascinating crossroads, where three fundamental challenges demand our attention.

- The first is the question of scale. As our models grow increasingly powerful, like GPT-3 with its 175 billion parameters, traditional embedding approaches strain against the limits of computational feasibility. We're forced to confront difficult questions about efficiency and scalability that will shape the next generation of AI systems.

- The second challenge cuts to the heart of artificial intelligence: the grounding problem. While our current embedding techniques capture linguistic patterns with remarkable sophistication, they still struggle to bridge the gap between statistical patterns and genuine understanding. A model might learn perfect word associations without ever truly grasping what those words mean in the real-world. This disconnect between symbol and meaning echoes long-standing questions in cognitive science and AI.

- The third and perhaps most pressing issue is the challenge of bias. Our embedding systems, learning from human-generated text, have become mirrors reflecting societal biases. These reflections sometimes distort and amplify problematic associations, raising crucial questions about fairness and representation in AI systems that will increasingly shape our world.

Emerging Directions

The future of embeddings is taking shape at the intersection of multiple modalities. Researchers are pushing beyond pure text to create representations that unify understanding across different types of information. Imagine embeddings that capture not just the word "cup," but link it to visual appearances, physical properties, and functional uses. These multimodal approaches promise a richer, more grounded understanding of concepts.

Simultaneously, new architectural innovations are reimagining how we can make embeddings more computationally efficient. Rather than representing every concept with dense vectors, emerging approaches activate only relevant dimensions for each concept. These sparse, hierarchical representations might offer a path to scaling embedding systems while maintaining their expressive power.

The Bridge to General AI

What makes embeddings particularly fascinating is their role as a potential bridge to more general artificial intelligence. The way these systems learn to combine concepts, transfer knowledge between domains, and exhibit emergent capabilities at scale offers intriguing parallels to human cognition. As embedding systems grow more sophisticated, we're seeing hints of compositional reasoning and unexpected abilities that suggest we're just beginning to tap their potential.

DISCUSSION

The journey of embeddings from simple vector representations to sophisticated contextual systems reveals a profound truth about artificial intelligence: the representation of knowledge is just as crucial as the processing of it. The mathematical foundations we explored in Chapter 1 find their most elegant expression in how embeddings transform symbolic meaning into geometric relationships. This isn't merely a technical achievement - it's a fundamental breakthrough in how we can represent and manipulate meaning in computational systems.

What makes embeddings particularly fascinating is their role as a bridge between abstract mathematical concepts and practical implementation challenges. When we observe how contextual embeddings capture nuanced meanings of words, we're witnessing the convergence of theoretical elegance and engineering pragmatism. This convergence becomes even more critical when we consider the storage and computational challenges discussed in Chapter 4 – the way we represent meaning must not only be mathematically sound but also computationally efficient. The evolution from static to contextual embeddings demonstrates how theoretical advances in representation learning must be balanced against practical constraints of memory usage and computational resources.

As we'll explore in Chapter 5, these embedding representations form the foundational input layer for modern deep learning architectures. The success of transformer models and their attention mechanisms builds directly upon our ability to represent words and concepts in rich, high-dimensional spaces. The challenges we face - from grounding these representations in real-world understanding to addressing inherent biases - aren't just theoretical considerations but practical hurdles that influence architecture design, training strategies, and model optimization. The future of language models depends not just on scaling existing architectures, but on developing more sophisticated ways to represent, store, and manipulate the patterns that underlie human understanding.

KEY TAKEAWAYS:

1. Word embeddings map words to dense vector representations, enabling models to capture semantic relationships.
2. The evolution from static to contextual embeddings has revolutionized language understanding in LLMs.
3. Embedding spaces in neural networks creates powerful, learnable representations for processing language.

REFLECTIVE PROMPTS

1. How do the geometric properties of embedding spaces, such as similarity and analogy, reflect the way humans understand and reason about language? What are the implications of this connection for the development of more human-like AI systems?
2. As LLMs become more sophisticated in their ability to capture nuanced meaning through contextual embeddings, what new challenges might arise in terms of interpretability and transparency?

3. How might the continued evolution of embedding techniques impact the field of knowledge representation and reasoning in artificial intelligence?

Building on these insights into representation learning, in the next Chapter we will delve into the data structures and storage optimizations necessary to efficiently process and manipulate these embeddings at scale.

DATA STRUCTURES AND STORAGE OPTIMIZATION FOR LARGE LANGUAGE MODELS

Reflective Prompt: The model requires over 700 GB of memory to store its parameters. Explain how the immense scale of Large Language Models highlights the computational challenges in deploying these AI systems.

INTRODUCTION

Efficient data structures and storage techniques are crucial for the successful implementation and deployment of Large Language Models (LLMs). Given the vast number of parameters in these models, often in the billions, traditional storage methods and data structures can prove inefficient, leading to slow training times, high memory consumption, and suboptimal inference performance. This chapter explores the theoretical background and key concepts related to data structures and storage optimization, and how these concepts are applied in the context of LLMs.

Having explored the mathematical foundations and embedding representations in previous chapters, we now confront a critical challenge: how do we efficiently store and manipulate these complex mathematical structures? This question becomes particularly crucial as we scale to billions of parameters in modern language models.

THEORETICAL FOUNDATIONS

The efficient storage and manipulation of embeddings, which we explored in the previous chapter, require careful consideration of computational complexity and data structure design. Let's examine the theoretical tools that help us analyse and optimise these systems.

Big O Notation and Complexity Analysis

Big O notation is used to describe the performance or complexity of an algorithm. It specifically describes the worst-case scenario and can be used to describe the execution time required or the space used (e.g. in memory or on disk) by an algorithm.

In the context of LLMs, complexity analysis is crucial for understanding the scalability and efficiency of the underlying data structures and algorithms. For example, the time complexity of the attention mechanism in transformer-based models is $O(n^2)$ with respect to the sequence length, which can become a bottleneck for very long sequences.

Data Structures

Data structures are a fundamental concept in computer science. They are a way of organising and storing data so that it can be accessed and modified efficiently. Some fundamental data structures include:

- Arrays: A linear collection of elements, each identified by an array index.
- Linked Lists: A linear collection of data elements, where each element points to the next.
- Trees: A hierarchical structure where each node has a parent (except the root) and zero or more children.
- Hash Tables: A data structure that implements an associative array, mapping keys to values.

The choice of data structure can have a significant impact on the efficiency of algorithms in terms of both time and space complexity.

Sparse vs. Dense Representations

In many LLMs, particularly transformer-based models, the learned parameters (weights) can exhibit a high degree of sparsity - meaning a significant portion of the weights are zero or near-zero.

- Dense representations store all elements, regardless of their value. They are simple and allow for efficient fixed-size operations, but can be memory-inefficient for sparse data.
- Sparse representations store only non-zero elements, along with an index indicating their position. They are memory-efficient for sparse data, but can lead to more complex and slower operations.

The choice between sparse and dense representations is a key consideration in LLMs and often involves a trade-off between memory efficiency and computational simplicity.

STORAGE OPTIMIZATION TECHNIQUES

The dense vector representations we discussed in Chapter 3 pose unique storage challenges. While these vectors capture rich semantic meaning, they also demand significant memory resources. This tension between representational power and computational efficiency drives the following optimization techniques.

Quantization

Quantization is a technique used to compress the model by reducing the number of bits required to store each weight. The most common quantization techniques are:

- FP16 (16-bit floating-point): Reduces the memory usage by half compared to FP32, often with minimal impact on accuracy.
- INT8 (8-bit integer): Provides even greater compression, though it may require more careful calibration to maintain model performance.

Quantization can significantly reduce the memory footprint of LLMs, making them more feasible to store and deploy.

Pruning

Pruning is a technique to remove (prune) unnecessary weights or connections in a neural network. The idea is that by removing these connections, we can reduce the model size and computational requirements, often with minimal impact on performance.

There are different pruning strategies:

- Unstructured Pruning: Removes individual weights based on some criterion (e.g., magnitude of the weight).
- Structured Pruning: Removes entire structures (e.g., neurons, channels, layers) based on some criterion.

Pruning can lead to sparser models, which can then be more efficiently represented using sparse data structures.

Knowledge Distillation

Knowledge distillation is a compression technique in which a smaller "student" model is trained to reproduce the behaviour of a larger "teacher" model. The idea is that the knowledge of the complex model can be "distilled" into a simpler model.

In the context of LLMs, knowledge distillation can be used to create smaller, more memory-efficient models that still capture much of the knowledge of the larger model.

DATA STRUCTURES IN LLMS

The theoretical concepts and optimization techniques we've explored find their practical application in several key data structures used in modern LLMs. These structures must efficiently handle both the static components (like embedding tables) and dynamic components (like attention masks) of the model.

Embedding Tables

In LLMs, words or tokens are often represented by dense vectors, known as embeddings. These embeddings are learned during the training process and stored in embedding tables. Given the large vocabulary sizes in LLMs (often in the tens or hundreds of thousands), these embedding tables can become very large. Efficient storage and retrieval of these embeddings are crucial for the performance of the model. Techniques like quantization and pruning can be applied to embedding tables to reduce their memory footprint. Additionally, techniques like hashing or clustering can be used to efficiently store and retrieve embeddings.

Sparse Attention Masks

In transformer-based models, attention masks are used to indicate which tokens should attend to which other tokens. In many cases, especially with long sequences, these attention masks can be quite sparse (i.e. most tokens do not attend to most other tokens). Representing these sparse attention masks efficiently is important for reducing memory usage and computational requirements. Sparse data structures, such as sparse matrices or sparse tensor representations, can be used to efficiently store and manipulate these masks.

Efficient Checkpointing

During the training of LLMs, it's often necessary to save intermediate activations for use in the backward pass. However, storing all these activations can be prohibitively memory-intensive. Efficient checkpointing techniques, such as gradient checkpointing or activation precomputation, can be used to trade-off memory for computation. The idea is to only store a subset of activations and recompute the others as needed during the backward pass. Choosing which activations to store and which to recompute is an important consideration and can be based on heuristics or learned during the training process.

FUTURE DIRECTIONS AND CHALLENGES

As we'll see in the next chapter on deep learning fundamentals, the choice of data structures and storage optimizations directly impacts model architecture decisions and training strategies. The future developments in this area will likely co-evolve with advances in neural network architectures.

As LLMs continue to grow in size and complexity, efficient data structures and storage techniques will become increasingly important. Some key challenges and future directions include:

- Developing more efficient and scalable sparse data structures and algorithms, particularly for attention mechanisms and embedding tables.
- Improving quantization and pruning techniques to achieve better compression ratios while maintaining model performance.
- Exploring novel architectures and training paradigms that are more memory-efficient, such as reversible networks or activation-efficient transformers.
- Developing better tools and frameworks for monitoring and optimizing the memory usage and storage requirements of LLMs during training and inference.

DISCUSSION

The art of implementing Large Language Models lies not just in their mathematical foundations or embedding representations, but in the crucial intersection of theoretical elegance and practical constraints. As we've seen, the way we structure and store model components fundamentally shapes what's possible with these systems. The marriage of efficient data structures with careful storage optimization transforms abstract mathematical concepts into practical, deployable systems.

This bridge between theory and implementation reveals a deeper truth about large-scale AI systems: their effectiveness depends not just on model architecture or training strategies, but on the foundational decisions about how we represent and access data. The careful balance between memory efficiency and computational access patterns, between sparse and dense representations, represents more than just engineering trade-offs – it defines the practical limits of what we can achieve with these models. As we move forward to explore deep learning fundamentals in the next chapter, we'll see how these storage and structural decisions ripple through every aspect of model design and training, from gradient flow to optimization strategies.

The future of language models will likely be shaped as much by innovations in efficient storage and data structures as by breakthroughs in architecture or training methods. Success in pushing the boundaries of AI capabilities will require not just understanding the mathematical principles or mastering deep learning techniques, but developing increasingly sophisticated approaches to managing the fundamental resource constraints that underpin these systems.

KEY TAKEAWAYS:

1. Efficient data structures and storage techniques are crucial for the successful implementation and deployment of Large Language Models.

2. The choice of data structure can have a significant impact on the efficiency of algorithms in terms of both time and space complexity.
3. Sparse representations, quantization, and knowledge distillation are key optimisation techniques for reducing the memory footprint of LLMs.

REFLECTIVE PROMPTS:

1. What are the trade-offs between memory efficiency and computational complexity when it comes to the design of data structures for LLMs? How might these trade-offs evolve as hardware capabilities continue to improve?
2. How can the principles of data structure optimization explored in this chapter be applied to other domains of artificial intelligence beyond language processing?
3. What are the potential societal implications of developing highly efficient and compact LLM architectures? How might these advancements impact the accessibility and democratisation of advanced AI capabilities?

With a firm grasp of data structures and storage optimizations, we're now ready to explore the fundamental building blocks that make deep learning possible. Chapter 5 will provide a comprehensive overview of key concepts, architectures, and mechanisms that form the foundation of modern Large Language Models.

DEEP LEARNING FUNDAMENTALS: A PRIMER

Reflective Prompt: Consider a neural network with three hidden layers. Describe how the architectural choices, such as activation functions and optimization algorithms, reflect the fundamental principles of information processing in the human brain.

BACKGROUND

Before diving into Large Language Models (LLMs), it's essential to understand the fundamental building blocks of deep learning. This chapter provides a comprehensive overview of key concepts, architectures, and mechanisms that form the foundation of modern LLMs.

Deep learning, a subset of machine learning, uses artificial neural networks inspired by the human brain's structure. These networks learn hierarchical representations of data through multiple layers of processing, enabling them to understand complex patterns and relationships.

WHY THIS PRIMER MATTERS

- Foundation for understanding LLM architectures
- Context for key terminology used throughout the book
- Essential concepts for grasping scaling laws and training dynamics
- Background for development and deployment considerations

Before diving into advanced architectures and training methods, let's establish the core building blocks that make deep learning possible. Understanding these fundamentals will provide crucial context for more sophisticated concepts we'll explore later.

NEURAL NETWORK FUNDAMENTALS

Basic Architecture

A neural network consists of interconnected layers of neurons, as illustrated in Fig. 5.1. The journey of data through a neural network begins at the input layer. This layer serves as the gateway, welcoming the raw input data into the network. Each neuron in the input layer represents a unique feature of the data, eagerly awaiting its chance to contribute to the overall understanding. However, the input layer is merely a distributor, passing the data along without performing any computations of its own.

As the data ventures deeper into the neural network, it enters the realm of the hidden layers. These mysterious layers are where the true magic happens. They take the input data and transform it, molding it through a series of weighted connections. Each connection bears a specific weight, determining the strength and importance of the data flowing through it. The hidden layers apply non-linear activation functions, allowing the network to capture complex patterns and relationships within the data. These layers can be stacked, forming a deep network of multiple hidden layers, each contributing its own unique perspective to the data's transformation.

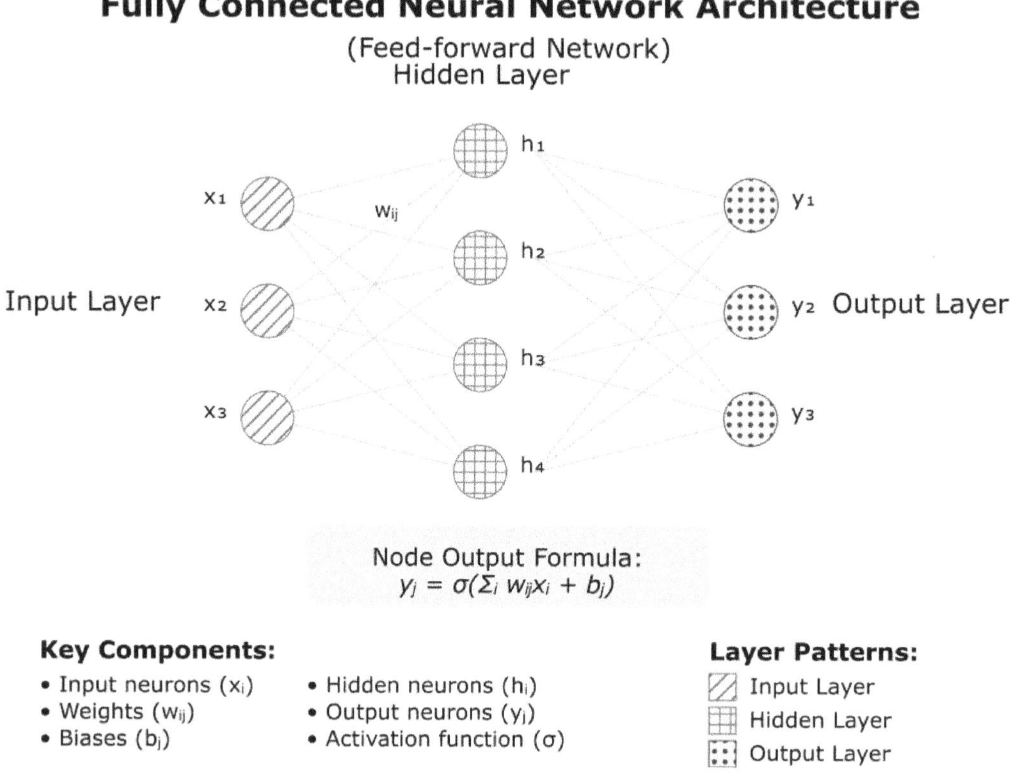

Fig. 5.1: Architecture of a fully connected feed-forward neural network where each neuron connects to every neuron in the subsequent layer through weighted connections (w_{ij}). The network processes information from the input layer (left) through the hidden layer (middle) to the output layer (right), with each node applying an activation function σ to its inputs. There can be multiple hidden layers, each having the same activation function.

Finally, the data reaches its destination: the output layer. This layer is responsible for producing the network's final output, the culmination of all the computations and transformations that have taken place. The number of neurons in the output layer depends on the specific task at hand. For example, in a classification task, each neuron might represent a different class or category. The output layer employs task-specific activation functions to interpret the incoming data and generate the desired output format. It is here that the neural network reveals its final predictions or decisions, based on the patterns and insights it has learned from the input data.

Together, these three components—the input layer, hidden layers, and output layer—form the backbone of a neural network. They work in harmony, passing data from one layer to the next, gradually refining and transforming it until the final output is achieved. It is through this intricate dance of data and computation that neural networks can tackle complex problems and uncover hidden patterns, making them a powerful tool in the world of artificial intelligence.

Key Components

Weights and Biases

- **Weights (w)**: Numbers that define the strength of connections between neurons
- **Biases (b)**: Additional parameters that allow the network to represent the data better

Together, they form the network's learnable parameters

Activation Functions

Common activation functions include:

- ReLU (f(x) = max(0, x)): Keeps positive values unchanged but replaces all negative values with zero, helping create sparse activations and reduce the vanishing gradient problem.
- Sigmoid ($\sigma(x) = 1/(1 + e^{-x})$): Squishes any input value into an output between 0 and 1, making it useful for representing probabilities or binary classifications.
- Tanh (($e^x - e^{-x})/(e^x + e^{-x}$)): Squishes input values to outputs between -1 and 1, providing zero-centered outputs which can help with training in deeper networks.
- Softmax: Converts inputs into a probability distribution (commonly used in classification output layers)

The choice of activation functions depends on the type of problem addressed. A few cases are shown in the Table below.

Types of problems and corresponding recommended activation functions

Selection Criteria	Activation Function	Use Case Examples	Why This Choice
1. Type of Problem			
Classification (Binary)	Sigmoid (Output)	- Email Spam Detection - Medical Diagnosis - Fraud Detection	Outputs between [0,1] represent probability
Classification (Multi-class)	Softmax (Output)	- Image Classification - Language Detection - Document Categorization	Converts outputs to a probability distribution
Regression (Unbounded)	Linear (Output)	- House Price Prediction - Temperature Forecasting - Stock Price Prediction	Allows any range of output values.
Regression (Bounded)	Tanh (Output)	- Normalised Predictions - Control Systems - Signal Processing	Bounds outputs between [-1, 1].
2. Layer Location			
Early Hidden Layers	ReLU	- Feature Detection Layers - Initial Convolution Layers - Input Processing	- Fast computation - Good gradient flow. - Sparse activations
Deep Hidden Layers	Leaky ReLU	- Deep CNNs - Advanced Feature Layers - Complex Pattern Detection	Prevents dying neurons in deep networks.
Output Layer	Depends on Problem: - -Sigmoid (Binary) - Softmax (Multi-class) - Linear (Regression)	- Final Classification Layer - Decision Layer - Prediction Layer	Matches the output requirements of the task.
3. Characteristics Needed			
Smooth Gradients	- Tanh - Sigmoid - ELU	- Control Systems - Signal Processing - Continuous Mappings	Differentiable everywhere with smooth transitions

Range Requirements	- Sigmoid [0,1] - Tanh [-1,1] - ReLU [0,∞)	- Probability Outputs - Normalized Values - Positive Values	Matches the required output range
Gradient Flow	- ReLU Family - Leaky ReLU - ELU	- Deep Networks - Complex Architectures - Training Stability	Prevents vanishing/exploding gradients.
4. Architecture			
CNNs	ReLU	- Image Classification - Object Detection - Computer Vision Tasks	Fast, sparse activations are good for visual features.
RNNs	Tanh/Sigmoid	- Language Processing - Time Series - Sequential Data	Controls information flow in gates.
Transformers	GELU	- BERT - GPT - Modern NLP Models	Better performance in attention mechanisms
Autoencoders	ReLU in Encoder Similar in Decoder	- Image Reconstruction - Dimensionality Reduction - Feature Learning	Maintains information flow symmetry

Modern LLMs typically use GELU as the primary activation function in transformer blocks, with Softmax in attention layers for weight distribution, as this combination handles the massive self-supervised learning task well and provides stable gradients across the deep architecture. Some newer models like PaLM use SwiGLU variants for potentially better performance. For downstream task fine-tuning, the original activation functions (GELU/Softmax) are usually kept in the transformer blocks, but the output layer's activation is adapted to the specific task: Softmax for classification tasks (like sentiment analysis), Sigmoid for binary decisions (like yes/no question answering), or Linear for regression-type tasks (like text similarity scoring).

Forward Propagation

The process of computing outputs from inputs:
1. Multiply inputs by weights
2. Add biases
3. Apply activation function
4. Pass the result to the next layer

Mathematical representation for a single neuron: output = $\sigma(\sum_i w_i x_i + b)$ where σ is the activation function.

Dense vs Sparse Vectors: The Foundation of Modern Deep Learning and Their Dimensionality

In the world of deep learning and neural networks, the distinction between dense and sparse vectors represents a fundamental shift in how we represent and process information. Imagine you're in a vast library where every book needs to be uniquely identified. The traditional approach – sparse vectors – is like giving each book a unique number and representing it as a vector where only one position holds a value (1) while all others are zero. It's similar to saying "this book is number 1242 out of 50,000 books." While this uniquely identifies the book, it tells us nothing about its content, genre, or relationship to other books.

Now, consider dense vectors – the cornerstone of modern deep learning. Instead of using a single position to identify our book, we describe it using multiple meaningful characteristics simultaneously.

Each dimension in our vector contributes to the overall description. Think of it as describing a book using multiple attributes: how romantic it is (0.7), how adventurous (0.3), how scientific (0.2), and so on. This rich representation allows us to capture complex relationships and similarities between different items.

Mathematical Foundation and Creation

The mathematical foundation for this transformation is rooted in the concept of embedding spaces. In sparse representations, we operate in a high-dimensional space where most dimensions are zero. For instance, in language models, a vocabulary of 50,000 words would require 50,000-dimensional vectors, with each word represented by a single '1' and 49,999 zeros. This is mathematically inefficient and computationally expensive. Dense vectors, typically ranging from 100 to 1000 dimensions, pack more information into each dimension through learned representations.

The creation process of these dense vectors begins with random initialization – each word starts with random values in each dimension. Through training, these vectors are gradually refined. When processing sentences like "The king ruled the kingdom" or "The queen addressed her subjects," the model learns to adjust these vectors based on context. Words appearing in similar contexts develop similar patterns in their dense representations.

The Art of Dimensionality Selection

The choice of vector dimensionality is a crucial decision that impacts both model performance and computational efficiency. This process requires careful consideration of several key factors:

Domain-Specific Baselines

Different applications require different dimensional spaces:

- Text and language processing typically starts with 100-300 dimensions for basic word embeddings, expanding to 512-768 for contextual embeddings in transformer models
- Image feature vectors often use 512-2048 dimensions to capture visual complexities
- Audio processing commonly employs 128-512 dimensions for spectral features
- Recommendation systems might use 32 to 256 dimensions for user behaviour modelling

Data-Driven Decisions

The amount of training data significantly influences optimal dimensionality. With limited data, higher dimensions can lead to overfitting – where vectors memorise noise rather than learning meaningful patterns. Consider the following relationship:

- Small datasets (thousands of examples): Start with lower dimensions (32-128)
- Medium datasets (millions of examples): Moderate dimensions (256-512)
- Large datasets (billions of examples): Higher dimensions (512+)

Practical Implementation

Modern language models demonstrate this balance beautifully. BERT-base uses 768 dimensions to capture rich linguistic relationships, while GPT-3 expands to 12,288 dimensions to model more complex patterns across larger context windows. This scaling isn't arbitrary – it's based on empirical evidence of performance improvements and computational constraints.

Validation Approach

To find the optimal dimensionality:

1. Start with a baseline dimension based on your domain
2. Implement systematic testing with different dimensions (usually powers of 2)
3. Monitor key metrics: training convergence, validation performance, memory usage
4. Look for the elbow point where additional dimensions yield diminishing returns
5. Consider practical constraints like inference speed requirements

The Power of Dense Representations

The power of dense vectors becomes evident in their ability to capture semantic relationships. In the sparse representation world, the words "king" and "queen" would be as different as "king" and "bicycle" – their vectors would have 1s in completely different positions. However, in dense vector space, these relationships are captured through the patterns of numbers across dimensions. This is why we can perform remarkable vector arithmetic: king - man + woman $\approx$ queen.

Modern transformer-based language models take this concept further by learning contextual dense representations. Instead of having a fixed vector for each word, they generate context-dependent representations. The word "bank" would have different dense vectors when appearing in "river bank" versus "bank account." This is achieved through sophisticated attention mechanisms that consider the entire context when generating these representations.

Practical Considerations and Future Directions

As systems evolve, dimensionality choices may need to be revisited. Modern techniques allow for progressive dimensionality expansion, starting small and growing vector spaces as needed. The key is maintaining the balance between expressiveness and efficiency while considering:

- Model interpretability needs
- Computational resources
- Data growth patterns
- Performance requirements

The shift from sparse to dense vectors, combined with careful dimensionality selection, represents a fundamental evolution in how we enable machines to understand and process information, making possible the remarkable capabilities we see in modern AI systems.

With the basic neural architecture established, we can now explore how these networks actually represent and manipulate information. This understanding is crucial for grasping more advanced concepts like attention mechanisms and generative models.

UNDERSTANDING REPRESENTATION

Latent Space

At its core, representation learning transforms raw data into meaningful mathematical abstractions where semantic relationships emerge as geometric properties. This latent space – a high-diemnsional mathematical landscape - encodes concepts as dense vectors where proximity indicates similarity, directions encode transformations and vector operations reveal conceptual relationships. Through the training process, neural networks progressively refine these representations, distributing information across dimensions to capture both explicit features and implicit patterns, ultimately enabling machines to process information in ways that mirror human understanding.

Core Concept

Latent space represents a continuous, high-dimensional mathematical space where data is represented through dense vectors. While dense vectors distribute information across dimensions, latent space provides the structured environment where these vectors interact and derive meaning through their relationships. This organization emerges through neural network training, where network weights learn to map inputs to meaningful representations.

Structure and Mathematical Properties

The latent space encodes meaning through geometric properties:

- Distance represents similarity: Dense vectors of similar concepts are positioned closer together in space. The distance between vectors v1 and v2 becomes a measurable indicator of their semantic similarity.
- Direction encodes transformation: Paths between dense vectors represent meaningful changes. Vector direction (v2 - v1) captures the transformation between concepts.
- Vector arithmetic enables analogies: Relationships between concepts can be manipulated through vector operations: king - man + woman ≈ queen works because difference vectors capture semantic relationships.

Formation through Neural Network Training

The organisation of latent space emerges through neural network weight adjustments. The process connects raw inputs to dense vector representations through multiple layers:

1. Forward Propagation: Input data transforms through weight matrices W and bias vectors b:

Layer Output = activation(W * input + b)

Each layer contributes to the final dense vector representation through:

- Embedding layer: Initial dense vector lookup
- Hidden layers: Progressive refinement
- Final layers: Task-specific adjustments
2. Loss Computation: The network evaluates representation quality through:
- Prediction accuracy

- Reconstruction quality
- Similarity preservation
3. Backpropagation: Weight adjustments modify:
- Input to dense vector mappings
- Vector transformations through layers
- Contextual influence patterns

Context Processing

Modern architectures, particularly transformers, handle context through attention mechanisms:

1. Initial Representation:
   word_vector = embedding_layer[word_id]
2. Context processing
   attention_scores = (Q * K^T) / sqrt(d_k)
   attention_weights = softmax(attention_scores)
   context vectors = attention weights * V
3. Vector adjustment
   contextual_vector = LayerNorm(word_vector + context_vectors)

This process repeats at multiple layers, capturing different aspects of context from syntactic patterns to abstract concepts.

Technical Considerations

- Dimensionality: Balance between expressiveness and computational efficiency determines vector dimensions.
- Regularization: Techniques ensure well-structured representations and prevent degenerate solutions.
- Architecture: Network design influences information distribution across vector dimensions and contextual adjustments.

Applications

The geometric properties of latent space enable:

- Language understanding through semantic vector relationships
- Image generation via smooth transitions between vectors
- Scientific applications like molecular structure representation

Recent Developments

Current research focuses on:

- Interpretable vector representations
- Controlled manipulation of latent space directions
- Multi-modal vector spaces
- Efficient architectures for representation learning

The power of latent space lies in its ability to capture meaning through geometric properties, enabling deep learning models to perform sophisticated tasks through mathematical operations on dense vectors.

Introduction to Word Embeddings

What are Word Embeddings?

Word embeddings are dense vector representations of words that capture semantic meanings in a continuous vector space. They serve as the foundational input representation for modern language models. This is illustrated in Fig. 5.2.

Word Embeddings

Converting Words to Dense Vector Representations

Input Words

"cat" → [0.2, -0.5, 0.1, ..., 0.8]

"kitten" → [0.3, -0.4, 0.2, ..., 0.7]

"dog" → [0.1, -0.6, 0.0, ..., 0.9]

Dense Vectors (e.g., 768 dimensions)

Semantic Properties

- Similar words cluster together
- Captures analogies:
  king - man + woman ≈ queen
- Preserves relationships:
  cat → kitten ≈ dog → puppy
- Handles multiple meanings

Applications:

- Natural Language Processing (NLP)
- Machine Translation
- Text Classification
- Document Similarity
- Question Answering

Fig. 5.2: Visualization of the word embedding process, where discrete words are mapped to dense vectors in continuous space. The example shows the word 'cat' being transformed into a high-dimensional vector representation (e.g., 768 dimensions) that captures semantic meaning.

Key Concepts
1. **Words to Vectors**
   - Convert discrete words into continuous vectors
   - Example: "cat" → [0.2, -0.5, 0.3,..., 0.1]
   - Typically 100-1000 dimensions
2. **Properties.**
   - Similar words have similar vectors
   - Capture semantic relationships
   - Enable mathematical operations on words
   - Form the input layer of neural language models
3. **Basic Types.**
   - Static embeddings (Word2Vec, GloVe)
   - Contextual embeddings (modern transformer-based)

Why They Matter for LLMs

- Form the first layer of transformation in language models
- Enable models to process textual input
- Provide a foundation for understanding semantic relationships
- Bridge the gap between human language and machine processing

Vector Spaces in Neural Networks

The mathematical foundations of vector spaces we explored in Chapter 1 and their application to embeddings in Chapter 3 find their practical implementation in neural network architectures. In the context of deep learning, these vector spaces serve as the computational backbone where transformations occur and information flows.

Consider a neural network layer with input $x \in \mathbb{R}^n$ and output $y \in \mathbb{R}^m$. The layer performs a transformation $T: \mathbb{R}^n \to \mathbb{R}^m$, mapping vectors from the input space to the output space. It combines the linear operations we studied earlier with non-linear activations:

$$y = \sigma(Wx + b)$$

where $W \in \mathbb{R}^{m \times n}$ represents the weight matrix, $b \in \mathbb{R}^m$ the bias vector, and σ the activation function. Each row of W effectively defines a direction in the input vector space along which the network learns to project the input data.

The power of this representation becomes apparent in how neural networks learn to organise their internal vector spaces. Consider the hidden layers of a network processing word embeddings:

1. Early layers operate in spaces that capture low-level features (e.g., syntactic patterns)
2. Middle layers transform these into increasingly abstract representations.
3. Final layers organise the space to optimise for the target task

This hierarchical organization of vector spaces explains why techniques like transfer learning work. The learned transformations create generally useful vector space organizations that can be repurposed for new tasks.

For implementation, this translates directly to tensor operations:

```
1.   class VectorSpaceLayer(nn.Module):
2.      def __init__(self, input_dim, output_dim):
3.         super().__init__()
4.      # Define the learnable transformation
5.         self.W = nn.Parameter(torch.randn(output_dim, input_dim) /
6.         np.sqrt(input_dim))
7.         self.b = nn.Parameter(torch.zeros(output_dim))
8.      def forward(self, x):
9.      # Transform input vector space to output vector space
10.        return F.relu(F.linear(x, self.W, self.b))
```

Code Exhibit 5.1: The code implements a basic neural network layer that transforms vectors between spaces while maintaining the geometric relationships we explored in vector space mathematics.

This implementation demonstrates how the theoretical concepts of vector spaces materialise in practical deep learning architectures, setting the foundation for the more complex transformations we'll explore in attention mechanisms and modern architectures.

TRAINING NEURAL NETWORKS

Activation Functions

Neural networks use activation functions to introduce nonlinearity into the model, enabling them to learn complex patterns. Important activation functions are shown in Fig. 5.3.

Loss Functions

Loss functions measure how well the network's predictions match the desired outputs:

1. **Mean Squared Error (MSE)**
   - o Used for regression problems
     $$L = 1/n \, \Sigma(y\_pred - y\_true)^2$$
2. **Cross-Entropy Loss**
   - o Used for classification problems
     $$L = -\Sigma(y\_true * \log(y\_pred))$$

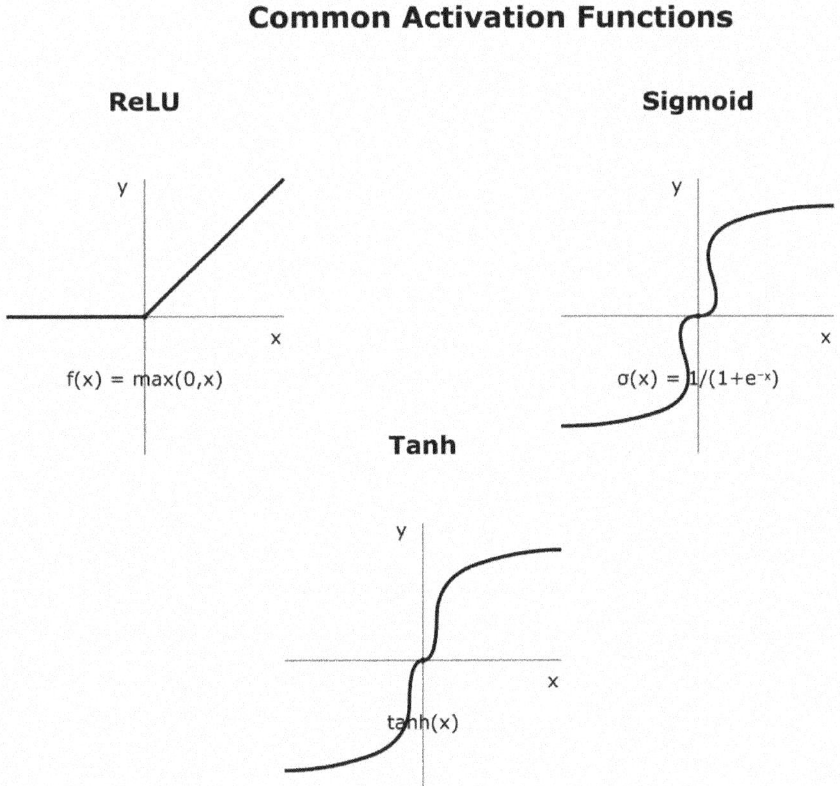

Fig. 5.3: Visualization of three fundamental activation functions (ReLU, Sigmoid, and Tanh) showing their characteristic shapes and mathematical formulas.

Training Process

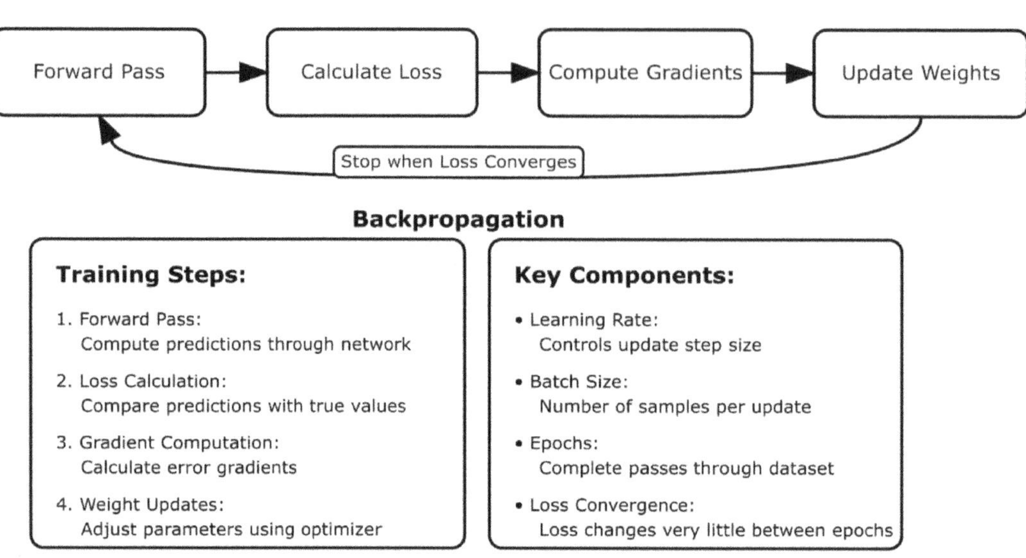

Fig. 5.4: Circular flow diagram illustrating the four key steps of neural network training: forward pass, loss calculation, gradient computation, and weight updates through backpropagation.

Gradient Descent and Backpropagation

The training process, illustrated in Fig. 5.4, consists of two main phases:

1. **Forward Pass**
- Input data flows through the network
- Each layer computes: output = activation (weights × input + bias)
- Final layer produces a prediction
2. **Backward Pass (Backpropagation)**
- Calculate the loss between the prediction and the true value
- Compute gradients of weights with respect to loss
- Update weights using gradient descent: $w = w - \eta \nabla w$ where η is the learning rate

Optimization Techniques

Different types of gradient descent are illustrated in Fig.5.5.

1. **Batch Gradient Descent:** Batch gradient descent, the reliable workhorse, embraces the entire dataset for each update. It ensures stability but comes at the cost of computational expense and slower convergence. A steady and comprehensive approach for those who value reliability over speed.
2. **Stochastic Gradient Descent (SGD):** SGD, the adventurous explorer, fearlessly updates parameters using a single training example at a time. It moves swiftly, but its updates can be noisy and erratic. However, this noise allows SGD to escape local minima and discover unexpected solutions.

3. **Mini-batch Gradient Descent:** Mini-batch gradient descent, the balanced negotiator, strikes a compromise between batch and SGD. It updates parameters using small batches of examples, typically ranging from 32 to 128 samples. This approach achieves a sweet spot of efficiency and effectiveness, making it the most commonly used technique in practice.

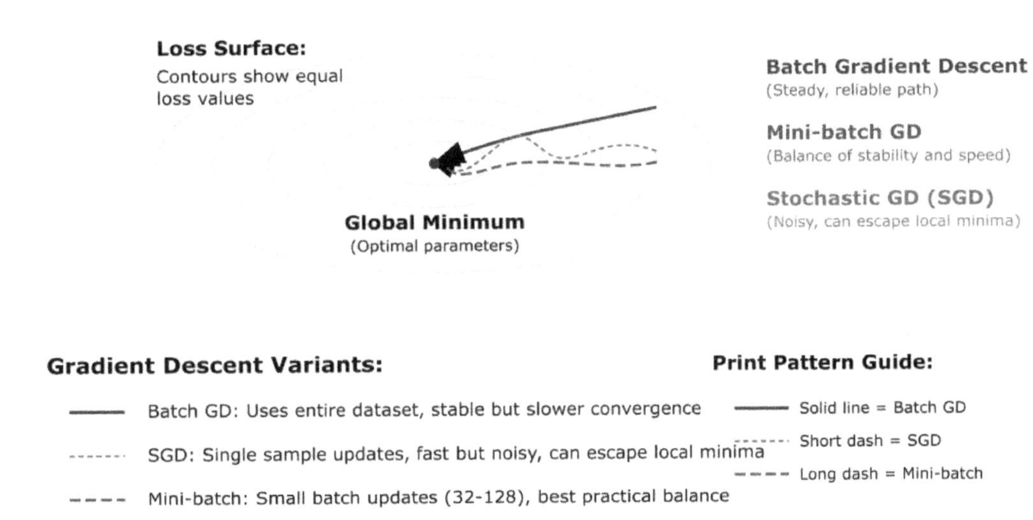

Fig. 5.5: The figure illustrates three variants of gradient descent: Batch GD (solid line) takes a steady, reliable path but moves slowly. SGD (short dash) follows a noisy path that can escape local minima, and Mini-batch GD (long dash) strikes a practical balance between stability and speed in reaching the global minimum.

Advanced Optimizers

1. **Adam (Adaptive Moment Estimation):** Adam, the intelligent optimizer, combines the best of both worlds by incorporating momentum and adaptive learning rates. It automatically adjusts the updates for each parameter based on their historical gradients and second moments. Adam's adaptability and efficiency make it a popular default choice for many deep learning tasks.
2. **RMSprop:** RMSprop, the gradient whisperer, adapts the learning rates based on the recent history of gradients for each parameter. It pays close attention to the magnitudes of recent gradients, allowing it to handle non-stationary objectives with ease. RMSprop's ability to adapt to changing landscapes makes it a valuable tool in the optimization arsenal.

Modern LLMs typically use AdamW optimizer (a variant of Adam with weight decay) with mini-batch training. They often employ learning rate warm-up followed by cosine decay scheduling, and gradient clipping to prevent exploding gradients. This combination has proven particularly effective for the massive-scale of LLM training. We will discuss more detail in the following chapters.

Training Challenges
The challenges and their solutions are described in the following Table.

Challenge	Description	Solutions
Overfitting	Model performs well on training data but poorly on new data	• **Dropout**: Temporarily removes random neurons during training, forcing network to learn redundant patterns • **L1/L2 regularization**: Penalizes large weights to prevent over-reliance on any single feature • **Early stopping**: Monitors validation performance and stops training when performance starts to degrade • **Data augmentation**: Increases training data variety through transformations like rotation, scaling, and noise addition
Vanishing/Exploding Gradients	• Vanishing: Gradients become too small in early layers, preventing effective learning. • Exploding: Gradients become too large, causing unstable updates	• **Proper initialisation**: Uses techniques like Xavier/Glorot to set initial weights that maintain good gradient flow • **Gradient clipping**: Sets a maximum threshold for gradients to prevent explosive updates • **Batch normalization**: Standardizes layer outputs to stabilise training and improve gradient flow • **Residual connections (Skip connections)**: Create direct pathways for gradients to flow backward, especially helpful in very deep networks
Learning Rate Issues	• Too high: Results in unstable training and missed optima. • Too low: Leads to slow convergence and potential stuck states.	• **Learning rate scheduling**: Systematically decreases the learning rate over time (e.g., step decay, cosine decay) • **Adaptive optimizers**: Use algorithms like Adam/RMSprop that automatically adjust learning rates based on gradient history. • **Learning rate warm-up**: Starts with a very small learning rate and gradually increases it to find optimal training dynamics
Poor Initialization	Bad initialisation can lead to: • Dead neurons (always output zero). • Saturated activations • Poor gradient flow	• **Xavier/Glorot initialization**: Scales weights based on layer dimensions, ideal for tanh/sigmoid activations. • **He initialization**: Modified version of Xavier that works better with ReLU activations. • **Orthogonal initialization**: Initializes weights as orthogonal matrices to maintain gradient magnitudes, particularly useful in deep networks

The evolution of sequential processing in neural networks reflects our growing understanding of how to handle temporal and contextual information. This journey from simple RNNs to modern architectures like Transformers and Mamba reveals key insights about deep learning's development.

SEQUENTIAL MODELS AND THEIR CHALLENGES

Introduction to Sequential Data

Neural networks processing sequential data (like text or time series) need to:

- Handle variable-length inputs
- Maintain the context/memory of previous inputs
- Capture temporal dependencies
- Process information step-by-step

Recurrent Neural Networks (RNNs)

RNNs, explained in Fig. 5.6, process sequential data by maintaining a 'hidden state' that gets updated at each time step. The key equation is: $h\_t = \tanh(W\_h \cdot h\_{t-1} + W\_x \cdot x\_t + b)$

Where:

- h_t is the current hidden state
- h_{t-1} is the previous hidden state
- x_t is the current input
- W_h, W_x are weight matrices
- b is the bias term

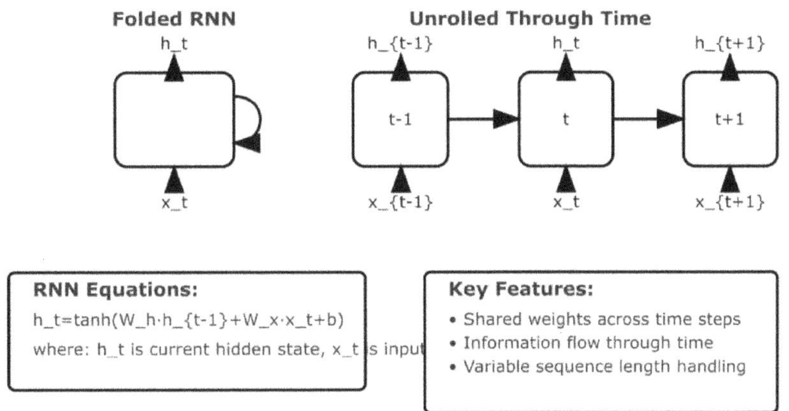

Fig. 5.6: Visualization of a Recurrent Neural Network (RNN) showing both its compact form with a feedback loop and its unrolled representation through time steps.

THE VANISHING GRADIENT PROBLEM

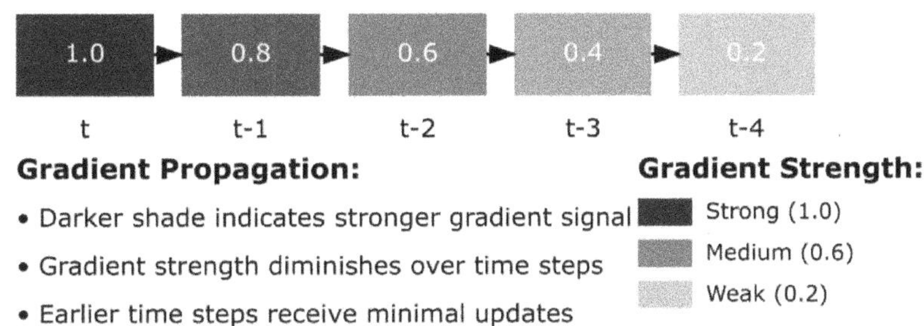

Fig. 5.7: Illustration of how the gradient signal weakens as it propagates backward through time steps in RNNs, leading to the vanishing gradient problem.

When training RNNs, gradients are multiplied many times through the time steps during backpropagation. This leads to two issues:

1. **Vanishing Gradients**
   o Gradients become extremely small as they are propagated back in time
   o Earlier time steps receive minimal updates
   o Network can't learn long-term dependencies
   o Occurs when gradients are repeatedly multiplied by small numbers (<1)

2. **Exploding Gradients**
   - o Gradients become extremely large
   - o Causes unstable training
   - o Results in large weight updates
   - o Occurs when gradients are repeatedly multiplied by large numbers (>1)

LONG SHORT-TERM MEMORY (LSTM)

LSTMs were designed to address the vanishing gradient problem through a gating mechanism:

1. **Forget Gate (f_t)**
   - o Decides what information to discard from the cell state
   - o $f\_t = \sigma(W\_f \cdot [h\_{t-1}, x\_t] + b\_f)$
2. **Input Gate (i_t)**
   - o Controls what new information to store in the cell state
   - o $i\_t = \sigma(W\_i \cdot [h\_{t-1}, x\_t] + b\_i)$
   - o Creates new candidate values: $\tilde{c}\_t = \tanh(W\_c \cdot [h\_{t-1}, x\_t] + b\_c)$
3. **Output Gate (o_t)**
   - o Controls which parts of the cell state to output
   - o $o\_t = \sigma(W\_o \cdot [h\_{t-1}, x\_t] + b\_o)$

Key advantages of LSTM:
- Better gradient flow through the cell state pathway
- Selective memory retention and forgetting
- Ability to learn long-term dependencies
- More stable training compared to vanilla RNNs

ATTENTION MECHANISMS AND TRANSFORMERS

Introduction to Attention

Attention mechanisms allow models to focus on relevant parts of input sequences when producing outputs. Unlike RNNs/LSTMs that must compress all information into a fixed-size hidden state, attention lets the model dynamically focus on different parts of the input.

Self-Attention

Self-attention allows a sequence to attend to itself, capturing relationships between different positions in the sequence. This is illustrated in Fig. 5.8.

Key Components:
1. **Queries (Q)**: What we're looking for
2. **Keys (K)**: What we match against
3. **Values (V)**: What we retrieve

Formula: $\text{Attention}(Q, K, V) = \text{softmax}(QK^T/\sqrt{d\_k})V$

where d_k is the dimension of the keys (scaling factor)

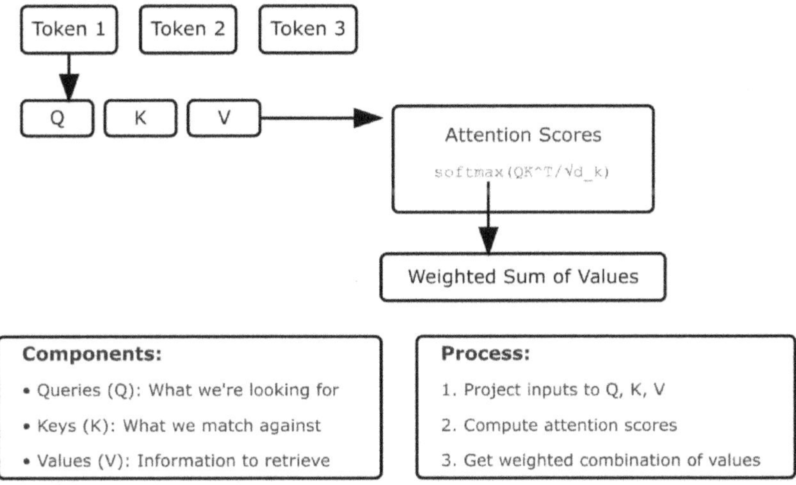

Fig. 5.8: Illustration of the self-attention mechanism showing how input tokens are projected to queries, keys, and values to compute attention scores and weighted outputs.

Multi-Head Attention

Multi-head attention runs multiple attention operations in parallel:
- Each head can focus on different aspects of the input
- Heads are concatenated and projected to the final output
- Typically uses 8-16 attention heads

Formula: MultiHead(Q,K,V) = Concat(head_1, ..., head_h)W^O

where head_i = Attention(QW_i^Q, KW_i^K, VW_i^V)

Transformer Architecture

Key components: These are illustrated in Fig. 5.9.

1. **Encoder**
   - Self-attention layer
   - Feed-forward neural network
   - Layer normalisation
   - Residual connections

2. **Decoder**
   - Masked self-attention (prevents looking at future tokens)
   - Cross-attention to encoder output
   - Feed-forward neural network
   - Layer normalisation

3. **Positional Encoding**
   - Adds position information to tokens
   - Uses sine and cosine functions of different frequencies
   - Enables model to understand token order

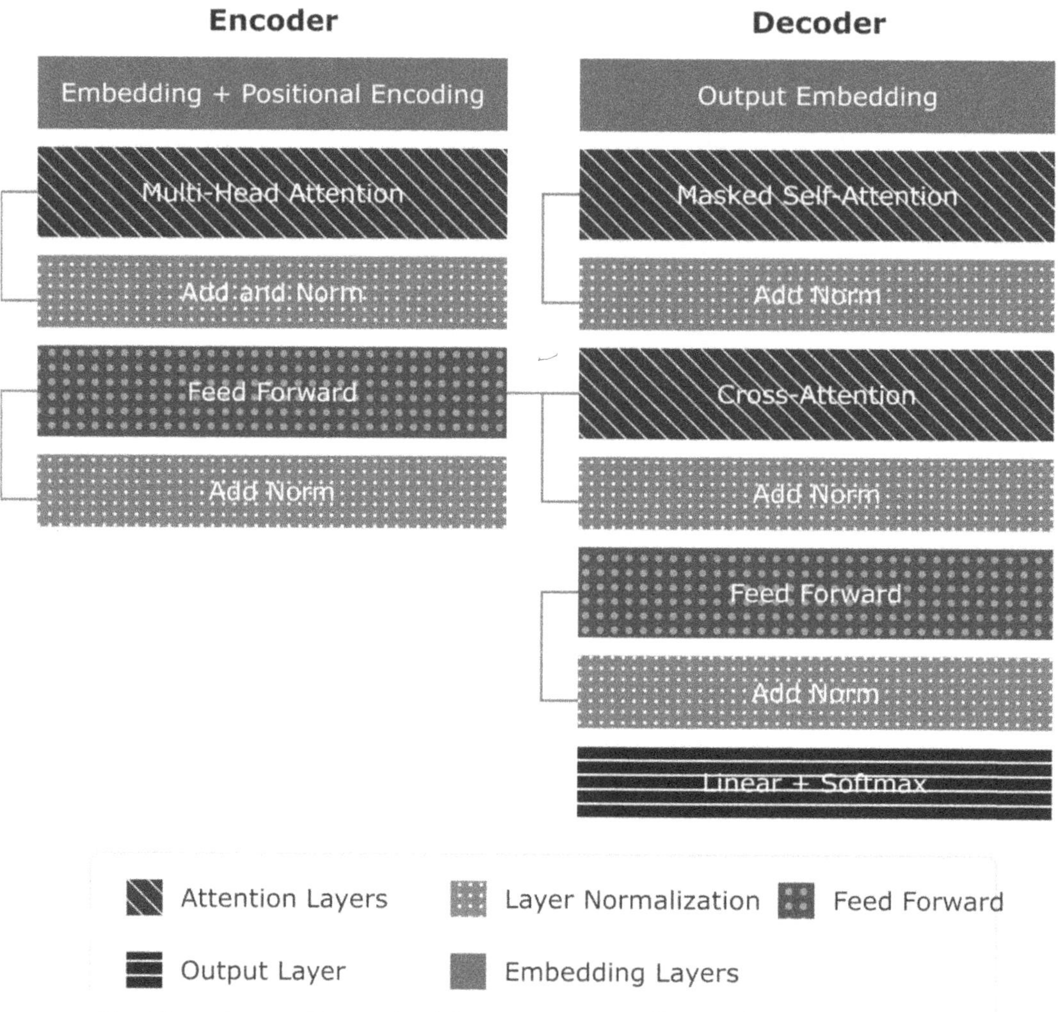

Fig. 5.9: Complete transformer architecture showing encoder and decoder stacks with multi-head attention, feed-forward networks, and normalization layers.

Advantages Over RNNs/LSTMs
1. Parallel Processing: No sequential computation required
2. Global Dependencies: Direct connections between any positions
3. Better Gradient Flow: Shorter paths between dependencies
4. Scalability: More efficient for longer sequences

MAMBA: REIMAGINING SEQUENTIAL PROCESSING BEYOND ATTENTION

Since the introduction of the Transformer architecture in 2017, attention mechanisms have dominated the landscape of language modelling. However, late 2023 brought a paradigm shift with the introduction of Mamba, a fundamentally different approach to sequence processing that challenges our assumptions about how language models should work. A comparison of Mamba and Transformer is illustrated in Fig. 5.10.

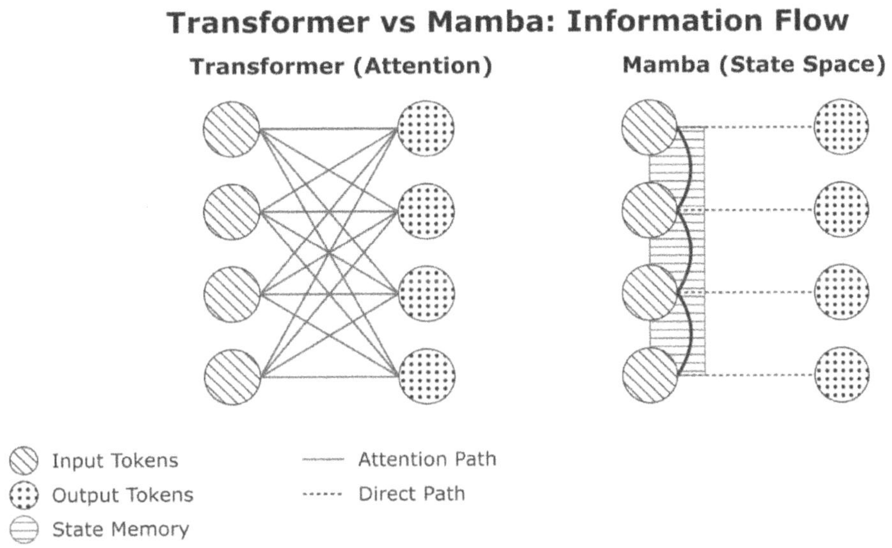

Transformer vs Mamba: Information Flow

Transformer (Attention)   **Mamba (State Space)**

Fig. 5.10: A side-by-side comparison of information processing in Transformers (left) versus Mamba (right), illustrating Transformer's quadratic attention connections versus Mamba's efficient linear state-based processing. The visualization highlights how Mamba achieves comparable capabilities with significantly reduced computational complexity.

Understanding Mamba Through Analogy

Imagine reading a complex novel with multiple characters and plotlines. There are two fundamentally different ways to process this information:

1. **The Transformer Way**: Like a meticulous reader who continuously flips back through previous pages to connect every new piece of information with everything that came before. While thorough, this becomes increasingly time-consuming as the story progresses.

2. **The Mamba Way**: Like an efficient reader who maintains a running mental summary, selectively updating it with new information. Instead of constant backward references, this reader maintains a compressed yet informative state of understanding that evolves with the narrative.

This fundamental difference in approach leads to significant implications for computational efficiency and scalability.

A Practical Example: News Article Analysis

Let's see how Mamba processes a news article excerpt differently from a Transformer. Consider this text:

"Breaking News: Tech startup OpenAI launches GPT-4. The new AI model shows significant improvements over its predecessor. CEO Sam Altman says this represents a major breakthrough in artificial intelligence. Early testing demonstrates exceptional performance in coding and analysis tasks."

Transformer Processing

When processing "CEO Sam Altman says," a Transformer would:

1. Look back at "OpenAI" (first sentence)

2. Look back at "GPT-4" (first sentence)
3. Look back at "new AI model" (second sentence)
4. Compute attention scores between ALL these elements
5. Make connections across all previous tokens

This results in $O(n^2)$ computations as each new token needs to attend to all previous tokens

Mamba Processing (State-Based Approach)

Mamba maintains and updates a state vector as it processes the text. This is shown in Code Exhibit 5.2.

Key Differences:
1. **Memory Efficiency**: Mamba maintains a fixed-size state vector regardless of sequence length
2. **Selective Updates**: Only relevant parts of the state are significantly modified
3. **Linear Scaling**: Computational cost grows linearly with sequence length
4. **Context Preservation**: Important information persists in the state while irrelevant details fade

This example demonstrates Mamba's efficient processing of sequential information through selective state updates rather than exhaustive attention computation. The state acts as a dynamic summary of relevant information, updated based on the importance of new inputs.

Mathematical Foundations: Elegance in Simplicity

At its core, Mamba implements a selective state space model, expressed through two key equations:

```
1.    # Simplified state evolution example
2.    Initial State = {
3.    'entity': None,
4.    'topic': None,
5.    'key_info': None
6.    }
7.
8.    # After "Breaking News: Tech startup OpenAI launches GPT-4"
9.    State_1 = {
10.   'entity': 'OpenAI', # Company identification
11.   'topic': 'product launch', # Main event
12.   'key_info': 'GPT-4' # Product detail
13.   }
14.
15.   # After "The new AI model shows significant improvements"
16.   State_2 = {
17.   'entity': 'OpenAI',
18.   'topic': 'product launch',
19.   'key_info': ['GPT-4', 'improvements'] # Selectively updated
20.   }
21.
22.   # Processing "CEO Sam Altman says"
23.   importance = calculate_importance("CEO Sam Altman")
24.   # High importance for 'entity' dimension as it's leadership information
25.   # Lower importance for existing product details.
```

```
26.
27.  State_3 = {
28.  'entity': ['OpenAI', 'Sam Altman (CEO)'], # Updated with high importance
29.  'topic': 'product launch',              # Maintained
30.  'key_info': ['GPT-4', 'improvements'] # Maintained }
31.  The selective update mechanism determines how much to modify each aspect of the state:
32.  def selective_update(current_state, new_info, importance):
33.  # Importance scores between 0 and 1 for each state dimension
34.  importance_scores = {
35.  'entity': 0.9, # High importance for a new entity
36.  'topic': 0.1, # Low importance (topic unchanged)
37.  'key_info': 0.3 # Moderate importance
38.      }
39.
40.  # Update each dimension based on importance
41.  new_state = {}
42.  for key in current_state:
43.  new_state[key] = (
44.  importance_scores[key] * new_info[key] +
45.  (1 - importance_scores[key]) * current_state[key]
46.      )
47.  return new state
```

Code Exhibit 5.2: A selective state update mechanism for tracking and prioritizing information during conversational context evolution.

State Update: $x(t+1) = A(u)x(t) + Bu(t)$

Output Generation: $y(t) = Cx(t) + Du(t)$

Where:

- $x(t)$ represents the current state
- $u(t)$ is the input at time t
- $A(u)$ is the selective update matrix (input-dependent)
- B, C, and D are learnable parameters

Why This Matters: Practical Implications

The significance of Mamba's approach extends beyond theoretical elegance. Its design offers several practical advantages:

1. **Computational Efficiency.**
- Linear scaling with sequence length ($O(n)$) versus Transformer's quadratic scaling ($O(n^2)$)
- More efficient memory utilisation through state compression
- Better hardware utilisation due to simplified computation patterns
2. **Improved Long-Range Processing**
- Natural handling of long-range dependencies through state updates
- No artificial context window limitations
- More efficient processing of sequential patterns
3. **Adaptive Processing**
- Input-dependent parameter generation allows for content-aware processing

- Flexible allocation of computational resources based on input complexity
- More natural handling of varying content types

Mamba represents a fundamental rethinking of how we process sequential information in deep learning. By moving away from attention mechanisms towards selective state space models, it achieves comparable or superior performance with significantly reduced computational complexity. This breakthrough reminds us that even in well-established fields, revolutionary approaches can emerge by questioning fundamental assumptions and exploring alternative paradigms.

As the field continues to evolve, Mamba's innovations may well influence the next generation of language models, potentially leading to more efficient and capable architectures that can process ever-longer sequences with greater efficiency.

GENERATIVE MODELS IN DEEP LEARNING

Generative models represent a fundamental shift in deep learning, moving beyond discriminative tasks (like classification) to actually creating new data that matches the patterns learned from training examples. These models learn to approximate the underlying probability distribution of the training data, enabling them to generate new, synthetic examples that maintain the characteristics of the original dataset. The evolution of Generative AI Architecture is illustrated in Fig. 5.11.

Here's a clearer technical explanation focusing on the core mechanisms and intuition.

Core Architectures of Generative Models

The First Building Blocks: Autoencoders

Autoencoders learn through a compression-decompression mechanism: the encoder network compresses input data into a compact latent representation, while the decoder attempts to reconstruct the original input from this compressed form. The network's architecture forces learning by deliberately constraining the latent space size (like forcing information through a narrow tunnel), compelling it to discover efficient data encodings. This bottleneck architecture essentially teaches the network to understand what features are truly essential for reconstruction - if it can rebuild the input accurately from a compressed state, it has learned the data's fundamental patterns.

The Probabilistic Revolution: VAEs

VAEs enhance autoencoders by learning probability distributions rather than fixed encodings. Instead of compressing input to exact points, the encoder outputs parameters (mean and variance) defining a probability distribution for each input. This allows sampling different latent values for the same input, enabling controlled variation in generation. The key technical innovation was making random sampling differentiable through the reparameterization trick, allowing the network to learn smooth latent spaces where similar inputs map to overlapping distributions, enabling meaningful interpolation and controlled generation.

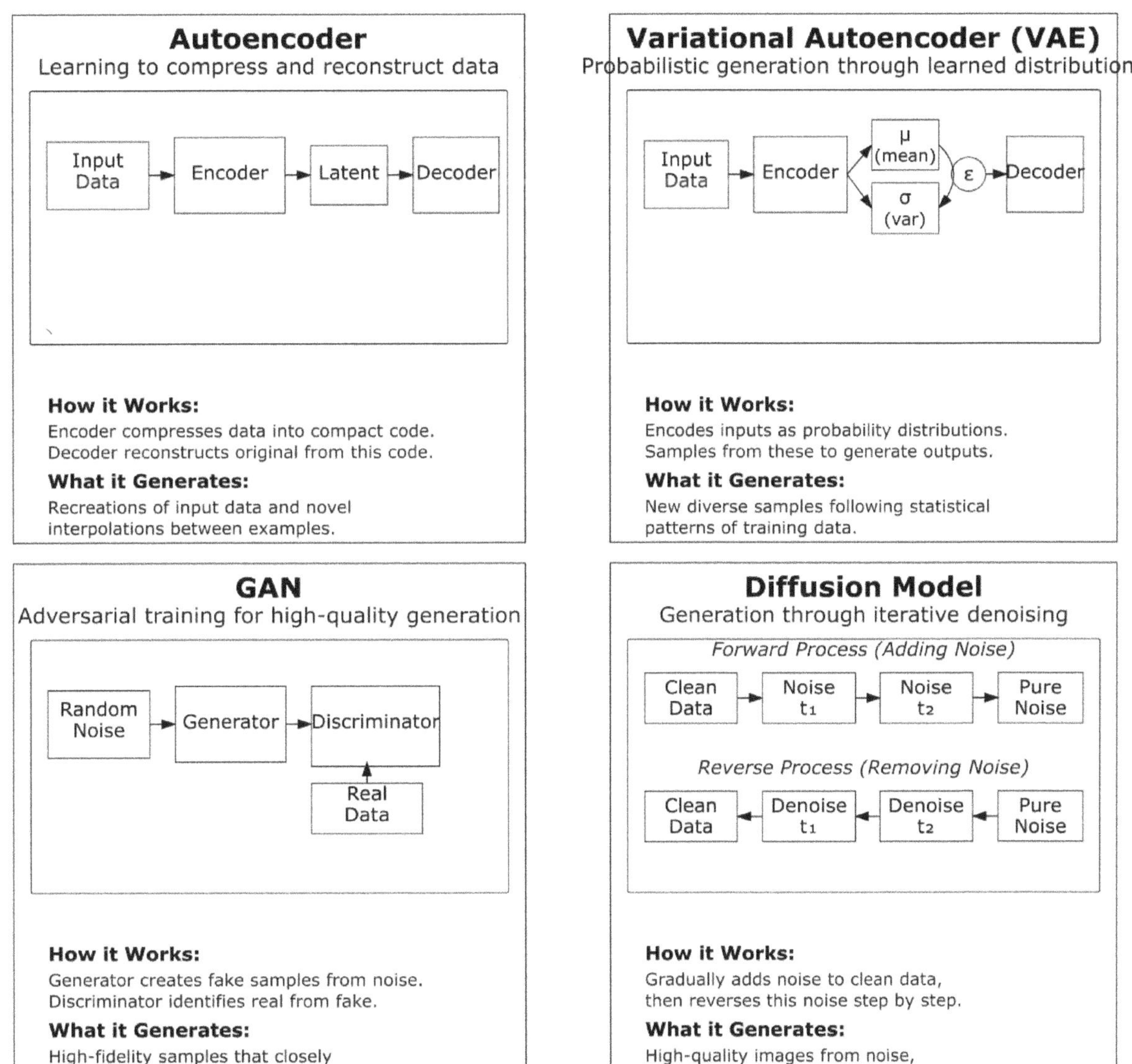

Fig. 5.11: The diagram illustrates the evolution of generative AI architectures, showing how each model approaches data generation differently: Autoencoders through compression and reconstruction, VAEs through probabilistic sampling, GANs through adversarial training, and Diffusion Models through gradual denoising.

The Adversarial Breakthrough: GANs

GANs operate through a two-network competition: a generator creates data samples from random noise, while a discriminator learns to distinguish real from generated samples. As training progresses, the generator improves at creating realistic samples to fool an increasingly sophisticated discriminator, while the discriminator becomes better at detecting subtle flaws. This adversarial feedback loop drives both networks to improve - the generator learns the true data distribution through the discriminator's feedback, while the discriminator learns increasingly nuanced features that differentiate real and fake samples.

The Modern Renaissance: Diffusion Models

Diffusion models work by learning to reverse a gradual noise addition process. The training happens in two phases: first, progressively adding random noise to real data samples in small steps until they become pure noise; then learning to reverse this process. The model learns to estimate the direction towards the original data at each noise level, allowing it to gradually denoise random noise into coherent samples. This step-by-step approach makes the generation process more controlled and stable than GANs, while the multiple noise levels allow the model to learn features at different scales, from fine details to overall structure.

Comparative Analysis

Architecture	Best For	Limitations	Training Stability	Output Quality
Autoencoders	• Dimensionality reduction. • Feature learning	• Blurry generations • Limited generative capabilities	High	Moderate
VAEs	• Probabilistic modelling • Controlled generation	• Less sharp outputs than GANs. • Limited complexity in generations	Good	Good
GANs	• High-fidelity generation • Realistic outputs	• Training instability. • Mode collapse • Hard to achieve convergence	Low to Medium	Excellent (when successful)
Diffusion Models	• High-quality generation • Controlled synthesis	• Slower generation process • Computationally intensive	Excellent	Excellent

Each architecture represents a different approach to the generation problem, with its own trade-offs between quality, control, and training stability. The choice of architecture depends heavily on the specific requirements of your application, available computational resources, and desired output characteristics.

Understanding these fundamental generative architectures is crucial for working with modern language models, as many of their principles evolve in the current LLM designs and training approaches. The evolution from simple autoencoders to sophisticated diffusion models parallels the development of increasingly capable language models, with each advance in generative modelling contributing to our understanding of how to create more powerful and reliable AI systems.

DISCUSSION

The journey through deep learning fundamentals reveals how the mathematical principles we explored earlier manifest in practical neural architectures. From the vector spaces that enable representation learning to the optimization techniques that make training possible, these concepts don't just exist in theory – they form the building blocks of modern AI systems. The progression from basic neural networks to sophisticated architectures like Transformers and Mamba demonstrates not just technological evolution, but deeper insights into how we can structure systems to process information more effectively.

What makes deep learning particularly fascinating is its elegant synthesis of multiple mathematical disciplines. The linear algebraic operations we explored in Chapter 1 combine with the embedding concepts from Chapter 3 and the efficient data structures from Chapter 4 to create systems capable of learning increasingly complex patterns. This synthesis isn't just theoretical – it manifests in practical architectural choices that determine both the capabilities and limitations of our models. As we move forward to explore Large Language Models in the next chapter, these fundamentals will prove crucial in understanding why certain architectures succeed where others fail, and how we might push the boundaries of what's possible in artificial intelligence.

The shift from traditional neural networks to modern architectures like Transformers and Mamba represents more than just architectural innovation – it reflects a deeper understanding of how to structure computations for learning from data. Success in developing and deploying these systems requires not just mastering individual concepts, but understanding how they interplay in creating systems that can learn, adapt, and generalise. This foundation will prove essential as we delve into the specific challenges and opportunities presented by Large Language Models.

Key Takeaways:

1. Neural networks learn hierarchical representations of data through multiple layers of processing, enabling them to understand complex patterns and relationships.
2. Activation functions, loss functions, and optimization techniques are crucial components in training neural networks effectively.
3. The transition from traditional neural networks to modern architectures like Transformers and Mamba reflects a deeper understanding of how to structure computations for learning from data.

Reflective Prompts:

1. How do the architectural choices in neural networks, such as the selection of activation functions and optimization algorithms, reflect the fundamental principles of information processing in the human brain? What insights can be gained from this connection?
2. As neural network architectures become increasingly complex, what are the potential challenges in maintaining interpretability and transparency? How might future developments address these concerns?
3. The evolution of sequential processing approaches, from RNNs to Transformers and Mamba, demonstrates a shift in how AI systems handle temporal and contextual information. What are the broader implications of these advancements for the field of artificial intelligence and its ability to mimic human-like reasoning?

With a firm grasp of deep learning fundamentals, we're now ready to delve into the world of Large Language Models in Chapter 6, exploring their definition, historical context, and the key characteristics that define these powerful AI systems.

INTRODUCTION TO LARGE LANGUAGE MODELS

Reflective Prompt: The LLM has been trained and is ready for deployment. Discuss how the computational and memory demands of these models shape the ethical considerations around their development and deployment, with potential societal implications.

INTRODUCTION

In the rapidly evolving landscape of artificial intelligence, few developments have captured the imagination and transformed the field quite like Large Language Models (LLMs). These sophisticated AI systems have revolutionized how we interact with machines, process information, and approach complex language tasks. This chapter aims to provide a comprehensive introduction to LLMs, exploring their definition, historical context, importance, and the fundamental concepts that underpin their functionality.

HISTORICAL CONTEXT AND EVOLUTION OF LANGUAGE MODELS

The journey to today's Large Language Models has been long and marked by significant milestones, see Fig.6.1. Understanding this evolution provides crucial context for appreciating the current state and future potential of LLMs.

Evolution of Language Models

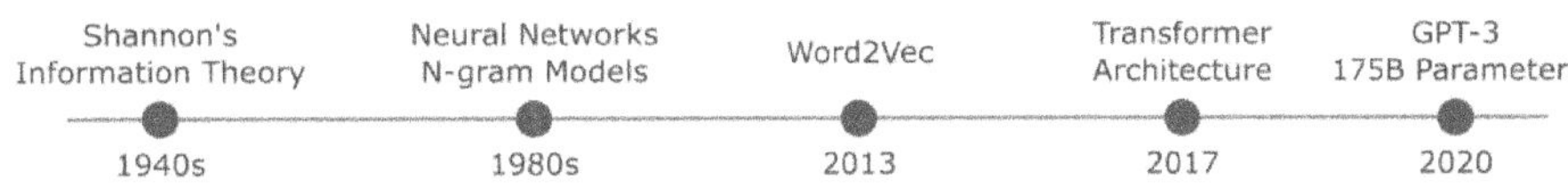

Fig. 6.1: The figure traces the key milestones in language model development, from Shannon's foundational Information Theory in the 1940s through neural networks and n-grams in the 1980s, to the transformative introduction of Word2Vec (2013) and Transformer architecture (2017), culminating in GPT-3's breakthrough scale in 2020.

1. Early Language Models (1940s-1980s):

The foundations of language modelling can be traced back to Claude Shannon's work on information theory in the 1940s. Shannon introduced the concept of using probability distributions to model language, laying the groundwork for future developments.

In the 1980s, n-gram models became popular. These statistical models predict the probability of a word based on the (n-1) previous words. While simple, n-gram models were effective for many tasks and remained dominant for decades.

2. Statistical Machine Translation (1990s-2000s):

The 1990s and 2000s saw the rise of statistical approaches to machine translation. These models used large parallel corpora of translated texts to learn translation probabilities. While not directly language models, they contributed significantly to the field of NLP.

3. Neural Network Renaissance (2010s):

The 2010s marked a turning point with the resurgence of neural networks, thanks to increased computational power and the availability of large datasets.

- 2013: Word2Vec introduced neural word embeddings, representing words as dense vectors in a continuous space.
- 2014: Sequence-to-sequence models with attention mechanisms revolutionised machine translation and other sequence tasks.
- 2018: BERT (Bidirectional Encoder Representations from Transformers) introduced by Google, marked a significant leap in language understanding.

4. The Age of Large Language Models (Late 2010s-Present):

- 2018: GPT (Generative Pre-trained Transformer) by OpenAI showed the potential of large-scale language models.
- 2019: GPT-2 demonstrated impressive text generation capabilities.
- 2020: GPT-3, with 175 billion parameters, showcased remarkable few-shot learning abilities.
- 2022: ChatGPT brought conversational AI to the mainstream, demonstrating human-like dialogue capabilities.

This timeline illustrates the rapid acceleration in the field, with models growing exponentially in size and capability over just a few years.

This evolution from simple statistical models to sophisticated neural architectures reveals not just technological progress, but a fundamental shift in how we approach language understanding. Building on this historical foundation, let's explore what defines modern LLMs and their core characteristics.

DEFINITION AND BASIC CONCEPTS

A Large Language Model (LLM) is a type of artificial intelligence system designed to understand, generate, and manipulate human language in a way that is both coherent and contextually appropriate. These models are "large" in two primary aspects: the amount of data they're trained on and the number of parameters they contain.

To better grasp the concept of an LLM, imagine a vast library where every book, article, and webpage ever written is stored. Now picture a librarian who has read and memorised all of this information. This librarian can answer questions, write essays, and even create new stories based on all this knowledge. An LLM is like this librarian, but in the form of a computer program. It has been trained on enormous amounts of text data and can use this training to perform a wide variety of language tasks.

Key characteristics of LLMs include

1. Scale: LLMs typically contain billions of parameters and are trained on massive datasets, often hundreds of gigabytes or even terabytes of text.
2. Generalisation: They can perform well on a wide range of tasks without task-specific training.
3. Context understanding: LLMs can understand and generate language based on context, often capturing nuances and subtleties in communication.
4. Transfer learning: Knowledge gained from pre-training on large datasets can be applied to new, specific tasks with minimal additional training.

Having established what LLMs are, we must understand what makes them "large." At their core, these models' capabilities emerge from their parameters - the learnable components that transform raw text into meaningful representations using the mathematical principles we explored in earlier chapters.

Understanding Parameters in LLMs

A crucial aspect of Large Language Models is the concept of "parameters." In the context of LLMs, parameters are the adjustable parts of the model that are learned during the training process, see Fig.6.2. They are essentially the "knowledge" of the model, encoding patterns and information from the training data.

Parameters in Neural Networks

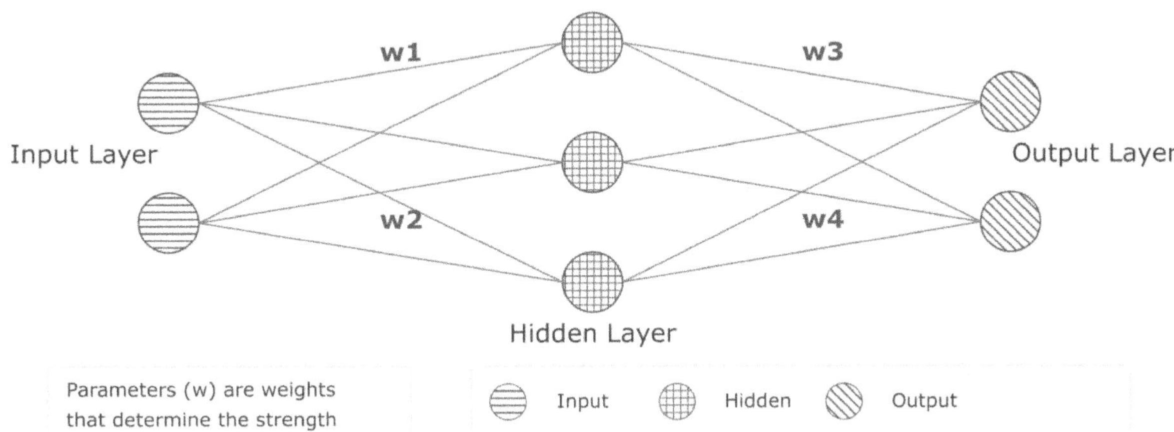

Fig. 6.2: The figure illustrates the basic structure of a neural network showing parameters (weights) as connections between neurons across three layers: input layer, hidden layer, and output layer. Each connection represents a learnable parameter that determines how strongly neurons influence each other, with the total number of these connections (weights) contributing to the model's capacity to learn patterns.

To understand parameters, let's break it down:

1. Definition: In mathematical terms, parameters are the variables in the model that are adjusted to minimise the difference between the model's predictions and the actual data.
2. What they represent: In an LLM, parameters typically represent weights in the neural network. These weights determine how input data (like words or tokens) is transformed and combined to produce outputs.

3. Scale: Modern LLMs can have billions or even trillions of parameters. Fig.6.3 gives an idea of the scale. For example:
   - GPT-3 has 175 billion parameters
   - GPT-4 is estimated to have over a trillion parameters
   - BERT-Large has 340 million parameters
4. Why "large" matters: Generally, more parameters allow the model to capture more complex patterns and relationships in the data. This increased capacity often translates to better performance across a wide range of tasks.
5. Types of parameters: In a typical transformer-based LLM, parameters are found in various components:
   - Embedding layers (converting tokens to vectors)
   - Attention mechanisms (determining which parts of the input to focus on)
   - Feed-forward neural networks (processing the attention outputs)
   - Layer normalisation (stabilising the learning process)

To visualise this, imagine a vast network of interconnected nodes, where each connection has a weight (a parameter). The input text travels through this network, with each parameter influencing how the information flows and is transformed.

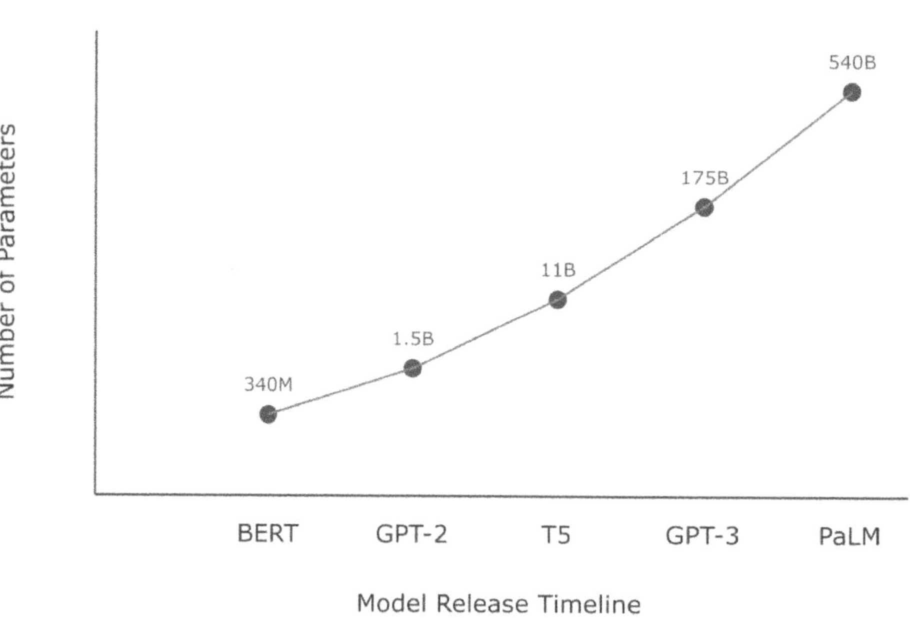

Fig. 6.3: The figure illustrates the exponential growth in the size of language models over time, from BERT's 340 million parameters to PaLM's 540 billion parameters, demonstrating the rapid scaling of model complexity in recent years. The upward trend highlights how language models have grown by several orders of magnitude, with each new model significantly larger than its predecessors.

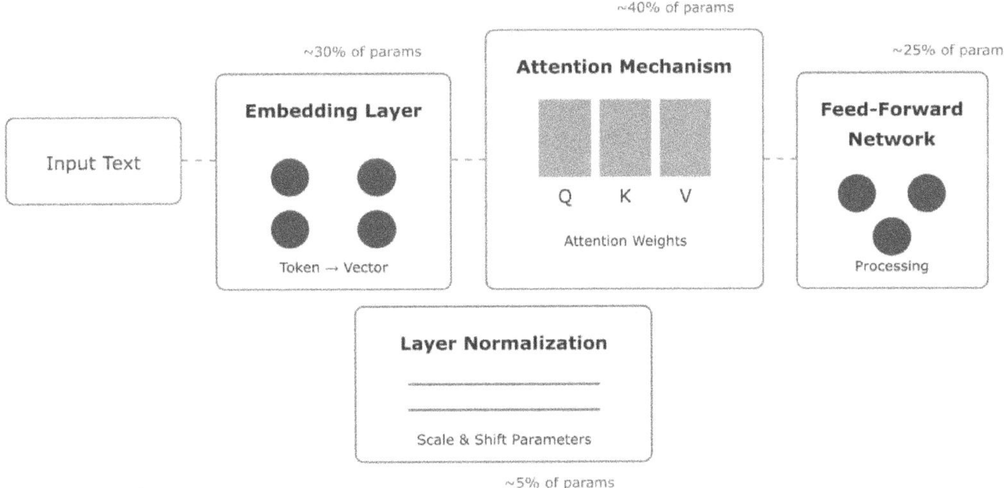

Fig. 6.4: The figure illustrates the different types of parameters in transformer-based LLMs and their roles across key architectural components: embedding layer (converting tokens to vectors), attention mechanism (Q, K, V matrices for computing attention), feed-forward network (processing transformed representations), and layer normalization (scaling and shifting for stable training).

Example calculation:

Let's say we have a simple feed-forward layer in our model with 1000 input neurons and 1000 output neurons. The number of parameters in just this layer would be:

1000 * 1000 = 1,000,000 (1 million) parameters

Now, consider that LLMs have many such layers, plus additional components, each with their own parameters. This is how we quickly reach billions of parameters.

It's important to note that while having more parameters generally allows for more complex models, it also increases:

- Computational requirements for training and inference
- The amount of data needed for effective training
- The risk of overfitting (memorising training data rather than learning general patterns)

Balancing the number of parameters with model performance and efficiency is an active area of research in the field of LLMs.

Overview of LLM Architecture

The Large Language Model architecture, shown in Fig. 6.5, implements a sophisticated sequence-to-sequence transformer framework that processes input through multiple stages of feature extraction and contextual understanding. The input layer begins with tokenization, converting raw text into subword units through byte-pair encoding (BPE) or WordPiece tokenization, followed by learned embeddings that map these tokens to high-dimensional vector spaces (typically 768 to 4096 dimensions). These embeddings are augmented with sinusoidal or learned positional encodings to maintain sequential information. The core processing occurs in the transformer blocks, which utilise multi-head self-attention mechanisms allowing each token to attend to the full sequence through scaled dot product attention (Query-Key-Value projections). Each attention head captures different semantic relationships, with their outputs concatenated and projected through a linear transformation. This is followed by a position-wise feed-forward network (FFN) consisting of two linear transformations with a GeLU or ReLU activation, enabling non-linear feature processing. Layer normalisation and residual connections surround both the self-attention and FFN components, stabilising deep network training. This transformer block is repeated N times (ranging from 12 to hundreds of layers), with each layer progressively building more sophisticated representations. The final output layer projects these representations through a linear transformation to logits matching the vocabulary size, followed by a softmax operation to produce a probability distribution over possible next tokens, enabling autoregressive generation or task-specific predictions. We will deep dive into the architecture in the next chapter.

LLM Architecture

1. Input Processing Layer
Purpose: Converts raw text into a format the model can process
- Tokenization: Breaks text into smaller units (tokens)
- Embedding: Converts tokens into vector representations
- Adds positional information to maintain sequence order

2. Transformer Layers (Core Processing)
Purpose: Processes and transforms the input representations
Key Components:
- Self-Attention: Captures relationships between all tokens
- Feed Forward Networks: Processes each token's representation
- Layer Normalization: Stabilizes training
- Repeated N times for deeper processing

3. Output Layer
Purpose: Generates final predictions or outputs
- Linear transformation: Projects to vocabulary size
- Softmax: Converts to probability distribution

Fig.6.5: The diagram illustrates the fundamental architecture of a Large Language Model (LLM), showing the three main components: input processing, transformer layers (purple), and output generation.

Before diving deeper into how LLMs process language, we need to understand the fundamental NLP concepts that form their foundation. These building blocks, when combined with the deep learning techniques we explored in Chapter 5, enable LLMs' sophisticated language processing capabilities.

OVERVIEW OF NATURAL LANGUAGE PROCESSING BASICS

To fully appreciate how Large Language Models work, it's crucial to understand some fundamental concepts in Natural Language Processing (NLP). These are the building blocks upon which more complex language understanding is built.

1. Tokenization:

Tokenization is the process of breaking down text into smaller units called tokens. These can be words, subwords, or even characters. For example:

Sentence: "OpenAI released GPT-3 in June 2020."

Tokens: ["Open", "AI", "released", "GPT", "-", "3", "in", "June", "2020", "."]

Tokenization is crucial because it's often the first step in processing text for an NLP system.

2. Part-of-Speech (POS) tagging:

POS tagging involves identifying the grammatical part-of-speech for each word in a sentence (e.g., noun, verb, adjective). This helps in understanding the structure and meaning of the sentence.

3. Named Entity Recognition (NER):

NER is the task of identifying and classifying named entities (such as persons, organizations, locations) in text.

4. Syntactic Parsing:

This involves analysing the grammatical structure of a sentence, often represented as a parse tree.

Let's look at a code example that demonstrates these basic NLP tasks:

```
1.   import nltk
2.   from nltk import word_tokenize, pos_tag, ne_chunk
3.   from nltk.tree import Tree
4.   # Download necessary NLTK data
5.   nltk.download('punkt')
6.   nltk.download('averaged_perceptron_tagger')
7.   nltk.download('maxent_ne_chunker')
8.   nltk.download('words')
9.   # Example sentence
10.  sentence = "OpenAI released GPT-3 in June 2020."
11.  # Tokenization
12.  tokens = word_tokenize(sentence)
13.  print("Tokens:", tokens)
14.  # Part-of-speech tagging
15.  pos_tags = pos_tag(tokens)
16.  print("POS Tags:", pos_tags)
17.  # Named Entity Recognition
18.  ner_tree = ne_chunk(pos_tags)
19.  print("Named Entities:")
20.  for subtree in ner_tree:
21.  if isinstance(subtree, Tree):
22.  print(subtree.label(), ' '.join([token for token, pos in subtree.leaves()]))
23.  # Simple demonstration of syntactic parsing (using POS tags)
24.  print("\nSimplified Syntactic Structure:")
25.  for token, pos in pos_tags:
26.     print(f"{token} ({pos})")
```

Code Exhibit 6.1: NLTK (Natural Language Toolkit) is a comprehensive Python library for natural language processing that provides tools and interfaces for working with human language data. In this code, NLTK is being used to perform three fundamental NLP tasks: tokenization (breaking text into words), part-of-speech tagging (labeling words with their grammatical roles like nouns, verbs), and named entity recognition (identifying and classifying named entities like organizations, dates), demonstrating basic text analysis capabilities on the sample sentence "OpenAI released GPT-3 in June 2020."

This code demonstrates:

1. Tokenization: The `word_tokenize()` function splits the sentence into individual words and punctuation marks.

2. POS Tagging: `pos_tag()` assigns a part-of-speech tag to each token (e.g., NNP for proper noun, VBD for past tense verb).

3. Named Entity Recognition: `ne_chunk()` identifies and classifies named entities in the text.

4. A simplified view of syntactic structure using the POS tags.

Output:

```
Tokens: ['OpenAI', 'released', 'GPT-3', 'in', 'June', '2020', '.']
POS Tags: [('OpenAI', 'NNP'), ('released', 'VBD'), ('GPT-3', 'NNP'), ('in', 'IN'), ('June', 'NNP'),
('2020', 'CD'), ('.', '.')]
Named Entities:
ORGANIZATION: OpenAI
GPT-3
Simplified Syntactic Structure:
OpenAI (NNP)
released (VBD)
GPT-3 (NNP)
in (IN)
June (NNP)
2020 (CD)
. (.)
```

This example illustrates how basic NLP tasks break down and analyse text, forming the foundation for more complex language understanding in LLMs.

The practical implementation of LLMs relies on sophisticated machine learning techniques that build upon both traditional NLP approaches and modern neural architectures. This synthesis of methods enables the remarkable capabilities we see in current systems.

THE ROLE OF MACHINE LEARNING IN LLMS

Large Language Models (LLMs) represent a sophisticated application of machine learning principles, showcasing how different learning paradigms work together to create systems that can understand and generate human-like text. The development and training of LLMs involve several fundamental machine learning concepts that build upon each other to create increasingly sophisticated language understanding capabilities.

Training Pipeline and Model Development

The LLM training pipeline, illustrated in Fig.6.6, represents a sophisticated approach to developing powerful language models through several distinct yet interconnected stages. At its foundation, the process begins with pre-training on vast corpora of text data, where models learn fundamental language understanding through self-supervised learning tasks like next token prediction. This initial phase creates a base model equipped with broad linguistic knowledge and pattern recognition capabilities, serving as the foundation for all subsequent adaptations.

The adaptation of these models for specific tasks primarily occurs through transfer learning approaches. These include few-shot learning (adaptation with minimal examples), zero-shot learning (task performance without specific training examples), and multi-task learning (simultaneous learning of multiple objectives). These approaches can be implemented through two main methods: full model fine-tuning or Parameter-Efficient Fine-Tuning (PEFT). Full fine-tuning updates all model parameters but requires significant computational resources. PEFT methods offer resource-efficient alternatives: LoRA (Low-Rank Adaptation) injects trainable rank decomposition matrices while keeping most parameters frozen, prompt tuning optimizes soft prompts that guide the model's behaviour, and adapters insert small trainable modules between existing model layers.

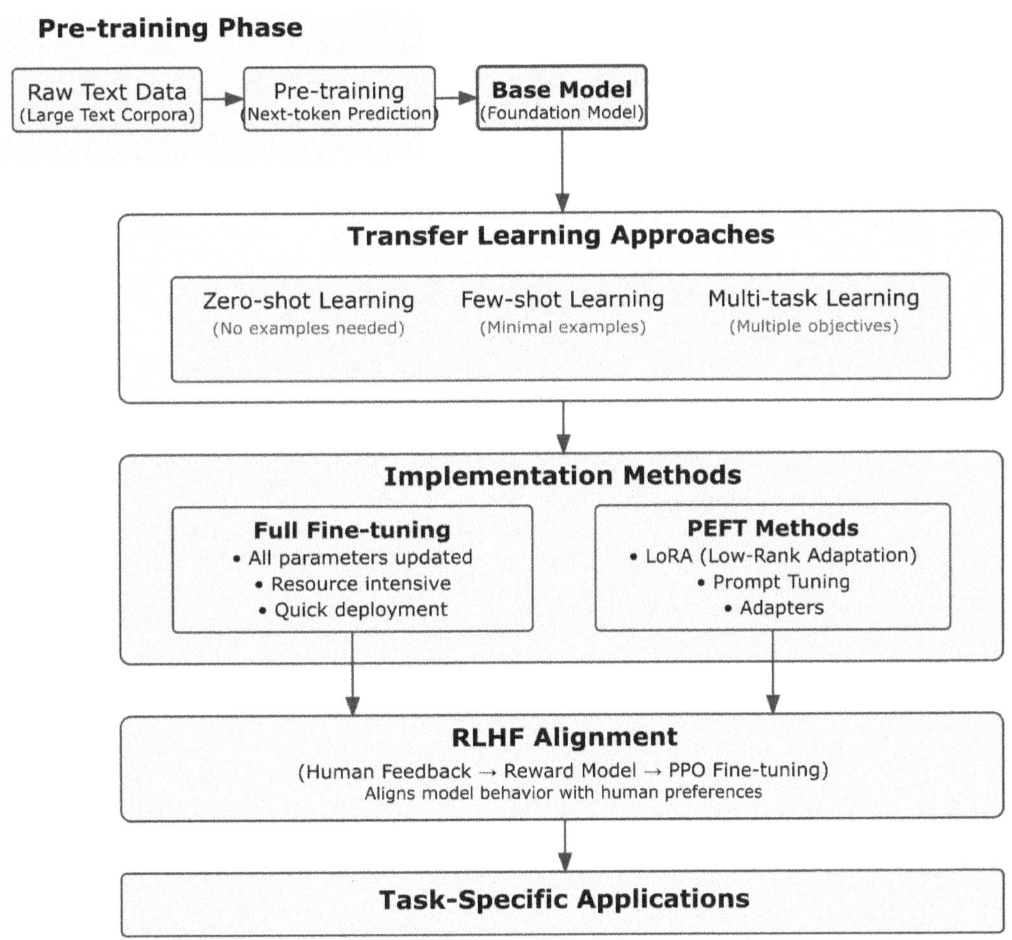

Fig. 6.6: LLM Training Pipeline demonstrates how knowledge transfers from pre-training (using raw text) through different adaptation methods (PEFT, LoRA, adapters) to various task learning approaches (few-shot, zero-shot, multi-task), showing the progressive specialization of the model.

A crucial component in modern LLM development is Reinforcement Learning from Human Feedback (RLHF), which aligns model outputs with human preferences and values. RLHF operates through a three-stage process: first, collecting human feedback on model outputs to create a dataset of preferred responses; second, training a reward model that learns to predict human preferences; and finally, using Proximal Policy Optimization (PPO) to fine-tune the model. PPO, a reinforcement learning algorithm, carefully updates the model's policy to maximise the reward signal while preventing too large policy changes that could destabilise training. This process is typically applied after initial task adaptation and helps ensure that the model not only performs tasks effectively but does so in a way that aligns with human values and preferences.

This comprehensive pipeline combines transfer learning principles with efficient adaptation methods and human feedback alignment, enabling LLMs to develop both task-specific capabilities and appropriate behaviour patterns. The result is models that can effectively tackle specific tasks while maintaining alignment with human preferences, all achieved with varying degrees of computational efficiency depending on the chosen implementation methods.

Core Learning Paradigms

At the heart of LLM development are three distinct learning paradigms, illustrated in Fig.6.7, each playing a crucial role. Self-supervised learning serves as the primary approach, where models learn by predicting parts of their input data - typically predicting masked or next tokens in text sequences. This approach is particularly powerful because it allows models to create their own supervisory signals from raw text data, effectively learning from vast amounts of unlabelled text while maintaining a clear training objective. This differs from traditional supervised learning, which requires human-annotated data, and unsupervised learning, which focuses on discovering patterns without explicit training signals. The self-supervised approach has proven transformative, enabling models to learn rich language representations from the virtually unlimited text available on the internet.

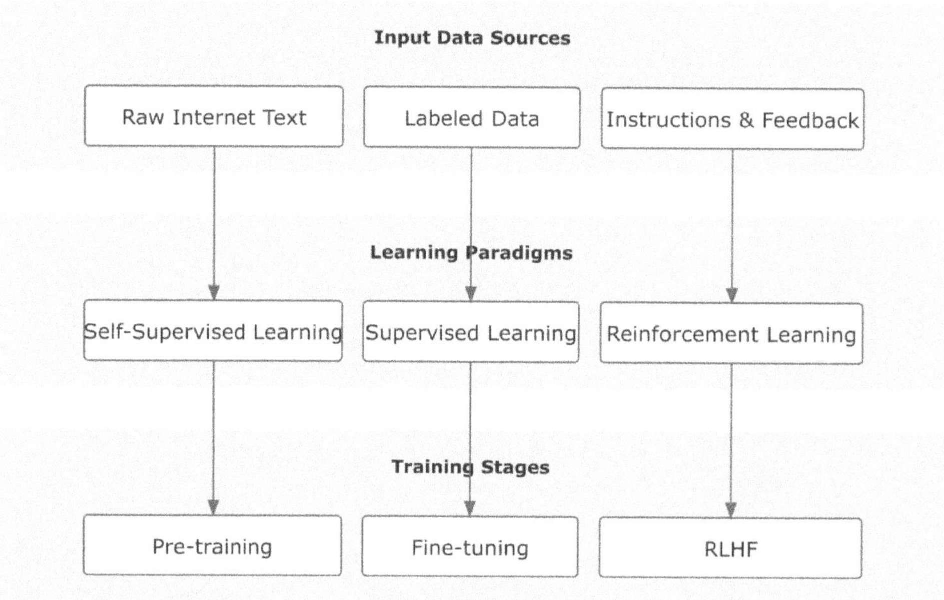

Fig. 6.7: LLM Learning Flow (Input ➡ Paradigms ➡ Training): Shows how raw data, labelled data, and feedback flow through different learning approaches (self-supervised, supervised, and reinforcement learning) to create the final training stages (pre-training, fine-tuning, and RLHF), illustrating the complete learning pipeline of LLMs.

Neural Network Architectures

Underlying all these learning processes are sophisticated neural network architectures, particularly transformer models. These architectures use self-attention mechanisms to process text, allowing models to weigh the importance of different words in context. The self-attention mechanism enables models to capture complex dependencies and relationships within text, contributing to their impressive language understanding capabilities.

Through this layered approach to learning - from basic pattern recognition to sophisticated task adaptation - LLMs develop their ability to understand and generate human-like text. This progression from general language understanding to specific task capabilities demonstrates how different machine learning concepts work together to create increasingly sophisticated AI systems.

IMPORTANCE AND APPLICATIONS OF LLMS

The importance of Large Language Models cannot be overstated. They have transformed various fields and opened up new possibilities in how we interact with technology and process information. Here are some key areas where LLMs have made significant impacts:

1. Natural Language Understanding and Generation:

LLMs have dramatically improved machines' ability to understand and generate human-like text. This has applications in:

- Chatbots and virtual assistants
- Content creation (articles, stories, poems)
- Text summarisation
- Sentiment analysis

2. Translation and Multilingual Capabilities:

LLMs can perform high-quality translations between numerous languages, often capturing nuances and context that previous systems struggled with.

3. Content Creation and Summarization:

LLMs can generate human-like text on a wide range of topics, as well as summarise long documents while retaining key information.

4. Code Generation and Analysis:

Some LLMs are trained on code repositories and can assist in writing, debugging, and explaining code across various programming languages.

5. Question Answering and Information Retrieval:

LLMs can understand complex queries and provide relevant, contextualised answers, making them powerful tools for information retrieval and knowledge management.

Example of Real-world Application:

In customer service, LLMs power chatbots that can understand and respond to customer queries in natural language, handling a wide range of topics without needing pre-programmed responses for every possible question. For instance, a customer might ask:

"I received my order yesterday, but the blue shirt I ordered looks more like navy. Can I exchange it for a different colour?"

An LLM-powered chatbot could understand the context of the query, recognise the issue (colour discrepancy), and provide a relevant response:

"I'm sorry to hear that the colour of the shirt wasn't what you expected. Yes, you can certainly exchange it for a different colour. Our return policy allows exchanges within 30 days of purchase. Would you like me to guide you through the exchange process or provide information on other available colours?"

This demonstrates the LLM's ability to understand context, extract relevant information, and generate a helpful, human-like response.

CHALLENGES AND LIMITATIONS OF CURRENT LLMS

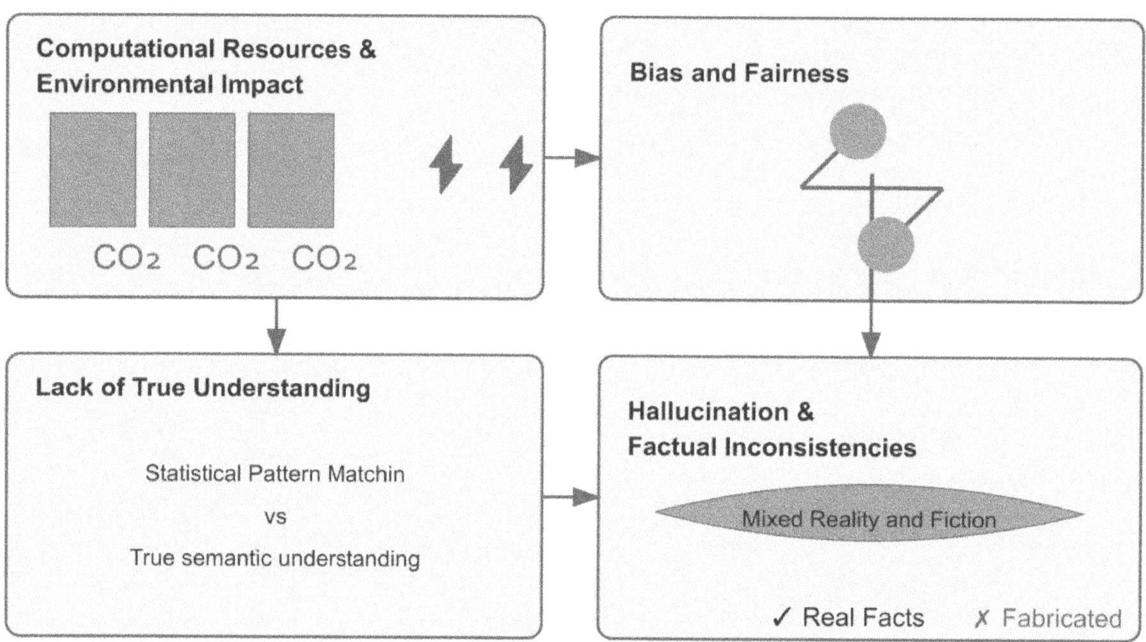

Fig. 6.8: A visual overview of key challenges in LLM development, highlighting the interplay between computational demands, fairness concerns, understanding limitations, and reliability issues. These fundamental challenges underscore both the current limitations and areas for future improvement in LLM technology.

While LLMs have achieved remarkable capabilities, they also face significant challenges and limitations, see Fig.6.8:

1. Computational Resources and Environmental Impact:

Training and running LLMs require enormous computational power, raising concerns about energy consumption and carbon footprint.

2. Bias and Fairness:

LLMs can perpetuate and amplify biases present in their training data, leading to unfair or discriminatory outputs.

3. Lack of True Understanding:
Despite their impressive outputs, LLMs fundamentally operate on statistical patterns rather than true understanding. This can lead to nonsensical or inconsistent responses when pushed beyond their training boundaries.

4. Hallucination and Factual Inconsistencies:
LLMs can generate plausible-sounding but entirely fabricated information, a phenomenon known as "hallucination."

Example: An LLM might confidently generate a detailed biography of a fictional person, demonstrating its ability to create coherent text but also highlighting its tendency to "hallucinate" information that seems plausible but is entirely fabricated.

LOOKING AHEAD: THE FUTURE OF LLMS

As we look to the future of Large Language Models, several exciting trends and considerations emerge:

1. Increased Model Size and Efficiency:
While models have been growing larger, there's also a push for more efficient architectures that can achieve similar performance with fewer parameters.

2. Multimodal Models:
Future LLMs may integrate text with other data types such as images, audio, and video, leading to a more comprehensive understanding and generation capabilities.

3. Ethical Considerations and Responsible Development:
As LLMs become more powerful and ubiquitous, there's a growing focus on developing them responsibly, with considerations for privacy, security, and societal impact.

4. Specialised Models:
We may see more LLMs fine-tuned for specific domains or tasks, balancing the benefits of large-scale pretraining with domain-specific expertise.

Thought Experiment: Imagine a future where LLMs are seamlessly integrated into every aspect of digital interaction. How might this change the way we work, learn, and communicate? What new possibilities and challenges might arise in fields like education, healthcare, or creative arts?

DISCUSSION

The introduction to Large Language Models reveals a fascinating convergence of multiple technological streams. Building on the mathematical foundations we explored in Chapter 1, the embedding techniques from Chapter 3, the efficient data structures from Chapter 4, and the deep learning fundamentals from Chapter 5, these models represent a quantum leap in artificial intelligence.

Their emergence wasn't just a matter of scaling existing systems - it required fundamental innovations in how we represent, process, and generate language.

What makes LLMs particularly intriguing is their probabilistic nature. Unlike traditional rule-based systems, these models operate on distributions of meaning, leveraging the geometric properties of high-dimensional spaces we discussed earlier to capture the fluid, contextual nature of language. This probabilistic foundation explains both their remarkable capabilities and their limitations - from their ability to generate coherent text across diverse domains to the phenomenon of hallucination, which becomes more understandable when viewed through the lens of probability distributions and pattern matching.

As we move forward to explore LLM architectures in Chapter 7, this foundational understanding will prove crucial. The technical choices in architecture design - from attention mechanisms to layer normalization - directly reflect the theoretical principles we've covered. Success in developing and deploying these systems requires not just understanding individual components, but appreciating how they work together to create models that can process language with unprecedented sophistication. The future of LLMs lies not just in scaling existing architectures, but in finding novel ways to combine these fundamental principles to create more efficient, reliable, and capable systems.

KEY TAKEAWAYS:

1. Large Language Models are AI systems designed to understand, generate, and manipulate human language in a coherent and contextually appropriate way.
2. The scale of LLMs, in terms of both model parameters and training data, is a key characteristic that enables their remarkable capabilities.
3. The evolution of language models, from early statistical approaches to the current transformer-based architectures, highlights the field's rapid progress and the fundamental shift in how we approach language understanding.

REFLECTIVE PROMPTS:

1. How do the computational and memory demands of LLMs, as discussed in this chapter, shape the ethical considerations around their development and deployment? What are the potential societal implications of these resource-intensive AI systems?
2. The historical progression of language models demonstrates a shift from rule-based to data-driven approaches. What are the advantages and limitations of each paradigm, and how might future LLMs balance these perspectives to achieve more robust and versatile language understanding?
3. As LLMs become more prominent in our daily lives, what are the potential risks and benefits of these systems being integrated into various industries and applications? How can we ensure that the transformative power of LLMs is harnessed responsibly and for the greater good of humanity?

Building on this foundational understanding, Chapter 7 will explore the core architectural components and design choices that define the structure of modern Large Language Models.

THE ARCHITECTURE OF LARGE LANGUAGE MODELS

Reflective Prompt: You are tasked with deploying an LLM in a production environment. Explain the trade-offs between model performance, computational efficiency, and resource requirements, and how they highlight the fundamental challenges in scaling these systems.

INTRODUCTION TO NEURAL NETWORK ARCHITECTURES IN NLP

The field of Natural Language Processing (NLP) has been revolutionized by the advent of neural network architectures. These architectures have enabled machines to process and generate human language with unprecedented accuracy and fluency. In this chapter, we'll explore the fundamental building blocks of Large Language Models (LLMs) and how they work together to create powerful language understanding and generation systems.

The evolution from simple feed-forward networks to sophisticated transformer architectures reflects not just technological progress, but a fundamental shift in how we approach language processing. This is illustrated in Fig.7.1. Each advancement addressed specific limitations of its **predecessors**, culminating in the transformer architecture that forms the backbone of modern LLMs. Understanding this evolution provides crucial context for appreciating the architectural choices in today's models.

Brief History of Neural Networks in NLP

Evolution of Neural Networks in NLP

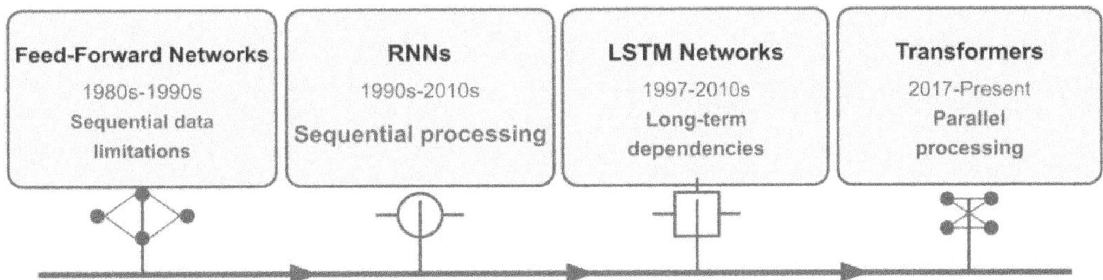

Fig. 7.1: A chronological progression of neural network architectures in NLP, showcasing the evolution from simple feed-forward networks to modern transformers, with each advancement addressing specific limitations of its predecessors. The timeline highlights key architectural innovations that have shaped the field's development from the 1980s to the present.

The journey of neural networks in NLP has been marked by several key milestones:

1. Feed-Forward Neural Networks (1980s-1990s): Early attempts at using neural networks for NLP tasks involved simple feed-forward architectures. While these showed promise, they struggled with sequential data and long-range dependencies in language.
2. Recurrent Neural Networks (RNNs) (1990s-2010s): RNNs introduced the ability to process sequential data, making them well-suited for tasks like language modelling and machine translation. However, they faced challenges with long sequences due to the vanishing gradient problem.
3. Long Short-Term Memory (LSTM) Networks (1997-2010s): LSTMs, a special kind of RNN, were designed to overcome the vanishing gradient problem. They became the go-to architecture for many NLP tasks for over a decade.
4. Transformer Architecture (2017-Present): The introduction of the Transformer model in the paper "Attention Is All You Need" by Vaswani et al. marked a paradigm shift in NLP. Transformers effectively addressed the limitations of RNNs and LSTMs, particularly in handling long-range dependencies and enabling parallel processing.

Transition from RNNs and LSTMs to Transformer-based Models

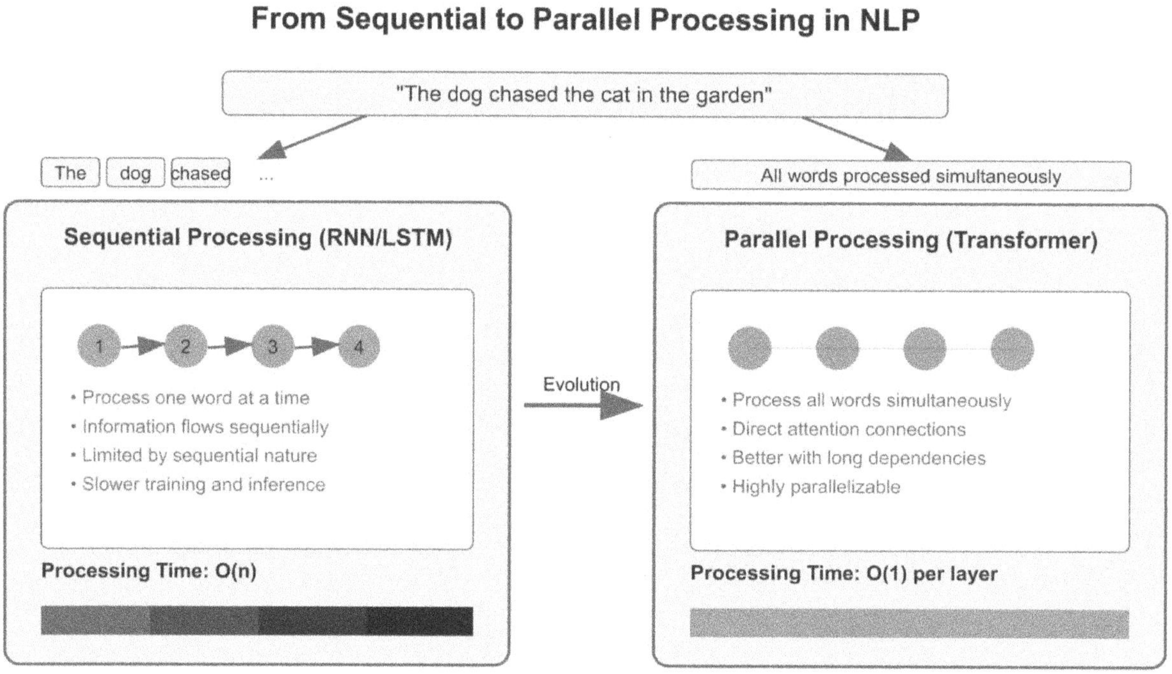

Fig. 7.2: A comparative visualization illustrating the fundamental shift from sequential processing in RNNs/LSTMs to parallel processing in Transformers, highlighting how the same input sentence is handled differently by each architecture. The diagram emphasises the key advantages of Transformer's parallel processing and attention mechanisms over traditional sequential approaches.

The transition from RNNs and LSTMs to Transformer-based models, as illustrated in Fig.7.2, represented a significant leap forward in NLP. Here's why:

1. Parallelization: RNNs and LSTMs process text sequentially, word by word. This makes them slow to train on large datasets. Transformers, on the other hand, can process entire sequences in parallel, dramatically speeding up training and inference.

2. Long-range Dependencies: While LSTMs improved upon basic RNNs in capturing long-range dependencies, they still struggled with very long sequences. Transformers, through their attention mechanisms, can directly model relationships between any two words in a sequence, regardless of their distance.

3. Scalability: Transformer architectures have proven to be highly scalable. As we increase the size of these models (in terms of parameters and training data), their performance continues to improve across a wide range of tasks.

4. Transfer Learning: The Transformer architecture enabled effective pretraining on large corpora of unlabelled text, followed by fine-tuning on specific tasks. This transfer learning approach has led to significant improvements in performance across numerous NLP tasks.

Consider this example to illustrate the difference:

Imagine trying to understand the sentence: "The dog, which had a red collar and was wagging its tail enthusiastically, chased the cat."

An RNN or LSTM would process this sentence word by word, potentially struggling to connect "dog" with "chased" due to the long dependent clause in between. A Transformer, however, can directly attend to "dog" when processing "chased," easily capturing this long-range dependency.

As we delve deeper into the architecture of Large Language Models in the following sections, we'll see how the Transformer architecture and its subsequent innovations have enabled the creation of increasingly powerful language models.

FUNDAMENTAL CONCEPTS

These historical developments led to key insights about processing sequential data, particularly the importance of parallel processing and attention mechanisms. Let's examine these fundamental concepts that form the building blocks of modern LLM architectures, starting with how models represent and process information.

High-Level LLM Architecture Overview

Large Language Models (LLMs) are composed of several key architectural components working together to process and generate text, see Fig.7.3. Understanding this high-level architecture provides a foundation for diving deeper into individual components.

Self-Attention

- Multi-head attention mechanism for capturing relationships between tokens
- Layer normalisation for stabilising learning
- Residual connections for better gradient flow

While attention mechanisms provide the means for information exchange between tokens, the overall information flow in LLMs follows a carefully designed path through multiple processing stages. This flow, from input embedding through multiple transformer layers to output generation, ensures efficient processing while maintaining the rich relationships captured by attention mechanisms.

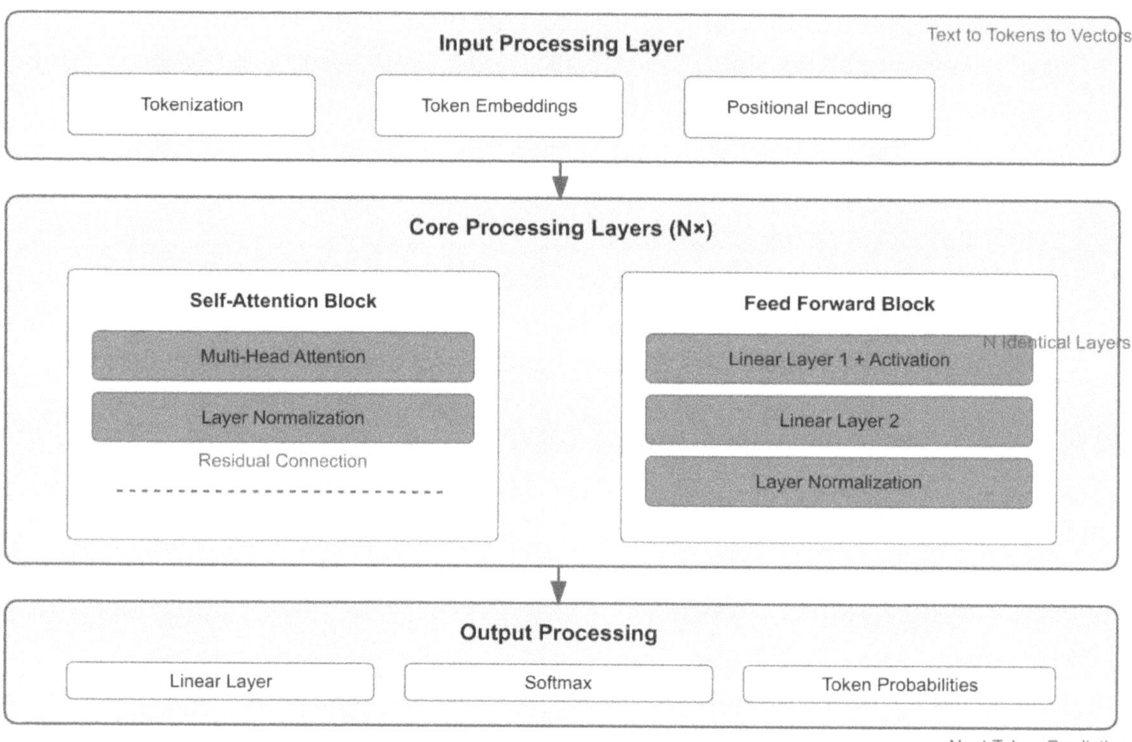

Fig. 7.3: Comprehensive overview of LLM's three-tier architecture: input processing (tokenization, embeddings, and positional encoding), core processing (multiple transformer layers with self-attention and feed-forward blocks), and output processing layers. The diagram illustrates how these components work together to transform raw text into meaningful representations and generate predictions, showing the model's parallel processing capabilities and deep architectural structure.

Information Flow
1. Forward Pass:
- Text is tokenized and embedded with position information
- Embeddings pass through multiple transformer layers
- Each layer processes information through:
  o Self-attention to capture token relationships
  o Feed-forward networks for transformation
  o Final layer produces output representations
2. Key Characteristics:
- Parallel Processing: Processes all tokens simultaneously in the attention layer
- Deep Architecture: Typically 12-96+ layers depending on model size.
- Residual Connections: Allow information to flow directly through the network.
- Layer Normalization: Stabilises training in deep networks

CORE LLM ARCHITECTURE

With these foundational elements established, we can now explore how modern LLMs integrate them into a coherent architecture. The design choices in each component - from input processing through core layers to output generation - reflect careful consideration of how to best leverage these fundamental concepts. Let's begin with how raw text is transformed into a format the model can process.

Input Processing

Tokenization and Embeddings

Before a Large Language Model can process text, the input needs to be converted into a form that the model can understand. This is where tokenization and embeddings come into play. These processes transform human-readable text into numerical representations that can be processed by the neural network.

Tokenization Strategies

Tokenization is the process of breaking down text into smaller units called tokens. There are several strategies for tokenization, each with its own advantages and trade-offs, see Fig.7.4:

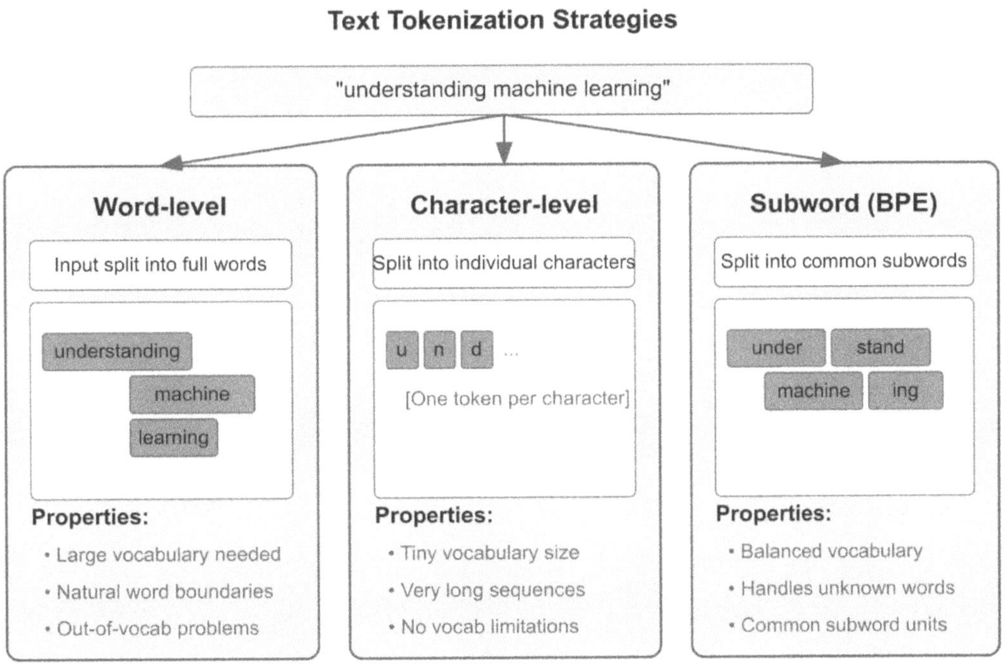

Fig. 7.4: Comparison of Word-level, Character-level, and Subword Tokenization approaches, showing how each method breaks down text differently with their respective advantages and limitations.

1. Word-level Tokenization:
- Splits text into words based on whitespace and punctuation.
- Pros: Intuitive, preserves word boundaries.
- Cons: Large vocabulary size; struggles with out-of-vocabulary words.
Example: "I love NLP!" → ["I", "love", "NLP", "!"]

2. Character-level Tokenization:
- Splits text into individual characters.
- Pros: Small vocabulary size, no out-of-vocabulary issues.
- Cons: Very long sequences; loses word-level semantics.

Example: "I love NLP!" → ["I", " ", "l", "o", "v", "e", " ", "N", "L", "P", "!"]

3. Subword Tokenization:
- Breaks words into smaller units, balancing between word and character-level approaches.
- Popular algorithms: Byte-Pair Encoding (BPE), WordPiece, SentencePiece.
- Pros: Handles out-of-vocabulary words, balances vocabulary size and sequence length.
- Cons: May split words in unintuitive ways.

Example (using BPE): "I love NLP!" → ["I", "love", "NL", "P", "!"]

Most modern LLMs use subword tokenization strategies. For instance, GPT models use a variant of BPE, while BERT uses WordPiece.

Word Embeddings vs. Subword Embeddings

Once text is tokenized, each token needs to be represented as a vector of numbers. This is where embeddings come in (see Fig. 7.5).

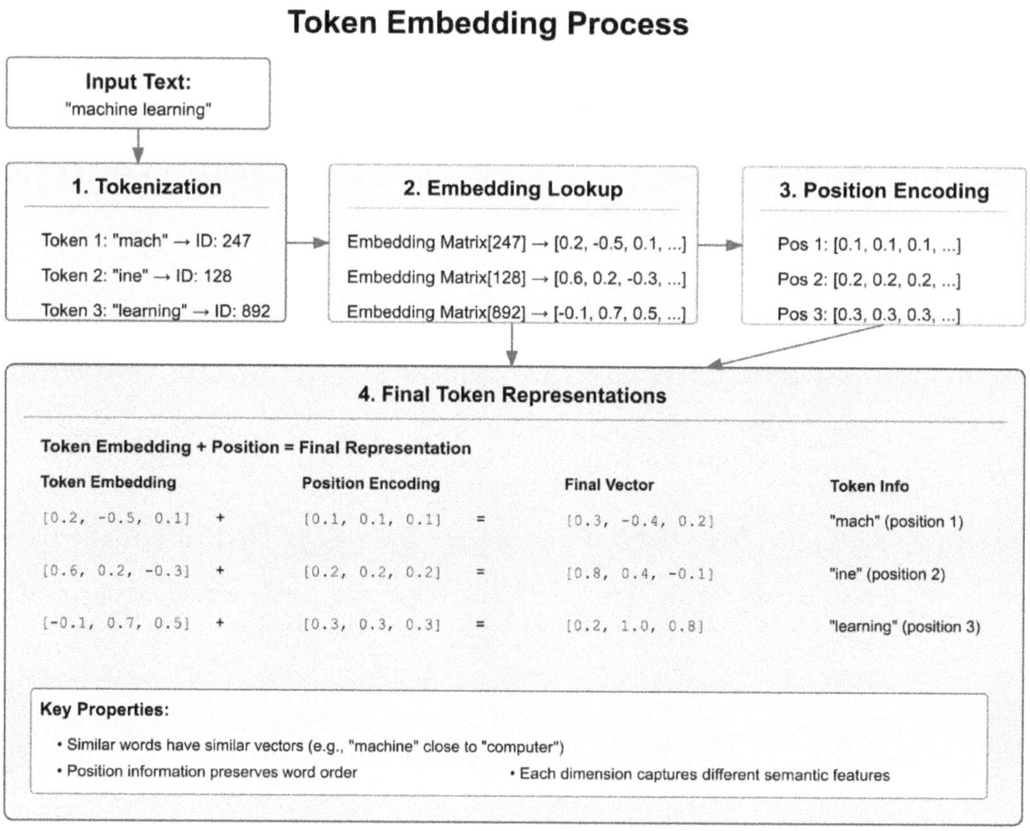

Token Embedding Process

Fig. 7.5: Comprehensive visualisation of the token embedding process, from raw text to final vector representations, showing how tokens are converted to numerical vectors and combined with positional information to create context-aware embeddings.

1. Word Embeddings:
- Each word in the vocabulary is assigned a dense vector representation.
- Examples: Word2Vec, GloVe.
- Pros: Captures semantic relationships between words.
- Cons: Struggles with out-of-vocabulary words, doesn't handle polysemy well.
2. Subword Embeddings:
- Used in conjunction with subword tokenization.
- Each subword unit is assigned a vector representation.
- Pros: Can handle out-of-vocabulary words, more flexible.
- Cons: May lose some word-level semantic information.

In practice, most modern LLMs use subword embeddings. The embedding layer is typically the first layer of the model and is learned during the training process.

Positional Encodings

One challenge with the Transformer architecture is that it processes all tokens in parallel, potentially losing information about the order of tokens in the sequence. To address this, positional encodings are added to the token embeddings.

Positional encodings are vectors that represent the position of each token in the sequence. They have two key properties:
1. They should be unique for each position.
2. The relative positions of tokens should be consistently represented across sequences of different lengths.

In the original Transformer paper, the authors used sine and cosine functions of different frequencies:

PE(pos, 2i) = sin(pos / 10000^(2i/d_model))
PE(pos, 2i+1) = cos(pos / 10000^(2i/d_model))

Where 'pos' is the position in the sequence, 'i' is the dimension, and 'd_model' is the embedding dimension.

These positional encodings are added to the token embeddings before they are passed to the first layer of the Transformer.

Example:

Let's consider a simple sentence: "I love machine learning"

1. Tokenization (using a hypothetical subword tokenizer):

["I", "love", "mach", "ine", "learning"]

2. Each of these tokens would be converted to an embedding vector, let's say of dimension 4 for simplicity:

I: [0.1, -0.2, 0.3, 0.4]
love: [0.5, 0.6, -0.7, 0.8]
mach: [-0.1, 0.2, 0.3, -0.4]
ine: [0.5, -0.6, 0.7, 0.8]
learning: [-0.9, 0.1, -0.2, 0.3]

3. Positional encodings (simplified for illustration) might look like:
Position 1: [0.1, 0.2, 0.3, 0.4]
Position 2: [0.2, 0.3, 0.4, 0.5]
Position 3: [0.3, 0.4, 0.5, 0.6]
Position 4: [0.4, 0.5, 0.6, 0.7]
Position 5: [0.5, 0.6, 0.7, 0.8]
4. The final input to the first Transformer layer would be the sum of the token embeddings and the positional encodings:

I: [0.2, 0.0, 0.6, 0.8]
   love: [0.7, 0.9, -0.3, 1.3]
   mach: [0.2, 0.6, 0.8, 0.2]
   ine: [0.9, -0.1, 1.3, 1.5]
   learning: [-0.4, 0.7, 0.5, 1.1]

This process allows the model to understand both the meaning of the tokens and their positions in the sequence.

Core Processing Layer

The Transformer Architecture

The Transformer architecture, introduced in 2017, has become the foundation for most modern Large Language Models. Its innovative design allows for efficient processing of sequential data without the need for recurrence, enabling parallel computation and better capture of long-range dependencies.

Overview of the Transformer Model

In the previous chapter, we briefly covered the transformer and attention, but given its importance, we will cover it in detail in this chapter. The Transformer model is based on the encoder-decoder architecture, as illustrated in Fig.7.6, which was commonly used in sequence-to-sequence tasks like machine translation. However, it replaces the traditional recurrent layers with multi-head self-attention mechanisms.

Key features of the Transformer include:

1. Parallelization: Unlike RNNs, Transformers can process all elements of the input sequence in parallel.
2. Attention Mechanisms: These allow the model to weigh the importance of different parts of the input when producing each part of the output.
3. Positional Encodings: Since the model has no recurrence, positional encodings are added to provide the model with information about the sequence order.

Key Components: Encoder and Decoder

The original Transformer consists of two main components: the encoder and the decoder.
1. Encoder:
- Processes the input sequence
- Consists of a stack of identical layers

- Each layer has two sub-layers:
- Multi-head self-attention mechanism
- Position-wise fully connected feed-forward network

2. Decoder:
- Generates the output sequence
- Also consists of a stack of identical layers
- Each layer has three sub-layers:
- Masked multi-head self-attention mechanism
- Multi-head attention over the encoder's output
- Position-wise fully connected feed-forward network

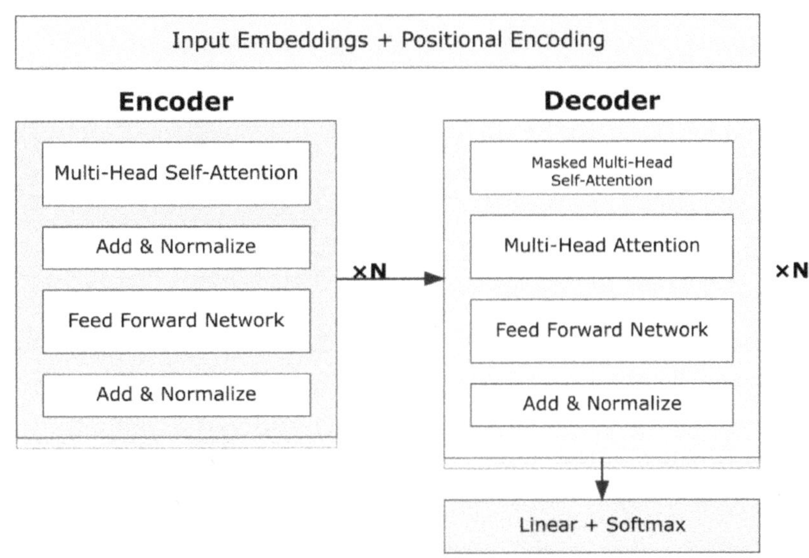

Fig. 7.6: The diagram illustrates the complete Transformer architecture, showing how information flows from input through parallel encoder (left, red) and decoder (right, green) stacks, with each containing repeated layers of attention mechanisms, feed-forward networks, and normalization layers, ultimately producing output through a final linear and SoftMax layer.

Output Processing Layer: From Hidden States to Next Token Prediction

The output processing layer is the final stage of an LLM's architecture, where rich internal representations are transformed into meaningful predictions. This layer plays the crucial role of converting complex hidden states into probabilities over the model's vocabulary, consisting of three key components working in sequence:

1. Linear Layer (Projection)
- Takes the high-dimensional hidden states (e.g., 768 or 1024 dimensions)
- Projects them to match vocabulary size (e.g., 50,000 tokens)
- Learns mappings between features and token probabilities

Example: Converting a 1024D vector to a 50,000D vector of logits
Each dimension represents the model's "confidence score" for a token

2. Softmax Function
   - Converts raw logits into proper probability distributions
   - Ensures all probabilities are between 0 and 1
   - Makes probabilities sum to 1 across vocabulary

Formula: $P(x\_i) = \exp(x\_i/T) / \Sigma \exp(x\_j/T)$
x_i represents the logit (raw score) for a specific token i in the vocabulary.

Let me break this down: x_i is the unnormalized score (logit) that comes from the linear layer for token i. For example, if we're predicting the next word and "cat" is token i, then x_i would be the raw score for "cat". The subscript i refers to a specific position in the vocabulary. If vocabulary size is 50,000, then i can be any number from 1 to 50,000. Each i corresponds to a different token in the vocabulary

Here, T is the "temperature" parameter that controls the randomness of predictions:
- Lower temperature (T < 1) makes predictions more focused and deterministic
- Higher temperature (T > 1) makes predictions more diverse and exploratory
- T = 1 maintains the original distribution

3. Token Probabilities.
   o Uses the probability distribution to select the next token.
   o Can use different sampling strategies:
     - Greedy: Always choose highest probability token (like low temperature)
     - Sampling: Choose tokens based on their probabilities, influenced by temperature
     - Higher temperatures encourage more creative and varied outputs
     - Lower temperatures produce more consistent and focused outputs

This architecture allows the model to both generate reliable, focused text when needed (low temperature) and explore more creative possibilities (high temperature) while maintaining coherent outputs.

ADVANCE ARCHITECTURAL COMPONENTS

While attention mechanisms and feed-forward networks form the basic building blocks of transformer layers, stable and efficient processing at scale requires additional architectural innovations. Layer normalization and residual connections are crucial components that enable deep networks to learn effectively.

Layer Normalization and Residual Connections

As we've seen, Large Language Models are composed of many layers of attention mechanisms and feed-forward networks. Training such deep networks can be challenging due to issues like vanishing or exploding gradients. Two techniques that have proven crucial in addressing these challenges are layer normalization and residual connections.

Layer Normalization

Layer normalization is a technique used to normalise the inputs to each layer in a neural network, see Fig.7.7. It helps in stabilising the learning process and reducing the training time.

Layer Normalization and Residual Connection

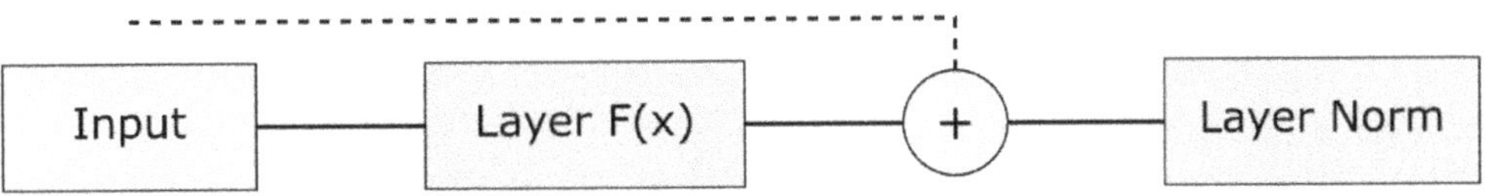

Fig. 7.7: The figure demonstrates how residual connections create a direct path for information flow by adding the input directly to the layer's output (x + F(x)), followed by layer normalization, which stabilizes training by normalizing the combined output, forming a fundamental building block of transformer architectures.

Purpose of Layer Normalization

1. Stabilize Training: By normalising the inputs to each layer, layer normalisation helps to reduce the internal covariate shift (changes in the distribution of layer inputs during training).
2. Faster Convergence: Normalised inputs tend to result in faster convergence during training.
3. Reduce Dependence on Initialization: Layer normalization makes the network less sensitive to the initial weight values.

Implementation of Layer Normalization

Layer normalization computes the mean and variance used for normalization from all of the summed inputs to the neurons in a layer on a single training case.

Mathematically, for an input vector $x = (x_1,..., x_m)$, layer normalization is defined as:

$$LN(x) = \alpha \odot (x - \mu) / (\sigma + \varepsilon) + \beta$$

Where:
- μ is the mean of the inputs
- σ is the standard deviation of the inputs
- α and β are learnable parameters.
- $\odot$ represents element-wise multiplication.
- ε is a small constant added for numerical stability. It will be a small value constant to prevent division by zero in the normalization step.

Example:

Consider a layer with input [2, 4, 6]:

1. Calculate the mean: $(2 + 4 + 6) / 3 = 4$
2. Calculate variance: $((2\text{-}4)^2 + (4\text{-}4)^2 + (6\text{-}4)^2) / 3 = 4$
3. Normalize: $[(2\text{-}4)/\sqrt{(4+\varepsilon)}, (4\text{-}4)/\sqrt{(4+\varepsilon)}, (6\text{-}4)/\sqrt{(4+\varepsilon)}] \approx [-1, 0, 1]$
4. Scale and shift: $\alpha \odot [-1, 0, 1] + \beta$

The values of α and β are learned during training

Residual Connections

Residual connections, also known as skip connections, are another key component in modern LLMs. They allow information to flow directly from earlier layers to later layers.

Purpose of Residual Connections

1. Mitigate Vanishing Gradients: By providing a direct path for gradients to flow backwards, residual connections help combat the vanishing gradient problem in deep networks.
2. Enable Training of Very Deep Networks: Residual connections make it possible to train networks with hundreds or even thousands of layers.
3. Preserve Information: They allow the network to easily learn identity functions, preserving important information throughout the network.

Implementation of Residual Connections

In a residual connection, the output of a layer is added to its input before being passed to the next layer. Mathematically:

$y = F(x) + x$
Where:
- x is the input to the layer
- $F(x)$ is the function learned by the layer
- y is the output
In the context of Transformer-based LLMs, residual connections are typically applied around both the attention mechanism and the feed-forward network within each Transformer layer.
Example:
In a Transformer layer:
1. Input: x
2. After attention: $y = Attention(x) + x$
3. After feed-forward: $z = FFN(y) + y$

This structure allows the model to learn residual functions with reference to the layer inputs, rather than having to learn the entire transformation.

Having understood the high-level architecture, let's dive deeper into attention mechanisms - the innovation that makes modern LLMs possible. Attention allows models to dynamically focus on relevant information, mimicking how humans process language by emphasising different parts of input based on context.

Attention Mechanisms

Attention mechanisms are a crucial component of modern Large Language Models. They allow the model to focus on different parts of the input when producing each part of the output, mimicking the way humans pay attention to specific details when processing information.

What is Attention and Why is it Important?

At its core, attention in neural networks is a way to assign importance weights to different parts of the input data. In the context of NLP, this means giving different weights to different words or tokens in a sequence.

Importance of attention:

1. Handling variable-length inputs: Attention allows models to process input sequences of any length effectively.

2. Capturing long-range dependencies: It enables the model to directly connect distant parts of the input, addressing a key limitation of RNNs.

3. Interpretability: Attention weights can often be visualised to understand which parts of the input the model is focusing on for a particular output.

Types of Attention: Self-Attention and Multi-Head Attention

1. Self-Attention:

Self-attention, also known as intra-attention, is a mechanism that relates different positions of a single sequence in order to compute a representation of the sequence. This is illustrated in Fig.7.8.

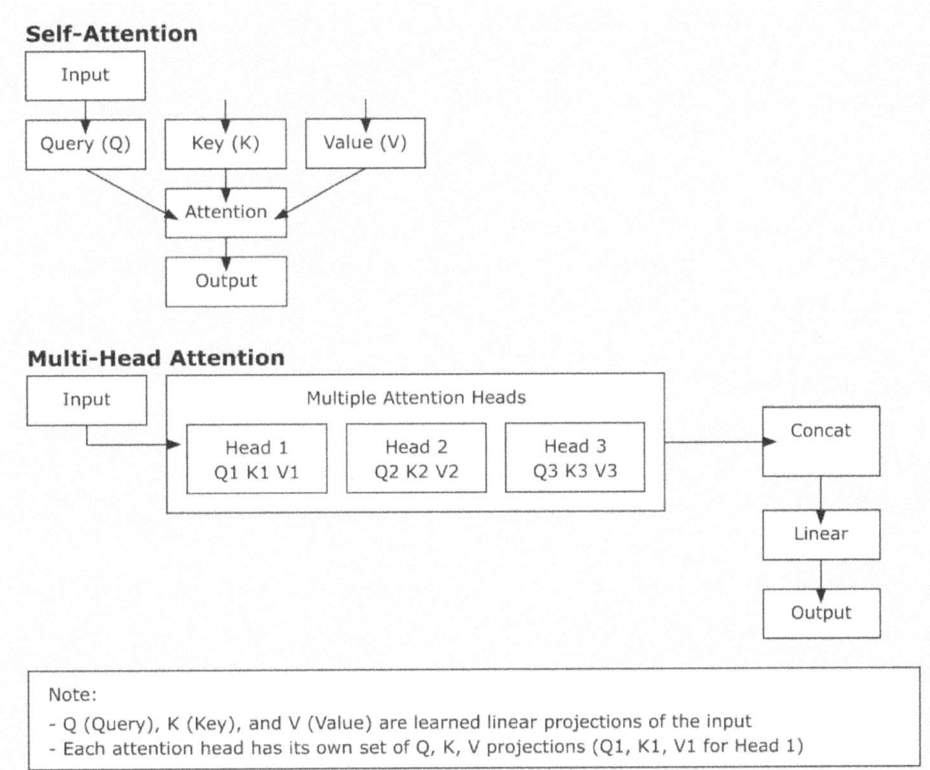

Fig. 7.8: The diagram illustrates the architectures of self-attention (single-head attention) and multi-head attention, highlighting the key components such as Query (Q), Key (K), Value (V), and the flow of data through the attention layers to produce the output.

Here's how self-attention works:

1. For each word in the input sequence, three vectors are created:
- Query vector (Q)
- Key vector (K)
- Value vector (V)

2. These matrices are created by multiplying the embedding of the word with three matrices that are learned during the training process.

3. To calculate the attention for a word:
• Take the dot product of its query vector with the key vectors of all words (including itself)

- Scale the results and apply a softmax function to obtain attention weights
- Multiply these weights by the value vectors

4. The result is a weighted sum of the value vectors, where the weights represent how much focus to place on other parts of the input sequence when encoding a particular word.

> Mathematically, this can be represented as:
> Attention(Q, K, V) = softmax((QK^T) / √d_k)V
> Where d_k is the dimension of the key vectors.

This process allows the model to attend to different parts of the input sequence differently for each word, enabling it to capture complex relationships and dependencies within the data.

While single-head self-attention provides the basic mechanism for capturing relationships between tokens, modern LLMs use multiple attention heads operating in parallel. This multi-head approach allows the model to capture different types of relationships simultaneously, much like how humans process multiple aspects of language at once.

2. Multi-Head Attention:

Multi-head attention is an extension of the self-attention mechanism that adds more power and flexibility to the attention layer. Instead of performing a single attention function, multi-head attention performs multiple attention operations in parallel.

Let's dive deeper into multi-head attention:

Multi-Head Self-Attention in Detail

Multi-head attention consists of several attention layers running in parallel. Each of these attention layers is called a "head". Here's how it works:

1. Multiple Sets of Q, K, V: Instead of having a single set of Query (Q), Key (K), and Value (V) matrices, multi-head attention creates multiple sets. If we have h heads, we'll have h sets of Q, K, and V.
2. Parallel Processing: Each head performs its attention calculation independently, using its own set of Q, K, and V matrices.
3. Different Aspects of Representation: Each head can potentially focus on different aspects of the input. For example, one head might capture syntactic relationships, while another focuses on semantic relationships.
4. Concatenation and Linear Transformation: The outputs from all heads are concatenated and then passed through a final linear transformation to produce the final output.

Mathematically, multi-head attention can be expressed as:

> MultiHead(Q, K, V) = Concat(head_1,..., head_h)W^O
> where head_i = Attention(QW_i^Q, KW_i^K, VW_i^V)
> Here, W^O and W_i^Q, W_i^K, W_i^V are learned parameter matrices.

Advantages of Multi-Head Attention

1. Richer Representations: By allowing the model to jointly attend to information from different representation subspaces, multi-head attention captures more complex patterns in the data.

2. Increased Model Capacity: Multiple heads increase the model's capacity to learn without a substantial increase in computational cost, as the operations can be parallelized.

3. Improved Performance: In practice, multi-head attention has been shown to outperform single-head attention across various NLP tasks.

Feed-Forward Neural Networks in LLMs

While attention mechanisms are a key innovation in Transformer-based LLMs, feed-forward neural networks still play a crucial role in these architectures. In this section, we'll explore how feed-forward networks are used in Transformer-based LLMs and why they're important, see Fig.7.9.

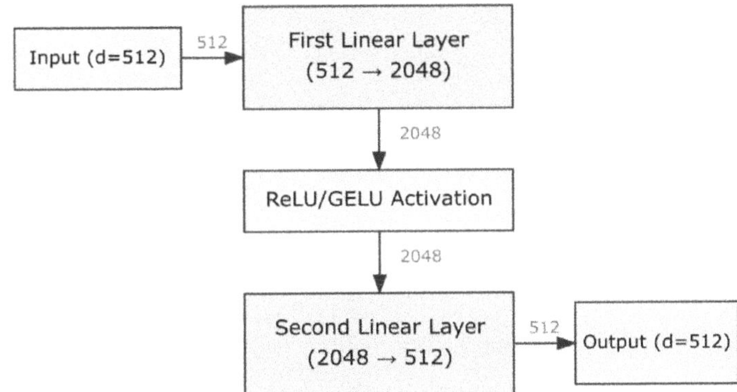

Fig. 7.9: The diagram illustrates the feed-forward network structure in transformers, showing how input vectors (dimension 512) are first projected to a higher dimension (2048) through a linear layer, passed through an activation function (ReLU/GELU), and then projected back to the original dimension (512) through a second linear layer.

Structure and Function of Feed-Forward Layers

In the context of Transformer-based LLMs, feed-forward neural networks typically refer to fully connected layers that are applied to each position separately and identically. These layers are sometimes called "position-wise feed-forward networks."

Structure:

1. The feed-forward network usually consists of two linear transformations with a non-linear activation function in between.

2. It's applied to each position (token) in the sequence independently.

Mathematically, this can be expressed as:

$$\text{FFN}(x) = \max(0, xW\_1 + b\_1)W\_2 + b\_2$$
Where:
- x is the input vector
- W_1 and W_2 are weight matrices
- b_1 and b_2 are bias vectors
- $\max(0,...)$ represents the ReLU activation function

Function:

The primary roles of the feed-forward network in LLMs include:

1. Introducing Non-linearity: While attention mechanisms are essentially weighted sums (linear operations), the feed-forward network introduces non-linearity, allowing the model to learn more complex functions.
2. Increasing Model Capacity: The feed-forward layers typically project the data to a higher-dimensional space and then back down, effectively increasing the model's capacity to represent complex patterns.
3. Position-wise Processing: By applying the same transformation to each position independently, the model can learn position-specific features.

Example:

Let's say we have a sequence of 5 tokens, each represented by a vector of dimension 512 after the attention layer. The feed-forward network might:

1. Project each 512-dimensional vector to a 2048-dimensional space (first linear transformation)
2. Apply ReLU activation.
3. Project back to 512 dimensions (second linear transformation).

This process is repeated for each of the 5 tokens independently.

Activation Functions Commonly Used in LLMs

Activation functions introduce nonlinearity into the model, allowing it to learn more complex patterns. In LLMs, several activation functions are commonly used:

1. ReLU (Rectified Linear Unit):

- Function: $f(x) = \max(0, x)$

  - Pros: Simple, computationally efficient, helps mitigate the vanishing gradient problem
  - Cons: "Dying ReLU" problem (neurons can sometimes get stuck in a state where they never activate)

2. GELU (Gaussian Error Linear Unit):

- Function: $f(x) = x * \Phi(x)$, where $\Phi(x)$ is the cumulative distribution function of the standard normal distribution

  - Pros: Smooth function, often performs better than ReLU in language models
  - Cons: More computationally expensive than ReLU

3. Swish:

- Function: $f(x) = x * \mathrm{sigmoid}(x)$

  - Pros: Smooth, non-monotonic function that often outperforms ReLU
  - Cons: More computationally expensive than ReLU

Many modern LLMs, including BERT and GPT models, use GELU as their activation function.

The Role of Feed-Forward Networks in the Overall LLM Architecture

In a typical Transformer layer, the feed-forward network is applied after the attention mechanism:

1. Multi-head attention is computed
2. Add & Norm (residual connection and layer normalisation)
3. Feed-forward network is applied

    4.   Another Add & Norm

This sequence allows the model to:

    1.   Capture complex relationships between tokens (via attention)

    2.   Process this information in a position-wise manner (via feed-forward network)

The combination of these operations enables LLMs to learn highly sophisticated language representations.

By stacking multiple such layers (often 12, 24, or more in large models), LLMs can learn to perform a wide variety of language tasks with high proficiency.

SCALING AND EFFICIENCY

With the core architectural components established, a key question emerges: how do we scale these models to achieve better performance? Scaling isn't simply about making everything bigger - it requires careful consideration of multiple dimensions and their interactions. This is illustrated in Fig.7.10. Let's examine each scaling dimension and its implications.

Four Dimensions of Scaling LLM architecture

Depth Scaling: Computing Through Layers

At the heart of LLMs lies the question of depth - the number of transformer layers through which information flows. With linear computational complexity O(L), depth scaling presents a deceptively simple growth pattern. Each layer adds to the model's reasoning capacity through successive transformations of the input representation.

The computational cost grows predictably: each layer introduces self-attention ($2d^2 \times n$ operations) and feed-forward transformations ($4d^2 \times n$ operations). While this linear scaling appears manageable, the reality is more nuanced. Beyond 50 layers, gradient flow becomes increasingly unstable, requiring sophisticated normalization techniques and carefully tuned residual connections. Models like GPT-3 (175B) with 96 layers represent a careful balance between depth and stability.

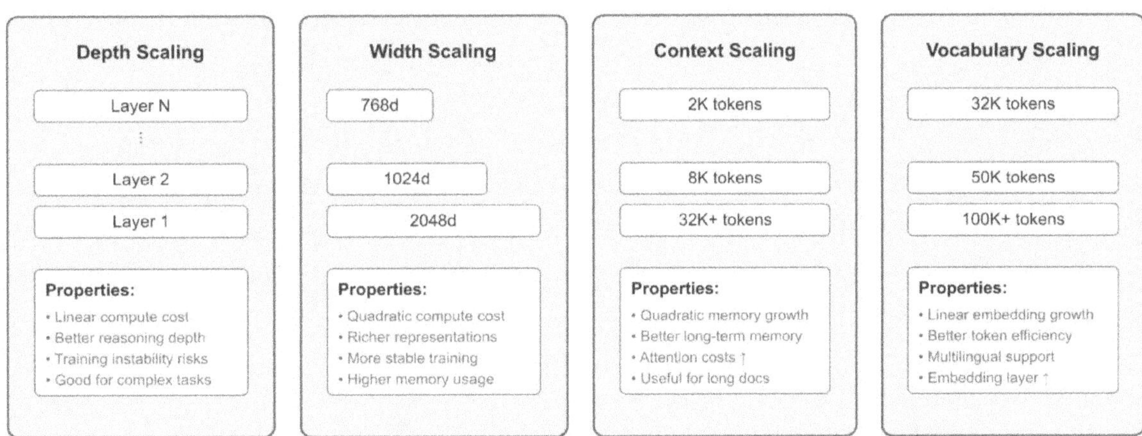

Fig. 7.10: Visualization of key LLM scaling dimensions - depth, width, context, and vocabulary size - showing their computational implications and growth patterns. Each dimension presents distinct trade-offs between model capabilities and resource requirements, influencing architecture decisions for specific deployment scenarios.

It is best suited for tasks requiring sequential reasoning and complex logical steps. Mathematical problem-solving, code generation, and structured analysis benefit most from increased depth.

Width Scaling: The Representational Capacity

Model width - the dimension of hidden representations - influences computational complexity quadratically $O(d^2)$. This dimension affects every major computation in the transformer architecture: attention mechanisms, feed-forward transformations, and embedding projections. The quadratic cost manifests in both computation and memory usage, making width scaling particularly resource-intensive.

Consider PaLM's 18,432-dimensional representations compared to BERT-base's 768 dimensions. This expansion enables richer feature capture but comes at a steep computational cost. The trade-off becomes evident in attention computations, where the quadratic scaling of query-key interactions can quickly dominate computational requirements.

This scaling strategy is particularly effective for tasks demanding rich feature representation and parallel processing of multiple concepts. Language translation, semantic analysis, and tasks requiring nuanced understanding of context benefit from wider models. The increased representational capacity helps capture subtle variations in meaning and complex relationships between concepts.

Context Length: The Memory Horizon

Perhaps the most challenging scaling dimension is context length, with its quadratic memory scaling $O(n^2)$. This impacts both attention computations and memory requirements for key-value caches. The progression from early models handling 512 tokens to modern architectures managing 32K+ tokens illustrates both the importance and complexity of context scaling.

This scaling strategy is critical for tasks involving long-form content analysis and generation. Document summarisation, legal contract analysis, and long-form question-answering see dramatic improvements with increased context length.

Vocabulary Scaling: The Token Space

Vocabulary size presents a linear scaling challenge $O(V)$, primarily affecting the embedding and output layers. While this might seem like the most manageable scaling dimension, its implications are significant. Multilingual models often require vocabularies exceeding 250K tokens, substantially increasing the parameter count in embedding layers.

This scaling strategy is essential for multilingual applications and domain-specific tasks with specialised terminology. Technical documentation, medical analysis, and cross-lingual transfer benefit most from expanded vocabularies. Also crucial for models handling multiple scripts or specialised notation systems. However, general conversational tasks might see minimal benefits beyond a certain vocabulary threshold.

Balancing Act: General-Purpose LLMs

General-purpose LLMs face a unique challenge in balancing these scaling dimensions to maintain versatility across diverse tasks. Models like GPT-4 and PaLM exemplify sophisticated scaling strategies that optimise for broad applicability while managing computational constraints.

These models typically employ a balanced scaling approach: moderate depth (24-96 layers) provides reasonable sequential reasoning capability, substantial width (2048-12288 dimensions) enables rich feature capture, and extended context windows (8K-32K tokens) support various document lengths. The vocabulary size usually settles around 50K-100K tokens for English-centric models, expanding to 250K+ for multilingual capabilities.

Scaling Laws in LLMs

Research has shown that the performance of language models tends to follow predictable "scaling laws" as we increase model size, dataset size, and compute resources, as shown in Fig.7.11. These laws, first comprehensively described by OpenAI researchers, provide crucial insights into the behaviour of LLMs at scale.

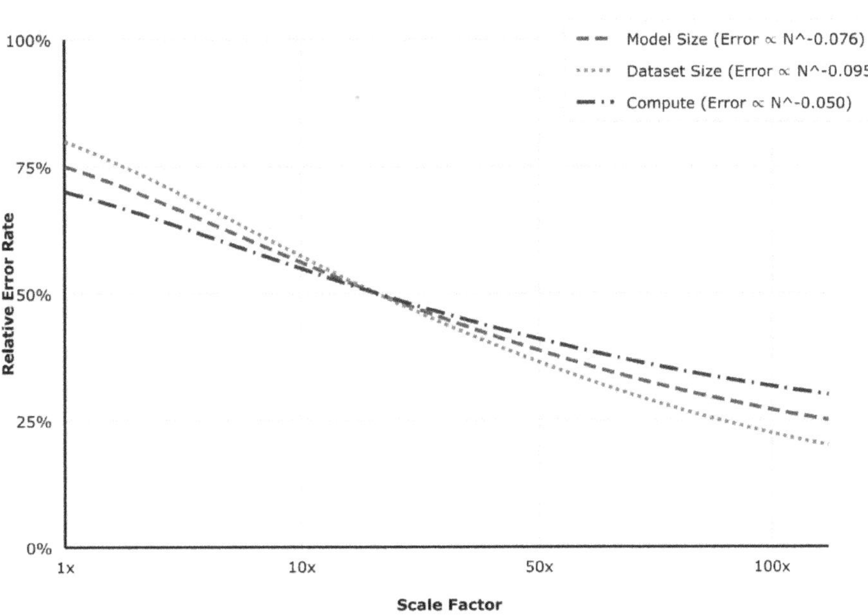

Fig. 7.11: Visualization of LLM scaling laws demonstrating how error rates decrease with increased resources. Dataset size shows the steepest improvement (dotted line), followed by model size (dashed line)while compute scaling (dash-dot) requires the largest increase to achieve similar gains.

Key Scaling Relationships

1. Model Size (Number of Parameters)
- As model size increases, performance improves following a power-law relationship.
- Mathematically: Error ∝ (Number of Parameters)^(-0.076)
- This means that to halve the error rate, you need to increase the model size by about 10 times.
2. Dataset Size
- Similar to model size, increasing the dataset size also improves performance following a power-law.
- Mathematically: Error ∝ (Dataset Size)^(-0.095)

- This indicates that to halve the error rate, you need to increase the dataset size by about 7 times.

3. Compute Resources

- The relationship between computing and performance also follows a power-law.
- Mathematically: Error $\propto$ (Compute)$^{(-0.050)}$
- This suggests that to halve the error rate, you need to increase computing power by about 20 times.

Implications of Scaling Laws

1. Smooth Scaling: Performance improves smoothly as we scale up, without sudden jumps or plateaus. This suggests that continuing to scale up models will likely lead to further improvements.
2. Trade-offs: There's a trade-off between compute-efficient and data-efficient scaling. Larger models are more compute-efficient (they require less data to reach a given level of performance), while smaller models trained on more data are more data-efficient.
3. Diminishing Returns: While performance continues to improve with scale, the rate of improvement slows down. Each doubling of model size or dataset size yields a smaller improvement than the previous doubling.
4. Predictability: These laws allow researchers to predict how much a model's performance will improve with increased scale, helping to guide resource allocation and research directions.

Practical Example

Let's consider a hypothetical scenario to illustrate these laws:

Suppose we have a language model with 1 billion parameters, trained on 10 billion tokens, achieving a certain performance level.

1. To improve performance by reducing errors by about 20%:
   - We could increase the model size to about 10 billion parameters, or
   - Increase the dataset size to about 70 billion tokens or
   - Increase the compute used in training by about 20 times
2. If we wanted to halve the error rate:
   - We'd need to increase the model size to about 100 billion parameters, or
   - Increase the dataset size to about 490 billion tokens, or
   - Increase the computing power by about 400 times

This example illustrates why recent trends have favoured increasing model size and dataset size simultaneously, as it's often more practical than exponentially increasing compute resources.

Limitations and Considerations

1. Upper Limits: It's unclear whether these scaling laws will continue indefinitely or if there's an upper limit to performance improvements from scaling.
2. Task Dependence: While these laws hold broadly, the exact coefficients can vary depending on the specific task or benchmark.
3. Architectural Innovations: New architectural designs might alter these scaling relationships. For instance, sparse models like Switch Transformers aim to improve the efficiency of scaling.

4. Real-World Constraints: Practical constraints like memory limitations, inference time requirements, and energy consumption considerations often limit how much we can scale in practice.

5. Data Quality: These laws assume high-quality, diverse data. In practice, as datasets grow extremely large, maintaining quality becomes challenging and may affect scaling efficiency.

Understanding these scaling laws is crucial for researchers and practitioners in the field of LLMs. They guide decisions about resource allocation, help in predicting the benefits of scaling up models, and inform the search for more efficient architectures and training methods. As the field continues to evolve, refining our understanding of these scaling behaviours remains an active area of research.

While scaling laws provide insights into performance improvements through raw scale, architectural innovations offer ways to achieve better efficiency and effectiveness. These techniques represent creative solutions to the challenges posed by scaling traditional transformer architectures.

Architectural Innovations for Scaling

As models have grown, researchers have developed new techniques to make scaling more efficient:

1. Sparse Attention Mechanisms

- Instead of attending to all tokens, sparse attention selectively attends to a subset.
- This can reduce computational complexity from $O(n^2)$ to $O(n \log n)$ or even $O(n)$, where n is the sequence length.

  Examples: Sparse Transformer, Longformer, BigBird

2. Model Parallelism

- Distributing different parts of the model across multiple devices.
- This allows for training models that are too large to fit on a single GPU.

3. Activation Checkpointing

- Saving computation by recomputing activations during the backward pass instead of storing them.
- This trades off increased compute for reduced memory usage.

4. Mixed Precision Training

- Using lower precision (e.g., 16-bit) for some computations to save memory and increase speed.

MODERN ARCHITECTURE AND FUTURE DIRECTIONS

The theoretical understanding of scaling and architectural components manifests in various ways across different LLM implementations. Each major language model represents specific architectural choices and trade-offs. Let's examine how different organizations have approached these challenges in their implementations.

Popular LLM Architectures

A set of popular LLMs as on date are given in the Table below. This table represents information available as of model release dates. Many details for recent models are not publicly disclosed. The field continues to evolve rapidly.

Model	Developer	Release Date	Param eters	Architectur e	Training Data	Key Features
GPT-3	OpenAI	June 2020	175B	Decoder-only	Common Crawl, WebText2, Books1 & 2, Wikipedia	•Few-shot learning •2048-token context •45TB training data •Wide application range
GPT-4	OpenAI	March 2023	Not disclos ed	Decoder-only (presumed).	Not fully disclosed.	•Multimodal capabilities •Improved reasoning •Enhanced task performance
BERT	Google	October 2018	Base: 110M Large: 340M	Encoder-only	BookCorpus (800M words), Wikipedia (2.5B words).	•Bidirectional training •MLM & NSP objectives •Strong fine-tuning capabilities
T5	Google	October 2019	60M - 11B	Encoder-decoder	C4 (Colossal Clean Crawled Corpus)	•Unified text-to-text format •Transfer learning support •Strong benchmark performance
DALL-E 2	OpenAI	April 2022	Not disclos ed	Transformer + Diffusion	Millions of image-text pairs.	•Text-to-image generation • Image editing • CLIP integration
LaMDA	Google	May 2021	137B	Decoder-only	Public dialogue data, web documents	•Specialized for dialogue •Safety-focused. •1.56 trillion words training
PaLM	Google	April 2022	540B	Decoder-only	780B tokens from the web, books, and code	•Few-shot learning •Multilingual support •Strong reasoning
Megatron-Turing NLG	NVIDIA & Microsoft	October 2021	530B	Decoder-only	The Pile + web data	•Large-scale distribution •Zero-shot capabilities •270B tokens training
BLOOM	BigScience	July 2022	176B	Decoder-only	ROOTS corpus (46 languages).	• Open-source • 46 languages support • Ethical focus
Claude	Anthropic	March 2023	Not disclos ed	Not disclosed	Not fully disclosed.	•Strong reasoning • Safety-focused. •Coding capabilities

Emerging Architectures and Future Directions

Architecture Type	Key Aspects	Examples	Benefits	Challenges
Sparse Models	• Mixture of Experts (MoE) with a gating mechanism • Dynamic Sparsity	• GShard • Switch Transformer • DeepSpeed-MoE	• Better scaling without a proportional increase in computation • More energy-efficient	• Complex training and deployment • Inconsistent performance across inputs
Retrieval-Augmented Models	• External Knowledge Integration • Retrieval Mechanisms	• REALM (Google, 2020) • RAG (Facebook, 2020) • RETRO (DeepMind, 2021)	• Access to current information • Better interpretability with trackable sources	• Increased architectural complexity • Needs efficient retrieval mechanisms

Multimodal Models.	• Cross-modal Understanding • Unified Architectures	• DALL-E and CLIP • Wu Dao 2.0	• Comprehensive understanding • Human-like processing capabilities	• Complex architecture and training • Requires new evaluation metrics
Efficient Attention Mechanisms	• Linear Attention • Local Attention. • Sparse Attention.	• Linformer • Longformer • BigBird	• Handles longer sequences • Reduced computational needs	• Potential performance trade-offs. • May affect generalisation
Neuro-symbolic AI	• Reasoning Capabilities. • Interpretability.	• Neuro-Symbolic Concept Learner	• More robust and interpretable • Can incorporate prior knowledge	• Complex integration of AI paradigms • Balancing neural and symbolic approaches

Looking ahead, several trends seem likely to shape the future of LLM architectures:

Trend Category	Description
Sustainable AI	Growing emphasis on developing more energy-efficient and environmentally sustainable models
Personalization	Architectures that can efficiently adapt to individual users or specific domains
Continual Learning	Models that can update their knowledge without full retraining
Ethical AI	Architectural choices that promote fairness, reduce bias, and enhance privacy
Quantum Machine Learning	Potential development of quantum-inspired or quantum-accelerated LLM architectures as quantum computing matures

As we conclude this chapter, it's clear that while the Transformer architecture has been transformative for NLP, the field continues to evolve rapidly. Future LLMs are likely to be more efficient, adaptable, and capable across a broader range of tasks and modalities. However, with these advances come new challenges in terms of ethics, interpretability, and responsible development. As practitioners and researchers in this field, it's crucial to stay informed about these emerging trends and to consider their implications carefully.

DISCUSSION

The architecture of Large Language Models represents a remarkable synthesis of mathematical principles, computational efficiency, and cognitive inspiration. Building upon the mathematical foundations explored in earlier chapters, these architectures demonstrate how carefully designed components can work together to create systems of extraordinary capability. The transformer architecture, in particular, stands as a testament to how rethinking fundamental assumptions about sequence processing can lead to breakthrough advances.

What makes these architectures particularly fascinating is their scalability and adaptability. From the elegant mathematics of attention mechanisms to the practical considerations of layer normalization and residual connections, each component plays a crucial role in enabling models to scale to billions of parameters while remaining trainable. This scalability isn't just about size – it's about creating architectures that can effectively learn and leverage patterns in language at an unprecedented scale. As we've seen, the interplay between different scaling dimensions reveals deep insights about the nature of language learning itself.

Looking ahead to the training and deployment challenges we'll explore in subsequent chapters, these architectural foundations will prove crucial. Success in developing and deploying LLMs requires not just understanding individual components, but appreciating how they work together as an integrated system. Whether optimizing attention mechanisms for efficiency, developing better normalization techniques, or exploring new architectural paradigms, the principles we've examined will continue to guide innovation in the field. The future of LLMs lies not just in scaling existing architectures, but in finding novel ways to combine and enhance these components while maintaining their mathematical elegance and computational efficiency.

KEY TAKEAWAYS:

1. The transformer architecture, with its self-attention mechanism and feed-forward networks, forms the backbone of most modern large language models.
2. Scaling LLMs involves carefully balancing dimensions like model depth, width, context length, and vocabulary size, each with its own computational trade-offs.
3. Architectural innovations like sparse attention, mixture of experts, and retrieval-based models are enabling more efficient and capable LLM implementations.

REFLECTIVE PROMPTS:

1. The architectural choices in LLMs, such as the use of attention mechanisms and feed-forward networks, reflect a deeper understanding of how language is processed in the human brain. What insights can be drawn from this connection and how might it inform future developments in artificial general intelligence?
2. As LLMs continue to scale in size and complexity, what are the potential implications for their environmental impact in terms of energy consumption and carbon footprint? How can the field of AI address these concerns proactively?
3. The trade-offs between model performance, computational efficiency, and resource requirements, as discussed in this chapter, highlight the challenges in deploying LLMs at scale. What creative solutions or alternative approaches might emerge to overcome these fundamental constraints?

As we continue our journey, Chapter 8 will delve into the intricacies of training Large Language Models, examining the data preparation, pretraining objectives, and optimization strategies that are crucial for developing these powerful AI systems.

TRAINING LARGE LANGUAGE MODELS

Reflective Prompt: You are training a Large Language Model. Explain how the training techniques, such as self-supervised learning and efficient optimization strategies, enable the development of sophisticated language understanding capabilities in the model.

INTRODUCTION TO LLM TRAINING

Imagine teaching a student who needs to learn not just facts, but the entire pattern and structure of human knowledge and communication. This student needs to understand everything from basic grammar to complex reasoning, from poetry analysis to scientific discourse. Now imagine this student needs to learn from billions of examples, process them perfectly, and be able to apply this knowledge in entirely new situations. This is essentially what we're doing when training a Large Language Model (LLM).

The training of Large Language Models (LLMs) represents one of the most complex and resource-intensive processes in the field of artificial intelligence. It's a journey that transforms vast amounts of raw text data into a sophisticated AI system capable of understanding and generating human-like text across a wide range of topics and tasks. In this chapter, we'll explore the intricacies of this process, from data preparation to advanced training techniques and evaluation methods.

Overview of the Training Process

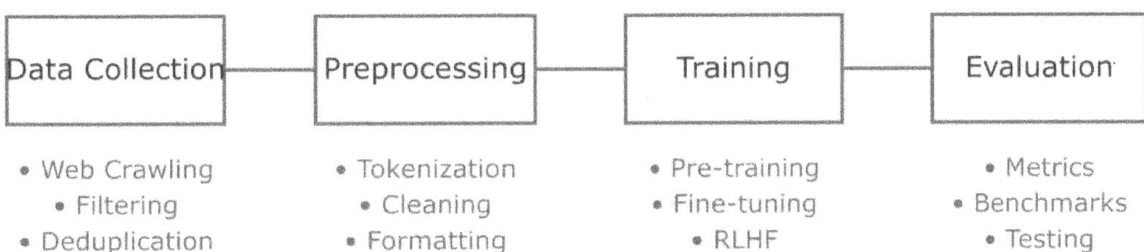

Fig. 8.1: Overview of the LLM training pipeline showing the four main stages: data collection, preprocessing, training, and evaluation, with key subtasks for each stage.

The LLM training pipeline, shown in Fig.8.1, represents a complex, multi-staged process that transforms raw internet data into sophisticated language models. It begins with massive-scale data collection, where web crawlers systematically gather text from diverse sources including books, articles, websites, and academic papers, followed by careful filtering and deduplication to ensure quality and uniqueness. The preprocessing stage then transforms this raw data through tokenization, cleaning, and formatting – converting human-readable text into structured sequences that machines can process efficiently.

The heart of the pipeline lies in the training phase, which typically occurs in three distinct stages: pre-training, where the model learns general language understanding from vast amounts of text; fine-tuning, where it's specialised for specific tasks or domains; and RLHF (Reinforcement Learning from Human Feedback), where human preferences help refine the model's outputs to be more helpful and aligned with human values. The final evaluation phase rigorously tests the model's capabilities through multiple benchmarks, assessing everything from basic comprehension to complex reasoning, while also checking for potential biases and safety concerns.

This entire pipeline requires immense computational resources, often running on large clusters of GPUs or TPUs, and can take weeks or months to complete, depending on the model's size and complexity. The process is typically iterative, with insights from evaluation feeding back into earlier stages to continuously improve the model's performance and reliability.

Differences Between Training LLMs and Other Neural Networks

Aspect	Large Language Models (LLMs)	Traditional Neural Networks
Scale	• Billions of parameters • Terabytes of training data • Requires specialised infrastructure	• Usually, millions of parameters or less • Gigabytes of data or less • Can run on standard hardware
Training Approach	• Two-phase: pre-training + fine-tuning • General language understanding first • Task-specific adaptation later	• Single-phase training • Directly trained for a specific task • No general pre-training needed
Architecture Needs	• Must handle long-range dependencies • Requires Transformer architecture • Complex attention mechanisms	• Simpler architectures are often sufficient • Shorter input sequences • Local pattern recognition
Computational Resources	• Hundreds or thousands of GPUs • Training takes weeks or months • Massive parallel processing	• Single or few GPUs are often sufficient • Hours/days of training • More manageable computing needs
Generalisation	• Expected to handle many tasks • Few/zero-shot learning capabilities • Broad knowledge application	• Task-specific performance. • Requires task-specific training data. • Limited to the trained domain
Ethical Considerations	• Privacy concerns with web-crawled data • Bias in large-scale datasets • Complex societal implications	• Usually domain-specific data • More controlled data sources • Limited ethical scope

As we delve deeper into this chapter, we'll explore each aspect of the LLM training process in detail. We'll discuss the challenges faced by researchers and practitioners, the cutting-edge techniques used to overcome these challenges, and the ongoing efforts to make LLM training more efficient, effective, and ethically sound.

Whether you're a researcher looking to advance the state-of-the-art, a practitioner aiming to apply LLMs to real-world problems, or simply an enthusiast eager to understand these powerful AI systems, this chapter will provide you with a comprehensive understanding of how Large Language Models are brought to life through the training process.

DATA PREPARATION AND PREPROCESSING

Imagine you're tasked with creating a digital library that encompasses all human knowledge and expression. Now, picture doing this not just for human readers, but for an AI that's trying to understand and emulate human language. This is essentially what we're doing when preparing data for a Large Language Model. It's a monumental task that requires careful planning, sophisticated tools, and a deep understanding of both language and technology.

The journey begins with data collection, a process that's akin to a digital archaeological expedition. Web crawlers, the workhorses of this expedition, tirelessly scour the internet, archiving everything from scientific papers to social media posts. Take Common Crawl, for instance, a non-profit organization that regularly crawls the web and freely provides its archive for research purposes. Many LLMs, including GPT-3, have used Common Crawl data as a substantial part of their training corpus.

But the internet isn't the only source. Digital books, academic journals, and even transcripts of spoken conversations all find their way into the mix. The goal is diversity – a rich tapestry of language use that covers everything from casual chat to formal discourse, from creative writing to technical documentation.

However, not all that glitters is gold in this digital landscape. Much of what we collect is unusable in its raw form. It's like panning for gold in a river – you need to sift through a lot of mud to find the nuggets. This is where data cleaning comes into play.

Imagine you've scraped a webpage that looks like this:

```
html
<div class="article">
    <h1>The Future of AI</h1>
    <p>Artificial Intelligence is rapidly evolving. <span class="highlight">Machine learning</span> and <span class="highlight">deep learning</span> are at the forefront of this revolution.</p>
    <!-- User Comment -->
    <div class="comment">
      <p>Great article! Can't wait to see what's next in AI.</p>
    </div>
</div>
```

We don't want our LLM to learn HTML tags or distinguish between article text and user comments. So, we need to clean this up. We might use a tool like BeautifulSoup in Python to parse the HTML and extract just the main text: which will give us:

"The Future of AI

Artificial Intelligence is rapidly evolving. Machine learning and deep learning are at the forefront of this revolution."

Notice how we've stripped away all the HTML tags and excluded the user comment. This cleaned text is much more suitable for training an LLM.

But cleaning isn't just about removing HTML tags. It's also about handling different character encodings, normalizing whitespace, and dealing with special characters. For instance, we might want to convert all text to UTF-8 encoding to ensure consistency across our dataset.

Once we have clean text, we move on to tokenization – the process of breaking text into smaller units that our model can process. This is where things get really interesting.

Modern LLMs typically use subword tokenization methods. One popular approach is Byte-Pair Encoding (BPE), used by models like GPT-3. BPE starts with a basic vocabulary of individual characters and iteratively merges the most frequent pairs of tokens to form new tokens.

Let's see how this might work in practice. Imagine we're tokenizing the word "unbelievable" using a simplified BPE process:

1. Start with character-level tokens: ["u", "n", "b", "e", "l", "i", "e", "v", "a", "b", "l", "e"]
2. Find the most common pair: "e" appears most often
3. Merge this pair: ["u", "n", "b", "e", "l", "i", "ev", "a", "b", "l", "e"]
4. Repeat: ["u", "n", "b", "e", "li", "ev", "a", "b", "le"]
5. Repeat: ["un", "b", "e", "li", "ev", "a", "b", "le"]

This process continues until we reach a desired vocabulary size or until no more merges are possible.

In practice, tokenization is usually done using pre-trained tokenizers. Here's how you might tokenize text using the GPT-2 tokenizer:

```
1.  from transformers import GPT2Tokenizer
2.  tokenizer = GPT2Tokenizer.from_pretrained('gpt2')
3.  text = "Unbelievable! The AI wrote a novel."
4.  tokens = tokenizer.encode(text)
5.  print(tokenizer.convert_ids_to_tokens(tokens))
```

Code Exhibit 8.1: This code takes a sentence ("Unbelievable! The AI wrote a novel.") and breaks it down into smaller pieces (token) using a library from transformers that the AI can understand - similar to how we might break down a long word into syllables to help someone read it.

This might output for an unbelievable token

['Un', 'bel', 'ievable', '!', 'The', 'AI', 'wrote', 'a', 'novel', '.']

Notice how "Unbelievable" is split into subwords, while common words like "The" are kept as single tokens.

The final step in our data preparation journey is formatting the data for efficient training. When you're dealing with terabytes of text, you need to think carefully about how to store and access this data during training.

One popular approach is to use TFRecord files, a binary file format that allows for efficient storage and reading of training data. Here's a simplified example of how you might create a TFRecord file:

```
1.  import tensorflow as tf
2.  def create_tf_example(text, tokens):
3.      feature = {
4.      'text': tf.train.Feature(bytes_list=tf.train.BytesList(value=[text.encode()])),
5.      'tokens': tf.train.Feature(int64_list=tf.train.Int64List(value=tokens))
6.      }
7.  return tf.train.Example(features=tf.train.Features(feature=feature))
8.
9.  with tf.io.TFRecordWriter('data.tfrecord') as writer:
10. text = "Unbelievable! The AI wrote a novel."
11. tokens = tokenizer.encode(text)
12. tf_example = create_tf_example(text, tokens)
13. writer.write(tf_example.SerializeToString())
```

Code Exhibit 8.2: Using TensorFlow (a popular AI library), this code takes our text and its broken down pieces (tokens) and packages them into a special format (TFRecord) that can be efficiently stored and loaded during AI training - like creating a compressed file that's optimized for machine learning.

This creates a TFRecord file containing our tokenized text, ready for efficient loading during the training process.

Data preparation for LLMs is a complex, multifaceted process that combines web scraping, text cleaning, sophisticated tokenization, and efficient data storage. It's a process that requires not just technical skill, but also careful consideration of linguistic nuances and computational efficiency.

With our data properly prepared - cleaned, tokenized, and efficiently formatted - we're ready to begin the actual training process. However, just as a student needs different types of exercises and assignments to develop a comprehensive understanding, an LLM needs different training objectives to develop robust language capabilities. This brings us to the crucial concept of pre-training objectives and self-supervised learning.

PRE-TRAINING OBJECTIVES AND SELF-SUPERVISED LEARNING

Self-supervised learning forms the cornerstone of LLM pre-training, where the model learns from unlabelled data by automatically generating supervisory signals from the input itself. This approach allows models to learn general language understanding without explicit human annotation, making it possible to train on vast amounts of text data.

Core Principle: Prediction as Supervision

The fundamental idea behind self-supervised learning in LLMs is to create prediction tasks from the input data itself. Each pre-training technique essentially defines different ways to construct these prediction tasks. The model learns by:

1. Creating artificial gaps or predictions in the input data
2. Using the surrounding context to predict the missing or next elements
3. Learning representations that capture linguistic patterns and relationships

Pre-training Objectives and Their Roles

1. Masked Language Modelling (MLM)

MLM is a bidirectional context learning technique where the model learns to predict masked tokens using both left and right context.

```
# Technical implementation of MLM pre-training objective
1.    def create_mlm_batch(text, tokenizer, mask_prob=0.15):
2.        tokens = tokenizer.tokenize(text)
3.        masked_tokens = tokens.copy()
4.        labels = [-100] * len(tokens)  # -100 indicates non-masked positions
5.
6.        # Randomly select tokens to mask
7.        mask_indices = torch.bernoulli(torch.full((len(tokens),), mask_prob)).bool()
8.
9.        for idx in range(len(tokens)):
10.           if mask_indices[idx]:
11.               rand = torch.rand(1).item()
12.
13.               if rand < 0.8:
14.                   masked_tokens[idx] = "[MASK]"
```

```
15.              elif rand < 0.9:  # 10% chance to replace with a random token
16.                  masked_tokens[idx] = tokenizer.convert_ids_to_tokens(
17.                      torch.randint(len(tokenizer), (1,)).item()
18.                  )
19.
20.              labels[idx] = tokenizer.convert_tokens_to_ids([tokens[idx]])[0]
21.
22.      return masked_tokens, labels
```

Code Exhibit 8.3: In this code, it takes a piece of text and randomly masks (hides) 15% of the words. For each masked word: 80% chance to replace with [MASK] token, 10% chance to replace with a random word, 10% chance to keep unchanged. Think of it like creating a fill-in-the-blank exercise where some words are hidden, replaced, or kept as is.

2. Causal Language Modelling (CLM)

CLM learns to predict the next token given previous tokens, making it particularly suited for generative tasks.

```
1.   # Technical implementation of CLM pre-training objective
2.   def create_clm_batch(text, tokenizer, sequence_length=512):
3.       # Tokenize and create input/output pairs
4.       tokens = tokenizer.encode(text)
5.       input_ids = tokens[:-1]  # Input is all tokens except last
6.       labels = tokens[1:]      # Labels are all tokens except first
7.
8.       # Create an attention mask to prevent looking at future tokens
9.       attention_mask = torch.tril(torch.ones((len(input_ids), len(input_ids))))
10.
11.      return {
12.          'input_ids': input_ids,
13.          'labels': labels,
14.          'attention_mask': attention_mask
15.      }
16.
```

Code Exhibit 8.4: This code takes text and prepares it for next word prediction where each input is a sequence of words, and the target is the next word. It is like teaching the model to complete sentences by showing it partial sentences and asking it to predict what comes next.

3. Span Corruption

A more sophisticated approach that masks consecutive tokens and predicts them as a single unit.

```
1.   def create_span_corruption_batch(text, tokenizer, mean_span_length=3):
2.       tokens = tokenizer.tokenize(text)
3.       corrupted = tokens.copy()
4.
5.       # Geometric distribution for span lengths
6.       span_lengths = torch.geometric(1/mean_span_length, (len(tokens),))
7.
8.       current_idx = 0
9.       while current_idx < len(tokens):
10.          span_length = min(int(span_lengths[current_idx].item()), len(tokens) - current_idx)
```

```
11.
12.        if torch.rand(1).item() < 0.15:  # 15% corruption rate
13.            corrupted[current_idx:current_idx + span_length] = ["<X>"]
14.
15.        current_idx += span_length
16.
17.    return corrupted, tokens  # Fixed return statement to include both values
```

Code Exhibit 8.5: This code, instead of masking single words, masks groups of consecutive words. It randomly selects sequences of about 3 words and replaces them with a single mask token, similar to asking someone to fill in entire phrases rather than just single words.

Achieving General-Purpose Capabilities

Modern general-purpose models like ChatGPT achieve their versatility through several key strategies:

1. *Multi-Task Pre-training*

```
1.    class MultiTaskPreTraining:
2.        def __init__(self, model, tasks):
3.            self.model = model
4.            self.tasks = {
5.                'mlm': self.mlm_forward,
6.                'clm': self.clm_forward,
7.                'span': self.span_forward
8.            }
9.
10.       def forward(self, batch):
11.           # Randomly select task for each batch
12.           task = random.choice(list(self.tasks.keys()))
13.           return self.tasks[task](batch)
```

Code Exhibit 8.6: This code sets up a system to train the model on multiple types of tasks simultaneously. It randomly switches between different training objectives (masking words, predicting next words, etc.). It is like teaching a student multiple subjects in random order to maintain versatility.

2. Scale and Data Diversity

- Use of massive datasets (hundreds of billions to trillions of tokens)
- Careful data curation and mixing strategies
- Dynamic batch construction to maintain balanced exposure

3. Pre-training Process

The actual pre-training process involves several key components:

```
1.    class PreTrainer:
2.        def __init__(self, model, optimizer, scheduler):
3.            self.model = model
4.            self.optimizer = optimizer
5.            self.scheduler = scheduler
6.
7.        def train_step(self, batch):
8.            self.optimizer.zero_grad()
9.
```

```
10.        # Forward pass with multiple objectives
11.        mlm_loss = self.model.mlm_forward(batch)
12.        clm_loss = self.model.clm_forward(batch)
13.
14.        # Combined loss
15.        loss = mlm_loss * 0.5 + clm_loss * 0.5
16.
17.        # Backward pass and optimization
18.        loss.backward()
19.        self.optimizer.step()
20.        self.scheduler.step()
21.
22.        return loss.item()
23.
24.    def train(self, dataloader, epochs):
25.        for epoch in range(epochs):
26.            epoch_loss = 0
27.            for batch in dataloader:
28.                loss = self.train_step(batch)
29.                epoch_loss += loss
30.
31.            # Logging and checkpointing
32.            self.save_checkpoint(epoch)
33.            self.log_metrics(epoch_loss)
```

*Code Exhibit 8.7: This code **manages** the entire training process from start to finish. It combines different learning objectives and updates the model's knowledge. It tracks progress and saves checkpoints along the way, like running a complete education program with regular assessments and progress reports.*

Practical Applications and Selection Guide

The theoretical understanding of pre-training objectives must be paired with practical knowledge of when to use each technique. These pre-training objectives form the foundation of how LLMs learn to understand and generate language, developing sophisticated language understanding through repeated exposure to massive datasets.

Choosing the Right Pre-training Technique

The selection of pre-training techniques should be guided by your specific application requirements:

For Generative Applications (CLM)

Use Cases:

- Code generation (GitHub Copilot)
- Conversational AI (ChatGPT)
- Creative writing tools

For Understanding Tasks (MLM)

Use Cases:

- Sentiment analysis
- Information extraction
- Search systems

For Document Analysis (NSP/Span Corruption)

Use Cases:

- Legal document analysis
- Academic research tools
- Document coherence checking

Decision Tree for Technique Selection

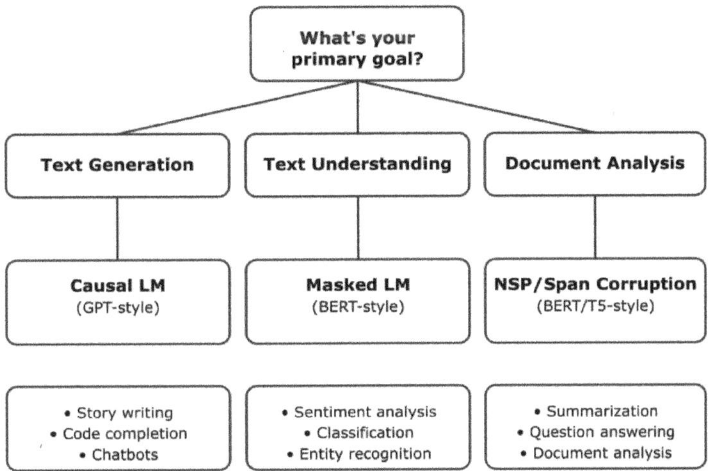

Fig. 8.2: The decision tree illustrates the selection process for LLM pretraining techniques based on three primary goals: text generation (like ChatGPT), text understanding (like sentiment analysis), and document analysis (like summarization). Each path leads to specific techniques (Causal LM, Masked LM, or NSP/Span Corruption) with practical use cases shown at the bottom, making it easy to choose the right approach for your specific AI application.

Combining Techniques in Modern Applications

Modern LLM applications often leverage multiple pre-training techniques to achieve more robust performance. Here's an example of how to implement a multi-technique training approach:

```
1.   class MultiTechniqueTrainer:  # Fixed class name to remove hyphen
2.     def __init__(self):
3.       self.techniques = {
4.         'clm': CausalLMTrainer(),
5.         'mlm': MaskedLMTrainer(),
6.         'nsp': NextSentencePredictor()
7.       }
8.
9.     def train_step(self, batch):
10.      losses = {}
11.      # Apply each technique with appropriate weighting
12.      for technique, trainer in self.techniques.items():
13.        losses[technique] = trainer.forward(batch)
14.
15.      # Combine losses based on application needs
16.      total_loss = (
17         0.4 * losses['clm'] +  # Emphasis on generation
18.        0.4 * losses['mlm'] +  # Strong understanding
19.        0.2 * losses['nsp']    # Document coherence
20.      )
```

```
21.         return total_loss
22.
23.
24.    # Example usage in a customer service AI
25.    class CustomerServiceAI:
26.      def __init__(self):
27.        self.understanding = MLMProcessor()   # For query understanding
28.        self.generation = CLMProcessor()      # For response generation
29.        self.coherence = NSPProcessor()       # For conversation flow
30.
31.      def process_query(self, query):
32.        understanding = self.understanding.process(query)
33.        context = self.coherence.check(query, conversation_history)
34.        response = self.generation.generate(understanding, context)
35.        return response
```

Code Exhibit 8.8: In this code, the first part creates a training program that teaches the AI three different skills at once (like teaching someone to listen, speak, and remember conversations). The second part uses these learned skills in real-world situations - when a customer asks something, the AI understands the question, remembers past conversations, and creates a helpful response, just like a well-trained customer service representative would do.

This combined approach allows models to develop a more comprehensive understanding of language, making them more versatile and effective across different types of tasks. The key is to balance these techniques based on your specific application requirements while maintaining computational efficiency.

The sophisticated training techniques we've discussed require equally sophisticated computing infrastructure. Just as a research university needs specialised laboratories and equipment for advanced experiments, training LLMs demands purpose-built computing environments. Let's explore the critical infrastructure components that make LLM training possible.

REINFORCEMENT LEARNING FROM HUMAN FEEDBACK (RLHF)

Introduction: Teaching AI to Align with Human Intent

Reinforcement Learning from Human Feedback (RLHF) is a training methodology that teaches language models to generate responses that align with human preferences and values. At its core, RLHF uses human feedback to

create a reward system that guides the model toward more helpful, accurate, and appropriate outputs. Think of it as teaching an AI system not just what it can do, but what it should do based on human judgment.

Large Language Models, after pre-training and fine-tuning, possess extraordinary capabilities in processing and generating text. However, having vast knowledge doesn't necessarily translate to using it wisely or helpfully. A model might be able to generate perfectly grammatical text that is nevertheless inappropriate, unhelpful, or misaligned with human values and intentions. This gap between capability and desirability is what RLHF addresses.

The significance of RLHF in modern AI development cannot be overstated. It represents the crucial step that transformed models like GPT from powerful but potentially unreliable systems into more controlled, helpful assistants. By incorporating human preferences directly into the training process,

RLHF helps create AI systems that are not just knowledgeable, but also more aligned with human values and expectations.

The Implementation Mechanics

At its core, RLHF transforms the way a language model generates responses through a three-stage process, each building upon the previous one.

Stage 1: Building the Human Feedback Dataset

The process begins with collecting human preferences. Here's how it works:

1. The base LLM generates multiple responses (usually 2-4) for each prompt.
2. Human evaluators rank these responses or choose between pairs.
3. These comparisons create a dataset such as:
    a. Prompt: "Explain climate change"
    b. Response A: [A detailed, technical explanation]
    c. Response B: [A clear, accessible explanation]
    d. Human Choice: B (more helpful and accessible)
4. This process is repeated thousands of times across diverse prompts

Stage 2: Creating the Reward Model

The reward model learns to mimic human judgments. Here's the actual implementation:

1. Take a copy of the original language model
2. Add a new final layer (the "reward head") that outputs a single number representing quality
3. Train this model on the human preference data:
    a. Input: A prompt-response pair
    b. Output: A score predicting how humans would rate this response
    c. Training goal: Learn to assign higher scores to preferred responses
4. The model learns patterns such as:
    a. Clear explanations get higher scores than confusing ones
    b. Polite responses score better than rude ones
    c. Safe responses rate higher than harmful ones

Stage 3: Training the Language Model with PPO

This is where the original language model learns to generate better responses:

1. Initial Response Generation:
    a. The model receives a prompt
    b. It generates multiple response variations
    c. The reward model scores each response
2. Learning Loop:
    a. High-scoring responses teach the model what patterns to reinforce
    b. Low-scoring responses show what patterns to avoid
    c. A special constraint (KL divergence) ensures the model doesn't forget its original knowledge
    d. This process repeats many times for each prompt

3. Fine-tuning Process:
    a.   Start with small adjustments to model behaviour
    b.   Gradually increase the influence of the reward signal
    c.   Continuously monitor output quality to prevent degradation
    d.   Regular evaluation against original model capabilities

The Transformation Process

To understand how this changes the model, consider a simple example:

Original Model Response to "Explain quantum physics":

-   Might give: A technically accurate but overwhelming explanation with advanced terminology

After RLHF Training:

1. The model first generates multiple potential responses
2. The reward model evaluates each for clarity, helpfulness, and appropriateness
3. The model learns to favour responses that:
    a.   Start with basic concepts
    b.   Use the appropriate level of technical detail
    c.   Include relevant examples
    d.   Match the apparent knowledge level of the questioner

Key Technical Components

1. The Reward Model Architecture:
    a.   Uses the same base architecture as the LLM
    b.   Adds a regression layer to produce quality scores
    c.   Processes both the prompt and response together
    d.   Outputs a single quality score
2. The PPO Training Process:
    a.   Small batches of prompts for exploration
    b.   Multiple response generations per prompt
    c.   Immediate reward scoring
    d.   Careful policy updates to maintain model stability
3. Training Stability Measures:
    a.   Gradient clipping to prevent extreme updates
    b.   Value function normalisation
    c.   Adaptive learning rates
    d.   Regular evaluation checkpoints

Challenges and Future Directions

While RLHF has proven remarkably effective in improving model behaviour, significant challenges remain. The process requires large amounts of high-quality human feedback, which is expensive and time-consuming to collect. There's also the challenge of ensuring consistency across different human evaluators and preventing the model from learning to game the reward system. Future developments focus on automated feedback mechanisms, more sophisticated reward modelling architectures, and improved optimisation techniques that better preserve model knowledge while enhancing alignment.

TRAINING INFRASTRUCTURE AND OPTIMIZATION

Imagine you're tasked with building the world's largest jigsaw puzzle. Not only is the puzzle enormous, but you also need to complete it as quickly as possible. Oh, and the pieces keep changing shape as you work. This analogy gives you a glimpse into the challenges of training Large Language Models. The compute requirement for various models is shown in Fig.8.3.

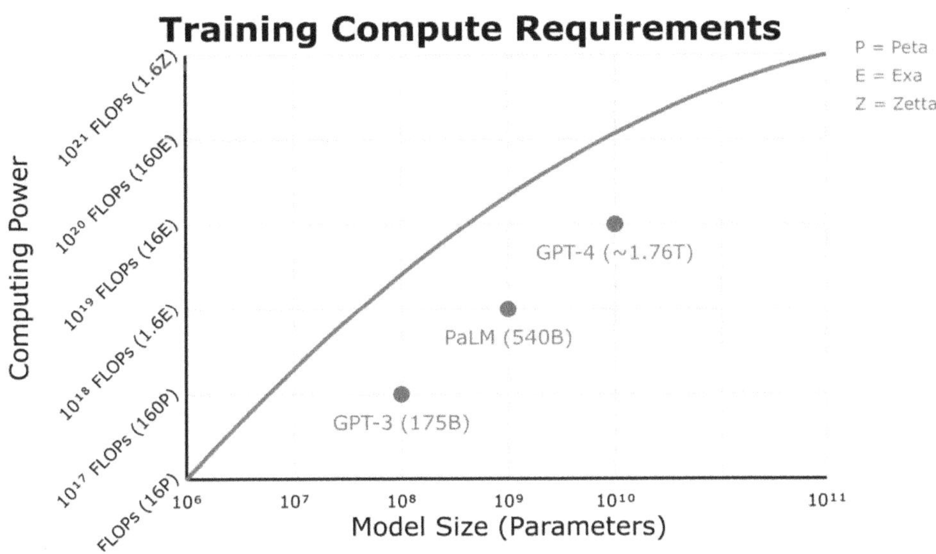

Fig. 8.3: Visualization of how computing requirements (FLOPS) scale with model size, showing exponential growth in computational needs as models get larger.

Training an LLM is a herculean task that pushes the boundaries of our computational capabilities. It requires not just powerful hardware, but also sophisticated software techniques to make the most of that hardware. Let's dive into the world of LLM training infrastructure and optimization techniques.

Distributed Training

When you're dealing with models that have billions of parameters, a single GPU, no matter how powerful, just won't cut it. This is where distributed training comes in. It's like having a team of master puzzle solvers working on different sections of our giant jigsaw puzzle simultaneously.

One popular approach to distributed training is data parallelism. In this method, we divide our training data among multiple GPUs or machines. Each device has a copy of the entire model but works on a different subset of the data. After each forward and backward pass, the gradients from all devices are averaged, and the model is updated accordingly.

Here's a simplified example using PyTorch's DistributedDataParallel:

```
1.   import torch
2.   import torch.distributed as dist
3.   from torch.nn.parallel import DistributedDataParallel as DDP
4.
5.   def setup(rank, world_size):
6.       dist.init_process_group("nccl", rank=rank, world_size=world_size)
7.
```

```
 8.  def cleanup():
 9.      dist.destroy_process_group()
10.
11.  class LargeLanguageModel(torch.nn.Module):
12.    def __init__(self):
13.        super().__init__()
14.        # Define your model architecture here
15.
16.  def train(rank, world_size):
17.      setup(rank, world_size)
18.      model = LargeLanguageModel().to(rank)
19.      ddp_model = DDP(model, device_ids=[rank])
20.
21.      # Training loop
22.      for epoch in range(num_epochs):
23.          for batch in dataloader:
24.              outputs = ddp_model(batch)
25.              loss = criterion(outputs, targets)
26.              loss.backward()
27.              optimizer.step()
28.
29.      cleanup()
30.
31.  if __name__ == "__main__":
32.      world_size = torch.cuda.device_count()
33.      torch.multiprocessing.spawn(
34.          train,
35.          args=(world_size,),
36.          nprocs=world_size,
37.          join=True
38.      )
```

Code Exhibit 8.9: This code demonstrates distributed data parallel training for Large Language Models using PyTorch's DistributedDataParallel (DDP). It distributes model training across multiple GPUs by replicating the model on each GPU and automatically synchronizing gradients during training. For instance, if you have 4 GPUs, each processes a different batch of data in parallel, effectively multiplying your training throughput by 4.

Mixed Precision Training

Another key optimization technique is mixed precision training. It's like using a mix of fine-tipped pens and broad markers in our puzzle-solving analogy – we use high precision where it's needed most, and lower precision where we can get away with it.

In practice, this often means using 16-bit floating-point numbers (FP16) for most computations, while keeping a master copy of the weights in 32-bit (FP32) precision. This not only reduces memory usage but can also speed up training, especially on modern GPUs designed for mixed precision arithmetic.

Here's how you might set up mixed precision training using NVIDIA's Apex library:

```
1.  from apex import amp
2.
3.  model = LargeLanguageModel().cuda()
4.  optimizer = torch.optim.Adam(model.parameters())
5.  model, optimizer = amp.initialize(model, optimizer, opt_level="O1")
6.
```

```
7.    for epoch in range(num_epochs):
8.       for batch in dataloader:
9.          outputs = model(batch)
10.         loss = criterion(outputs, targets)
11.
12.         with amp.scale_loss(loss, optimizer) as scaled_loss:
13.            scaled_loss.backward()
14.
15.         optimizer.step()
```

Code Exhibit 8.10: This code implements mixed precision training (using both 16-bit and 32-bit numbers) with NVIDIA's Apex library – a technique that speeds up model training and reduces memory usage while maintaining accuracy by automatically switching between different numerical precisions.

Gradient Accumulation

When you're working with enormous models, sometimes even a single training example doesn't fit in GPU memory. This is where gradient accumulation comes in handy. It's like solving our puzzle piece by piece, but only rearranging the overall layout after we've placed several pieces.

In technical terms, gradient accumulation involves performing several forward and backward passes, accumulating the gradients, and then updating the model weights only after a certain number of steps. Here's a simple implementation:

```
1.    model = LargeLanguageModel()
2.    optimizer = torch.optim.Adam(model.parameters())
3.    accumulation_steps = 4  # Update weights every 4 steps
4.
5.    for epoch in range(num_epochs):
6.       for i, batch in enumerate(dataloader):
7.          outputs = model(batch)
8.          loss = criterion(outputs, targets)
9.          loss = loss / accumulation_steps  # Normalize the loss
10.         loss.backward()
11.
12.         if (i + 1) % accumulation_steps == 0:
13.            optimizer.step()
14.            optimizer.zero_grad()
```

Code Exhibit 8.11: This code shows the core training loop of a large language model where it processes data in batches, accumulates gradients over 4 steps before updating model weights – a technique used to handle large models with memory constraints.

This technique allows us to effectively increase our batch size without increasing memory usage.

Optimization Algorithm

The choice of optimization algorithm can significantly impact the training process. While standard Stochastic Gradient Descent (SGD) can work, most state-of-the-art LLMs use more advanced optimizers.

Adam (Adaptive Moment Estimation) and its variants are particularly popular. These algorithms adapt the learning rate for each parameter, which can lead to faster convergence. Here's a simple example using **AdamW**, a variant of Adam with decoupled weight decay:

```
1.   from transformers import AdamW
2.
3.   model = LargeLanguageModel()
4.   optimizer = AdamW(
5.       model.parameters(),
6.       lr=5e-5,
7.       correct_bias=False
8.   )
9.
10.  for epoch in range(num_epochs):
11.     for batch in dataloader:
12.         outputs = model(batch)
13.         loss = criterion(outputs, targets)
14.         loss.backward()
15.
16.         optimizer.step()
17.         optimizer.zero_grad()
```

Code Exhibit 8.12: This code shows the basic training loop of a language model using the AdamW optimizer (a popular optimization algorithm for transformers). It processes data in batches, calculates errors, and updates the model's knowledge using a specialised learning rate and bias correction technique.

In practice, you'd often combine this with a learning rate scheduler to adjust the learning rate over the course of training.

Checkpointing

When you're training a model that takes weeks or even months, you need a way to save your progress. This is where checkpointing comes in. It's like taking a snapshot of your partially completed puzzle so you can resume work later if you're interrupted.

Here's a basic implementation of checkpointing:

```
1.   def save_checkpoint(model, optimizer, epoch, path):
2.       torch.save({
3.           'epoch': epoch,
4.           'model_state_dict': model.state_dict(),
5.           'optimizer_state_dict': optimizer.state_dict(),
6.       }, path)
7.
8.   def load_checkpoint(model, optimizer, path):
9.       checkpoint = torch.load(path)
10.      model.load_state_dict(checkpoint['model_state_dict'])
11.      optimizer.load_state_dict(checkpoint['optimizer_state_dict'])
12.      return checkpoint['epoch']
13.
14.  # During training
15.  if epoch % save_every == 0:
```

```
16.    save_checkpoint(model, optimizer, epoch, f"checkpoint_{epoch}.pt")
17.
18.    # To resume training
19.    start_epoch = load_checkpoint(model, optimizer, "checkpoint_latest.pt")
```

Code Exhibit 8.13: This code handles the saving and loading of model checkpoints during training. It periodically saves the complete state of the model and optimizer, allowing training to be resumed from any saved point without losing progress. This is useful for long training runs and preventing loss of work from interruptions.

This allows us to resume training from where we left off, which is crucial for long-running training jobs.

Training Large Language Models is a complex dance of hardware and software optimizations. It requires not just powerful GPUs and high-speed networking, but also sophisticated techniques to make the most of these resources. As models continue to grow in size and complexity, innovations in training infrastructure and optimization will play a crucial role in pushing the boundaries of what's possible with AI.

FINE-TUNING LLMS FOR SPECIFIC TASKS

Imagine you've spent years studying general medicine, absorbing vast amounts of knowledge about the human body and its ailments. Now, you decide to specialize in cardiology. You don't start from scratch – instead, you build upon your broad medical knowledge, focusing it on the intricacies of the heart. This is essentially what we're doing when we fine-tune a Large Language Model for a specific task.

Fine-tuning allows us to take a pre-trained LLM – a model that has already learned the general patterns and structures of language – and adapt it for a particular application. This process is crucial because it bridges the gap between the broad capabilities of LLMs and the specific requirements of real-world tasks.

The Fine-tuning Process

At its core, fine-tuning involves training the pre-trained model on a smaller, task-specific dataset. This process adjusts the model's weights to optimize its performance for the target task. Let's walk through a simple example of fine-tuning a model for sentiment analysis using the Hugging Face Transformers library:

```
1.    from transformers import (
2.        AutoModelForSequenceClassification,
3.        AutoTokenizer,
4.        Trainer,
5.        TrainingArguments
6.    )
7.    from datasets import load_dataset
8.
9.    # Load pre-trained model and tokenizer
10.   model_name = "distilbert-base-uncased"
11.   model = AutoModelForSequenceClassification.from_pretrained(model_name, num_labels=2)
12.   tokenizer = AutoTokenizer.from_pretrained(model_name)
13.
```

```
14.   # Load and preprocess the dataset
15.   dataset = load_dataset("imdb")
16.
17.   def tokenize_function(examples):
18.     return tokenizer(
19.       examples["text"],
20.       padding="max_length",
21.       truncation=True
22.     )
23.
24.   tokenized_datasets = dataset.map(tokenize_function, batched=True)
25.
26.   # Define training arguments
27.   training_args = TrainingArguments(
28.     output_dir="./results",
29.     num_train_epochs=3,
30.     per_device_train_batch_size=16,
31.     per_device_eval_batch_size=64,
32.     warmup_steps=500,
33.     weight_decay=0.01,
34.     logging_dir="./logs",
35.   )
36.
37.   # Create Trainer instance
38.   trainer = Trainer(
39.     model=model,
40.     args=training_args,
41.     train_dataset=tokenized_datasets["train"],
42.     eval_dataset=tokenized_datasets["test"],
43.   )
44.
45.   # Fine-tune the model
46.   trainer.train()
```

Code Exhibit 8.14: This code shows how to adapt a general-purpose language model for a specific task (sentiment analysis) using the Hugging Face transformers library. It takes a pre-trained model, configures the training process with specific parameters, and fine-tunes it on movie reviews to learn to identify sentiment.

In this example, we're fine-tuning a DistilBERT model on the IMDB dataset for sentiment analysis. The process involves loading a pre-trained model, preparing the task-specific dataset, and then training the model on this new data.

Language Tasks and Model Selection

Task Category	Specific Tasks	Example Models	Key Characteristics
Text Generation	• Story writing • Code generation • Translation • Paraphrasing	• GPT-4 (OpenAI) • Codex • BLOOM • PaLM	• Causal LM architecture • Large context windows • Strong next-token prediction
Text Understanding	• Sentiment analysis • Topic classification • Named Entity Recognition • Intent detection	• BERT • RoBERTa • DeBERTa • XLNet	• Bidirectional context • Masked LM pre-training • Fine-grained understanding

Question Answering	• Open-domain QA • Reading comprehension • Factual retrieval	• T5 • UnifiedQA • REALM • RAG	• Cross-attention mechanisms • Knowledge integration • Context processing
Document Processing	• Summarisation • Document classification • Information extraction • Text structuring	• BART • Longformer • BigBird • LED	• Long document handling • Hierarchical processing • Efficient attention mechanisms
Dialogue Systems	• Open dialogue • Task-oriented chat • Multi-turn conversation	• LaMDA • BlenderBot • DialoGPT • Claude	• Context retention • Personality consistency • Multi-turn coherence
Code Understanding	• Code completion • Code review • Bug detection • Documentation	• CodeBERT • GraphCodeBERT. • Codex • StarCoder	• AST understanding • Multi-language support • Context-aware completion
Multimodal Tasks	• Image captioning • Visual QA • Text-to-image • Cross-modal retrieval	• DALL-E • GPT-4V • PaLM-E • LLaVA	• Multi-modal embeddings • Cross-modal attention • Joint understanding

Efficient Fine-tuning Techniques

As LLMs have grown larger, fine-tuning the entire model has become increasingly computationally expensive. This has led to the development of more efficient fine-tuning techniques:

1. Adapter Layers: This technique involves adding small, trainable layers to the pre-trained model while keeping the original model weights frozen. Here's a conceptual example using the adapter-transformers library:

```
1.    from transformers import AutoModelWithHeads
2.    from adapters import AdapterConfig
3.
4.    model = AutoModelWithHeads.from_pretrained("bert-base-uncased")
5.    model.add_adapter("sentiment", config="pfeiffer")
6.    model.train_adapter("sentiment")
```

Code Exhibit 8.15: This code demonstrates adapter-based fine-tuning, a memory-efficient alternative to full model fine-tuning. Using the adapter-transformers library, it loads a pre-trained BERT model and adds a small trainable "adapter" layer for sentiment analysis using the Pfeiffer configuration (a popular adapter architecture). Instead of updating all model parameters, only the adapter layers are trained, significantly reducing memory requirements and training time.

2. Prompt Tuning: This method fine-tunes continuous prompt embeddings while keeping the rest of the model fixed. It's particularly effective for very large models. Here's a simplified example:

```
1.    import torch
2.
3.    class PromptTuningModel(torch.nn.Module):
4.        def __init__(self, base_model, prompt_length):
5.            super().__init__()
6.            self.base_model = base_model
7.            self.prompt_embeddings = torch.nn.Parameter(
8.                torch.randn(prompt_length, base_model.config.hidden_size)
9.            )
```

```
10.
11.    def forward(self, input_ids, attention_mask):
12.       batch_size = input_ids.shape[0]
13.       prompt_embeddings = self.prompt_embeddings.repeat(batch_size, 1, 1)
14.       inputs_embeds = self.base_model.embeddings(input_ids)
15.       inputs_embeds = torch.cat([prompt_embeddings, inputs_embeds], dim=1)
16.       outputs = self.base_model(
17.          inputs_embeds=inputs_embeds,
18.          attention_mask=attention_mask
19.       )
20.       return outputs
```

Code Exhibit 8.16: This code implements prompt tuning, a technique for adapting language models where instead of fine-tuning the entire model, we only train a small set of continuous prompt embeddings. The model adds learnable prompt tokens to the input embeddings before processing, similar to adding a prefix to your input but with trainable vectors. These prompt embeddings are updated during training while keeping the base model frozen, making it a parameter-efficient fine-tuning method.

3. LoRA (Low-Rank Adaptation): This technique adapts the model by adding pairs of rank decomposition matrices to existing weights. It's highly parameter-efficient and has shown impressive results. Here's how you might use it with the Hugging Face PEFT library:

```
1.    from transformers import AutoModelForCausalLM
2.    from peft import get_peft_model, LoraConfig, TaskType
3.
4.    model = AutoModelForCausalLM.from_pretrained("gpt2")
5.    peft_config = LoraConfig(
6.       task_type=TaskType.CAUSAL_LM,
7.       r=8,
8.       lora_alpha=32,
9.       lora_dropout=0.1
10.   )
11.   model = get_peft_model(model, peft_config)
```

Code Exhibit 8.17: This code is implementing LoRA (Low-Rank Adaptation), a technique to efficiently fine-tune large language models. It loads GPT-2 as the base model, then applies LoRA configuration which adds trainable "adapter" layers while keeping most of the original model frozen. This makes fine-tuning much more memory-efficient and faster compared to full model fine-tuning.

Challenges in Fine-tuning

While fine-tuning is powerful, it comes with its own set of challenges:

1. Catastrophic Forgetting: This occurs when the model "forgets" its general language understanding while learning the specific task. One way to mitigate this is through regularization techniques:

```
1.    from transformers import AutoModelForSequenceClassification
2.
3.    class RegularizedModel(AutoModelForSequenceClassification):
4.       def __init__(self, *args, **kwargs):  # Fixed kwargs syntax
5.          super().__init__(*args, **kwargs)
```

```
6.        self.pretrained_weights = {
7.           n: p.clone().detach()
8.           for n, p in self.named_parameters()
9.        }
10.
11.    def get_regularization_loss(self, lambda_reg=0.1):
12.       reg_loss = 0.0
13.       for name, param in self.named_parameters():
14.          reg_loss += lambda_reg * torch.sum(
15.             (param - self.pretrained_weights[name]) ** 2  # Fixed power operator
16.          )
17.       return reg_loss
```

Code Exhibit 8.18: This code creates a specialized model class that maintains the balance between learning new tasks and retaining original knowledge - it adds a penalty term that discourages the model's parameters from moving too far from their pre-trained values, helping prevent catastrophic forgetting.

2. Limited Data: Often, we have limited labelled data for the specific task. Techniques like few-shot learning and data augmentation can help:

```
1.    from nlpaug import naf
2.
3.    def augment_text(text):
4.       aug = naf.WordNetAug()
5.       augmented_text = aug.augment(text)
6.       return augmented_text  # Fixed variable name
7.
8.    augmented_dataset = [
9.       augment_text(text)
10.      for text in original_dataset
11.   ]
```

Code Exhibit 8.19: This code implements data augmentation using WordNet (a dictionary of word relationships) - it automatically generates more training examples by substituting words with their synonyms, helping the model learn robust language understanding.

3. Overfitting: With smaller datasets, there's a risk of overfitting to the task-specific data. Techniques like early stopping and cross-validation are crucial:

```
1.    from sklearn.model_selection import KFold
2.
3.    kf = KFold(n_splits=5, shuffle=True, random_state=42)
4.    for train_index, val_index in kf.split(dataset):
5.       train_dataset = dataset.select(train_index)
6.       val_dataset = dataset.select(val_index)
```

Code Exhibit 8.20: This code divides the training data into 5 different train/validation splits using k-fold cross-validation - a technique that helps assess how well the model will perform on unseen data by training and evaluating it on different subsets of the data.

Fine-tuning is where the rubber meets the road in LLM applications. It's the process that turns a general-purpose language model into a specialised tool for specific tasks. As we continue to develop more efficient and effective fine-tuning techniques, we're expanding the range of applications where LLMs can make a significant impact.

EVALUATING LLM PERFORMANCE

Imagine you've trained a world-class chef. They claim to be proficient in cuisines from around the globe, capable of creating everything from delicate French pastries to spicy Thai curries. How would you evaluate their skills? You might have them prepare a variety of dishes, assess the flavour profiles, presentation, and technique. You might also gather feedback from diners with different tastes and cultural backgrounds. Evaluating a Large Language Model is not so different – we need a diverse set of tasks and metrics to truly gauge its capabilities.

Evaluation is a critical step in the development of LLMs. It helps us understand the model's strengths and weaknesses, guides further improvements, and allows us to compare different models objectively. Let's explore the various ways we evaluate LLMs, from intrinsic metrics to task-specific evaluations.

Perplexity and Intrinsic Evaluation Metrics

One of the most fundamental metrics for language models is perplexity. In essence, perplexity measures how "surprised" the model is by new text. A lower perplexity indicates that the model is better at predicting the next word in a sequence.

Here's how you might calculate perplexity using PyTorch:

```
1.    import torch
2.    import torch.nn.functional as F
3.    from transformers import GPT2LMHeadModel, GPT2Tokenizer
4.
5.    def calculate_perplexity(model, tokenizer, text):
6.    encodings = tokenizer(text, return_tensors='pt')
7.    max_length = model.config.n_positions
8.       stride = 512
9.    seq_len = encodings.input_ids.size(1)
10.    nlls = []
11.    for i in range(0, seq_len, stride):
12.    begin_loc = max(i + stride - max_length, 0)
13.    end_loc = min(i + stride, seq_len)
14.       trg_len = end_loc - i
15.       input_ids = encodings.input_ids[:, begin_loc:end_loc].to(model.device)
16.    target_ids = input_ids.clone()
17.    target_ids[:, :-trg_len] = -100
18.    with torch.no_grad():
19.    outputs = model(input_ids, labels=target_ids)
20.    neg_log_likelihood = outputs[0] * trg_len
21.       nlls.append(neg_log_likelihood)
22.    ppl = torch.exp(torch.stack(nlls).sum() / end_loc)
23.    return ppl.item()
24.
25.    model = GPT2LMHeadModel.from_pretrained('gpt2')
26.    tokenizer = GPT2Tokenizer.from_pretrained('gpt2')
```

```
27.  text = "The quick brown fox jumps over the lazy dog."
28.  perplexity = calculate_perplexity(model, tokenizer, text)
29.  print(f"Perplexity: {perplexity}")
```

Code Exhibit 8.21: This code calculates perplexity (a measure of how well the model predicts text) by processing text in smaller chunks - like assessing how confident and accurate the model is in predicting each word, where lower scores indicate better performance.

While perplexity is useful, it's not always intuitive and doesn't directly measure the model's performance on specific tasks. This is where task-specific evaluation metrics come in.

Task-Specific Evaluation Metrics

Different NLP tasks require different evaluation metrics. Let's look at a few common ones:

1. Text Classification (e.g. Sentiment Analysis)

For classification tasks, we often use metrics like accuracy, precision, recall, and F1 score. Here's an example using scikit-learn:

```
1.   from sklearn.metrics import accuracy_score, precision_recall_fscore_support
2.
3.   def evaluate_classification(y_true, y_pred):
4.       accuracy = accuracy_score(y_true, y_pred)
5.       precision, recall, f1, _ = precision_recall_fscore_support(  # Fixed asterisk to underscore
6.           y_true,
7.           y_pred,
8.           average='weighted'
9.       )
10.
11.      return {
12.          'accuracy': accuracy,
13.          'precision': precision,
14.          'recall': recall,
15.          'f1': f1
16.      }
17.
18.  # Assume y_true and y_pred are your true labels and model predictions
19.  metrics = evaluate_classification(y_true, y_pred)
20.  print(metrics)
```

Code Exhibit 8.22: This code calculates different metrics to evaluate how well the model performs classification tasks. It measures accuracy (overall correctness), precision (how many predictions were correct), recall (how many true cases were caught), and F1 (balance between precision and recall).

2. Question Answering

For question answering tasks, we often use metrics like Exact Match (EM) and F1 score. Here's a simplified implementation:

```
1.   def normalize_text(text):
2.     return ' '.join(text.lower().split())
3.
4.   def calculate_em_f1(pred, truth):
5.     pred = normalize_text(pred)
6.     truth = normalize_text(truth)
7.
8.     em = int(pred == truth)
9.
10.    pred_tokens = set(pred.split())
11.    truth_tokens = set(truth.split())
12.    common = pred_tokens & truth_tokens
13.
14.    precision = len(common) / len(pred_tokens) if pred_tokens else 0
15.    recall = len(common) / len(truth_tokens) if truth_tokens else 0
16.    f1 = 2 * precision * recall / (precision + recall) if (precision + recall) else 0
17.
18.    return {
19.       'em': em,
20.       'f1': f1
21.    }
22.
23.  # Example usage
24.  pred = "The quick brown fox"
25.  truth = "The brown fox"
26.  scores = calculate_em_f1(pred, truth)
27.  print(scores)
```

Code Exhibit 8.23: This code measures the similarity between predicted and true text responses in two ways - checking for exact matches (EM) and calculating word overlap (F1), helping assess how close the model's answers are to the correct ones even when they're not perfectly identical.

3. Text Generation (e.g. Summarization, Translation)

For text generation tasks, we often use metrics like BLEU (Bilingual Evaluation Understudy) or ROUGE (Recall-Oriented Understudy for Gisting Evaluation). Here's an example using the NLTK library for BLEU:

```
1.   from nltk.translate.bleu_score import sentence_bleu
2.
3.   reference = [
4.     ['the', 'quick', 'brown', 'fox', 'jumps', 'over', 'the', 'lazy', 'dog']
5.   ]
6.   candidate = ['the', 'fast', 'brown', 'fox', 'jumps', 'over', 'the', 'lazy', 'dog']
7.
8.   score = sentence_bleu(reference, candidate)
9.   print(f"BLEU score: {score}")
```

Code Exhibit 8.24: This code calculates the BLEU score to measure how similar the model's generated text is to a reference text. It compares sequences of words (like phrases) between the two texts, similar to how we might grade a language translation by comparing it to an expert's translation.

Benchmarks and Standardized Datasets

To compare different models objectively, the NLP community has developed several benchmarks and standardized datasets. Some popular ones include:

1. GLUE (General Language Understanding Evaluation)

GLUE is a collection of diverse NLP tasks designed to evaluate language understanding. Here's how you might evaluate a model on a GLUE task using the Hugging Face Datasets library:

```
1.   from datasets import load_dataset, load_metric
2.   from transformers import (
3.       AutoModelForSequenceClassification,
4.       AutoTokenizer,
5.       Trainer,
6.       TrainingArguments
7.   )
8.
9.   # Load dataset and metric
10.  dataset = load_dataset("glue", "mrpc")
11.  metric = load_metric("glue", "mrpc")
12.
13.  # Load pre-trained model and tokenizer
14.  model = AutoModelForSequenceClassification.from_pretrained("bert-base-uncased")
15.  tokenizer = AutoTokenizer.from_pretrained("bert-base-uncased")
16.
17.  # Tokenize dataset
18.  def tokenize_function(examples):
19.      return tokenizer(
20.          examples["sentence1"],
21.          examples["sentence2"],
22.          padding="max_length",
23.          truncation=True
24.      )
25.
26.  tokenized_datasets = dataset.map(tokenize_function, batched=True)
27.
28.  # Define compute_metrics function
29.  def compute_metrics(eval_pred):
30.      logits, labels = eval_pred
31.      predictions = np.argmax(logits, axis=-1)
32.      return metric.compute(
33.          predictions=predictions,
34.          references=labels
35.      )
36.
37.  # Define training arguments and trainer
38.  training_args = TrainingArguments(
39.      "test_trainer",
40.      evaluation_strategy="epoch"
41.  )
42.
43.  trainer = Trainer(
44.      model=model,
45.      args=training_args,
46.      train_dataset=tokenized_datasets["train"],
47.      eval_dataset=tokenized_datasets["validation"],
48.      compute_metrics=compute_metrics,
```

```
49.  )
50.
51.  # Evaluate
52.  results = trainer.evaluate()
53.  print(results)
```

Code Exhibit 8.25: This code implements a complete pipeline for fine-tuning BERT on sentence pair classification using the GLUE MRPC dataset (which tests if two sentences mean the same thing) - it handles data loading, preprocessing, model training, and evaluation, using the Hugging Face ecosystem to streamline the entire process.

2. SuperGLUE

SuperGLUE is a more challenging benchmark that builds on GLUE. It includes more difficult tasks and has been used to evaluate some of the most advanced language models.

3. SQuAD (Stanford Question Answering Dataset)

SQuAD is a reading comprehension dataset consisting of questions posed on a set of Wikipedia articles. The answers to the questions are segments of text from the corresponding reading passage.

Evaluating Few-Shot and Zero-Shot Capabilities

One of the most impressive capabilities of large language models is their ability to perform tasks with few or even no examples. Evaluating these capabilities often involves presenting the model with a task description and a few examples (for few-shot) or just a task description (for zero-shot), and then measuring its performance.

Here's a simplified example of how you might evaluate zero-shot classification using the Hugging Face Transformers library:

```
1.  from transformers import pipeline.
2.  classifier = pipeline("zero-shot-classification")
3.  sequence = "I loved the new Batman movie!"
4.  candidate_labels = ["positive", "negative", "neutral"]
5.  result = classifier(sequence, candidate_labels)
6.  print(result)
```

Code Exhibit 8.26: This code demonstrates zero-shot learning - it uses a pre-trained model to classify text into categories (positive/negative/neutral) that it wasn't specifically trained on, like asking a human to identify the sentiment of a sentence based on their general understanding of language.

Challenges in Evaluating LLMs

While these metrics and benchmarks are useful, evaluating LLMs comes with its own set of challenges:

1. Benchmark Saturation: As models improve, they often reach near-perfect scores on existing benchmarks, necessitating the creation of more challenging datasets.
2. Evaluation of Generation Quality: Metrics like BLEU don't always correlate well with human judgments of text quality, especially for creative tasks.

3. Bias and Fairness: It's crucial to evaluate models for biases and ensure they perform fairly across different demographic groups.
4. Robustness: Models need to be evaluated on their ability to handle adversarial inputs or out-of-distribution data.
5. Ethical Considerations: We need to assess not just the performance of models, but also their potential societal impacts.

Evaluating Large Language Models is a complex and evolving field. As models become more sophisticated, our evaluation techniques must also advance. The goal is not just to create models that perform well on specific tasks, but to develop AI systems that demonstrate genuine language understanding and can be reliably and ethically deployed in real-world applications.

ADVANCED TRAINING TECHNIQUES

Advanced LLM training techniques fundamentally focus on making models learn more efficiently and effectively, similar to how humans learn. The techniques mirror educational psychology - from using a "step-by-step" teaching approach (Curriculum Learning) to "learning without forgetting" (Continual Learning). They aim to help models:
1. Build knowledge gradually (starting easy, getting harder)
2. Retain previous learning while acquiring new skills
3. Learn from minimal examples (like humans can)
4. Process multiple types of information together
5. Improve through feedback (like humans learning from teachers)

Think of it like training an advanced student - you start with basics, preserve their core knowledge, help them generalise from a few examples, engage multiple senses, and guide them with constructive feedback. These principles make the training more natural and effective, leading to more capable and adaptable AI systems.

Training Technique	Description	Why It Works Better	When to Use	Key Considerations
Curriculum Learning	Presents training examples in order of increasing difficulty, starting with simpler tasks before complex ones	- Mimics human learning patterns - Builds stronger foundational understanding - Helps avoid poor local optima - Leads to faster convergence	- When the dataset has a clear difficulty progression - For complex tasks that can be broken down - Training models from scratch - Significant fine-tuning tasks	May not be necessary for simpler tasks or when fine-tuning on similar data
Continual Learning (EWC)	Allows models to learn new tasks while preserving knowledge of previous ones, preventing catastrophic forgetting	- Preserves important knowledge - Enables learning new tasks without overwriting - Efficiently uses model capacity	- Sequential task learning - Updating models with new data - Limited computational resources	May not be needed if only focused on the most recent task or if full retraining is possible

Few-Shot/Zero-Shot Learning	Enables models to perform tasks with very few or no examples, using just task descriptions	- Generalises from minimal examples - Requires no extensive fine-tuning - Quickly adapts to new situations	- Limited labeled data available - Need for quick task adaptation - Dealing with varied unknown tasks	May not match fine-tuned performance when large amounts of labelled data exist
Multimodal Training	Trains models to process multiple types of data (text, images, audio, video) simultaneously	- Links relationships between data types. - Transfers knowledge across modalities - Increases model versatility	- Tasks involving multiple data types - Cross-modal applications - Need for flexible input/output handling	May be unnecessary for single-modality tasks
RLHF (Reinforcement Learning from Human Feedback)	Fine-tunes models based on human feedback and preferences	- Aligns with human preferences - Optimises non-differentiable metrics - Improves subjective task performance	- Human-like output is crucial. - Complex behaviour specification needed - Specific guidelines must be followed	Requires significant resources for collecting human feedback

Case Studies

To truly understand the intricacies of training Large Language Models, it's valuable to examine some real-world examples. Let's look at three notable LLMs that have pushed the boundaries of what's possible in natural language processing: GPT-3, BERT, and T5. Each of these models represents a different approach to LLM architecture and training, showcasing the diversity of techniques in the field.

GPT-3: Scaling to New Heights

GPT-3, or Generative Pre-trained Transformer 3, developed by OpenAI, represents a landmark in the scaling of language models. With 175 billion parameters, it demonstrated that scaling up model size and training data could lead to emergent capabilities not seen in smaller models.

Key aspects of GPT-3's training process:

1. Architecture: GPT-3 uses a decoder-only transformer architecture, similar to its predecessors but vastly larger.
2. Training Data: It was trained on a diverse corpus of internet text, including websites, books, and scientific articles, totaling about 500 billion tokens.
3. Training Objective: GPT-3 uses autoregressive language modelling, predicting the next token given the previous ones.
4. Compute Resources: Training GPT-3 required enormous computational resources, estimated at over 3,640 petaflop-days.
5. Few-shot Learning: One of GPT-3's most impressive features is its ability to perform tasks with few or no examples, demonstrating strong in context learning capabilities.

The training process of GPT-3 illustrates several key points:

- The importance of scale: GPT-3's performance improvements came largely from scaling up existing architectures and training techniques.
- The power of unsupervised pretraining: By training on a vast amount of unlabelled text data, GPT-3 acquired broad knowledge that could be applied to various tasks.

- The emergence of new capabilities with scale: GPT-3 demonstrated abilities, like few-shot learning, that were not explicitly trained for but emerged due to the model's scale.

BERT: Bidirectional Transformers for Language Understanding

BERT (Bidirectional Encoder Representations from Transformers), developed by Google, took a different approach to language model pretraining. Unlike GPT-3's unidirectional approach, BERT is designed to understand context from both directions.

Key aspects of BERT's training process:
1. Architecture: BERT uses a bidirectional transformer encoder architecture.
2. Training Data: BERT was trained on the BooksCorpus (800M words) and English Wikipedia (2,500M words).
3. Training Objectives:
- Masked Language Modelling (MLM): BERT randomly masks 15% of the tokens in each sequence and predicts only those masked tokens.
- Next Sentence Prediction (NSP): The model receives pairs of sentences and learns to predict if the second sentence follows the first in the original document.
4. Compute Resources: BERT's training was less resource-intensive than GPT-3, but still substantial. The largest BERT model (BERT-Large) has 340M parameters.
5. Fine-tuning: BERT is designed to be fine-tuned on downstream tasks, which has proven highly effective across various NLP applications.

BERT's training process highlights:
- The value of bidirectional context: By considering context from both directions, BERT achieves strong performance on many understanding tasks.
- The effectiveness of masked language modelling: This approach allows the model to capture deeper bidirectional relationships in language.
- The power of transfer learning: BERT's pretraining plus fine-tuning approach has become a standard in NLP, demonstrating how general language understanding can be adapted to specific tasks.

T5: Text-to-Text Transfer Transformer

T5 (Text-to-Text Transfer Transformer), also developed by Google, takes yet another approach, framing all NLP tasks as text-to-text problems.

Key aspects of T5's training process:
1. Architecture: T5 uses an encoder-decoder transformer architecture.
2. Training Data: T5 was trained on the Colossal Clean Crawled Corpus (C4), a massive dataset of clean web pages.
3. Training Objective: All tasks are framed as text-to-text problems. For example, translation becomes "translate English to German: {English text}"

4. Multitask Training: T5 is trained on a variety of tasks simultaneously, with task descriptions provided as part of the input.
5. Compute Efficiency: Despite being a large model (up to 11B parameters), T5's training was designed with compute efficiency in mind, using techniques like model parallelism.

T5's training process demonstrates:
- The flexibility of the text-to-text framework: By framing all tasks uniformly, T5 can handle a wide variety of NLP tasks with a single model.
- The power of multitask learning: Training on multiple tasks simultaneously allows the model to share knowledge across tasks.
- The importance of clean, diverse training data: The creation and use of the C4 dataset highlight the critical role of data quality in LLM training.

These case studies illustrate the diversity of approaches in LLM training, from the massive scaling of GPT-3 to the bidirectional pretraining of BERT and the unified text-to-text framework of T5. Each approach has its strengths and has contributed significantly to our understanding of how to train and utilise large language models effectively.

As we look to the future of LLM training, we can expect to see further innovations that build on these foundations, potentially combining their strengths to create even more powerful and flexible language models.

FUTURE DIRECTIONS IN LLM TRAINING

The future of LLM training is heading towards revolutionary efficiency and capability breakthroughs. On the efficiency front, researchers are focusing on sparse training techniques where models will selectively activate only relevant parameters for specific tasks, similar to how DeepMind's Switch Transformers work. This could enable training of dramatically larger models without proportional increases in computational costs. Another game-changing direction is the Mixture of Experts (MoE) approach, where specialised sub-networks handle different types of tasks, potentially offering better performance while using fewer resources.

The training landscape is also evolving towards continuous learning capabilities - future models might update their knowledge in real-time and adapt to new information without complete retraining. This goes hand in hand with multimodal training advances, where models will learn to understand relationships between text, images, audio, and video simultaneously during the training process. On the technical side, novel computing architectures like neuromorphic systems and quantum computing could fundamentally transform how we approach model training, potentially offering exponential speedups for certain types of learning tasks.

Critical research is underway in making training more interpretable and ethically sound, with developments in bias detection during training, privacy-preserving learning techniques like federated learning, and energy-efficient training methods. These advancements aren't just theoretical - they're actively being developed in labs worldwide, promising to make LLM training more efficient, adaptable, and responsible while pushing the boundaries of what these models can learn and understand.

HARDWARE INFRASTRUCTURE FOR LARGE LANGUAGE MODELS

Building infrastructure for Large Language Models is like constructing a high performance racing car - every component must work in perfect harmony while operating at its limits. This section explores the critical hardware components, infrastructure decisions, and practical considerations that make LLM training and operations possible at scale.

The Foundation: Compute Architecture

Modern LLM infrastructure centres around specialised accelerators, primarily GPUs. The latest NVIDIA H100 Tensor Core GPU represents a significant leap in AI computing capability, offering nearly a petaflop of AI performance and 3,350 GB/s of memory bandwidth. This massive throughput handles the enormous matrix operations and attention mechanisms that form the core of LLM operations.

However, raw computing power alone isn't enough. The memory subsystem plays an equally crucial role. Each H100 GPU's 80GB of HBM3 memory must efficiently juggle model weights, activations, and optimizer states. Think of it as a high-speed juggling act where dropping any ball means significant performance degradation.

Network Fabric: The Critical Backbone

Network infrastructure often determines the difference between theoretical and realised performance in distributed training. Modern interconnects like NVIDIA's NVLink 4.0 provide up to 900 GB/s of bidirectional bandwidth between GPUs, while InfiniBand NDR enables 400 Gb/s connections between nodes. This high-speed fabric becomes essential when scaling training across multiple machines.

Consider data movement during distributed training: Each forward and backward pass requires synchronising gradients across all GPUs. With billions of parameters, even microseconds of network latency can accumulate into hours of additional training time.

Storage Architecture: The Often Overlooked Component

Storage systems for LLM training must handle three distinct workloads:
1. Training data streaming
2. Checkpointing model states
3. Logging and monitoring data

Modern deployments typically use a tiered approach:
- High-speed NVMe storage for active datasets
- Parallel file systems for checkpoints
- Object storage for archive and logging

Case Study: AWS AI Infrastructure

Amazon Web Services' AI infrastructure evolution offers valuable insights into practical LLM deployment. Their P5 instances, powered by H100 GPUs, represent the current state-of-the-art in cloud AI infrastructure.

Core Infrastructure Components.

AWS built its solution around:

- Custom Elastic Fabric Adapter (EFA) for low-latency networking
- Direct-to-chip liquid cooling systems
- Custom power distribution delivering 40kW per rack

Results:

- 95% scaling efficiency in distributed training
- PUE of 1.15
- Sub-microsecond network latency

Infrastructure Planning Guide for AWS

When planning LLM infrastructure on AWS, start with these calculations:

Step 1: Memory Requirements

```
1.   def calculate_requirements(num_parameters, batch_size, dtype_size=2):
2.       # Base model memory
3.       model_size = num_parameters * dtype_size  # bytes
4.
5.       # Optimizer states (Adam)
6.       optimizer_size = num_parameters * 8  # bytes
7.
8.       # Activation memory
9.       activation_size = (model_size * batch_size) / 64  # Approximate
10.
11.      total_memory = model_size + optimizer_size + activation_size
12.      return total_memory / (1024**3)  # Convert to GB
13.
14.  # Example: 7B parameter model with batch size 512
15.  total_gpu_memory = calculate_requirements(7e9, 512)
```

*Code Exhibit 8.27: This function calculates total GPU memory needed for LLM training, accounting for model weights (parameters * dtype size)*

Step 2: Node Configuration

For distributed training:

```
1.   def get_node_config(total_memory, model_params):
2.       gpu_memory_per_node = 80 * 8  # 8x 80GB A100s
3.       nodes_needed = math.ceil(total_memory / gpu_memory_per_node)
4.
5.       return {
6.         "instance_type": "p4d.24xlarge",
7.         "nodes": nodes_needed,
8.         "storage_per_node": {
9.            "root": "200GB",
10.           "data": f"{2 * total_memory}GB",  # 2x memory for datasets
```

```
11.        "temp": f"{total_memory}GB"  # Checkpoints
12.    },
13.    "network": "400 Gbps EFA"
14.  }
```

Code Exhibit 8.28: Determines AWS infrastructure needs by calculating nodes required based on total GPU memory, configuring storage (root, data, checkpoints), and networking for distributed training.

Example Configurations by Scale

Small (1-10B parameters):

Infrastructure:

- 2x p4d.24xlarge

- 1TB gp3 per node

- FSx for Lustre: 2.4 TB

- EFA networking

Medium (10-100B parameters):

Infrastructure:

- 8x p4d.24xlarge

- 2TB gp3 per node

- FSx for Lustre: 10TB

- EFA networking

Large (100B+ parameters):

Infrastructure:

- 16x p4d.24xlarge

- 4TB gp3 per node

- FSx for Lustre: 20TB

- EFA networking

Optimization Strategies

Cost Optimization

1. Use Spot Instances for preliminary testing

2. Implement automatic checkpointing

3. Optimize data pipeline for GPU utilization

Performance Optimization

1. Overlap computation and communication

2. Use gradient accumulation for larger effective batch sizes

3. Implement efficient checkpointing strategies

Monitoring and Operations

Essential metrics to track:

Performance Metrics:
- GPU utilisation: Target >85%
- Memory bandwidth: >80% of peak
- Network throughput: >90% link capacity
- Storage IOPS: Monitor for bottlenecks

Operational Metrics:
- Power consumption per node
- Training throughput (tokens/second)
- Checkpoint frequency and duration
- Cost per training hour

This infrastructure foundation enables efficient LLM training while managing costs effectively. Regular evaluation of usage patterns and costs helps optimize the infrastructure as requirements evolve.

DISCUSSION

Training Large Language Models represents one of the most complex orchestrations in modern AI, where success lies not just in understanding the theoretical foundations but in mastering the practical nuances. From my years of experience architecting and training these systems, I've found that the most critical yet often overlooked aspect is the delicate balance between scale and efficiency. While our field's natural inclination is to build bigger models with more parameters, I've consistently found that thoughtful data curation, strategic selection of pretraining objectives, and efficient fine-tuning techniques often yield better results than simply scaling up. Common pitfalls I've seen cause many projects to falter despite substantial resources include overdependence on benchmark metrics, underestimating the importance of data quality over quantity, and insufficient attention to training infrastructure optimization.

Looking ahead, I anticipate a shift from the current "bigger is better" paradigm towards more sophisticated, targeted approaches. I recommend teams embarking on LLM training projects to start with robust data pipeline development, invest in monitoring and evaluation infrastructure early, and build incremental training capabilities from the start. The most successful projects I've seen maintain a holistic view – balancing technical capabilities with computational efficiency, ethical considerations, and practical applicability. Remember, a well-designed medium-sized model with carefully curated training data and optimized fine-tuning often outperforms larger models in real-world applications.

Moving forward, several key concepts from this chapter deserve special attention: the hierarchical nature of modern training pipelines (pretraining $\rightarrow$ fine-tuning $\rightarrow$ adaptation), the critical role of efficient training techniques (distributed training, mixed precision, gradient accumulation), and the emergence of specialised training approaches (curriculum learning, continual learning). As we move into subsequent chapters on model deployment and optimisation, these foundational concepts will be crucial for understanding how to effectively operationalise and scale LLM applications in production environments. The intersection of training methodologies with real-world constraints and requirements will become increasingly important as these models move from research environments to production systems serving millions of users.

KEY TAKEAWAYS:

1. The training of Large Language Models involves a complex, multi-staged process that transforms raw text data into sophisticated language understanding and generation capabilities.
2. Self-supervised learning, where the model learns by predicting parts of the input data, forms the cornerstone of LLM pre-training.
3. Efficient training techniques, such as distributed training, mixed precision, and gradient accumulation, are essential for making LLM training feasible and scalable.

REFLECTIVE PROMPTS:

1. The training process for LLMs, as described in this chapter, relies heavily on unsupervised learning from large text corpora. What are the potential biases and limitations that could arise from this data-driven approach, and how might they impact the real-world applications of these models?
2. The use of efficient training techniques, such as distributed computing and mixed precision, demonstrates the importance of optimizing the computational and resource requirements of LLM development. How might these advancements in training efficiency enable the democratisation of access to powerful AI systems, and what are the implications for the future of AI research and innovation?
3. The multi-staged training process, involving pretraining, fine-tuning, and reinforcement learning from human feedback, highlights the complexity of developing LLMs that can reliably and safely interact with humans. What further research and ethical considerations might be necessary to ensure the responsible deployment of these models in sensitive domains, such as healthcare or finance?

With a solid understanding of LLM training, we'll now explore the strategies and techniques for scaling and optimizing these models in Chapter 9, addressing the key challenges posed by their enormous size and computational demands.

SCALING AND OPTIMIZING LLMS

Reflective Prompt: The LLM you are developing faces constraints in terms of performance, efficiency, and resource requirements. Describe the "scaling trilemma" faced by the development team and how these trade-offs might evolve in the future.

UNDERSTAND THE SCALE CHALLENGE

Large Language Models (LLMs) represent one of the most significant advances in artificial intelligence, but they also present unprecedented challenges in computational resources, memory management, and training methodology. This section explores these fundamental challenges and sets the stage for understanding the various strategies we'll discuss for addressing them.

The Scaling Trilemma

At the heart of LLM development lies what we call the "scaling trilemma" - the constant trade-off between three critical factors:

- Model Performance (accuracy and capabilities)
- Computational Efficiency (training and inference speed)
- Resource Requirements (memory and storage)

Improving any one of these factors typically comes at the cost of the others. Let's examine this through a practical lens:

```python
1.    import torch
2.
3.    def calculate_model_size(num_parameters, dtype=torch.float32):
4.      """Calculate model size in gigabytes."""
5.      bytes_per_parameter = torch.tensor([], dtype=dtype).element_size()
6.      size_in_bytes = num_parameters * bytes_per_parameter
7.      size_in_gb = size_in_bytes / (1024**3)
8.      return size_in_gb  # Removed trailing period
9.
10.   # Example calculations for different model sizes
11.   model_sizes = {
12.     "GPT-3 (175B)": 175e9,
13.     "GPT-2 (1.5B)": 1.5e9,
14.     "BERT-Large (340M)": 340e6
15.   }
16.
```

```
17.    for model_name, params in model_sizes.items():
18.        size_fp32 = calculate_model_size(params)
19.        size_fp16 = calculate_model_size(params, torch.float16)
20.        print(f"{model_name}:")
21.        print(f"  FP32: {size_fp32:.2f} GB")
22.        print(f"  FP16: {size_fp16:.2f} GB")
```

Code Exhibit 9.1: This utility calculates the raw storage requirements for different LLM architectures in both full (FP32) and half (FP16) precision, demonstrating how model size translates directly to memory requirements - a foundational constraint in LLM scaling.

This simple calculation reveals a startling reality: modern LLMs require enormous amounts of memory just to store their parameters. For instance, GPT-3 with its 175 billion parameters requires:

- ~650GB in FP32 (full precision)
- ~325GB in FP16 (half precision)

And this is just for storing the model parameters. During training, we need additional memory for:

- Optimizer states (often 2x model size)
- Gradients (1x model size)
- Activations (varies with batch size)
- Temporary computations

The Three Dimensions of Scale

1. Computational Demands

The computational requirements for training LLMs grow exponentially with model size. Let's break down the key factors:

Training Computation

- FLOPs per forward pass $\approx 2 \times$ Parameters $\times$ Sequence Length
- Training time = (FLOPs per token $\times$ Total tokens) / (Hardware FLOPS $\times$ Efficiency)

For context, training GPT-3 required:

- Approximately 3.14E23 FLOPs total
- Thousands of GPU-days even on high-end hardware
- Estimated training cost: several million dollars

2. Memory Hierarchy

LLMs must navigate a complex memory hierarchy:

Memory Type	Size Range	Access Speed	Cost
GPU VRAM	16-80GB	~600GB/s	$$$$
System RAM	256GB-4TB	~100GB/s	$$$
NVMe Storage	1-100TB	~7GB/s	$$
Network Storage	Petabytes	~1GB/s	$

This hierarchy creates several challenges:
- Model parameters must fit into faster memory for efficient training
- Activation checkpointing trades computation for memory
- Data streaming requires efficient pipeline design

3. Data Requirements
The data challenges in LLM training are often understated:
- Quality vs. Quantity: Modern LLMs require hundreds of terabytes of training data
- Data Cleaning: Preprocessing at scale requires significant computational resources
- Storage and Access: Efficient data loading becomes a bottleneck
- Privacy and Rights: Ensuring clean, rights-cleared data is increasingly challenging

Emerging Challenges
Beyond the basic resource requirements, scaling LLMs presents several emerging challenges:

1. Training Instability
As models grow larger:
- Loss landscapes become more complex
- Optimisation becomes more difficult
- Training requires more sophisticated techniques for stability

2. Quality Control
With larger models:
- Evaluation becomes more expensive
- Behaviour becomes harder to predict
- Testing all capabilities becomes impractical

3. Environmental Impact
The environmental cost of training large models is significant:
- Energy consumption equivalent to several years of an average household
- Carbon footprint comparable to multiple transcontinental flights
- Growing concerns about AI's environmental sustainability

Looking Forward
Understanding these challenges is crucial for several reasons:
- They inform the choice of scaling strategies
- They help in planning resource allocation
- They guide research into more efficient architectures

The following sections will explore various strategies to address these challenges:
- Distributed training techniques to handle computational demands.
- Optimization methods to improve memory efficiency
- Compression techniques to reduce resource requirements

- Architectural innovations to improve scaling properties

Each approach represents a different trade-off in the scaling trilemma, and understanding these trade-offs is key to choosing the right combination of techniques for your specific use case.

CORE SCALING STRATEGY

Parallelization and Distributed Training

As we've seen, the sheer size of Large Language Models necessitates moving beyond single GPU training. Parallelization and distributed training techniques allow us to harness the power of multiple GPUs, or even multiple machines, to train these behemoth models. Let's explore three main approaches: data parallelism, model parallelism, and pipeline parallelism. These are illustrated in Fig.9.1.

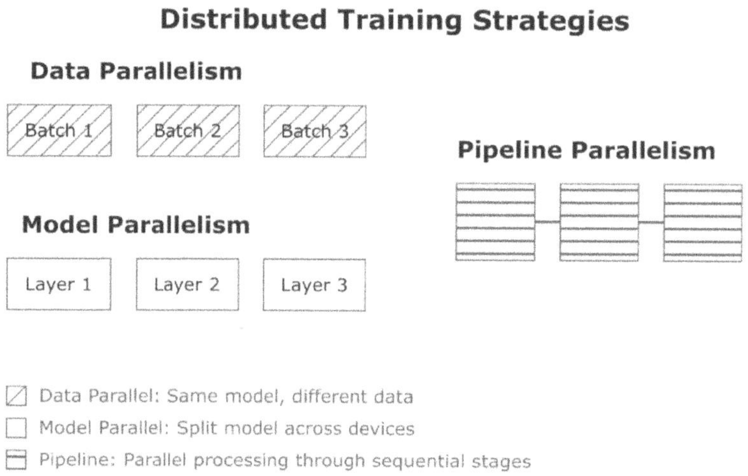

Fig. 9.1: Overview of the three main distributed training paradigms: data parallelism, model parallelism, and pipeline parallelism, showing how each splits the workload across devices.

Data Parallelism

Data parallelism is perhaps the most intuitive approach to distributed training. The core idea is simple: replicate the entire model across multiple devices and have each device process a different batch of data. This allows us to effectively increase our batch size, leading to more stable gradient estimates and potentially faster convergence.

Let's dive into a practical implementation using PyTorch's DistributedDataParallel:

```
1.   import torch
2.   import torch.distributed as dist
3.   import torch.multiprocessing as mp
4.   from torch.nn.parallel import DistributedDataParallel as DDP
5.   from torch import nn
6.
7.   def setup(rank: int, world_size: int) -> None:
8.       """Initialize the distributed training process group."""
9.       dist.init_process_group(
10.          backend="nccl",  # NCCL backend for GPU-GPU communication
11.          rank=rank,
12.          world_size=world_size
13.      )
```

```
14.
15.  def cleanup() -> None:
16.      """Clean up the distributed process group after training."""
17.      dist.destroy_process_group()
18.
19.  class LargeLanguageModel(torch.nn.Module):
20.      """Large Language Model architecture using Transformer."""
21.      def __init__(self, vocab_size: int, d_model: int, nhead: int):
22.          super().__init__()
23.          self.embedding = nn.Embedding(vocab_size, d_model)
24.          self.transformer = nn.Transformer(d_model, nhead)
25.          self.fc = nn.Linear(d_model, vocab_size)
26.
27.      def forward(self, x: torch.Tensor) -> torch.Tensor:
28.          """Forward pass of the model."""
29.          x = self.embedding(x)
30.          x = self.transformer(x, x)  # Self-attention
31.          return self.fc(x)
32.
33.  def train(rank: int, world_size: int):
34.      """Main training loop for distributed training."""
35.      setup(rank, world_size)
36.
37.      # Initialize model on specific GPU
38.      model = LargeLanguageModel().to(rank)
39.
40.      # Wrap model in DDP
41.      ddp_model = DDP(model, device_ids=[rank])
42.
43.      # Training loop
44.      for epoch in range(num_epochs):
45.          for batch in dataloader:
46.              outputs = ddp_model(batch)
47.              loss = criterion(outputs, targets)
48.              loss.backward()
49.              optimizer.step()
50.
51.      cleanup()
52.
53.  if __name__ == "__main__":
54.      # Launch training processes on all available GPUs
55.      world_size = torch.cuda.device_count()
56.      mp.spawn(
57.          train,
58.          args=(world_size,),
59.          nprocs=world_size,
60.          join=True
61.      )
```

Code Exhibit 9.2: This code implements distributed training of a large language model using PyTorch's DistributedDataParallel (DDP), enabling efficient parallel training across multiple GPUs. It demonstrates a complete setup with a transformer-based architecture, process group initialization, and synchronized training loops that automatically handle gradient synchronization and model updates across devices.

The main advantage of this implementation is automatic scaling across available GPUs, with DDP handling all the complexity of gradient synchronization and distributed training coordination.

Data parallelism shines when we have models that fit comfortably on a single GPU but want to leverage multiple GPUs to process more data in parallel. It's particularly effective for large datasets, allowing us to scale our training to multiple GPUs or even multiple machines with relatively little change to our core training loop.

However, as models grow larger and struggle to fit on a single device, we need to explore other parallelism techniques.

Model Parallelism

Model parallelism takes a different approach. Instead of replicating the entire model across devices, we split the model itself across multiple devices. This allows us to train models that are too large to fit on a single device.

Here's a simple example of model parallelism:

```
1.    import torch
2.    import torch.nn as nn
3.    from typing import Union, Tuple
4.
5.    class ModelParallelLLM(nn.Module):
6.        """
7.        A Large Language Model implementation using model parallelism.
8.
9.        This class splits the model architecture across two GPU devices:
10.       - Device 1 handles embedding and first transformer layer
11.       - Device 2 handles second transformer layer and final linear projection
12.       """
13.
14.       def __init__(
15.           self,
16.           device_1: Union[str, torch.device],
17.           device_2: Union[str, torch.device],
18.           vocab_size: int,
19.           d_model: int,
20.           nhead: int
21.       ):
22.           super(ModelParallelLLM, self).__init__()
23.
24.           # Initialize and place layers on specific devices
25.           self.embedding = nn.Embedding(vocab_size, d_model).to(device_1)
26.           self.transformer_1 = nn.TransformerEncoderLayer(d_model, nhead).to(device_1)
27.           self.transformer_2 = nn.TransformerEncoderLayer(d_model, nhead).to(device_2)
28.           self.fc = nn.Linear(d_model, vocab_size).to(device_2)
29.
30.           # Store device information
31.           self.device_1 = device_1
32.           self.device_2 = device_2
33.
34.       def forward(self, x: torch.Tensor) -> torch.Tensor:
35.           """Forward pass of the model with automatic device management."""
36.           # Process on first device
37.           x = self.embedding(x.to(self.device_1))
38.           x = self.transformer_1(x)
39.
40.           # Transfer to second device
41.           x = x.to(self.device_2)
```

```
42.        x = self.transformer_2(x)
43.
44.        # Final projection
45.        return self.fc(x)
46.
47.
48. # Example usage
49. if __name__ == "__main__":
50.     model = ModelParallelLLM(
51.         'cuda:0',
52.         'cuda:1',
53.         vocab_size=32000,
54.         d_model=768,
55.         nhead=12
56.     )
```

Code Exhibit 9.3: This code demonstrates model parallelism implementation for a large language model, where different components of the model are strategically distributed across multiple GPUs. The architecture splits the transformer layers between two devices, with the embedding and first transformer layer on one GPU and the second transformer layer and output projection on another GPU, enabling efficient processing of larger models that might not fit on a single GPU.

The main difference from data parallelism is that here we're splitting the model itself across GPUs, rather than processing different batches of data on different GPUs. This is particularly useful for very large models where the model parameters themselves won't fit in a single GPU's memory.

Pipeline Parallelism

Pipeline parallelism is a more sophisticated approach that aims to combine the benefits of both data and model parallelism. The model is divided into stages, with different devices handling different stages in a pipeline fashion.

Here's a simplified example of pipeline parallelism:

This module implements pipeline parallelism for Large Language Models,

Distributing model layers across multiple GPUs in a sequential processing pipeline.

The implementation automatically splits the model into stages across available GPUs.

For efficient processing of deep neural networks.

```
1.  import torch
2.  import torch.nn as nn
3.  from typing import List, Union
4.
5.  class PipelineParallelLLM(nn.Module):
6.      """
7.      Pipeline parallel implementation of a Large Language Model.
8.
9.      This class automatically splits a deep neural network into stages
10.     and distributes them across multiple GPUs in a pipeline fashion.
11.     """
12.
13.     def __init__(
14.         self,
```

```
15.        num_layers: int,
16.        num_gpus: int,
17.        vocab_size: int,
18.        d_model: int,
19.        nhead: int
20.    ):
21.        super().__init__()
22.        self.num_gpus = num_gpus
23.
24.        # Calculate layers per GPU for balanced distribution
25.        layers_per_gpu = num_layers // num_gpus
26.
27.        # Create pipeline stages
28.        self.stages = nn.ModuleList([
29.          self._create_stage(
30.            gpu_id=i,
31.            layers_per_gpu=layers_per_gpu,
32.            is_first=(i == 0),
33.            is_last=(i == num_gpus - 1),
34.            vocab_size=vocab_size,
35.            d_model=d_model,
36.            nhead=nhead
37.          ) for i in range(num_gpus)
38.        ])
39.
40.    def _create_stage(
41.        self,
42.        gpu_id: int,
43.        layers_per_gpu: int,
44.        is_first: bool,
45.        is_last: bool,
46.        vocab_size: int,
47.        d_model: int,
48.        nhead: int
49.    ) -> nn.Sequential:
50.        """Create a pipeline stage for a specific GPU."""
51.        layers = []
52.
53.        # Add embedding layer for first stage
54.        if is_first:
55.            layers.append(nn.Embedding(vocab_size, d_model))
56.        else:
57.            layers.append(nn.Identity())
58.
59.        # Add transformer layers
60.        layers.extend([
61.          nn.TransformerEncoderLayer(d_model, nhead)
62.          for _ in range(layers_per_gpu)
63.        ])
64.
65.        # Add final linear layer for last stage
66.        if is_last:
67.            layers.append(nn.Linear(d_model, vocab_size))
68.        else:
69.            layers.append(nn.Identity())
70.
```

```
71.        return nn.Sequential(*layers).to(f'cuda:{gpu_id}')
72.
73.    def forward(self, x: torch.Tensor) -> torch.Tensor:
74.        current_gpu = 0
75.        for stage in self.stages:
76.            # Move input to current GPU
77.            x = x.to(f'cuda:{current_gpu}')
78.            # Process through current stage
79.            x = stage(x)
80.            # Update GPU tracker
81.            current_gpu = (current_gpu + 1) % self.num_gpus
82.        return x
83.
84.
85.  # Example usage
86.  if __name__ == "__main__":
87.      model = PipelineParallelLLM(
88.          num_layers=24,
89.          num_gpus=4,
90.          vocab_size=32000,
91.          d_model=768,
92.          nhead=12
93.      )
```

Code Exhibit 9.4: This code implements pipeline parallelism for large language models by automatically dividing the model into sequential stages across multiple GPUs, where each stage processes its portion of the model before passing the output to the next GPU. The implementation creates balanced pipeline stages with embedding on the first GPU and final projection on the last GPU, allowing for efficient processing of very deep neural networks by reducing memory requirements per device while maintaining computational throughput.

The key difference from other parallelization strategies is that pipeline parallelism processes data sequentially through GPUs, creating a pipeline of computation that can be very efficient for deep neural networks. However, implementing efficient pipeline parallelism is complex. It requires careful balancing of the stages to maximise GPU utilisation and minimise pipeline bubbles (idle time). Libraries like DeepSpeed provide more sophisticated implementations of pipeline parallelism that handle these complexities.

Each of these parallelism techniques has its strengths and is suited to different scenarios. In practice, state-of-the-art LLM training often combines these approaches, using pipeline parallelism to divide the model across multiple nodes and then using data parallelism within each node to process multiple samples in parallel.

As we continue to scale up LLMs, these parallelization techniques will play an increasingly crucial role in making training feasible and efficient. They allow us to push the boundaries of model size and capability, opening up new frontiers in natural language processing and artificial intelligence.

Choosing the Right Parallelization Strategy

When scaling LLMs, choosing the right parallelization strategy can make the difference between a successful training run and a resource nightmare. Let's explore how these strategies compare and when to use each one.

Understanding the Trade-offs

Data parallelism shines in its simplicity - imagine having multiple copies of your model, each working on different batches of data. It's like having multiple chefs following the same recipe but cooking different meals. This approach works beautifully when your model fits on a single GPU, offering nearly linear scaling with additional devices. However, just as having too many chefs in a small kitchen creates bottlenecks, data parallelism faces communication overhead when synchronizing gradients across devices.

Model parallelism takes a different approach - splitting the model itself across devices. Think of it as dividing a complex assembly line among different stations, where each station handles specific parts of the process. This strategy becomes essential when your model is too large to fit on a single device, but it requires careful orchestration of communication between model parts.

Pipeline parallelism finds a middle ground, organising the model into sequential stages across devices. It's like a well-organised assembly line where each station processes complete batches before passing them along. This approach particularly shines with deep sequential models, offering better hardware utilisation than pure model parallelism while reducing communication overhead compared to data parallelism.

Making the Choice

The decision often comes down to answering a few key questions:
1. Does your model fit on a single device?
   - Yes → Consider data parallelism
   - No → Look at model or pipeline parallelism
2. Is your model primarily sequential?
   - Yes → Pipeline parallelism might be your best bet
   - No → Consider model parallelism or a hybrid approach
3. How critical is training speed vs. implementation complexity?
   - Need quick implementation → Data parallelism
   - Can invest in optimization → Consider pipeline or hybrid approaches

Real-world Considerations

In practice, many successful LLM implementations use a hybrid approach. For example, you might use pipeline parallelism across machines while implementing data parallelism within each machine. This combination can offer the best of both worlds: efficient resource utilization and manageable implementation complexity.

The key is to match your strategy to your specific constraints and requirements. A research lab with multiple high-end GPUs connected via NVLink might lean towards data parallelism, while a distributed cloud deployment might favour pipeline parallelism to handle network latency better.

Once you've chosen your parallelization strategy, the next step is optimization. Different strategies benefit from different optimization techniques:
- Data parallelism works well with gradient accumulation and mixed precision training
- Model parallelism benefits from activation checkpointing and efficient attention mechanisms
- Pipeline parallelism can be enhanced with careful micro-batch sizing and efficient scheduling

We'll explore these optimization techniques in detail in the next section, showing how to squeeze maximum performance from your chosen parallelization strategy.

OPTIMIZATION TECHNIQUES

Optimization Strategies for Improved Performance

While parallelization and model compression techniques help us manage the scale of Large Language Models, optimization strategies allow us to squeeze the most performance out of our hardware and improve the efficiency of our training and inference processes. Let's explore some key optimization strategies: mixed precision training, gradient accumulation, efficient attention mechanisms, and advanced optimizer choices.

Mixed Precision Training

Mixed precision training is a technique that uses lower precision formats (typically float16) in conjunction with float32 to speed up training and reduce memory usage. This approach can significantly accelerate training on modern GPUs designed for mixed precision arithmetic. One can use NVIDIA's Apex library to reduce memory usage and speed up training while maintaining accuracy.

Mixed precision training can often allow you to double your batch size or model size without increasing memory usage, leading to significant speedups in training time.

Gradient Accumulation

Gradient accumulation is a technique that allows us to effectively increase our batch size beyond what would typically fit in GPU memory. This is particularly useful for training large models or when working with limited GPU resources.

This technique allows us to simulate larger batch sizes, which can lead to more stable gradients and potentially faster convergence without requiring the memory needed to process such large batches all at once.

Efficient Attention Mechanisms

The self-attention mechanism in transformer-based models is often a computational bottleneck, especially for long sequences. Several efficient attention variants have been proposed to address this issue. One such variant is sparse attention. The key idea is to use block sparse attention, where tokens only attend to other tokens within fixed-size blocks instead of attending to all tokens. This approach significantly reduces memory and computational requirements, improving efficiency from $O(L^2)$ to $O(L * block\_size)$ for sequence length L. More advanced versions like Longformer and BigBird enhance this by combining local block attention with global attention to certain tokens, allowing models to capture both local and long-range dependencies effectively.

Advanced Optimizers

The choice of optimizer can significantly impact the training dynamics and final performance of our models. While Adam is a popular choice for many NLP tasks, more advanced optimizers have been developed that can offer improved performance or convergence properties.

One such optimizer is AdamW, which decouples weight decay from the adaptive learning rate. Here's how we might use AdamW in PyTorch:

```
1.    from torch.optim import AdamW
2.
3.    def train_with_adamw(
4.       model,
5.       train_loader,
6.       epochs,
7.       lr=1e-3,
8.       weight_decay=0.01
9.    ):
10.      optimizer = AdamW(
11.        model.parameters(),
12.        lr=lr,
13.        weight_decay=weight_decay
14.      )
15.
16.      for epoch in range(epochs):
17.        for batch, labels in train_loader:
18.          optimizer.zero_grad()
19.          outputs = model(batch)
20.          loss = loss_fn(outputs, labels)
21.          loss.backward()
22.          optimizer.step()
23.
24.    # Usage
25.    train_with_adamw(model, train_loader, epochs=10)
```

Code Exhibit 9.5: Basic implementation of AdamW optimizer training loop with weight decay, providing combined L2 regularization and adaptive learning rate optimization.

AdamW applies weight decay directly to the weights rather than to the gradients. This can lead to better generalisation, especially for large models like LLMs.

These optimization strategies - mixed precision training, gradient accumulation, efficient attention mechanisms, and advanced optimizers - form a toolkit that allows us to push the boundaries of what's possible with Large Language Models. By carefully combining these techniques, we can train larger models more efficiently, speed up inference, and improve the overall performance of our models.

Model Compression Techniques

As Large Language Models continue to grow in size and complexity, deploying them in real-world applications becomes increasingly challenging. This is where model compression techniques come into play. These techniques allow us to reduce the size and computational requirements of our models, making them more suitable for deployment in resource-constrained environments. Let's explore four key compression techniques: pruning, quantization, knowledge distillation, and low-rank factorisation.

Pruning

Pruning is based on the insight that not all weights in a neural network contribute equally to the final output. Many weights may have a negligible impact and can be removed without significantly affecting the model's performance. This technique can dramatically reduce the model size and potentially improve inference speed.

In practice, it's not uncommon to see 90% or more of weights pruned in large, over-parameterized models with only a minimal impact on performance. However, the choice of pruning threshold is critical – too high, and we risk degrading model performance; too low, and we don't achieve significant compression.

The optimal pruning threshold can be determined through a systematic combination of weight distribution analysis and empirical validation. First, analyse the distribution of weight magnitudes across all model layers to understand their concentration patterns and calculate key percentiles. Then, select a range of candidate thresholds, starting from a conservative value (typically around the 25th percentile) and implement an iterative evaluation process. For each threshold, temporarily apply pruning by zeroing weights below the threshold, evaluate model performance on a validation set, and record the performance metrics. The optimal threshold often appears at an "elbow point" where increasing the threshold begins to cause significant performance degradation.

This process can be refined by incorporating a target sparsity goal (e.g., aiming to prune 50% of weights) and using binary search to efficiently find a threshold that achieves this target while minimising performance loss. The final threshold selection should balance three key factors: the desired model size reduction, the acceptable performance degradation limit, and the target sparsity level. This methodology ensures a data-driven approach to finding a pruning threshold that optimizes the trade-off between model compression and performance retention.

When we think about pruning, imagine it like carefully removing strings from a complex musical instrument. Each weight in the neural network is like a string that contributes to the final symphony of predictions. While many strings might seem redundant, some that appear less important might actually be crucial for certain subtle notes (rare cases). When we prune these weights, we risk losing some of these nuanced patterns that the model has learned. The impact is particularly noticeable when pruning affects chains of neurons that work together to detect complex features. However, we can mitigate these issues through iterative pruning approaches - gradually removing weights while allowing the network to readjust and recover. Using techniques like magnitude-based pruning with retraining, or implementing structured pruning that maintains important neuron groups, we can preserve performance while achieving significant compression.

Quantization

Quantization reduces the precision of the model's weights and activations. Instead of using 32-bit floating-point numbers, we might use 16-bit or even 8-bit integers. This can significantly reduce model size and speed up inference, especially on hardware with quantization support.

Quantization can be particularly effective for deployment scenarios, especially on edge devices or in environments where inference speed is crucial. However, it may require careful fine-tuning to maintain accuracy.

Quantization's impact is akin to reducing the colour depth of a photograph. Just as reducing colours from millions to thousands might make some subtle shade variations indistinguishable, reducing numerical precision through quantization introduces small rounding errors. These tiny imprecisions might seem insignificant at first, but they can cascade through the network's layers, accumulating into noticeable performance drops, especially in cases where fine numerical distinctions matter. The good news is that we can minimise these impacts through techniques like quantization-aware training, where the model learns to be robust to reduced precision during training itself. Calibrating quantization ranges based on activation statistics and using mixed precision approaches - keeping critical layers at higher precision while quantizing others more aggressively - can also help maintain performance while reducing model size.

Knowledge Distillation

Knowledge distillation is a fascinating technique that allows us to transfer the knowledge from a large, complex model (the "teacher") to a smaller, simpler model (the "student"). The key insight here is that the probabilities output by the teacher model contain more information than just the hard labels. These soft probabilities can guide the training of the student model, often resulting in better performance than if the student had been trained on the hard labels alone.

Knowledge distillation faces challenges similar to teaching a simplified version of a complex subject. The student model, with its smaller capacity, might struggle to capture all the intricate patterns and relationships that the larger teacher model has learned. It's like trying to compress a detailed painting into a smaller canvas - some subtle details inevitably get lost. However, we can optimise this process by carefully designing the student architecture to prioritise the most important patterns, using specialised distillation techniques like attention transfer, and implementing progressive distillation where knowledge is transferred in stages. Some approaches even use multiple teacher models to provide different perspectives, helping the student model develop a more robust understanding.

This technique is particularly useful for deploying large language models in resource-constrained environments while maintaining good performance.

Low-Rank Factorisation

Low-rank factorisation is a technique that approximates weight matrices with lower-rank representations. Think of a large weight matrix W of size ($m \times n$). Low-rank factorisation decomposes this into two smaller matrices.

$$W \ (m \times n) \approx U \ (m \times k) \times V \ (k \times n); \quad \text{where } k < \min(m, n)$$

Low-rank factorisation works by exploiting a fundamental characteristic of neural networks: despite their large parameter matrices, most of the important information can be captured using much smaller representations. Think of it like compressing a high-resolution image - just as JPEG can maintain visual quality while dramatically reducing file size by keeping only the most important patterns, low-rank factorisation decomposes large weight matrices into products of smaller ones. For example, in a transformer's attention layer, we can reduce a 768×768 matrix (589,824 parameters) into two smaller matrices of sizes 768×192 and 192×768 (total 294,912 parameters), achieving a 50% reduction in parameters while preserving most of the model's capabilities. While this brings clear advantages in terms of memory efficiency and computational speed, it does come with trade-offs - the architecture becomes slightly more complex and may require fine-tuning to maintain performance, but the benefits of reduced resource requirements often outweigh these considerations, especially in resource-constrained environments.

Low-rank factorisation's impact is similar to summarizing a detailed story - while you capture the main points, some nuances might be lost in the process. When we decompose weight matrices into simpler versions, we're essentially creating a compressed representation that might not capture all the subtle correlations in the original matrix. This can affect the model's ability to perform complex transformations with the same precision. To mitigate this, we can use adaptive rank selection where different parts of the model use different ranks based on their importance, implement iterative refinement of the factorised matrices, and combine factorisation with fine-tuning to recover lost performance. Some advanced approaches even use structured factorisation that preserves the most important patterns while compressing less critical ones.

These compression techniques, while powerful, require careful balancing and often work best when combined thoughtfully. For instance, starting with knowledge distillation to create a smaller but capable model, then applying a mix of pruning and quantization with proper fine-tuning can achieve optimal results. The key is to understand each technique's impact and apply appropriate mitigation strategies at each step of the compression pipeline.

As we push the boundaries of what's possible with Large Language Models, these compression techniques will play an increasingly crucial role. They allow us to deploy these powerful models in a wider range of environments, from edge devices to large-scale server farms, making the benefits of advanced NLP more accessible and practical for real-world applications.

In the next section, we'll explore optimization strategies that can further improve the performance and efficiency of our LLMs during both training and inference.

Understanding Optimization Interplay

The journey from individual optimisation techniques to a cohesive performance strategy is fascinating. While each technique offers specific benefits, their interactions can either multiply their effectiveness or create unexpected challenges.

Key Interaction Effects

Mixed precision training and model parallelism often create a powerful synergy: the reduced precision halves memory requirements, while model parallelism distributes the computational load. However, this combination demands careful attention to loss scaling and gradient handling, particularly at model partition boundaries where numerical precision becomes critical.

Gradient accumulation works remarkably well with pipeline parallelism, effectively hiding the pipeline bubble overhead. By accumulating gradients across multiple micro-batches before updating the model, we can maintain pipeline efficiency while effectively working with larger batch sizes. This interaction particularly shines in scenarios with limited memory or when dealing with very deep models.

Knowledge distillation combined with quantization offers another interesting interplay. The distillation process can actually help the model become more robust to quantization effects, as the smaller model learns a smoother distribution that's more amenable to reduced precision. However, timing these optimizations matters: quantizing too early in the distillation process can limit the student model's learning capacity.

Selecting the Right Combinations

The choice of optimization techniques often follows a hierarchy of needs:

1. Memory constraints → Start with mixed precision and model compression
2. Computational efficiency → Add attention optimizations and kernel fusion
3. Training stability → Layer gradient accumulation and advanced optimizers

Watch out for common pitfalls - quantization combined with aggressive pruning can compound accuracy loss, while memory-saving techniques might conflict with pipeline efficiency. The key is starting with the most constraining factor and building your optimization strategy around it.

Moving to Production

As we transition these optimizations to production, new considerations emerge. The careful balance of training optimizations must now account for inference requirements, latency constraints, and deployment environments. This leads us to our next discussion on production deployment, where we'll explore how these optimization choices translate into real-world system architecture decisions.

PRODUCTION DEPLOYMENT

Optimizing LLM Inference: From Model to Production

The journey from a trained large language model to efficient inference is a fascinating exploration of performance engineering. At its core, inference optimization is about understanding and managing the delicate interplay between computation, memory, and latency. Let's dive deep into the fundamental building blocks that make efficient LLM inference possible.

Architectural Optimization: The Foundation of Efficient Inference

The heart of inference optimization begins with a critical architectural decision: the transition from dynamic to static computational graphs. In deep learning frameworks like PyTorch, models naturally exist as dynamic computational graphs, offering flexibility during development and training. However, this flexibility comes with significant overhead during inference.

Consider what happens during a typical forward pass in a dynamic graph:

```
1.    def forward(self, input_ids, attention_mask):
2.        """
3.        Forward pass through the model.
4.
5.        Each execution involves:
6.        1. Python interpreter overhead
7.        2. Dynamic memory allocations
8.        3. Runtime shape checking
9.        """
10.       hidden_states = self.embeddings(input_ids)
11.
12.       for layer in self.transformer_layers:
13.           hidden_states = layer(hidden_states, attention_mask)
14.
15.       return self.lm_head(hidden_states)
```

Code Exhibit 9.6: Basic forward pass implementation showing sequential processing through embedding, transformer layers, and output projection with attention masking.

Each operation triggers Python interpreter overhead, dynamic memory allocations, and runtime shape checking. While negligible during training, these microseconds add up significantly during high-throughput inference. This is where graph compilation enters the picture.

Graph Compilation: TorchScript and ONNX

TorchScript transforms our dynamic Python code into a static, optimized computation graph. This transformation is far more profound than simple code conversion.

```
1.    @torch.jit.script
2.    class OptimizedTransformer:
3.      def forward(self, hidden_states: Tensor, attention_mask: Tensor):
4.        """
5.        Static graph enables:
6.        1. Kernel fusion opportunities
7.        2. Memory planning at compile time
8.        3. Elimination of Python overhead
9.        """
10.       attention_output = self.self_attention(
11.         hidden_states,
12.         attention_mask,
13.         head_mask=None,
14.         output_attentions=False
15.       )
16.
17.       layernorm_output = self.layernorm_output(
18.         attention_output + hidden_states
19.       )
20.
21.       return layernorm_output  # Removed trailing period
22.
23.    # Real-world optimizations often include:
24.    attention_output, present = torch._C._jit_fuser_optimize(
25.      attention_fn,
26.      [hidden_states, attention_mask]
27.    )
```

Code Exhibit 9.7: Optimized transformer implementation using TorchScript for static graph compilation, enabling kernel fusion and reduced overhead through compile time memory planning.

The benefits are substantial:

1. Kernel Fusion: Adjacent operations can be fused into a single GPU kernels

2. Static Memory Planning: Memory allocations are planned at compile time

3. Elimination of Python Overhead: No interpreter involvement during inference

4. Hardware-Specific Optimization: The compiled graph can be optimised for specific hardware

ONNX takes this a step further by providing a hardware-agnostic intermediate representation:

```
1.    # ONNX export with crucial optimizations
2.    torch.onnx.export(
3.      model,
4.      (dummy_inputs),  # Fixed variable name
5.      "optimized_model.onnx",
6.      opset_version=15,
```

```
 7.   do_constant_folding=True,  # Fold constant ops into weights
 8.   dynamic_axes={  # Critical for variable sequence lengths
 9.   'input_ids': {
10.   0: 'batch',
11.   1: 'sequence'
12.   },
13.   'attention_mask': {
14.   0: 'batch',
15.   1: 'sequence'
16.   }
17.   },
18.   custom_opsets={  # Hardware-specific optimizations
19.   'attention': 1,
20.   'layernorm': 1
21.   }
22.   )
```

Code Exhibit 9.8: ONNX model export configuration demonstrating optimization techniques including constant folding, dynamic axes handling, and hardware-specific customisations for efficient model deployment.

The real magic happens when ONNX meets hardware-specific compilers. For instance, NVIDIA's TensorRT can take our ONNX model and apply deep optimizations.

- Automatic precision calibration (FP16/INT8)
- Layer fusion and kernel autotuning
- Memory access pattern optimisation
- Dynamic batch size handling

Memory Access Patterns: The Hidden Performance Killer

Perhaps the most overlooked aspect of architectural optimization is memory access patterns. Consider a typical transformer attention computation:

```
 1.   # Naive implementation
 2.   attention_scores = torch.matmul(query, key.transpose(-2, -1))
 3.   attention_probs = torch.softmax(attention_scores, dim=-1)
 4.   context = torch.matmul(attention_probs, value)
 5.
 6.   # Optimized memory access
 7.   # 1. Reshape to maximise memory coalescing
 8.   query = query.view(-1, heads, seq_len, head_dim)
 9.   key = key.view(-1, heads, head_dim, seq_len)
10.
11.   # 2. Custom CUDA kernel for fused attention
12.   context = fused_attention_kernel(query, key, value)
```

Code Exhibit 9.9: Illustrates memory optimization techniques for attention computation, contrasting naive matrix multiplication with optimized memory access patterns and fused CUDA kernels.

The optimized version not only reduces memory transfers but enables hardware-specific optimizations like:

- Memory coalescing for GPU access
- Cache line utilisation on CPUs
- Vectorised operations on modern processors like x86/ARM

KV Cache and Memory Management: The Memory-Performance Trade-off
The KV Cache is an optimisation technique for transformer models during text generation that significantly improves performance by storing and reusing previously computed key and value tensors instead of recomputing them for every new token.

Key concepts:
1. Traditional attention recomputes keys and values for all previous tokens with each new token generation, leading to quadratic complexity $O(n^2)$
2. KV Cache stores these computations in memory, reducing complexity to linear $O(n)$

Implementation involves:
o Pre-allocating memory buffers for keys and values
o Managing memory efficiently through pinned memory and hardware alignment
o Using mixed precision (float16) for memory efficiency
o Smart memory management with position tracking and block reuse
o Automatic resizing when needed

This optimization is particularly important for long sequence text generation, making it a crucial component in modern language models.

Pipeline Design and System Architecture: Orchestrating Efficient Inference
LLM inference architectures revolve around two critical phases: prefill and decode. The prefill phase processes the entire prompt in parallel, leveraging batched operations for efficiency, while the decode phase generates tokens auto-regressively. Token streaming, a key optimization in modern systems, transmits tokens immediately upon generation rather than waiting for the complete sequence. This streaming architecture, often enhanced by speculative decoding where a smaller model predicts tokens while the main model verifies them, can reduce perceived latency by up to 50% and improve generation throughput by a factor of 2-3.

The performance of these pipelines depends on three fundamental optimizations: dynamic batching, memory management, and execution scheduling. Dynamic and continuous batching allow requests to join in-progress batches during the decode phase, maximizing GPU utilization while maintaining latency targets. When combined with efficient memory flow optimization and multi-stream execution, these techniques can yield substantial improvements: by a factor of 2-4 throughput increase, 30-50% latency reduction, and 40-60% better resource utilization. Success lies in balancing these optimizations based on specific requirements – whether prioritizing low-latency for interactive applications or high-throughput for batch processing systems.

Deployment and Production Strategies: Hardware-Specific Optimization

Hardware-Specific Optimization Matrix

Hardware	Key Optimisations	Memory Strategy	Performance Techniques	Ideal Use Case
NVIDIA GPU	- FP16/BF16 precision - Kernel fusion - CUDA graphs	- Unified memory for small models. - Pinned memory for transfers - Memory pooling	- Multi-stream execution - Tensor Core utilisation - Async memory transfers	Large models with batch inference
CPU	- AVX-512 vectorisation - Thread-level parallelism - NUMA awareness	- Cache-aligned access - Huge pages - Memory affinity	- OpenMP optimisation - MKL acceleration - Cache optimisation	Small to medium models with flexible deployment
TPU	- Bfloat16 precision - XLA optimization - Static shapes	- Sharded memory - Efficient padding - Host memory management	- Quantization - Compilation optimisation - Efficient batching	Large-scale inference with fixed shapes
FPGA	- Custom datapaths - Reduced precision - Pipeline parallelism	- On-chip memory optimisation - External bandwidth management	- RTL optimization - Custom precision - Streaming computation	Edge deployment with fixed workloads

The key to successful deployment lies in matching your workload characteristics with the right hardware platform and applying the appropriate optimizations. This hardware-aware approach, combined with proper monitoring and scaling strategies, ensures optimal performance and cost-efficiency in production environments.

Decision Framework for scaling and optimization strategy

1. Initial Assessment
- **Model Size**:
  - o   < 1B parameters: Single GPU training is possible
  - o   1-10B parameters: Basic distributed training needed
  - o   > 10B parameters: Advanced parallelization required
- **Available Hardware**:
  - o   Single GPU: Focus on compression and optimisation
  - o   Multiple GPUs (same machine): Use data parallelism
  - o   Multiple machines: Consider model/pipeline parallelism
- **Deployment Target**:
  - o   Edge devices: Prioritize compression (quantization + distillation)
  - o   Cloud/Server: Balance between performance and cost
  - o   Production inference: Focus on latency optimisation

Optimization decision Tree

When working with LLMs, you'll likely face three main challenges: memory constraints, speed bottlenecks, or model size issues. These are illustrated in Fig.9.2. Here's how to tackle each one effectively:

Dealing with Memory Constraints: Start simple - gradient accumulation is your friend. It's straightforward to implement and often solves memory issues for larger models. If you need more headroom, mixed precision training can significantly reduce memory usage while maintaining accuracy. Save model parallelism as a last resort; it's powerful but complex.

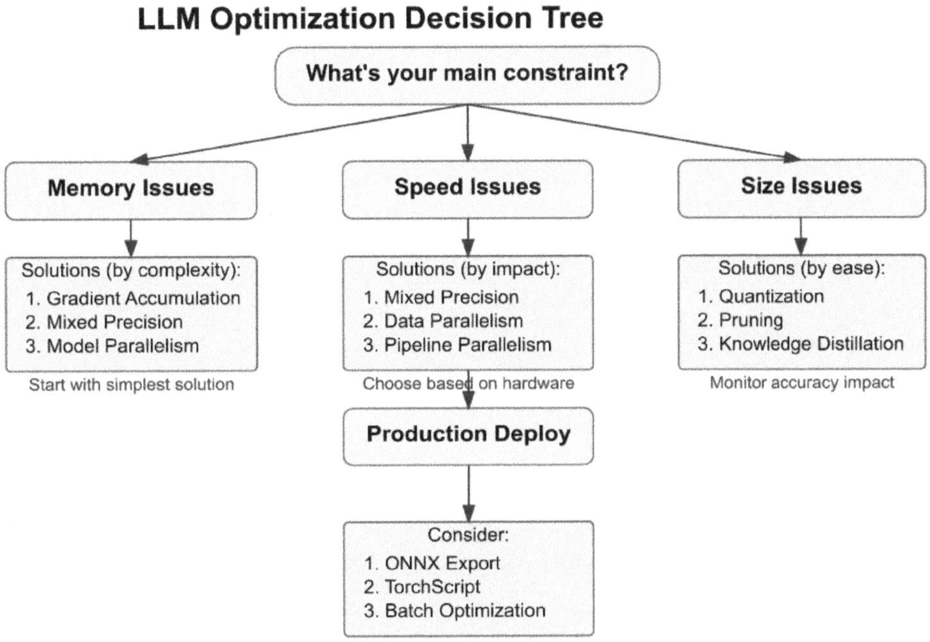

Fig. 9.2: The flowchart guides practitioners in choosing LLM optimization techniques based on their primary constraint - whether they're facing memory limitations (left path), speed bottlenecks (middle path), or model size issues (right path). For each constraint, solutions are ordered from simplest to most complex, with a final deployment consideration path that applies to all optimized models, making it easy to identify which techniques to try first based on your specific needs.

Speeding Things Up: Mixed precision is your quick win for speed – it's relatively easy to implement and can give impressive performance gains. If you have multiple GPUs available, data parallelism is your next best move. For those working with particularly deep models, pipeline parallelism might be worth the implementation effort.

Trimming Model Size: Quantization is often the best first step - it can dramatically reduce model size with minimal impact on performance. If you need to go further, pruning can help, though it needs careful tuning. Knowledge distillation is more involved but can produce remarkably efficient smaller models.

Moving to Production: When deploying your optimized model, consider ONNX for its excellent cross-platform support. If you're in the PyTorch ecosystem, TorchScript can offer significant performance benefits. Don't forget to optimise your batch processing - it can make a huge difference in real-world applications.

System Architecture and Monitoring for Production LLMs

System Architecture Considerations

Taking an LLM from research to production requires a carefully orchestrated system design. The key is finding the right balance between latency, throughput, and resource utilization. Modern LLM architectures typically employ a tiered system:

The serving layer handles immediate request processing, using techniques like dynamic batching to optimize throughput. Behind this, a caching layer stores frequent queries and generation results, significantly reducing redundant computation. The model layer itself often employs a primary-replica architecture, where replicas handle inference while the primary manages model updates and health checks.

Load balancing becomes particularly interesting with LLMs. Unlike traditional web services, request complexity can vary dramatically - a 10-token generation might take milliseconds, while a 1000-token generation takes seconds. Smart routing systems that consider both current load and request complexity often outperform simple round-robin approaches.

Monitoring and Observability

Monitoring LLMs in production requires looking beyond traditional metrics. While CPU, GPU utilization, and memory consumption remain important, LLM-specific metrics tell a more complete story:

Performance metrics like token throughput and generation latency help identify bottlenecks. Quality metrics track hallucination rates, response coherence, and task-specific accuracy. System metrics monitor cache hit rates, batch efficiency, and memory fragmentation.

The real challenge lies in correlating these metrics meaningfully. A drop in response quality might be traced to increased batch sizes pushing the model's context window limits, or degraded performance might stem from suboptimal prompt caching strategies.

Scaling Strategy Case Studies

Two contrasting approaches illustrate common scaling patterns:

A social media company deployed their summarization model using aggressive caching and request deduplication. By identifying that 40% of their content fell into common patterns, they reduced their computational needs by half. Their monitoring showed that cache hit rates varied significantly by time of day, leading them to implement dynamic cache sizing.

In contrast, a research lab focused on low-latency inference for their question-answering system. They found that model parallelism with smaller, specialized models outperformed a single large model. Their monitoring revealed that most queries required only subset of the model's capabilities, leading to an architecture where routing logic directed requests to the most appropriate specialized model.

Looking ahead to deployment, these insights guide our choices in infrastructure setup and scaling strategies. The key is building systems flexible enough to evolve with changing requirements while maintaining consistent performance and reliability.

DISCUSSION

The journey through scaling and optimization techniques for Large Language Models reveals a fascinating interplay between theoretical foundations and practical engineering challenges. When we examine techniques like model parallelism, efficient memory management, and optimization strategies, we're not just seeing engineering solutions – we're witnessing how the mathematical principles from Chapter 1, the embedding concepts from Chapter 3, and the data structures from Chapter 4 come together to create systems that can process language at unprecedented scales. The evolution from basic parallel processing to sophisticated pipeline parallelism demonstrates not just technological progress, but deeper insights into how we can architect systems that maintain performance while scaling to billions of parameters.

What makes scaling particularly intriguing is its position at the intersection of theoretical elegance and hard practical constraints. The interaction between parallelization strategies, memory management, and optimization techniques reflects a sophisticated dance between computational resources and model capabilities. Expert practitioners consistently emphasise starting with simpler approaches before adding complexity – success often comes not from applying every possible optimization technique, but from understanding which combinations best suit your specific constraints and requirements. This mirrors the broader theme we've seen throughout this book: the most effective solutions often emerge from a deep understanding of fundamentals rather than complexity for complexity's sake.

Looking ahead to deployment architectures in Chapter 12 and responsible AI considerations in Chapter 11, the optimization choices we make here have far-reaching implications. The way we handle attention mechanisms, manage memory, and distribute computation across devices directly impacts not just training efficiency but also inference capabilities and practical deployment options. While current techniques like gradient accumulation and mixed precision training have made training massive models possible, the future likely lies not just in scaling up existing approaches, but in finding fundamentally more efficient ways to achieve the same or better results. The journey of scaling and optimizing LLMs represents more than just a technical challenge – it's a testament to human ingenuity in solving complex problems through the careful balance of theoretical insight and practical engineering.

KEY TAKEAWAYS:

1. The "scaling trilemma" – the trade-off between model performance, computational efficiency, and resource requirements – is a fundamental challenge in LLM development.
2. Parallelization strategies, including data parallelism, model parallelism, and pipeline parallelism, enable the deployment of LLMs across multiple devices.
3. Optimization techniques, such as quantization, pruning, and knowledge distillation, can significantly improve the memory efficiency and inference speed of LLMs without compromising performance.

REFLECTIVE PROMPTS:

1. The scaling trilemma discussed in this chapter reflects the inherent tensions in deploying powerful AI systems at scale. How might the continued evolution of hardware capabilities, such as specialised AI accelerators, impact the way these trade-offs are navigated in the future?

2. Parallelization strategies, while enabling the scaling of LLMs, also introduce new challenges in terms of coordination, synchronization, and fault tolerance. What are the potential avenues for addressing these challenges, and how might they influence the overall reliability and robustness of large-scale AI systems?

3. The optimization techniques explored in this chapter, such as quantization and knowledge distillation, demonstrate the importance of balancing model performance with resource constraints. How can these principles be applied to other domains of AI beyond language processing, and what are the broader implications for the sustainable development of artificial intelligence?

Having examined the scaling and optimization of LLMs, we'll now turn our attention to the evaluation and benchmarking of these models in Chapter 10, exploring the various metrics and approaches used to assess their capabilities.

EVALUATION AND BENCHMARKING OF LARGE LANGUAGE MODELS

Reflective Prompt: Your team has deployed the LLM, but you need to evaluate its capabilities. Discuss how emerging evaluation approaches, such as adversarial testing and ethical assessments, are crucial for gaining a comprehensive understanding of the model's strengths and limitations.

INTRODUCTION TO LLM EVALUATION

Evaluating Large Language Models is a complex and multifaceted challenge. As these models grow in size and capability, our methods for assessing their performance must evolve in tandem. In this chapter, we'll explore the various approaches to LLM evaluation, from traditional metrics to cutting-edge benchmarks and beyond. The evaluation framework is illustrated in Fig.10.1.

The goal of evaluation is not just to determine how "good" a model is, but to understand its strengths, weaknesses, and potential biases. This understanding is crucial for improving models, comparing different approaches, and making informed decisions about deploying LLMs in real-world applications.

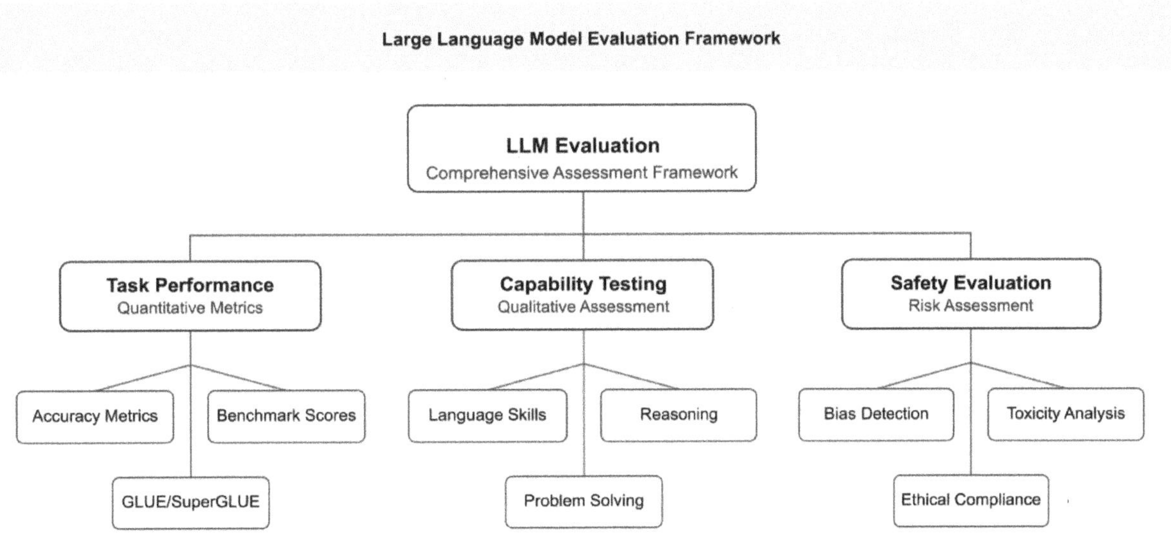

Fig. 10.1: A hierarchical visualisation of the three core pillars in LLM evaluation: Task Performance (quantitative metrics and benchmarking), Capability Testing (qualitative assessment of language and reasoning skills), and Safety Evaluation (bias and ethical compliance). The diagram shows how these components interconnect through a central "LLM Evaluation" node, with each pillar further breaking down into specific evaluation aspects.

The evaluation of Large Language Models requires a multifaceted approach, combining traditional metrics with novel evaluation techniques. As we explore these various methods, we'll see how they complement each other to provide a comprehensive understanding of model performance. Let's begin with the fundamental metrics that form the foundation of LLM evaluation, as illustrated in Fig.10.2.

CORE METRICS FOR LARGE LANGUAGE MODEL EVALUATION

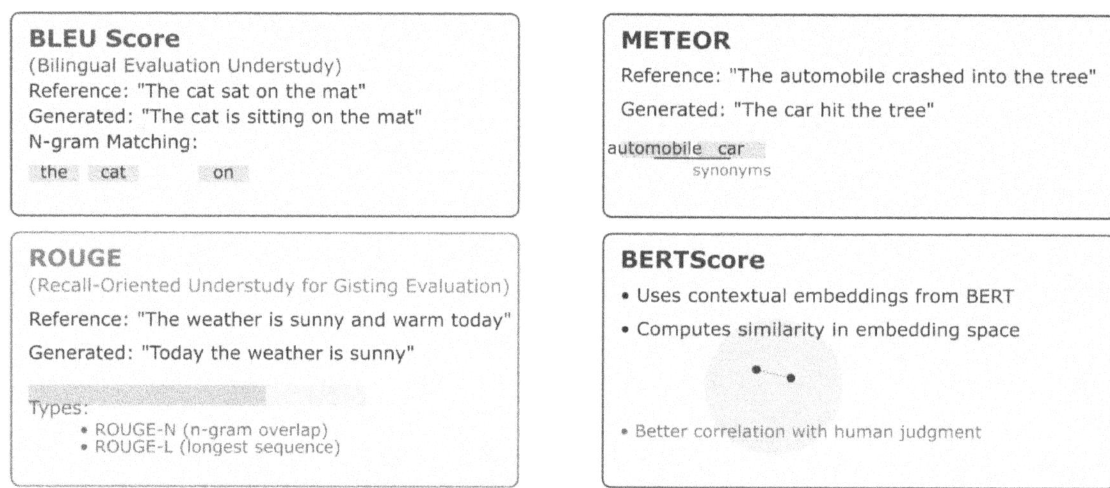

Fig. 10.2: This visualisation illustrates the three primary metrics used in evaluating text generation models: BLEU focuses on precision-based n-gram matching, ROUGE emphasises recall in text overlap, and Semantic Metrics (METEOR and BERTScore) capture deeper meaning similarities beyond exact word matches.

Perplexity: The Fundamental Quality Metric

Perplexity serves as the cornerstone metric for evaluating language models' predictive capabilities. Mathematically expressed as the exponential of the average negative log-likelihood of a sequence, perplexity quantifies how "surprised" a model is by new text. A lower perplexity score indicates that the model assigns higher probabilities to the correct tokens in the evaluation text.

Technical implementation:

$$PPL = \exp(-1/N * \Sigma(\log P(x\_i|x\_{<i})))$$

where N is the sequence length, and $P(x_i|x_{<i})$ represents the model's predicted probability of token x_i given the previous tokens. x_i is the ith token and $x_{<i}$ denotes all tokens before position i.

ROUGE (Recall-Oriented Understudy for Gisting Evaluation)

ROUGE metrics family evaluates generated text by comparing it against reference texts, particularly crucial for summarization tasks. The most commonly used variants are:
1. ROUGE-N: Measures n-gram overlap

    $ROUGE\text{-}N = \Sigma(\text{overlapping n-grams}) / \Sigma(\text{reference n-grams})$

2. ROUGE-L: Employs Longest Common Subsequence (LCS)
   ROUGE-L = LCS(reference, generated) / length(reference)

3. ROUGE-S: Considers skip-bigram co-occurrence

BLEU (Bilingual Evaluation Understudy)
BLEU score measures the precision of generated text against references, originally designed for machine translation but now widely used in general text generation tasks.
BLEU = BP * exp(Σ(wn * log pn))
where: BP: Brevity penalty, wn: Weights for different n-grams, pn: Modified n-gram precisions

BERTScore: Contextual Semantic Evaluation
BERTScore leverages contextual embeddings to compute similarity between generated and reference texts, offering a more nuanced semantic evaluation than surface-level metrics.

Technical process:
1. Token embedding extraction using BERT-like models
2. Optimal token pairing through greedy matching: For each token in generated text, select the most similar unmatched token from reference text-based on cosine similarity
3. Importance weighting using IDF scores
4. Aggregation into precision, recall, and F1 measures

F1 Score: Classification Performance
For classification tasks, the F1 score provides a balanced measure between precision and recall, crucial for evaluating LLMs on structured prediction tasks.

Mathematical formulation:
F1 = 2 * (precision * recall) / (precision + recall)
where:
precision = true positives / (true positives + false positives)
recall = true positives / (true positives + false negatives)

Implementation considerations:
- Macro vs. micro averaging
- Class imbalance handling
- Threshold selection
- Multi-class adaptation

While these core metrics provide essential quantitative measures, their true value emerges when applied to specific tasks and use cases. Let's examine how these metrics are employed in standard downstream tasks, where they help us understand model performance in real-world applications.

STANDARD DOWNSTREAM TASKS FOR LLM BENCHMARKING

When evaluating Large Language Models, researchers and practitioners often rely on a set of standard downstream tasks. These tasks are designed to assess various aspects of language understanding and generation, as illustrated in Fig.10.3. Let's explore some of the most common tasks used for benchmarking LLMs.

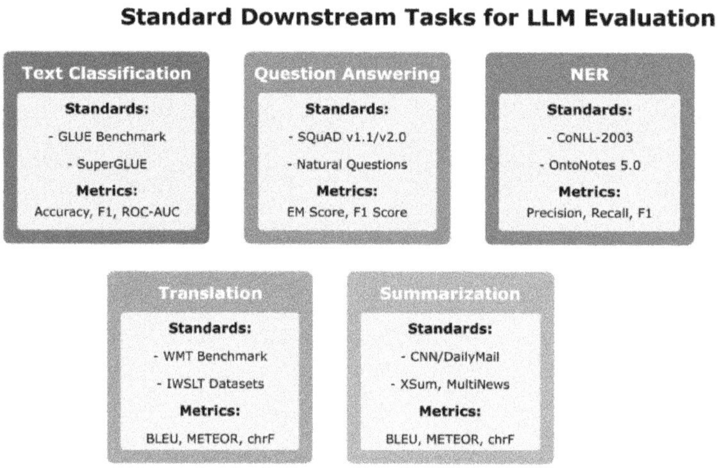

Standard Downstream Tasks for LLM Evaluation

Text Classification
Standards:
- GLUE Benchmark
- SuperGLUE
Metrics:
Accuracy, F1, ROC-AUC

Question Answering
Standards:
- SQuAD v1.1/v2.0
- Natural Questions
Metrics:
EM Score, F1 Score

NER
Standards:
- CoNLL-2003
- OntoNotes 5.0
Metrics:
Precision, Recall, F1

Translation
Standards:
- WMT Benchmark
- IWSLT Datasets
Metrics:
BLEU, METEOR, chrF

Summarization
Standards:
- CNN/DailyMail
- XSum, MultiNews
Metrics:
BLEU, METEOR, chrF

Fig. 10.3: The diagram illustrates the five primary downstream tasks used to evaluate LLMs: text classification, question answering, named entity recognition, translation, and summarization. Each task includes standardized benchmarks and evaluation metrics to assess model performance comprehensively.

The evaluation of Large Language Models (LLMs) relies heavily on a diverse set of downstream tasks that assess different aspects of language understanding and generation capabilities. These tasks form a comprehensive evaluation framework through five key categories. (i) Text Classification, evaluated through benchmarks like GLUE and SuperGLUE, tests the model's ability to categorise text into predefined classes, using metrics such as accuracy, F1 score, and ROC-AUC to measure performance. (ii) Question Answering capabilities are assessed using datasets like SQuAD and Natural Questions, where models must demonstrate reading comprehension by providing precise answers to queries, measured through Exact Match (EM) and F1 scores. (iii) Named Entity Recognition (NER), benchmarked through CoNLL-2003 and OntoNotes 5.0, evaluates the model's ability to identify and classify entities in text, using precision, recall, and F1 metrics.

The framework also includes generation-focused tasks. (iv) Machine Translation, evaluated through WMT benchmarks and IWSLT datasets, tests the model's ability to preserve meaning across languages, with performance measured using BLEU, METEOR, and chrF scores. (v) Text Summarization capabilities are assessed using datasets like CNN/DailyMail and XSum, where models must generate concise summaries while maintaining key information, evaluated through ROUGE metrics and BERTScore. Together, these tasks provide a structured approach to understanding an LLM's strengths and limitations across different linguistic challenges, offering a standardized way to compare different models and track improvements in language understanding and generation capabilities.

The application of these evaluation methods across various tasks reveals both the capabilities and limitations of our current evaluation approaches. These limitations lead us to several key challenges that the field must address.

CHALLENGES IN LLM EVALUATION

Key Challenges in LLM Evaluation

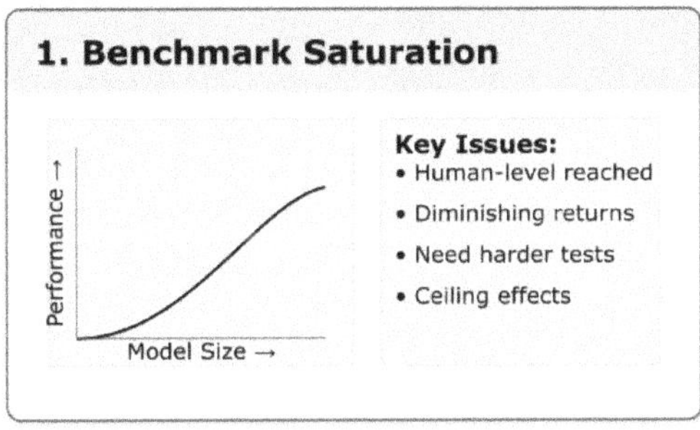

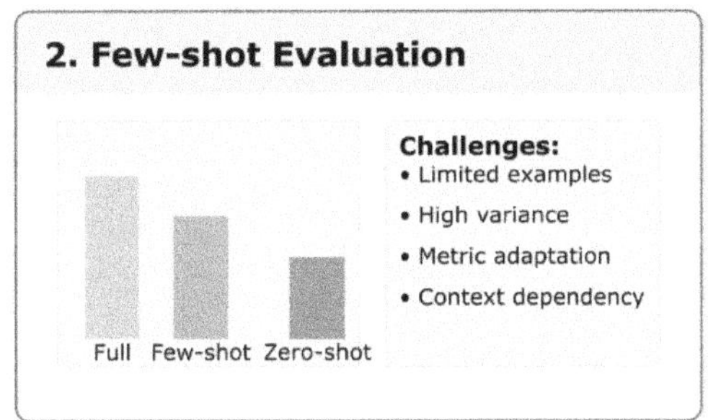

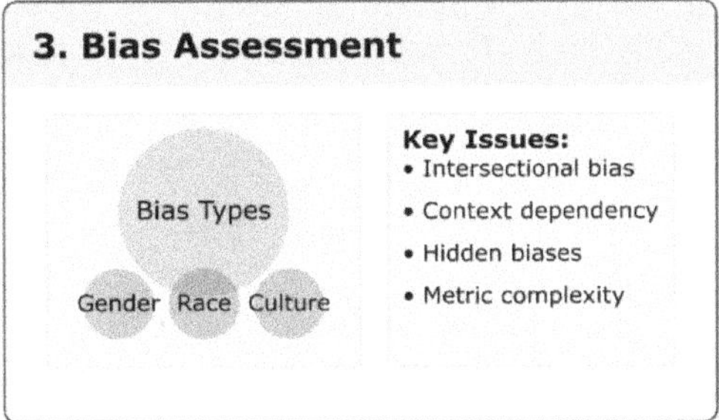

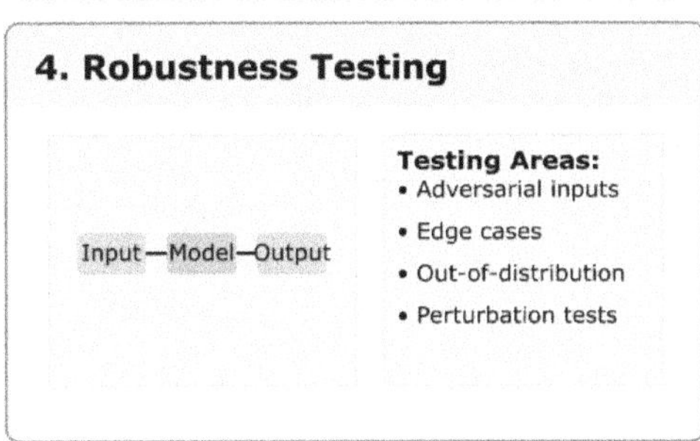

Fig. 10.4: A comprehensive visualization of four major challenges in evaluating Large Language Models: Benchmark Saturation (showing diminishing returns in model performance), Few-shot Evaluation (comparing different training regime performances), Bias Assessment (illustrating various types of biases), and Robustness Testing (demonstrating input-output testing flow). Each challenge is presented with its key issues and visual representations to illustrate the core concepts.

As Large Language Models become more sophisticated, several challenges emerge in their evaluation (see Fig.10.4). These are:

1. Benchmark Saturation: Top-performing models are approaching or exceeding human-level performance on many existing benchmarks, necessitating the development of more challenging evaluation tasks.

2. Evaluation of Few-shot and Zero-shot Capabilities: Traditional benchmarks often do not adequately assess a model's ability to perform tasks with minimal examples or task-specific training.

3. Assessing Reasoning and Logical Thinking: Many benchmarks focus on pattern recognition rather than deeper reasoning capabilities.

4. Ethical Considerations: Evaluating a model's tendency to produce biased or harmful content is crucial but challenging to quantify.

5. Robustness and Out-of-Distribution Performance: Assessing how well models perform on data that differs significantly from their training distribution is increasingly important.

To address these challenges, researchers are developing new evaluation approaches. Let's explore some of these emerging techniques.

These challenges have motivated the development of new evaluation methodologies. As we'll see in the next section, emerging approaches are attempting to address these limitations while providing more comprehensive evaluation frameworks.

EMERGING EVALUATION APPROACHES

Modern LLM evaluation has evolved beyond traditional metrics to include sophisticated approaches that assess models' robustness, ethical behaviour, and reasoning capabilities. These emerging approaches provide deeper insights into model limitations and potential risks, helping ensure safer and more reliable AI systems. The evaluation methods span across technical robustness, social impact, and cognitive capabilities. A set of evaluation approaches is listed in the Table below.

Evaluation Type	Methods	Description	Key Metrics	Challenges
Adversarial Testing				
	Input Perturbation	Systematically modifying input text by adding noise, changing words, or restructuring sentences to test model stability	- Robustness Score - Perturbation Sensitivity	- Maintaining semantic meaning - Natural text generation
	Word Replacement	Substituting key words with synonyms or adversarial terms to test meaning preservation	- Semantic Stability - Attack Success Rate	- Contextual appropriateness - Synonym selection
	Context Manipulation	Altering surrounding context while keeping target content the same to test contextual understanding	- Context Sensitivity - Response Consistency	- Context relevance - Natural transitions
Ethical Evaluation				
	Demographic Parity Testing	Comparing model outputs across different demographic groups to identify disparate treatment	- Bias Scores - Group Fairness Metrics	- Group definition: Intersectionality
	Stereotype Analysis	Examining model outputs for common stereotypes and biased associations	- Stereotype Score - Association Bias	- Cultural nuance - Context sensitivity
	Safety Boundary Testing	Probing model responses to increasingly sensitive prompts to find safety limitations	- Safety Violation Rate - Boundary Consistency	- Gray areas - Cultural variation
Reasoning Assessment				
	Multi-step Problem Solving	Presenting complex problems requiring sequential steps to test logical progression	- Step Accuracy - Solution Completeness	- Step granularity - Multiple valid paths
	Chain-of-Thought Analysis	Evaluating the model's explicit reasoning steps in problem-solving	- Reasoning Coherence - Logic Validity	- Evaluation criteria - Step validation
	Common Sense Scenarios	Testing response to everyday situations requiring practical judgment	- Plausibility Score - Reality Alignment	- Subjectivity - Cultural variation
Specialised Testing				
	Knowledge Consistency.	Testing model responses across related questions to check knowledge stability	- Consistency Score - Knowledge Graph Alignment	- Knowledge scope - Temporal consistency
	Cross-lingual Reasoning.	Evaluating logical consistency across different languages	- Translation Fidelity - Logic Preservation	- Cultural nuances - Language specifics
	Factual Accuracy	Verifying factual claims in model outputs against trusted sources	- Fact Accuracy Score - Source Agreement	- Source reliability - Time sensitivity

These emerging approaches, combined with traditional metrics and task-specific evaluations, create a more complete picture of LLM capabilities. As the field continues to evolve, the integration of these various evaluation methods will become increasingly important for developing and deploying effective language models.

DISCUSSION

The evaluation and benchmarking of Large Language Models represents more than just a technical challenge - it embodies our evolving understanding of artificial intelligence capabilities. The journey from simple metrics like perplexity and BLEU scores to sophisticated evaluation frameworks that assess reasoning, bias, and real-world applicability mirrors the field's growing maturity. This evolution reflects both our increasing expectations for these models and our deepening understanding of what constitutes meaningful language understanding and generation.

What makes LLM evaluation particularly fascinating is its position at the intersection of quantitative measurement and qualitative assessment. While traditional metrics provide important baselines, the emergence of more nuanced evaluation approaches - from few-shot capability testing to adversarial challenges - reveals the complexity of truly gauging artificial intelligence. This mirrors the broader theme we've seen throughout earlier chapters: the most effective approaches often emerge from combining multiple perspectives rather than relying on any single methodology. The careful balance between automated metrics and human evaluation, between testing specific capabilities and assessing general intelligence, has become increasingly crucial as these models grow in sophistication and real-world impact.

Looking ahead to ethical considerations in Chapter 11 and deployment strategies in Chapter 12, the insights gained from robust evaluation frameworks become essential for responsible AI development. The ability to comprehensively assess model capabilities, limitations, and potential biases directly informs both the technical and ethical decisions in deployment. Success in this domain will ultimately depend on developing evaluation approaches that are as sophisticated and adaptable as the models they assess, ensuring that   benchmarking serves not just as a measure of progress but as a guide for responsible advancement in the field.

KEY TAKEAWAYS:

1. Perplexity, ROUGE, BLEU, and BERTScore are core metrics used to evaluate the performance of Large Language Models.
2. Standardised downstream tasks, such as text classification, question answering, and information extraction, provide a structured framework for assessing LLM capabilities.
3. Emerging evaluation approaches, including adversarial testing, ethical considerations, and reasoning assessment, are crucial for gaining a comprehensive understanding of LLM strengths and limitations.

REFLECTIVE PROMPTS:

1. The evaluation metrics and benchmarks discussed in this chapter reflect a narrow set of capabilities, primarily focused on language processing tasks. How might the development of more holistic and multi-dimensional evaluation frameworks, incorporating aspects like common sense reasoning and real-world application performance, shape the future of LLM assessment?

2. As LLMs become increasingly sophisticated, the limitations of existing evaluation methods, such as benchmark saturation and the inability to capture complex reasoning abilities, become more apparent. What new evaluation paradigms or techniques might emerge to better assess the capabilities and limitations of these advanced AI systems?

3. The ethical considerations in LLM evaluation, as highlighted in this chapter, underscore the need for responsible development of these technologies. How can the integration of bias detection, safety testing, and transparency measures into the evaluation process help ensure that LLMs are deployed in a manner that benefits society as a whole?

As we've seen, the development and deployment of Large Language Models must be accompanied by a deep consideration of ethical implications. In Chapter 11, we'll explore the key aspects of responsible AI and safety considerations in the context of LLMs.

RESPONSIBLE AI AND SAFETY CONSIDERATIONS

Reflective Prompt: The LLM is ready for deployment, but you need to ensure it operates in an ethical and responsible manner. Outline the key aspects of bias identification and mitigation, privacy and security, and transparency and explainability that must be addressed.

BACKGROUND

As Large Language Models become increasingly integrated into society, their ethical implications extend beyond theoretical concerns to practical challenges that demand immediate attention. This chapter explores how we can systematically approach these challenges through three key dimensions: identifying and mitigating biases, ensuring privacy and security, and maintaining transparency and explainability.

As we've explored throughout this book, from the mathematical foundations in Chapter 1 to the sophisticated architectures in Chapter 7, LLMs represent immense technical achievement. However, with great power comes great responsibility. The ethical considerations we explore here are not separate from technical implementation but fundamentally intertwined with every aspect of LLM development and deployment.

INTRODUCTION: THE ETHICAL IMPERATIVE IN LLM DEVELOPMENT

As Large Language Models (LLMs) continue to advance at a breathtaking pace, their potential to reshape our world grows exponentially. With this great power comes an equally great responsibility. The development and deployment of LLMs raise a myriad of ethical concerns that we must address head-on. In this chapter, we delve into the critical domain of responsible AI and safety considerations in the context of LLMs.

The ethical framework for LLM development is illustrated in Fig.11.1. The ethical challenges posed by LLMs are not merely theoretical – they have real-world implications that affect individuals, communities, and societies at large. From perpetuating harmful biases to potentially infringing on privacy rights, the risks are as significant as the opportunities. As we navigate this complex landscape, we must strive to create AI systems that are not only powerful but also fair, transparent, and aligned with human values.

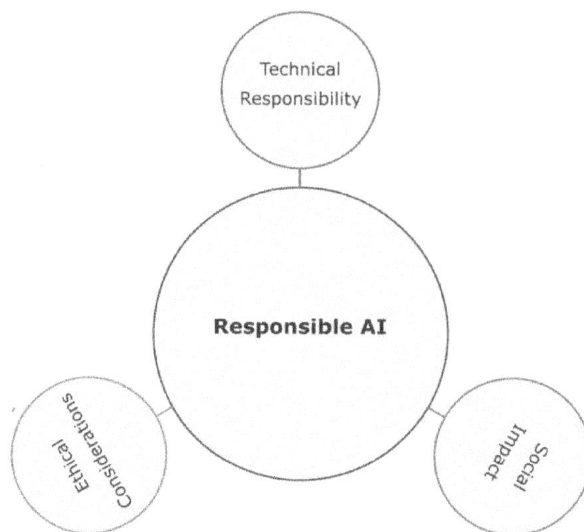

Fig. 11.1: A tripartite framework illustrating the core pillars of ethical LLM development: Technical Responsibility, Social Impact, and Ethical Considerations, all centred around Responsible AI. The circular design emphasises the interconnected nature of these elements and their equal importance in ethical AI development.

IDENTIFYING AND MITIGATING BIAS IN LLMS

At the foundation of responsible AI lies the critical task of understanding and addressing biases in LLMs. Like human biases that can unconsciously influence decision-making, model biases can systematically affect outputs in ways that perpetuate or amplify societal inequities. One of the most pressing concerns in the development of LLMs is the potential for these models to perpetuate or even amplify existing societal biases. LLMs, trained on vast corpora of human-generated text, can inadvertently learn and reproduce biases present in their training data.

The Scalable LLM Bias Identification and Mitigation Framework, illustrated in Fig.11.2, addresses the complex challenge of managing systematic bias in large language models through a comprehensive pipeline approach. At its core, the framework recognises that bias mitigation cannot be treated as a single-point solution but must be integrated throughout the entire LLM development lifecycle, from data preparation to production deployment.

The implementation journey begins at the data preparation stage, where the framework leverages distributed computing capabilities through Apache Spark to analyse massive datasets for pre-existing biases. This initial analysis focuses on detecting demographic distributions, representation imbalances, and content biases that could propagate through the model. Tools like HuggingFace datasets and AIF360 (IBM's AI Fairness 360 Toolkit) form the backbone of this analysis, enabling developers to quantify and address biases before they become embedded in the model architecture. This proactive approach to bias detection significantly reduces the computational cost of later-stage corrections.

Moving into the model training phase, the framework integrates bias mitigation strategies directly into the training pipeline. Through distributed training implementations using Ray or PyTorch Distributed, developers can scale their debiasing efforts across large model architectures. The training process incorporates debiased embeddings and adversarial debiasing techniques while maintaining model performance. MLflow's experiment tracking capabilities become crucial here, allowing teams to monitor the impact of various debiasing strategies on both model performance and bias metrics. This dual optimization approach ensures that bias mitigation doesn't come at the cost of model utility.

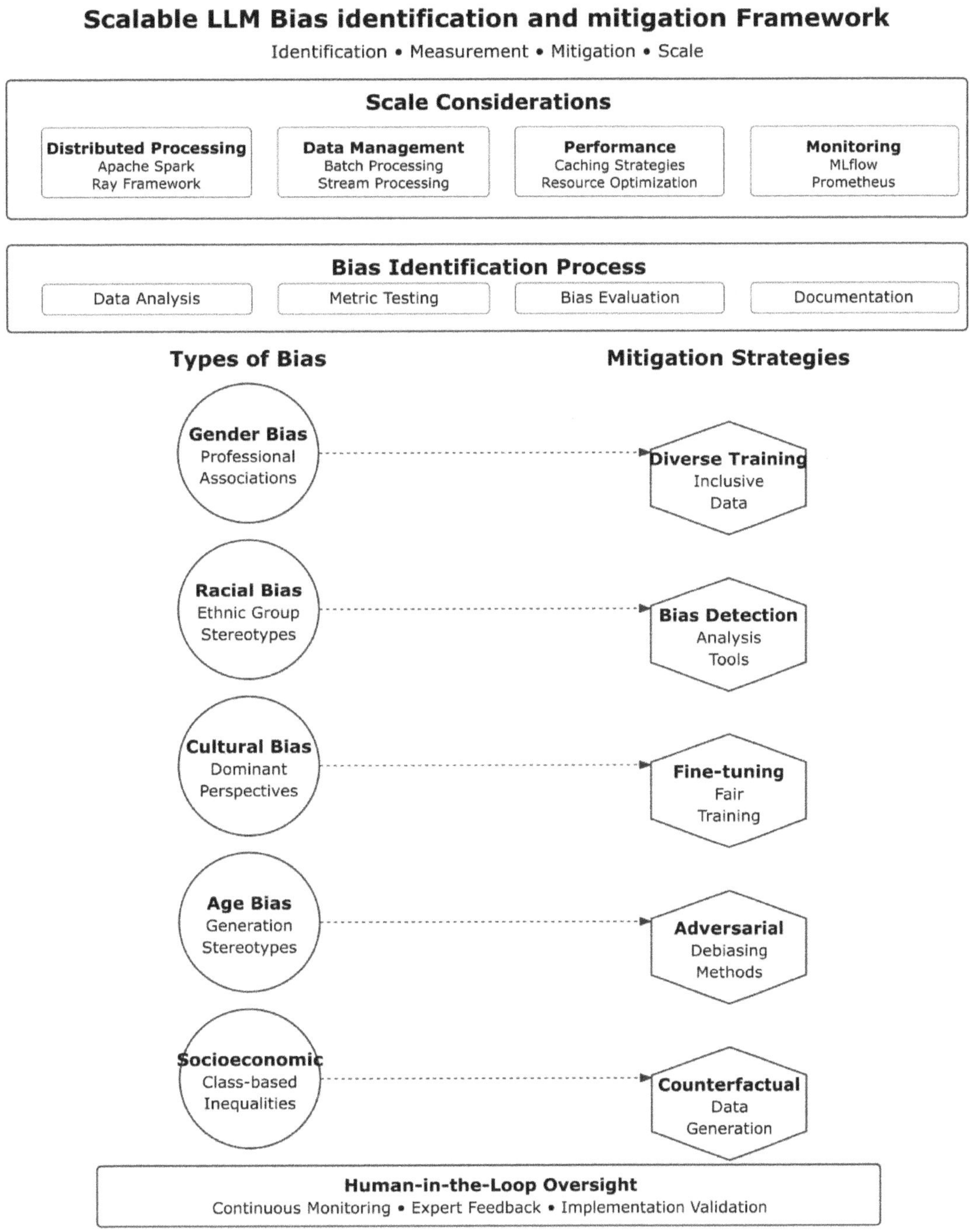

Scalable LLM Bias identification and mitigation Framework

Fig. 11.2: The visualisation presents a comprehensive framework for addressing bias in Large Language Models at scale, illustrating the interconnected layers of scale considerations, identification processes, bias types, and mitigation strategies. The framework flows from top to bottom, starting with scale considerations (distributed processing, data management, performance, monitoring), followed by the identification process, and then mapping specific types of bias (gender, racial, cultural, age, socioeconomic) to their corresponding mitigation strategies, all underpinned by human-in-the-loop oversight.

The evaluation and testing phase implements a systematic approach to bias assessment across multiple dimensions. Using tools like CheckList for behavioural testing and Robustness Gym for systematic evaluation, teams can quantify bias across gender, racial, cultural, age, and socioeconomic dimensions. This comprehensive evaluation strategy goes beyond simple accuracy metrics to understand the real-world implications of model outputs. The framework emphasises continuous evaluation through automated test suites, ensuring that bias metrics remain stable as models evolve.

Production deployment brings its own set of challenges, which the framework addresses through real-time bias detection and monitoring. The integration of Prometheus and Grafana enables teams to visualize bias metrics and set up alerting systems for unexpected behaviour. This production monitoring system creates a continuous feedback loop, where insights from real-world model usage inform further refinements to the bias mitigation strategy. The human-in-the-loop component ensures that critical decisions about bias thresholds and mitigation strategies remain grounded in practical considerations.

From a technical implementation perspective, the framework relies on a carefully selected stack of tools and libraries. The foundation is built on HuggingFace Transformers and either PyTorch or TensorFlow, with Ray providing distributed computing capabilities. Bias detection and mitigation leverage specialised libraries like AIF360 and Fairlearn (Microsoft's Fairness Library), while evaluation depends on CheckList and Robustness Gym. Production monitoring combines MLflow for experiment management with Prometheus and Grafana for real-time metrics.

The practical implementation of this framework should follow an incremental approach, starting with the most critical bias types for the specific use case. Organizations typically begin with basic bias detection in their data preparation pipeline, gradually incorporating more sophisticated mitigation strategies as they understand their model's bias patterns. This measured approach allows teams to build expertise with the tools and metrics while maintaining model performance and deployment schedules.

While addressing bias is crucial, it represents just one aspect of responsible AI development. Equally important is ensuring the privacy and security of these systems, particularly as they process increasingly sensitive information.

ENSURING PRIVACY AND SECURITY

Privacy and security considerations in LLMs extend beyond traditional data protection to encompass unique challenges posed by these powerful language understanding systems. The ability of LLMs to potentially reconstruct or infer sensitive information from training data requires a sophisticated, multi-layered approach to security. As LLMs process vast amounts of data, including potentially sensitive information, ensuring privacy and security becomes paramount.

Key Aspects of proposed LLM Security Framework

The LLM Privacy and Security Framework, illustrated in Fig.11.3, presents a systematic approach to implementing comprehensive protection measures throughout the LLM development and deployment lifecycle. This framework addresses the unique challenges posed by large language models, where traditional security measures must be adapted for massive-scale data operations, complex model architectures, and dynamic user interactions.

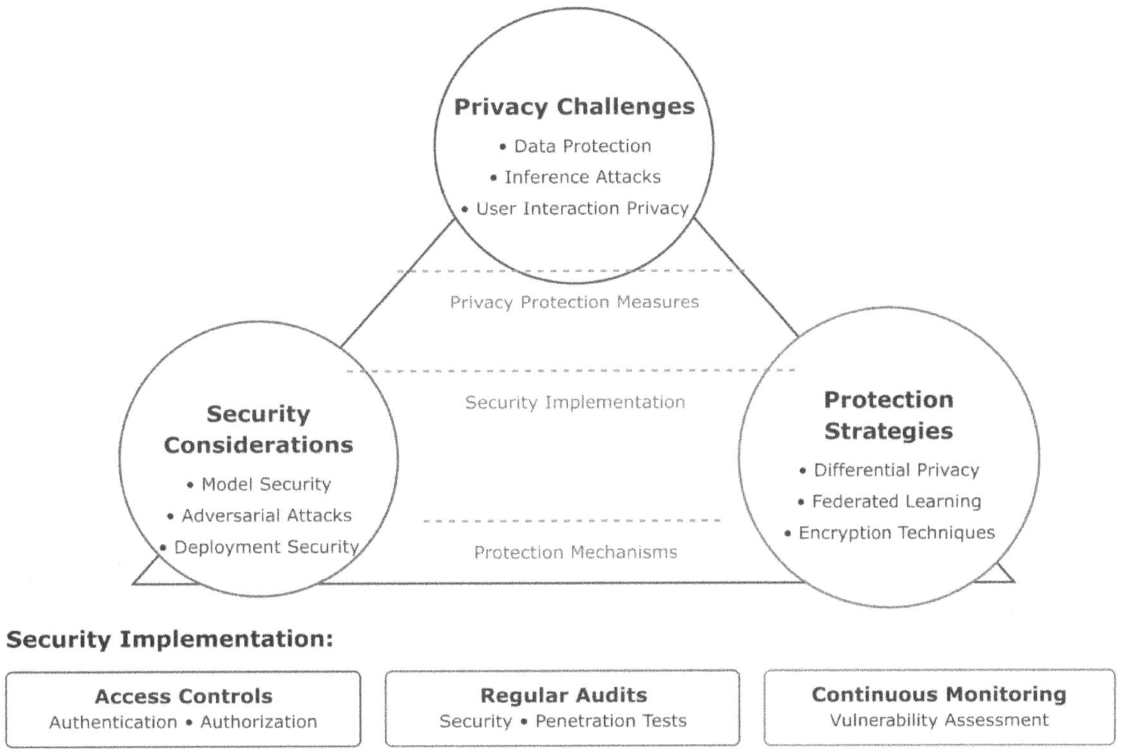

Fig.11.3: The visualization presents a triangular framework illustrating the three core pillars of LLM security: Privacy Challenges (data protection, inference attacks, user privacy), Security Considerations (model security, adversarial attacks, deployment), and Protection Strategies (differential privacy, federated learning, encryption). These interconnected components are unified through implementation layers of access controls, regular audits, and continuous monitoring, demonstrating a comprehensive approach to LLM system protection.

Framework Architecture and Core Principles:

The framework is structured around three interconnected pillars - Privacy Challenges, Security Considerations, and Protection Strategies - each addressing specific aspects of LLM protection while maintaining model utility. The implementation follows a layered security approach, with each layer providing specific protective measures that work in concert to create a robust defence system.

The theoretical understanding of bias, privacy, and security must be translated into practical implementation frameworks. These frameworks provide structured approaches to addressing ethical considerations throughout the LLM development lifecycle.

PRACTICAL IMPLEMENTATION GUIDE

Understanding Bias Detection in Practice

When implementing bias detection in LLMs, the first challenge lies in establishing robust measurement frameworks. Modern analysis leverages frameworks like AI Fairness 360 (AIF360) from

IBM and Google's What-If Tool for initial assessment. These tools provide foundation metrics, but scaling to LLM-specific needs requires careful adaptation.

The primary analysis begins with representation bias, where tools like Hugging Face's Transformers library combined with statistical packages (SciPy, NumPy) help quantify term distributions and associations. For instance, when analysing gender bias, we track not just term frequencies but contextual associations using embedding analysis through frameworks like spaCy or Stanford's NLP tools. This analysis becomes particularly crucial when scaling - you can't analyse every output, so strategic sampling becomes essential.

Let us look at the python function implementation for the same:

This module, The RepresentationBiasAnalyzer is a tool that examines text data for representation bias, particularly focusing on gender and professional associations, by analysing term frequencies, contextual relationships, and statistical patterns. Using advanced NLP techniques (BERT embeddings and spaCy), it quantifies bias through frequency analysis, semantic associations, and statistical validation, making it especially useful for evaluating LLM outputs and content for fairness.

```
1.    from transformers import AutoModel, AutoTokenizer
2.    import numpy as np
3.    from scipy import stats
4.    import spacy
5.    from collections import defaultdict
6.    from typing import List, Dict, Tuple
7.    import torch
8.
9.    class RepresentationBiasAnalyzer:
10.     def __init__(self):
11.         # Initialize models and tokenizers
12.         self.tokenizer = AutoTokenizer.from_pretrained('bert-base-uncased')
13.         self.model = AutoModel.from_pretrained('bert-base-uncased')
14.         self.nlp = spacy.load('en_core_web_sm')
15.
16.         # Define demographic and professional terms
17.         self.gender_terms = {
18.             'male': ['he', 'him', 'his', 'man', 'men', 'male'],
19.             'female': ['she', 'her', 'hers', 'woman', 'women', 'female']
20.         }
21.
22.         self.profession_terms = [
23.             'doctor', 'nurse', 'engineer', 'teacher', 'scientist', 'assistant',
24.             'programmer', 'manager', 'CEO', 'secretary', 'analyst'
25.         ]
26.
27.     def analyze_representation_bias(self, texts: List[str],
28.                         sample_size: int = 1000) -> Dict:
29.         """
30.         Analyzes representation bias in text samples using strategic sampling
31.         """
32.         # Strategic sampling if dataset is large
33.         if len(texts) > sample_size:
34.             # Stratified sampling to ensure representation
35.             sampled_indices = np.random.choice(
```

```
36.                len(texts), size=sample_size, replace=False
37.            )
38.            texts = [texts[i] for i in sampled_indices]
39.
40.        bias_metrics = {
41.            'term_frequencies': self._analyze_term_frequencies(texts),
42.            'contextual_associations': self._analyze_contextual_bias(texts),
43.            'statistical_significance': self._calculate_significance(texts)
44.        }
45.
46.        return bias_metrics
47.
48.    def _analyze_term_frequencies(self, texts: List[str]) -> Dict:
49.        """
50.        Analyzes frequency distribution of demographic terms
51.        """
52.        frequencies = defaultdict(int)
53.        total_terms = 0
54.
55.        for text in texts:
56.            doc = self.nlp(text.lower())
57.
58.            # Count demographic term occurrences
59.            for category, terms in self.gender_terms.items():
60.                for term in terms:
61.                    term_count = len([token for token in doc if token.text == term])
62.                    frequencies[category] += term_count
63.                    total_terms += term_count
64.
65.        # Calculate distribution metrics
66.        distribution = {
67.            category: count/total_terms if total_terms > 0 else 0
68.            for category, count in frequencies.items()
69.        }
70.
71.        return {
72.            'raw_frequencies': dict(frequencies),
73.            'distribution': distribution,
74.            'entropy': stats.entropy(list(distribution.values()))
75.        }
76.
77.    def _analyze_contextual_bias(self, texts: List[str]) -> Dict:
78.        """
79.        Analyzes contextual associations between demographics and professions
80.        """
81.        associations = defaultdict(lambda: defaultdict(list))
82.
83.        for text in texts:
84.            doc = self.nlp(text)
85.
86.            # Analyze sentence-level co-occurrences
87.            for sent in doc.sents:
88.                gender_mentions = []
89.                profession_mentions = []
90.
91.                for token in sent:
92.                    # Check for gender terms
```

```
93.                        for gender, terms in self.gender_terms.items():
94.                            if token.text.lower() in terms:
95.                                gender_mentions.append(gender)
96.
97.                        # Check for profession terms
98.                        if token.text.lower() in self.profession_terms:
99.                            profession_mentions.append(token.text.lower())
100.
101.                    # Record associations
102.                    for gender in gender_mentions:
103.                        for profession in profession_mentions:
104.                            associations[gender][profession].append(1)
105.
106.            # Calculate association strengths
107.            association_strengths = {
108.                gender: {
109.                    prof: np.mean(occurrences)
110.                    for prof, occurrences in prof_assoc.items()
111.                }
112.                for gender, prof_assoc in associations.items()
113.            }
114.
115.            return association_strengths
116.
117.        @torch.no_grad()
118.        def _calculate_embedding_bias(self, texts: List[str]) -> np.ndarray:
119.            """
120.            Calculates embedding-based bias metrics
121.            """
122.            # Tokenize and get embeddings
123.            encoded = self.tokenizer(texts, padding=True, truncation=True,
124.                          return_tensors='pt')
125.            outputs = self.model(**encoded)
126.            embeddings = outputs.last_hidden_state.mean(dim=1)
127.
128.            # Calculate bias scores using embedding similarities
129.            bias_scores = []
130.            for gender in self.gender_terms.keys():
131.                gender_emb = self._get_term_embedding(gender)
132.                similarities = torch.cosine_similarity(embeddings, gender_emb.unsqueeze(0))
133.                bias_scores.append(similarities.numpy())
134.
135.            return np.array(bias_scores).T
136.
137.        def _calculate_significance(self, texts: List[str]) -> Dict:
138.            """
139.            Calculates statistical significance of observed biases
140.            """
141.            frequencies = self._analyze_term_frequencies(texts)
142.
143.            # Chi-square test for distribution
144.            observed = np.array(list(frequencies['raw_frequencies'].values()))
145.            expected = np.array([np.mean(observed)] * len(observed))
146.            chi2, p_value = stats.chisquare(observed, expected)
147.
148.            return {
149.                'chi_square': chi2,
150.                'p_value': p_value,
```

```
151.          'significant': p_value < 0.05
152.      }
153.
154. # Usage example
155. analyzer = RepresentationBiasAnalyzer()
156. sample_texts = [
157.     "The doctor reviewed his patient's chart.",
158.     "The nurse prepared her medical supplies.",
159.     "The engineer presented their design solution."
160. ]
161.
162. results = analyzer.analyze_representation_bias(
163.     texts=sample_texts,
164.     sample_size=1000
165. )
```

Code Exhibit 11.1: This implementation demonstrates a comprehensive representation bias analysis system using BERT embeddings and spaCy, focusing on gender-profession associations and contextual bias detection through frequency analysis and statistical significance testing. The analyser employs strategic sampling and multiple bias metrics to provide a nuanced understanding of representation biases in text data.

Scaling Bias Analysis

The scale of LLM outputs presents unique challenges. Rather than attempting exhaustive analysis, implementing a stratified sampling approach proves more effective. Using distributed computing frameworks like Apache Spark or Ray, we can process sample batches while maintaining statistical significance. The key is identifying representative samples across different contexts and use cases.

For real-time analysis, streaming architectures using Kafka or RabbitMQ help process model outputs continuously. This allows for immediate bias detection while managing computational resources effectively. Tools like Elasticsearch can index and analyse patterns across massive output datasets, making trend analysis feasible at scale.

Framework Selection and Integration

Modern bias analysis implementations typically combine multiple frameworks. The foundational layer often uses AIF360 or Fairlearn for basic metrics, supplemented with custom analytics built on PyTorch or TensorFlow for model-specific analysis. These frameworks provide different strengths:

For base metrics, AIF360 excels at standardized fairness metrics. For custom analysis, PyTorch's ecosystem offers flexibility for embedding analysis. For visualization, What-If Tool helps in understanding bias patterns. For scaling, Ray provides distributed computing capabilities.

The integration of these tools requires careful architectural consideration. A typical pipeline might use Ray for distributed processing, feeding results into Elasticsearch for analysis, with Grafana dashboards for monitoring. This setup allows for both batch and real-time analysis while maintaining scalability.

Practical Mitigation Implementation

Mitigation strategies must be implemented thoughtfully, considering both effectiveness and computational cost. Using frameworks like Fairlearn, we can implement adversarial debiasing during training. However, the real challenge lies in continuous mitigation during model deployment.

A practical approach involves:
1. Using SageMaker or similar platforms for model deployment with built-in monitoring
2. Implementing A/B testing frameworks to validate mitigation strategies
3. Leveraging cloud infrastructure for scalable processing
4. Maintaining separate analysis pipelines for different types of bias

The deployment architecture typically involves multiple layers:
1. Stream processing for real-time analysis
2. Batch processing for deep analysis
3. Monitoring systems for trend detection
4. Alert systems for threshold violations

Scaling Considerations and Trade-offs

When scaling bias analysis to production LLMs, several strategic decisions become crucial. The first involves sampling strategy - random sampling often proves insufficient. Instead, implementing importance sampling focused on high-risk contexts and user interactions provides better coverage while managing computational costs.

Resource optimization becomes critical at scale. Using cloud platforms like AWS, GCP, or Azure allows for elastic scaling of analysis resources. However, this requires careful architecture:
1. Use container orchestration (Kubernetes) for analysis workloads
2. Implement caching strategies for frequent computations
3. Utilise serverless functions for event-driven analysis
4. Maintain separate pipelines for different analysis priorities

Monitoring and Continuous Improvement

Effective monitoring combines multiple tools:
1. Prometheus for metric collection
2. Grafana for visualisation
3. ELK stack for log analysis
4. Custom dashboards for bias-specific metrics

The key is establishing meaningful thresholds and alerts. Using time series analysis helps identify trends and patterns in bias manifestation, allowing for proactive mitigation rather than reactive responses.

While addressing bias is crucial, it represents just one aspect of responsible AI development. Equally important is ensuring the privacy and security of these systems, particularly as they process increasingly sensitive information.

Privacy Challenges and Implementation:

Privacy protection in LLM systems requires a multifaceted technical approach:

Data Protection:

- Implementation of differential privacy techniques using libraries like OpenDP or TensorFlow Privacy
- Configuration of epsilon values for privacy budgeting across training iterations
- Development of data anonymisation pipelines using tools like ARX or PRIPEL
- Integration of privacy-preserving record linkage (PPRL) techniques for data processing

Inference Attack Prevention:

- Deployment of membership inference attack prevention using ML Privacy Meter
- Implementation of model extraction defences through API rate limiting and query monitoring
- Usage of techniques like PATE (Private Aggregation of Teacher Ensembles) for knowledge transfer
- Integration of differential privacy in model responses using techniques like DP-SGD

User Interaction Privacy:

- Implementation of secure enclaves using technologies like Intel SGX or AMD SEV
- Development of privacy-preserving query logging systems
- Integration of homomorphic encryption for sensitive computations
- Implementation of secure multi-party computation (SMC) protocols

Security Considerations and Technical Implementation:
The security pillar requires robust implementation across three key areas:

Model Security:

- Deployment of model weight encryption using standard cryptographic libraries
- Implementation of secure model loading and verification procedures
- Integration of model integrity checking using checksums and digital signatures
- Development of secure parameter servers for distributed training

Adversarial Attack Protection:

- Implementation of input sanitisation and validation using custom preprocessing pipelines
- Integration of CERT Secure Coding Standards
- Deployment of real-time attack detection systems using tools like ART (Adversarial Robustness Toolkit)
- Implementation of model robustness techniques, like adversarial training.

Deployment Security:

- Configuration of container security using tools like Docker Security Scanning
- Implementation of secure API endpoints with rate limiting and authentication
- Integration of WAF (Web Application Firewall) rules specific to LLM vulnerabilities
- Deployment of continuous security monitoring using tools like Prometheus and Grafana

Protection Strategies Implementation:
The strategic implementation of protection measures involves:

Differential Privacy:
- Integration of DP-SGD optimizer in training pipelines
- Implementation of privacy accounting mechanisms
- Configuration of noise addition in model outputs
- Development of privacy budget management systems

Federated Learning:
- Implementation using frameworks like TensorFlow Federated or PySyft
- Development of secure aggregation protocols
- Integration of cross-silo federated learning architectures
- Implementation of federated evaluation systems

Encryption Techniques:
- Deployment of end-to-end encryption for data in transit
- Implementation of at-rest encryption for model weights and training data
- Integration of key management systems
- Development of secure encryption key rotation mechanisms

As we implement frameworks for bias mitigation and privacy protection, the need for transparency becomes paramount. Users and stakeholders must understand not only the capabilities of these systems but also how ethical considerations are being addressed.

TRANSPARENCY AND EXPLAINABILITY IN LLM

As LLMs become increasingly complex, ensuring transparency and explainability in their decision-making processes becomes crucial for building trust and accountability, explained in Fig. 11.4.

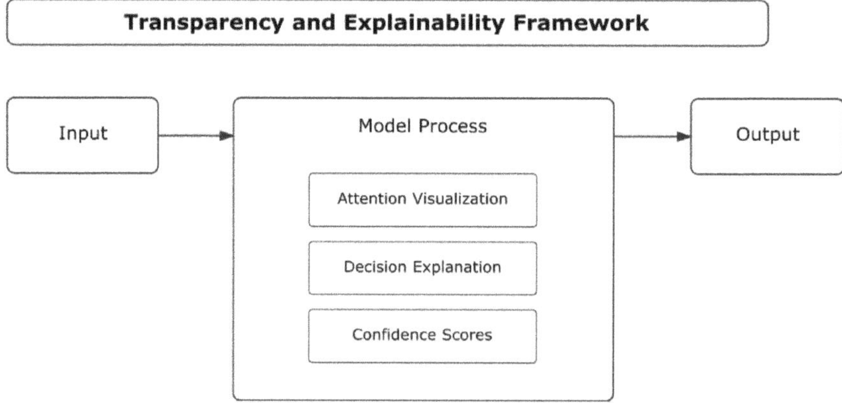

Fig. 11.4: A process flow diagram showing how LLM decisions are made transparent, from input through model processing to output, with key explainability components (attention visualization, decision explanation, and confidence scores) integrated into the model process.

Practical Approaches to Transparency

Understanding Attention Mechanisms

Attention mechanisms are like the model's "spotlight of focus." They show us which parts of the input the model considers most important when generating output. Here's how we can visualize this:

```python
1.   def visualize_attention(model_output, input_tokens):
2.       # Extract attention weights from the last layer
3.       attention_weights = model_output.attentions[-1].mean(dim=1)
4.
5.       # Create a heatmap of attention scores
6.       plt.figure(figsize=(10, 6))
7.       sns.heatmap(
8.           attention_weights.detach().numpy(),
9.           xticklabels=input_tokens,
10.          yticklabels=input_tokens
11.      )
12.      plt.title('Attention Weights Visualization')
13.      plt.show()
```

Code Exhibit 11.2: A utility function for visualizing self-attention patterns in transformer models using heatmaps, helping developers understand how the model attends to different input tokens during processing.

Making Sense of Model Decisions with LIME

LIME helps us understand individual predictions by creating simpler, interpretable models that approximate the LLM's behaviour locally. Think of it as creating a "simple explanation" for a complex decision.

Here's a practical implementation:

```python
1.   from lime.lime_text import LimeTextExplainer
2.
3.   class ModelExplainer:
4.     def __init__(self, model):
5.       self.model = model
6.       self.explainer = LimeTextExplainer(
7.         class_names=['negative', 'neutral', 'positive']
8.       )
9.
10.    def explain_prediction(self, text, num_features=5):
11.      """
12.      Explains model prediction for given text
13.
14.      Args:
15.        text (str): Text to explain
16.        num_features (int): Number of features to include in explanation
17.
18.      Returns:
19.        Dictionary containing original predictions and feature importance
20.      """
21.      # Get model prediction
22.      prediction = self.model.predict(text)
23.
24.      # Generate LIME explanation
```

```
25.        exp = self.explainer.explain_instance(
26.          text,
27.          self.model.predict_proba,
28.          num_features=num_features
29.        )
30.
31.        # Format results
32.        important_features = exp.as_list()
33.
34.        return {
35.          'prediction': prediction,
36.          'explanation': important_features,  # Fixed variable name
37.          'confidence': exp.score  # Fixed attribute access
38.        }
```

Code Exhibit 11.3: An implementation of LIME (Local Interpretable Model-agnostic Explanations) for explaining model predictions by identifying and ranking the importance of input features that contribute to specific classification decisions.

RESPONSIBLE DEVELOPMENT FRAMEWORKS

The Responsible Development Framework for LLMs, illustrated in Fig.11.5, presents a holistic approach structured around five essential pillars: Fairness, Transparency, Accountability, Privacy, and Safety (FTAPS). At its core, this framework emphasises the interconnected nature of responsible AI development, where each component reinforces and complements the others. Fairness ensures unbiased model behaviour across different demographic groups and use cases, while Transparency provides a clear understanding of model decisions and limitations. Accountability establishes clear responsibilities and mechanisms for monitoring and addressing model behaviour, with Privacy protecting user data and preventing unauthorised access or inference. Safety encompasses both technical robustness and societal impact considerations, ensuring reliable and beneficial model deployment.

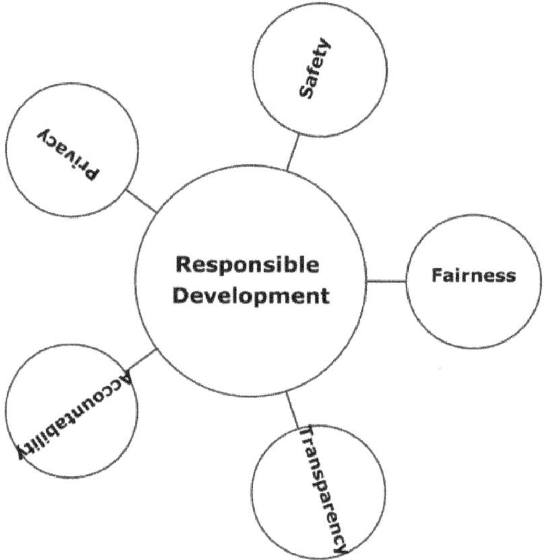

Fig. 11.5: A radial visualisation showing the five key components of responsible LLM development (Fairness, Transparency, Accountability, Privacy, and Safety) emanating from a central core, emphasising their interconnected nature and equal importance in the development process.

This framework aligns with and builds upon several established AI ethics and governance standards:
- IEEE's Ethically Aligned Design (EAD)
- EU's AI Act and Ethics Guidelines for Trustworthy AI
- UNESCO's Recommendation on AI Ethics
- ISO/IEC's Standards for AI Systems (ISO/IEC JTC 1/SC 42)
- NIST's AI Risk Management Framework (RMF)

While these standards provide broad guidelines, our framework offers practical implementation paths specifically tailored for LLM development, emphasising the unique challenges and requirements of large language models discussed throughout this chapter.

DISCUSSION

The examination of responsible AI and safety considerations in Large Language Models reveals the inseparable connection between technical capability and ethical responsibility. From the mathematical foundations explored in Chapter 1 through the architectural complexities detailed in Chapters 7 and 8, we've seen how ethical considerations must be woven into the very fabric of LLM development. The challenges of bias, privacy, and transparency aren't merely surface-level concerns but deeply technical problems that require sophisticated solutions at every level - from embedding spaces to attention mechanisms, from training pipelines to deployment architectures.

What makes responsible AI particularly fascinating is its position at the intersection of technical innovation and societal impact. While previous chapters focused on optimizing model performance and efficiency, this chapter demonstrates how those same techniques can be repurposed for ethical ends - using attention mechanisms to detect bias, leveraging efficient architectures for privacy-preserving computation, and applying careful prompt engineering for improved transparency. Expert practitioners consistently emphasise starting with ethical considerations during initial architecture design, integrating safety measures throughout the development process, and maintaining robust monitoring systems rather than treating these as afterthoughts.

Looking ahead to deployment architectures in Chapter 12 and emerging frontiers in Chapter 16, the principles of responsible AI become even more crucial. The success of LLM deployments will increasingly depend not just on technical performance but on their ability to operate fairly, transparently, and safely within real-world contexts. Current developments in techniques like federated learning and differential privacy show promise in addressing these challenges, but they also remind us that the future of LLMs lies not just in pushing the boundaries of what's possible, but in ensuring that what's possible serves the best interests of humanity. The path forward requires a careful balance between innovation and responsibility, treating ethical considerations not as constraints but as essential features that enhance these systems' real-world utility and trustworthiness.

KEY TAKEAWAYS:

1. Identifying and mitigating bias in LLMs is a critical challenge that requires a systematic, scalable approach spanning data preparation, model training, and production deployment.
2. Ensuring the privacy and security of LLM systems involves a multi-layered framework that addresses data protection, inference attack prevention, and model security.

3. Transparency and explainability are essential for building trust and accountability in LLM-powered applications, requiring the integration of interpretable techniques throughout the model development lifecycle.

REFLECTIVE PROMPTS:

1. The ethical challenges posed by LLMs, as outlined in this chapter, highlight the tension between technological advancement and societal responsibility. How might the principles of responsible AI development, such as fairness, transparency, and accountability, shape the future trajectory of LLM research and deployment?
2. Privacy and security concerns arising from the large-scale processing of sensitive data by LLMs present unique challenges. What innovative approaches or regulatory frameworks might emerge to strike a balance between the benefits of these powerful AI systems and the protection of individual and collective rights?
3. The integration of interpretable techniques and explainable AI into LLM architectures, as discussed in this chapter, suggests a shift towards more transparent and trustworthy AI systems. How might this trend influence the public's perception and acceptance of LLM-powered applications, and what are the implications for the broader adoption of these technologies?

With a strong foundation in responsible AI practices, we'll now dive into the advanced model serving architectures that enable the efficient deployment of Large Language Models in real-world scenarios, as explored in Chapter 12.

ADVANCED MODEL SERVING ARCHITECTURES FOR LARGE LANGUAGE MODELS

Reflective Prompt: You are tasked with designing the serving architecture for your LLM. Explain how the deployment strategies and architectural patterns highlight the challenges in transitioning powerful AI models from research to production-ready systems.

INTRODUCTION: THE CHALLENGE OF SERVING LLMS

Large Language Models (LLMs) have revolutionized natural language processing, but their sheer size presents unprecedented challenges in deployment. With parameters often numbering in the hundreds of billions, these models push the boundaries of what's possible with traditional serving architectures. This chapter progressively builds a comprehensive understanding of LLM serving: beginning with fundamental parallelization strategies that enable distributed computation, advancing to optimization techniques that improve efficiency, and culminating in complete serving architectures that integrate these approaches. We'll also explore how these concepts extend to edge deployment, bringing LLM capabilities directly to mobile and embedded devices.

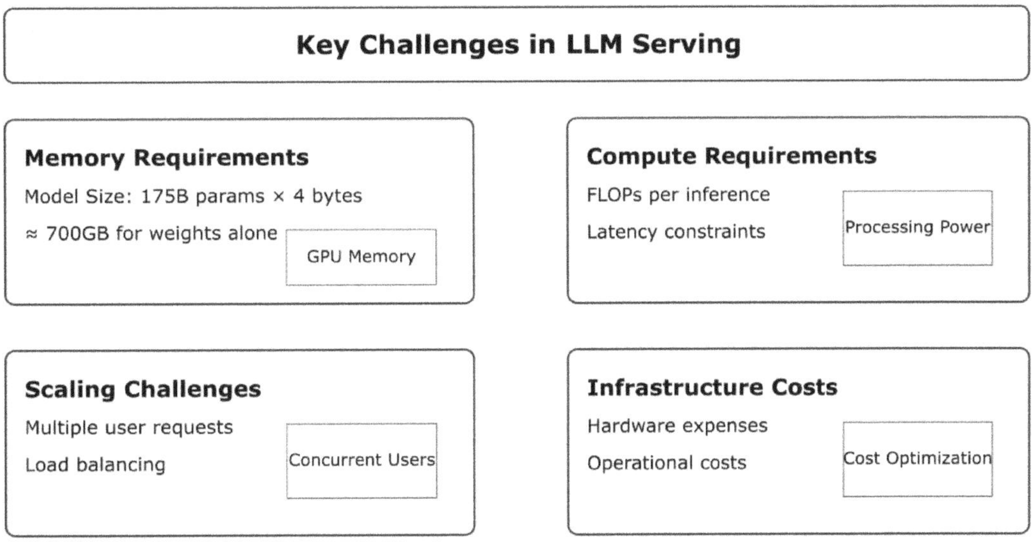

Key Challenges in LLM Serving

Memory Requirements

Model Size: 175B params × 4 bytes

≈ 700GB for weights alone

GPU Memory

Compute Requirements

FLOPs per inference

Latency constraints

Processing Power

Scaling Challenges

Multiple user requests

Load balancing

Concurrent Users

Infrastructure Costs

Hardware expenses

Operational costs

Cost Optimization

Fig. 12.1: A comprehensive visualisation of four critical challenges in deploying LLMs: memory requirements (700GB+ for weights), compute demands, scaling issues for multiple users, and infrastructure costs. The diagram illustrates how these challenges interconnect and impact deployment decisions.

Serving large language models (LLMs) presents several significant challenges, see Fig.12.1. One major challenge is the immense memory requirements. For example, the GPT-3 model with 175 billion parameters requires approximately 700 GB of memory to store the weights alone, with an estimated total memory requirement of 800 GB to 1 TB per GPU. Another challenge lies in the computational requirements, with each inference requiring billions of floating-point operations (FLOPs). To achieve a target latency of 100 milliseconds per inference, multiple GPUs, such as 8-16 NVIDIA A100 GPUs, are needed. Scaling LLM serving to handle 1,000 concurrent user requests may require 100-200 A100 GPUs, incurring hardware costs of $1 million - $4 million. Additionally, the operational costs associated with power consumption, cooling, and maintenance further contribute to the overall cost of LLM serving. Addressing these challenges requires careful system design, resource management, and optimization techniques to enable efficient and cost-effective LLM serving at scale.

THE EVOLUTION OF MODEL SERVING ARCHITECTURES

The journey of model serving architectures is one of constant adaptation to growing model sizes and increasing demand for low-latency, high-throughput inference. Traditional approaches, which worked well for smaller models, quickly hit their limits when faced with LLMs.

In the early days of machine learning deployment, a simple REST API served from a single machine was often sufficient. The entire model would be loaded into memory, ready to process incoming requests. This approach worked well for models with millions of parameters, but as we moved into the realm of billions and hundreds of billions, its limitations became glaringly apparent.

The primary challenge lies in the sheer size of LLMs. A model with 175 billion parameters, for instance, requires over 700GB of memory just to load. This exceeds the capacity of most server-grade GPUs and even many high-end server configurations. Even if we could load the model, the time taken to process a single request would be unacceptably high for most real-time applications.

Moreover, this approach doesn't scale well. As demand increases, the only option is to replicate the entire model across multiple machines – a strategy that quickly becomes prohibitively expensive both in terms of hardware costs and energy consumption.

These limitations have driven the development of more sophisticated serving architectures. The key insight driving this evolution is that we need to move from a paradigm of fitting the model to the machine to one of adapting our computing infrastructure to the model's needs.

This evolution from simple to sophisticated architectures sets the stage for modern parallelization strategies – the fundamental building blocks for distributed LLM serving. Understanding these parallelization approaches is crucial for implementing the advanced serving architectures we'll explore later in this chapter.

MODEL PARALLELISM: DIVIDE AND CONQUER

Model parallelism is a crucial technique for deploying LLMs that are too large to fit on a single device. Let's explore the different types of model parallelism and how they can be implemented in practice, as illustrated in Fig.12.2.

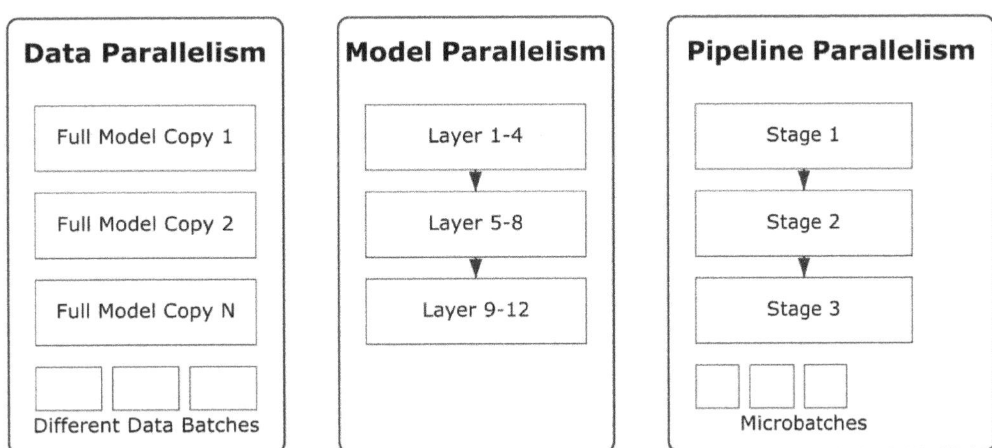

Fig. 12.2: Visual representation of three key parallelization strategies: Data Parallelism (same model, different data), Model Parallelism (divided model layers), and Pipeline Parallelism (staged processing), showing how each approach distributes the computational load across multiple devices.

LLM Parallelism Strategies Comparison

Aspect	Layer Parallelism	Tensor Parallelism	Pipeline Parallelism
Core Concept	Distributes model layers across multiple GPUs	Splits individual operations/tensors across GPUs	Divides model into sequential stages across GPUs
Data Flow	Sequential: Input flows through devices one after another	Parallel: Each GPU processes part of the same operation simultaneously	Pipelined:Multiple inputs processed at different stages simultaneously
Best Used For	•Very deep models •Sequential architectures •Models with clear layer boundaries	•Large matrix operations •Models with huge parameter matrices •Transformer attention layers	•Training with large batch sizes •Models that can be naturally segmented •Balanced workload distribution
Key Features	•Simple implementation •Direct layer-to-device mapping. •Straightforward communication pattern	•Efficient for large matrices •Reduces per-GPU memory requirements. •Parallel computation of operations	•Better hardware utilisation •Supports micro-batching • Built-in gradient checkpointing
Implementation Complexity	Low to Medium	Medium to High	High
Communication Pattern	•Unidirectional •Device-to-next-device	•All-to-all communication. • Synchronization is required	•Pipeline stages. •Micro-batch scheduling
Memory Efficiency	•Each GPU holds only its layers •Linear memory scaling	•Splits large tensors across GPUs •Sub-linear memory scaling	•Each GPU holds its stage • Efficient with micro-batching
Limitations	•Sequential processing bottleneck •Idle GPU time	•Communication overhead •Requires balanced splitting	•Bubble overhead • Complex scheduling
Common Tools	•PyTorch DDP (adapted) • Custom implementations	•DeepSpeed •Megatron-LM	•GPipe •PipeDream

Additional Considerations.

Optimization Area	Layer Parallelism	Tensor Parallelism	Pipeline Parallelism
Scaling Efficiency	Linear with the number of layers	Linear with matrix sizes	Sublinear due to bubbles
Load Balancing	Requires careful layer distribution	Natural balance with matrix splits	Needs balanced stage computation
Fault Tolerance	Moderate (sequential chain)	High (distributed computation)	High (isolated stages)
Resource Usage	•GPU Memory: Low •Communication: Low • Computation: Balanced	• GPU Memory: Distributed •Communication: High •Computation: Parallel	•GPU Memory: Balanced •Communication: Moderate •Computation: Pipelined

In practice, implementing efficient pipeline parallelism requires careful consideration of several factors:

1. Load Balancing: Ensuring each stage takes approximately the same amount of time to process.
2. Micro-batch Size: Balancing between reduced bubble overhead (larger micro-batches) and increased parallelism (smaller micro-batches).
3. Memory Management: Efficiently handling activations and gradients across the pipeline stages.

When implementing model parallelism, it's crucial to choose the right approach or combination of approaches based on your specific model architecture, hardware configuration, and performance requirements. Libraries like DeepSpeed, Megatron-LM, and Hugging Face's Accelerate provide high-level APIs that can significantly simplify the implementation of these complex parallelism strategies.

OPTIMIZED INFERENCE TECHNIQUES

While model parallelism helps us deploy large models across multiple devices, it's not the only tool in our arsenal. Several techniques allow us to optimize the inference process itself, reducing memory requirements and improving processing speed. These are illustrated in Fig.12.3.

Let us look in detail at the fundamental optimization methods.

Quantization

Quantization is a technique that reduces the precision of the model's weights and activations. Most models are trained using 32-bit floating-point numbers (FP32). Quantization might reduce this to 16-bit (FP16) or even 8-bit integers (INT8).

How does this help? Lower precision means less memory usage and faster computation. On some hardware, particularly those designed for AI workloads, low-precision operations can be significantly faster than their high precision counterparts.

The challenge with quantization is maintaining model accuracy. Naïve quantization can lead to a significant drop in model performance. However, techniques like quantization-aware training and post-training quantization have been developed to minimise this accuracy loss. In many cases, it's possible to achieve significant speed and memory improvements with minimal impact on model quality.

Pruning

Pruning is based on the observation that not all parameters in a model contribute equally to its outputs. Some may have a negligible impact and can be removed without significantly affecting model performance.

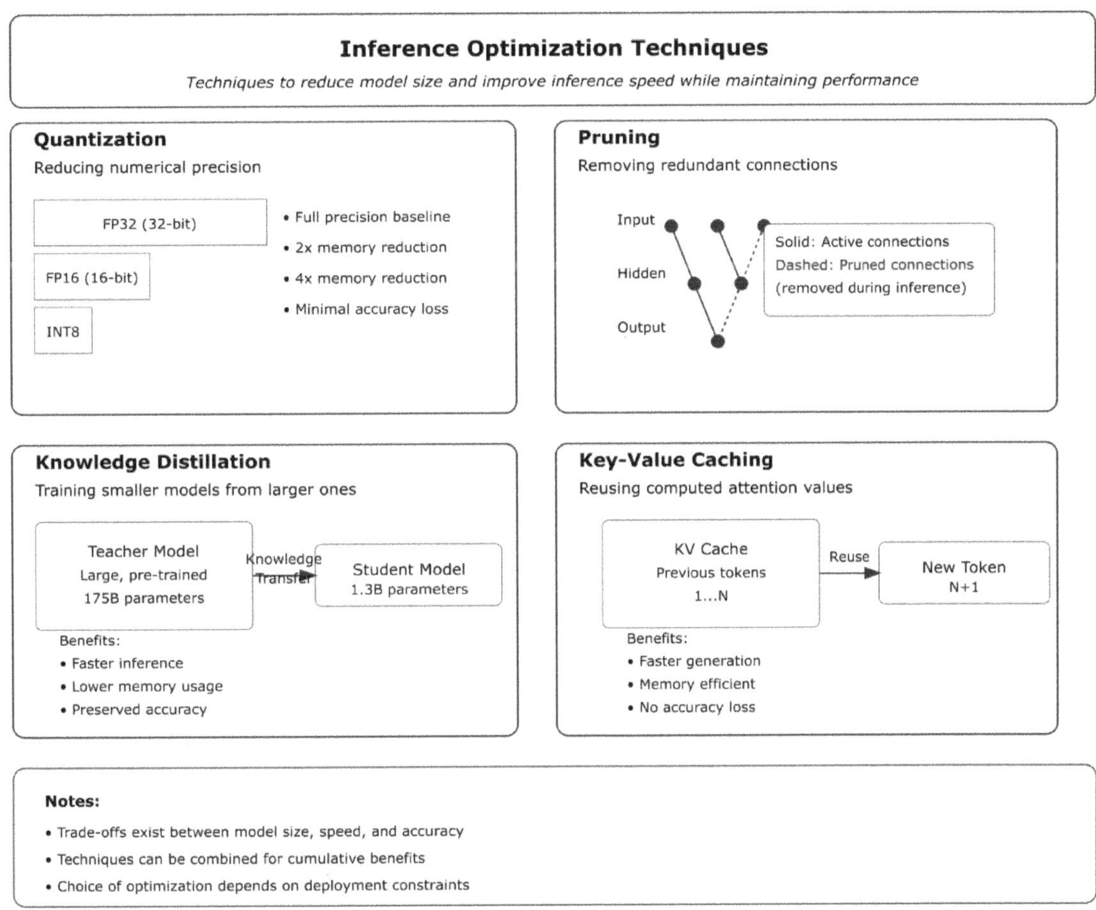

Fig. 12.3: Illustration of four fundamental optimization methods: Quantization (precision reduction), Pruning (connection removal), Knowledge Distillation (teacher-student transfer), and KV-Caching (computation reuse), demonstrating how each technique improves inference efficiency while maintaining model performance.

How does pruning work? There are various approaches, but one common method is magnitude-based pruning. This involves removing weights with the smallest absolute values, on the assumption that they contribute least to the model's outputs. More sophisticated techniques might consider the impact of removing weights on the loss function.

Pruning can lead to significantly smaller models, reducing both memory requirements and inference time. However, it requires careful tuning to balance model size reduction with performance preservation. In some cases, pruning can even improve generalisation by reducing overfitting.

Knowledge Distillation

Knowledge distillation is a technique where a smaller "student" model is trained to mimic a larger "teacher" model. The idea is to transfer the knowledge embedded in the large model to a smaller, more deployable model.

How does this work? The student model is trained on the same data as the teacher model, but instead of just looking at the ground truth labels, it also tries to match the output distributions of the teacher model. This allows the student to learn not just the correct answers, but also the nuanced "reasoning" of the teacher model.

The advantage of knowledge distillation is that it can produce models that are much smaller and faster than the original, while retaining much of the performance. This can be particularly valuable in scenarios where model size or inference speed is a critical constraint.

Key-Value Caching

Key-Value (KV) caching is an optimization technique specifically designed for transformer-based models that significantly improves inference speed during text generation. By storing and reusing previously computed key and value tensors from the attention mechanism, it eliminates redundant computations.

How does it work? In autoregressive generation, when generating each new token, the model needs to compute attention over all previous tokens. Without caching, this means recomputing key-value pairs for all previous tokens each time. With KV-caching, these computations are stored and reused, only computing new key-value pairs for the latest token.

The benefits are substantial:
- Reduces computation complexity from $O(n^2)$ to $O(n)$, where n is the sequence length
- No accuracy loss since it's just caching intermediate results
- Particularly effective for long sequence generation

This technique is now standard in most LLM inference implementations, providing a significant speedup with no drawbacks other than the memory needed to store the cache.

While these optimization techniques significantly improve individual model performance, deploying LLMs at scale requires incorporating them into broader distributed architectures. The following section explores how these optimizations can be integrated into comprehensive serving systems.

DISTRIBUTED SERVING ARCHITECTURES

As we move from optimising individual models to deploying them at scale, we need to consider the overall serving architecture. Modern LLM serving systems often employ sophisticated distributed architectures to manage the complexity of large-scale inference.

Microservices Architecture

A microservices architecture breaks down the serving system into smaller, specialised services. In the context of LLM serving, we might have separate services for preprocessing, inference, and postprocessing.

Why is this beneficial? It allows for greater flexibility and scalability. Each service can be scaled independently based on demand. For instance, if preprocessing is becoming a bottleneck, we can scale up that specific service without needing to scale the entire system.

Moreover, a microservices architecture makes it easier to update and maintain the system. New model versions can be deployed by updating just the inference service without disrupting the rest of the system. It also allows for easier integration of different models or serving strategies for different use cases.

Actor-based Systems

Actor-based systems treat different components of the serving pipeline as independent actors that can process messages asynchronously. This paradigm is particularly well-suited to the complex, distributed nature of LLM serving.

How does this work in practice? Each major component of the system – maybe a model shard, a preprocessing stage, or a caching layer – is represented as an actor. These actors can receive messages, perform computations, and send messages to other actors. They maintain their own state and operate concurrently.

The advantage of this approach is that it allows for high levels of concurrency and resilience. If one actor fails, it doesn't necessarily bring down the entire system. It's also a natural fit for the kind of distributed processing required in LLM serving.

Serverless Deployment

Serverless platforms offer a way to deploy models without having to manage the underlying infrastructure. In a serverless setup, the cloud provider takes care of provisioning and scaling the necessary resources.

How does this work for LLM serving? The model (or more likely, parts of the model in a sharded setup) is packaged as a serverless function. When a request comes in, the platform automatically allocates the necessary resources, runs the function, and returns the result.

The main advantage of serverless deployment is its simplicity and cost-efficiency. You only pay for the compute you use, and you don't have to worry about managing servers or scaling infrastructure. However, it also comes with challenges, particularly around cold starts (the delay when a new instance of the function is initialised) and maximum execution time limits imposed by many serverless platforms.

These architectural patterns - microservices, actor-based systems, and serverless deployment - provide the foundation for building complete LLM serving systems. The following reference architecture demonstrates how these patterns can be combined with the parallelisation and optimisation techniques discussed earlier to create a comprehensive serving solution.

Reference Architecture for model serving

The LLM Serving Reference Architecture is a comprehensive framework designed to facilitate the efficient deployment and management of large language models (LLMs) in production environments. This is illustrated in Fig.12.4. This architecture leverages a layered approach, ensuring scalability, reliability, and optimal performance while serving LLMs to various client applications. At the top level, the Client Layer offers multiple access points, such as web clients, mobile apps, and API clients, providing flexibility and support for both synchronous and asynchronous requests. The API Gateway layer acts as a central entry point, handling critical aspects like load balancing, rate limiting, authentication, request validation, and routing. This layer ensures efficient traffic management and robust security measures.

The Orchestration layer is the heart of the architecture, employing a microservices-based approach for independent scaling and fault tolerance. It includes components like the Request Router for intelligent traffic management, the Session Manager for stateful interactions, and the Model Registry for version control. The Actor System Coordinator facilitates distributed processing and enables efficient communication between services. In the Model Serving layer, a pipeline-based approach is adopted, with stages for preprocessing, model inference using sharded models, and postprocessing. The Cache layer optimizes performance by storing frequently accessed data, while the Model Manager handles versioning, A/B testing, and seamless updates. Real-time monitoring, dynamic scaling, and graceful degradation ensure high availability and responsiveness. The infrastructure layer underpins the entire architecture, leveraging GPU clusters for parallel processing, distributed storage systems for efficient data management, and serverless computing for flexibility and cost optimization. This reference architecture provides a solid foundation for organizations looking to deploy and scale LLMs effectively.

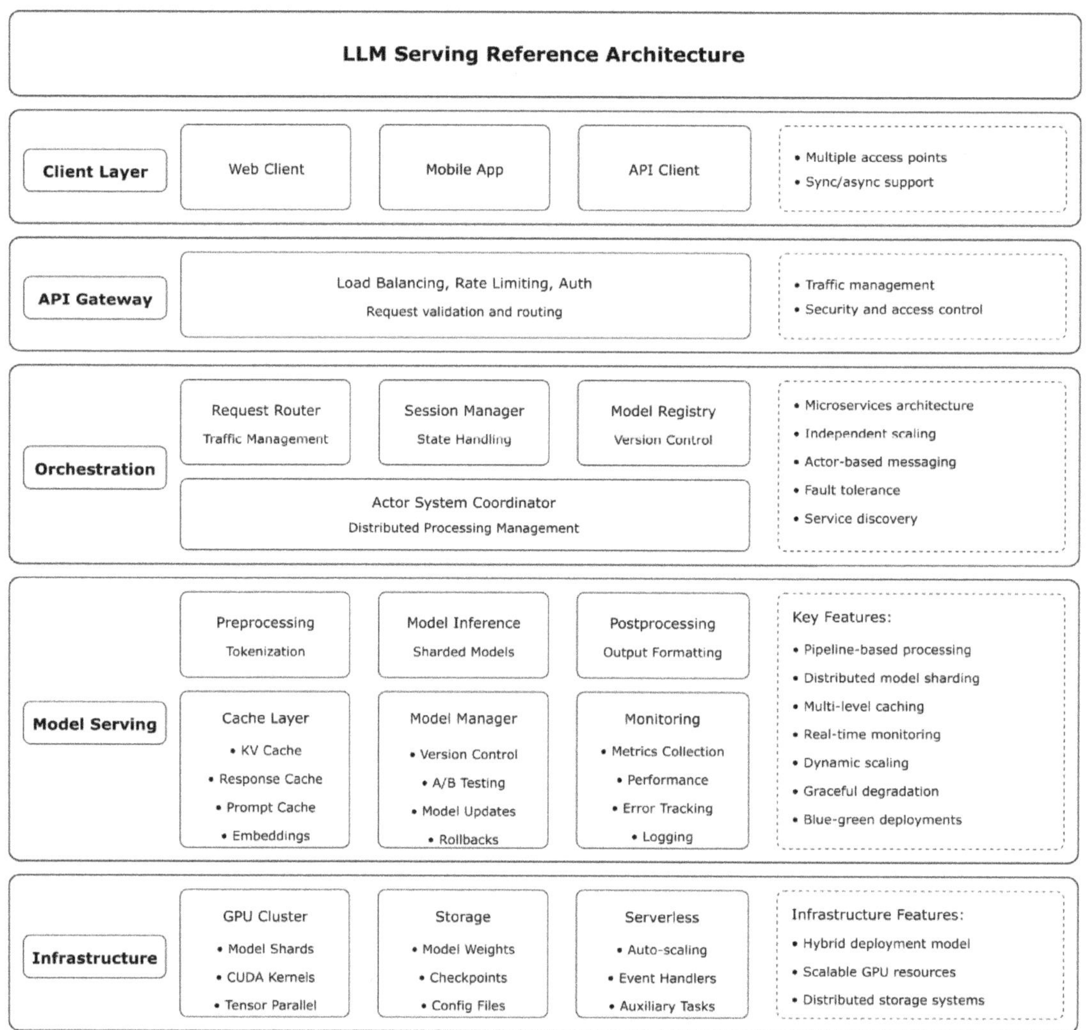

Fig. 12.4: A distributed system architecture for serving LLMs that implements microservices, actor-based processing, and pipeline parallelism across five key layers (Client, API Gateway, Orchestration, Model Serving, and Infrastructure) to handle high-throughput inference with features like caching, monitoring, and dynamic scaling.

This reference architecture demonstrates how the various concepts we've explored - from model parallelism to optimization techniques and distributed patterns - come together in a production-ready system. As we move from centralised architectures to edge deployment, many of these same principles will apply, albeit with additional constraints and considerations.

EDGE DEPLOYMENT AND MOBILE APPLICATIONS

Edge deployment of large language models (LLMs) presents unique challenges and opportunities for mobile and embedded applications. With the increasing demand for intelligent, responsive, and personalised user experiences, running LLMs directly on edge devices offers several advantages, such as reduced latency, enhanced privacy, and offline functionality. However, the limited computational resources, memory constraints, and power consumption of edge devices pose significant hurdles in deploying complex and resource-intensive models like LLMs.

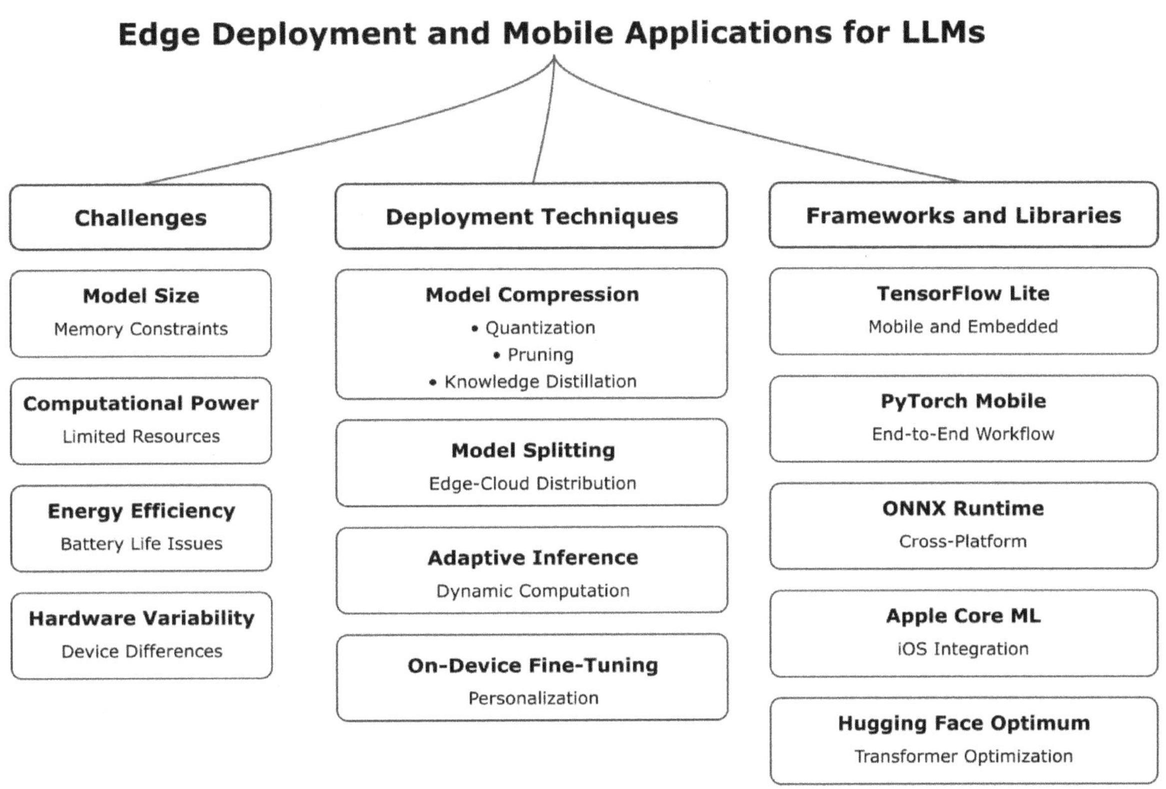

Fig. 12.5: The diagram illustrates the three key aspects of LLM edge deployment: the technical challenges (limited memory, compute, and battery life), solutions (compression, splitting, and fine-tuning techniques), and implementation tools (frameworks like TensorFlow Lite and PyTorch Mobile) – all organised in a clear, colour-coded structure showing their relationships and dependencies.

To address these challenges, developers can leverage various techniques and frameworks specifically designed for edge deployment. These are illustrated in Fig.12.5. Model compression techniques, such as quantization, pruning, and knowledge distillation, play a crucial role in reducing the model size and computational requirements while preserving the model's performance. Quantization reduces the precision of model weights and activations, leading to smaller model sizes and faster inference. Pruning removes redundant or less important connections in the model, further reducing its size. Knowledge distillation trains a smaller "student" model to mimic the behaviour of a larger "teacher" model, enabling the deployment of compact yet effective models on edge devices.

Another approach to edge deployment is model splitting, where the LLM is partitioned into smaller submodels that can be distributed across the edge device and the cloud. This hybrid approach allows for the offloading of computationally intensive tasks to the cloud while keeping the latency-sensitive and privacy-critical components on the edge device. Adaptive inference techniques dynamically adjust the model's computation based on the input complexity and available resources, optimizing the trade-off between performance and efficiency.

To facilitate the development and deployment of LLMs on edge devices, several frameworks and libraries have emerged. TensorFlow Lite and PyTorch Mobile provide lightweight versions of their respective deep learning frameworks, optimized for mobile and embedded platforms. These frameworks offer pre-built models, conversion tools, and APIs for efficient on-device inference. ONNX Runtime allows for the deployment of models in the Open Neural Network Exchange (ONNX) format, enabling interoperability across different frameworks and platforms. Apple's Core ML framework seamlessly integrates machine learning models into iOS applications, leveraging the device's CPU, GPU, and Neural Engine for optimized performance. Hugging Face's Optimum library focuses on the optimization of transformer-based models, including LLMs, for edge deployment.

By leveraging these techniques and frameworks, developers can successfully deploy LLMs on edge devices, enabling a wide range of intelligent applications. However, it is essential to carefully consider the specific requirements and constraints of the target devices, optimize the models accordingly, and extensively test the performance and resource utilization to ensure a smooth user experience. Developers should also keep in mind the potential privacy implications of on-device data processing and implement appropriate security measures. As the field of edge AI continues to evolve, staying updated with the latest advancements and best practices in edge deployment will be crucial for developers working with LLMs in mobile and embedded applications.

DISCUSSION

The journey through advanced model serving architectures for LLMs reveals a fascinating interplay between theoretical foundations and practical engineering. From model parallelism to optimised inference techniques, and from distributed architectures to edge deployment, each advancement builds upon core principles while addressing real-world constraints. The evolution from simple serving approaches to sophisticated distributed systems demonstrates not just technological progress, but deeper insights into how we can effectively deploy and scale these powerful models.

What makes LLM serving particularly intriguing is its position at the intersection of multiple disciplines - distributed systems, optimization theory, and hardware architecture. Expert practitioners consistently emphasise starting with simpler approaches before adding complexity, suggesting that success often comes not from implementing every possible optimization technique, but from understanding which combinations best suit specific deployment scenarios. This mirrors the broader theme we've seen throughout this book: the most effective solutions emerge from a deep understanding of fundamentals rather than complexity for complexity's sake.

Looking ahead to retrieval-augmented generation in Chapter 13 and prompt engineering in Chapter 14, the insights gained from serving architectures become crucial. The decisions we make in deployment architecture directly impact how effectively we can implement these advanced techniques. Current developments in efficient attention mechanisms and model compression show promise in addressing scaling challenges, but they also remind us that the future of LLM deployment lies not just in more sophisticated architectures, but in finding fundamentally more efficient ways to serve these models while maintaining their remarkable capabilities.

KEY TAKEAWAYS:

1. Distributing LLM computation across multiple devices, using strategies like model parallelism and pipeline parallelism, is crucial for handling the enormous scale of these models.
2. Optimization techniques, such as quantization, pruning, and key-value caching, can significantly improve the inference performance and efficiency of LLMs.
3. Sophisticated serving architectures, including microservices, actor-based systems, and serverless deployment, enable the scalable and reliable serving of LLMs in production environments.

REFLECTIVE PROMPTS:

1. The deployment strategies and architectural patterns discussed in this chapter highlight the challenges in transitioning powerful AI models from research prototypes to real-world, production-ready systems. What are the implications of these practical considerations for the pace of innovation and the democratisation of access to advanced AI capabilities?
2. The optimization techniques, such as quantization and pruning, aim to improve the efficiency and resource utilization of LLM serving. How might these advancements in model compression and edge deployment impact the environmental sustainability of AI systems, and what are the potential trade-offs that must be carefully considered?
3. The shift towards distributed and modular serving architectures, as described in this chapter, suggests a move towards more resilient and fault-tolerant AI infrastructure. What are the potential benefits and risks of this transition, and how might it influence the overall reliability and trustworthiness of LLM-powered applications?

Building upon the foundational understanding of LLM serving, Chapter 13 will introduce the concept of Retrieval-Augmented Generation (RAG), a powerful technique that enhances LLMs by dynamically incorporating external knowledge into the generation process.

EXTENDING LLMS: RETRIEVAL-AUGMENTED GENERATION (RAG)

Reflective Prompt: The LLM is capable, but you want to enhance its knowledge and accuracy. Describe how the integration of external knowledge retrieval with the LLM demonstrates the importance of grounding AI systems in real-world information and context.

INTRODUCTION AND CORE CONCEPTS

The landscape of Large Language Models (LLMs) has evolved dramatically, yet these powerful systems face fundamental limitations. Once trained, an LLM's knowledge remains static, frozen at its training cut-off date. This limitation becomes particularly apparent when models need to discuss current events or access specialised knowledge. Moreover, LLMs sometimes generate plausible-sounding but incorrect information – a phenomenon known as hallucination – especially when venturing beyond their training data.

Retrieval-Augmented Generation (RAG) represents a transformative architecture that enhances LLMs by dynamically incorporating external knowledge into the generation process. At its core, RAG works by first retrieving relevant documents or passages from a knowledge base when a query is received. These retrieved pieces are then injected into the LLM's prompt alongside the user's question, typically following patterns like "Given the following context: [retrieved information]... Answer the following question: [user query]". This approach essentially gives the LLM access to precise, relevant information at inference time, allowing it to ground its responses in specific sources rather than relying solely on its training data. This architecture delivers several crucial advantages: it enables real-time access to updated information, reduces hallucinations by providing explicit source material, and allows for domain adaptation by simply updating the knowledge base without model retraining. This is illustrated in Fig.13.1.

This chapter explores how RAG systems effectively bridge the gap between static LLM knowledge and dynamic information needs. We'll progress from fundamental components through advanced retrieval techniques to emerging frontiers, building a comprehensive understanding of how these systems can be implemented and optimized. Throughout our exploration, we'll see how RAG addresses core LLM limitations while introducing new possibilities for AI applications.

The concept behind RAG is straightforward yet powerful. When a user poses a query, the system first searches through a knowledge base for relevant information, then provides this context to the LLM along with the original query. This architecture ensures that every generation is informed by retrieved context, significantly improving response quality and factual accuracy.

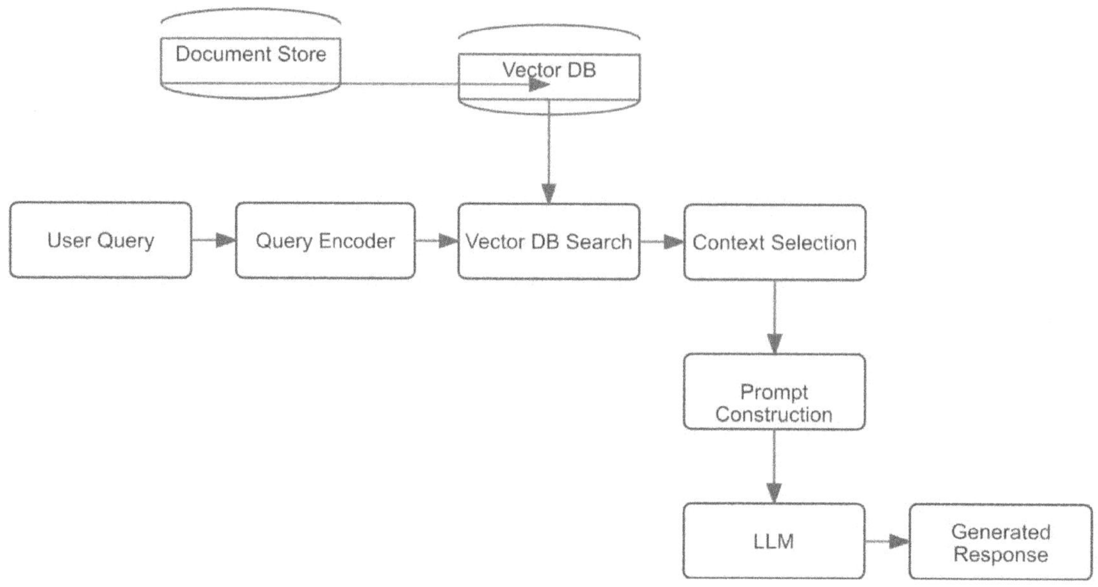

Fig. 13.1: The RAG (Retrieval-Augmented Generation) architecture illustrates how external knowledge is integrated into LLM responses. User queries trigger a retrieval process from a vector database (populated by a document store) which provides relevant context for the LLM to generate more accurate and informed responses.

To understand how it works, look at the minimalistic implementation.

```
1.    from typing import List, Dict
2.    from dataclasses import dataclass
3.    from sentence_transformers import SentenceTransformer
4.    import numpy as np
5.
6.    @dataclass
7.    class Document:
8.       content: str
9.       metadata: Dict = None
10.
11.   class SimpleRAG:
12.      def __init__(self):
13.         # Initialize embedding model
14.         self.encoder = SentenceTransformer('all-MiniLM-L6-v2')
15.         self.documents = {}
16.         self.embeddings = []
17.
18.      def add_documents(self, documents: List[Document]) -> None:
19.         """Process and store documents with their embeddings."""
20.         for doc in documents:
21.            # Generate embedding
22.            embedding = self.encoder.encode(doc.content)
23.
24.            # Store document and embedding
25.            doc_id = len(self.documents)
26.            self.documents[doc_id] = doc
27.            self.embeddings.append(embedding)
28.
```

```
29.    def query(self, question: str, top_k: int = 3) -> List[Document]:
30.        """Retrieve relevant documents for a query."""
31.        # Embed the query
32.        query_embedding = self.encoder.encode(question)
33.
34.        # Simple similarity search
35.        scores = np.dot(self.embeddings, query_embedding)
36.        top_indices = np.argsort(scores)[-top_k:]
37.
38.        return [self.documents[idx] for idx in top_indices]
```

Code Exhibit 13.1: A basic RAG (Retrieval-Augmented Generation) implementation that uses sentence embeddings to find relevant documents for a given query.

This basic implementation illustrates the core components of a RAG system. While simplified, it demonstrates the essential flow from document ingestion through retrieval.

The `SimpleRAG` class handles two main flows:

1. **Document Flow**: Using `add_documents()` method → converts `Document` objects (content + metadata) to embeddings via `SentenceTransformer` → stores in `self.documents` dictionary and `self.embeddings` list
2. **Query Flow**: Using `query()` method → converts question to embedding → finds similar docs through NumPy dot product → returns top-k matches from `self.documents`

Both flows use the same encoder (self.encoder) to ensure consistent vector representations for matching documents with queries.

To understand how RAG systems achieve this seamless integration of external knowledge with LLM capabilities, let's examine each critical component in detail. The effectiveness of a RAG system depends on how well these components work together, from initial document processing through efficient retrieval to final response generation.

KEY COMPONENTS

The power of RAG systems comes from the seamless integration of several key components. Understanding each component and making the right choices for your use case is crucial for building effective RAG applications. This is explained in Fig.13.2.

Vector Databases

At the heart of RAG systems lies the vector database, which enables efficient similarity search over embedded documents. The market offers several compelling options:

- **Pinecone**: A fully managed service ideal for production deployments.
- **Weaviate**: Open-source solution with strong multi-modal capabilities.
- **FAISS**: Meta's library offering high performance for research and custom needs.
- **Milvus**: Designed for large-scale distributed deployments.

The choice of vector database depends primarily on your scale, operational requirements, and development stage. Production systems often favour managed solutions like Pinecone for reliability and ease of maintenance, while research projects might opt for FAISS's flexibility.

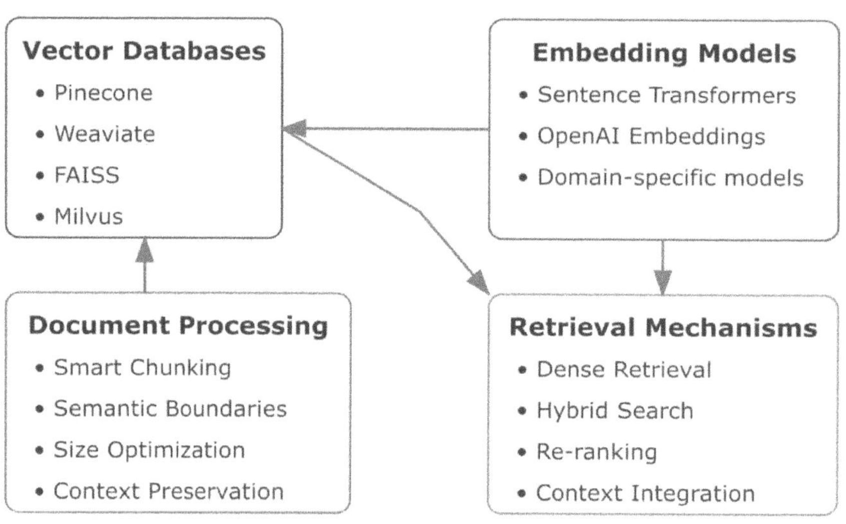

Fig. 13.2: This diagram illustrates the key components and flow of a typical Retrieval-Augmented Generation (RAG) system. The process starts with document processing, followed by embedding creation, storage in a vector database, and finally, efficient retrieval to augment language model outputs.

Embedding Models

Embedding models convert text into dense vector representations, enabling semantic search. Popular choices include:

- **Sentence Transformers**: Open-source models optimized for semantic similarity.
- **OpenAI Embeddings**: Production-ready embeddings with strong performance.
- **Domain-specific models**: Custom-trained for specific use cases.

Here's a simple example of generating embeddings:

```
from sentence_transformers import SentenceTransformer
model = SentenceTransformer('all-MiniLM-L6-v2')
embeddings = model.encode(texts, normalize_embeddings=True)
```

Code Exhibit 13.2: Uses SentenceTransformer model to create normalized text embeddings (dense vector representations) from input texts.

Document Processing

The way we process and chunk documents can make or break a RAG system. Think of document processing like breaking down a book - you wouldn't want to split it in the middle of sentences or important concepts, but you also can't keep it whole. See the illustration in Fig.13.3.

Document Chunking Approaches

Complete Concept
✓ Preserves meaning
Split
Concept
✗ Breaks context
Overlap
10-20% overlap

Chunking Size Guidelines

Content Type
Technical Docs: 400-500
Narrative: 800-1000
Code: Structure-based
Query Type
Factoid: Small (300-500)
Summary: Large (1000+)
Multi-hop: Medium + Overlap
System Limits
LLM Window
Embedding Limits
Response Time

Note: All sizes in tokens. Adjust based on specific use case requirements.

Fig. 13.3: The top section illustrates three chunking strategies: good chunking that preserves concept integrity, poor chunking that breaks context, and overlapping chunks for continuity. Below, it provides practical chunking size guidelines organised by content type (400-1000 tokens), query type (300-1000+ tokens), and system limitations to consider when implementing RAG systems.

Finding the right chunk size is crucial. Too small, and you lose important context. Too large, and your retrieval becomes less precise. The image above provides a comprehensive guide to chunking strategies and size recommendations based on different use cases.

Smart Chunking Implementation

Several libraries provide sophisticated chunking strategies that go beyond simple token counting: LangChain Text Splitters:

```
1.    from langchain.text_splitters import (
2.        RecursiveCharacterTextSplitter,
3.        SemanticTextSplitter
4.    )
5.
6.    # Recursive splitter - respects semantic boundaries
7.    text_splitter = RecursiveCharacterTextSplitter(
8.        chunk_size=500,
9.        chunk_overlap=50,
10.       separators=["\n\n", "\n", ".", " ", ""]  # Priority order
11.   )
12.   chunks = text_splitter.split_text(document)
```

```
13.
14.  # Semantic splitter - uses embeddings to ensure semantic coherence
15.  semantic_splitter = SemanticTextSplitter(
16.    embedding=sentence_transformers_embeddings
17.  )
18.  semantic_chunks = semantic_splitter.split_text(document)
```

Code Exhibit 13.3: Demonstrates two LangChain text splitting approaches - recursive (breaking by separators with overlap) and semantic (using embeddings to maintain meaning) splitting for document chunking.

Unstructured.io, For Different Document Types:

```
1.  from unstructured.partition.auto import partition
2.
3.  # Handles PDFs, Word docs, HTML intelligently
4.  elements = partition("document.pdf")
5.
6.  # Elements are pre-chunked by semantic boundaries
7.  chunks = [str(element) for element in elements]  # Added missing closing bracke
]
```

Code Exhibit 13.4: Uses Unstructured library to automatically detect and parse different document types (PDF, Word, HTML) while preserving semantic structure.

Custom Implementation with Best Practices:

```
1.  def smart_semantic_chunker(text: str, target_size: int = 512):
2.    """
3.    Chunks text while preserving semantic boundaries:
4.    - Respects paragraph and sentence boundaries
5.    - Maintains headers with content
6.    - Prevents split of enumerations
7.    """
8.    def is_header(line):
9.      return bool(re.match(r'^#+\s|^[A-Z].*:$', line))
10.
11.   paragraphs = text.split('\n\n')
12.   chunks = []
13.   current_chunk = []
14.   current_size = 0
15.
16.   for para in paragraphs:
17.     para_size = len(para.split())
18.
19.     # Keep headers with their content
20.     if is_header(para) and current_chunk:
21.       chunks.append('\n'.join(current_chunk))
22.       current_chunk = [para]
23.       current_size = para_size
24.       continue
25.
```

```
26.        # Check if adding paragraph exceeds target size
27.        if current_size + para_size > target_size and current_chunk:
28.            chunks.append('\n'.join(current_chunk))
29.            current_chunk = [para]
30.            current_size = para_size
31.        else:
32.            current_chunk.append(para)
33.            current_size += para_size
34.
35.    if current_chunk:
36.        chunks.append('\n'.join(current_chunk))
37.
38.    return chunks
```

Code Exhibit 13.5: Custom text chunking function that intelligently splits text while preserving semantic integrity by respecting headers, paragraphs, and maintaining enumerated lists together.

The key differences between these approaches:
- LangChain: Good for general-purpose, highly configurable
- Unstructured: Excellent for multiple document types
- Custom: Best when you need specific domain logic

Choose based on:
- Document structure (formatted text, code, PDFs)
- Processing requirements (speed vs. accuracy)
- Special domain needs (technical docs, legal texts)

Each approach tries to balance chunk size, semantic coherence, and processing efficiency.

Retrieval Mechanisms

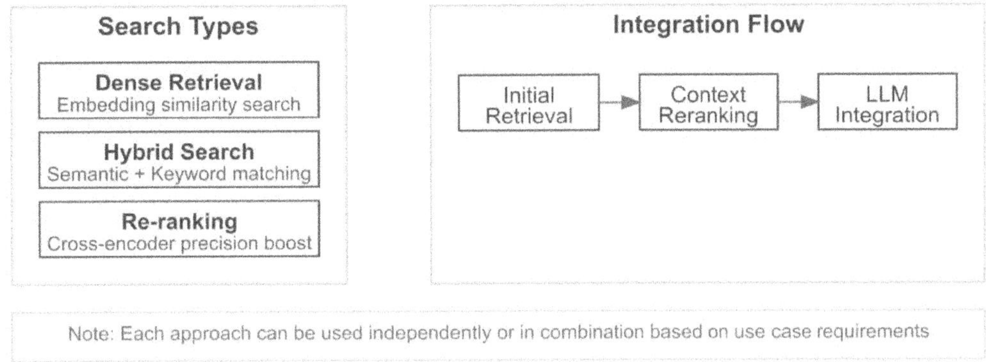

Fig. 13.4: The diagram illustrates the three main search strategies in RAG systems: dense retrieval using embeddings, hybrid search combining semantic and keyword matching, and re-ranking using cross-encoders for improved precision. The right side shows how these search results flow through context re-ranking before being integrated with the LLM for final response generation.

The retrieval component determines how relevant documents are found and ranked, see Fig.13.4. Common approaches include:

- **Dense Retrieval**: Using embedding similarity
- **Hybrid Search**: Combining semantic and keyword search
- **Re-ranking**: Using cross-encoders for better precision

For most applications, starting with simple dense retrieval and iterating based on performance is recommended. However modern vector databases offer multiple retrieval approaches:

```
1.    # Example using Weaviate hybrid search
2.    def hybrid_search(query: str, limit: int = 3):
3.      return client.query.get("Document", ["content"]).with_hybrid(
4.        query=query,          # Original query
5.        alpha=0.5,            # Balance between vector (0) and keyword (1)
6.        properties=["content"]
7.      ).with_limit(limit).do()
8.
9.    # Example using Pinecone with metadata filtering
10.   def filtered_search(query: str, metadata_filter: dict):
11.     xq = model.encode(query).tolist()
12.     return index.query(
13.       vector=xq,
14.       filter=metadata_filter,
15.       top_k=3,
16.       include_metadata=True
17.     )
```

Code Exhibit 13.6: # Demonstrates hybrid search (combining vector and keyword matching) using Weaviate and filtered vector search using Pinecone with metadata filtering capabilities

Key considerations:
- Vector search for semantic similarity
- Hybrid search when keyword matching is important
- Metadata filtering for domain-specific constraints
- Context re-ranking for better relevance
- Token management to fit LLM context window

Context Integration

The art of context integration determines how effectively retrieval information guides the LLM's response. Think of assembling a concise briefing document for LLM – too little context and the response lacks depth, too much and you risk overwhelming the model or exceeding token limits. This is illustrated in Fig.13.5.

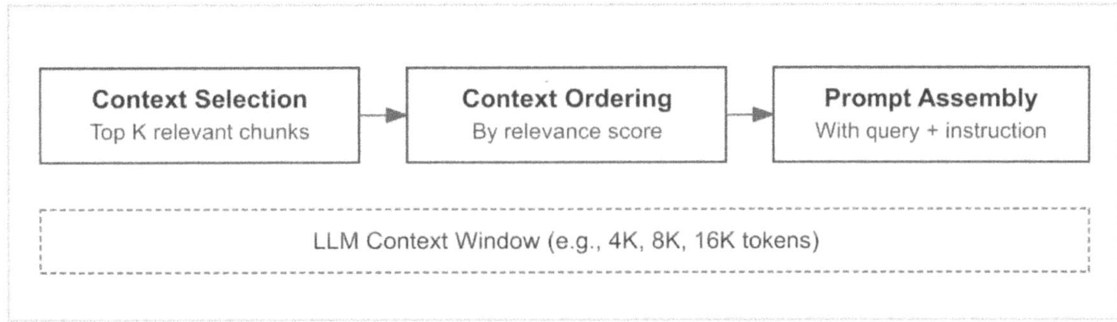

Fig. 13.5: The diagram shows the context integration pipeline, illustrating how retrieved chunks are selected, ordered, and assembled into a prompt while respecting LLM token limits, with each stage optimized for effective knowledge utilization.

Here's a practical implementation approach:

```
1.    def integrate_context(
2.      query: str,
3.      retrieved_chunks: List[dict],
4.      max_tokens: int = 3000
5.    ) -> str:
6.      # Order chunks by relevance score
7.      ordered_chunks = sorted(
8.        retrieved_chunks,
9.        key=lambda x: x['score'],
10.       reverse=True
11.     )
12.
13.     # Format context while respecting token limit
14.     context = []
15.     token_count = 0
16.     for chunk in ordered_chunks:
17.       chunk_tokens = len(chunk['text'].split())
18.       if token_count + chunk_tokens > max_tokens:
19.         break
20.       context.append(chunk['text'])
21.       token_count += chunk_tokens
22.
23.     # Assemble the final prompt
24.     prompt = f"""Use the following context to answer the question
25. Context: {' '.join(context)}
26. Question: {query}
27. Answer: """
28.
29.     return prompt
```

Code Exhibit 13.7: Processes retrieved text chunks by sorting them by relevance, managing token limits, and creating a formatted prompt that combines context and query.

The key is finding the right balance between comprehensive context and efficient token usage. For technical queries, prioritise accuracy and completeness. For general queries, focus on the most relevant chunks and clear instruction formatting.

While effective document processing and basic retrieval form the foundation of RAG systems, more sophisticated retrieval techniques can significantly enhance their capabilities. As we move from basic to advanced approaches, we'll see how different retrieval strategies can be combined and optimized for specific use cases.

ADVANCED RETRIEVAL TECHNIQUES

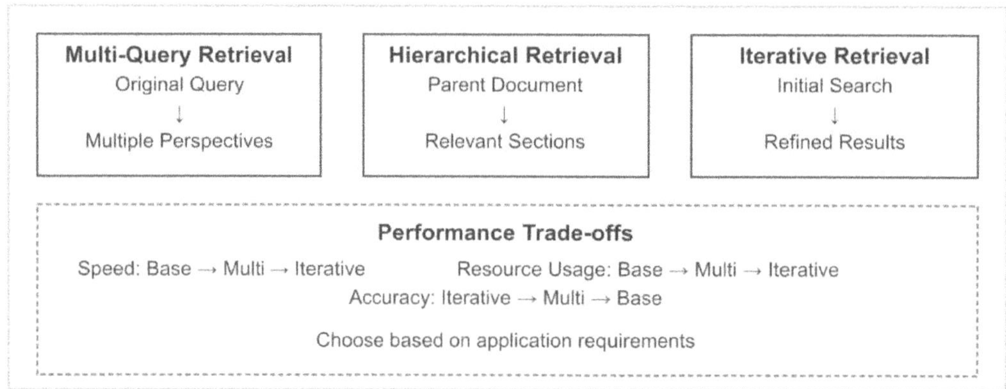

Fig. 13.6: The diagram illustrates three advanced retrieval strategies (multi-query, hierarchical, and iterative) and their performance trade-offs, helping developers choose the right approach based on their application's speed, accuracy, and resource requirements.

While basic retrieval serves simple queries well, real-world applications often demand more sophisticated approaches. Complex questions might require understanding from multiple angles, or answers might be scattered across different sections of documentation. Let's explore three powerful techniques that address these challenges, as illustrated in Fig.13.6.

Multi-Query Retrieval

Imagine asking about "the environmental impact of electric vehicles." A single query might miss important aspects. Multi-query retrieval automatically generates different perspectives of the same question: one focusing on manufacturing impacts, another on operational emissions, and perhaps a third on end-of-life recycling. By decomposing complex queries into multiple focused searches, we cast a wider net while maintaining precision.

```
1.   def multi_query_retrieve(original_query: str):
2.   # Generate variations of the query
3.       queries = [
4.   "manufacturing process environmental impact of electric vehicles",
5.   "carbon emissions from electric vehicle operation",
6.   "electric vehicle battery recycling: environmental effects"
7.       ]
```

```
8.
9.      results = []
10.  for query in queries:
11.  docs = retrieve_documents(query)
12.  results.extend(docs)
13.  return deduplicate_and_rank(results)
```

Code Exhibit 13.8: Executes multiple variations of a query to improve retrieval coverage and combines results after removing duplicates and ranking them.

Hierarchical Retrieval

Sometimes context is everything. Instead of treating documents as flat collections of chunks, hierarchical retrieval maintains their structure. When searching through technical documentation, it first identifies relevant sections before diving deeper into specific details. This preserves the contextual relationship between high-level concepts and their implementation details.

Think of reading a programming language's documentation – you first find the right module, then the appropriate class, and finally the specific method. Hierarchical retrieval mirrors this natural way of seeking information.

Iterative Retrieval

Perhaps the most sophisticated approach is iterative retrieval, which mimics how humans refine their search process. It starts with an initial query, analyses the results, and automatically formulates follow-up queries to fill information gaps or clarify ambiguous points.

For instance, when researching a technical implementation:
1. First query finds a relevant API
2. Analysis shows missing configuration details
3. System automatically queries for configuration options
4. Final results combine both the API usage and setup information

The effectiveness of these techniques comes with trade-offs. Multi-query retrieval increases coverage but requires more processing time. Hierarchical retrieval maintains context but needs structured data. Iterative retrieval often provides the most complete results but has the highest latency.

Choosing the Right Approach

Selection depends on your specific needs:
- For complex analytical questions, multi-query retrieval excels
- For technical documentation, hierarchical retrieval provides better context
- For research-oriented queries, iterative retrieval offers the most thorough results

In practice, many sophisticated RAG systems combine these approaches. They might use multi-query retrieval for initial search, apply hierarchical context preservation, and then refine results iteratively. The key is understanding your use case's requirements for speed, accuracy, and resource utilisation.

Here's a practical example combining multiple techniques:

```
1.    class AdvancedRetriever:
2.      def retrieve_with_context(self, query: str) -> List[Document]:
3.          # Generate multiple perspectives
4.          query_variants = self.generate_query_variants(query)
5.
6.          # Initial retrieval round
7.          initial_results = []
8.          for variant in query_variants:
9.              docs = self.base_retrieve(variant)
10.             initial_results.extend(docs)
11.
12.          # Analyze gaps in initial results
13.          missing_aspects = self.identify_gaps(query, initial_results)
14.
15.          # Perform focused follow-up queries if needed
16.          if missing_aspects:
17.              follow_up_results = self.retrieve_missing_aspects(missing_aspects)
18.              initial_results.extend(follow_up_results)
19.
20.          return self.rank_and_deduplicate(initial_results)
```

Code Exhibit 13.9: Performs advanced retrieval by generating multiple query variants, identifying information gaps, executing follow-up queries for missing aspects, and returning deduplicated ranked results.

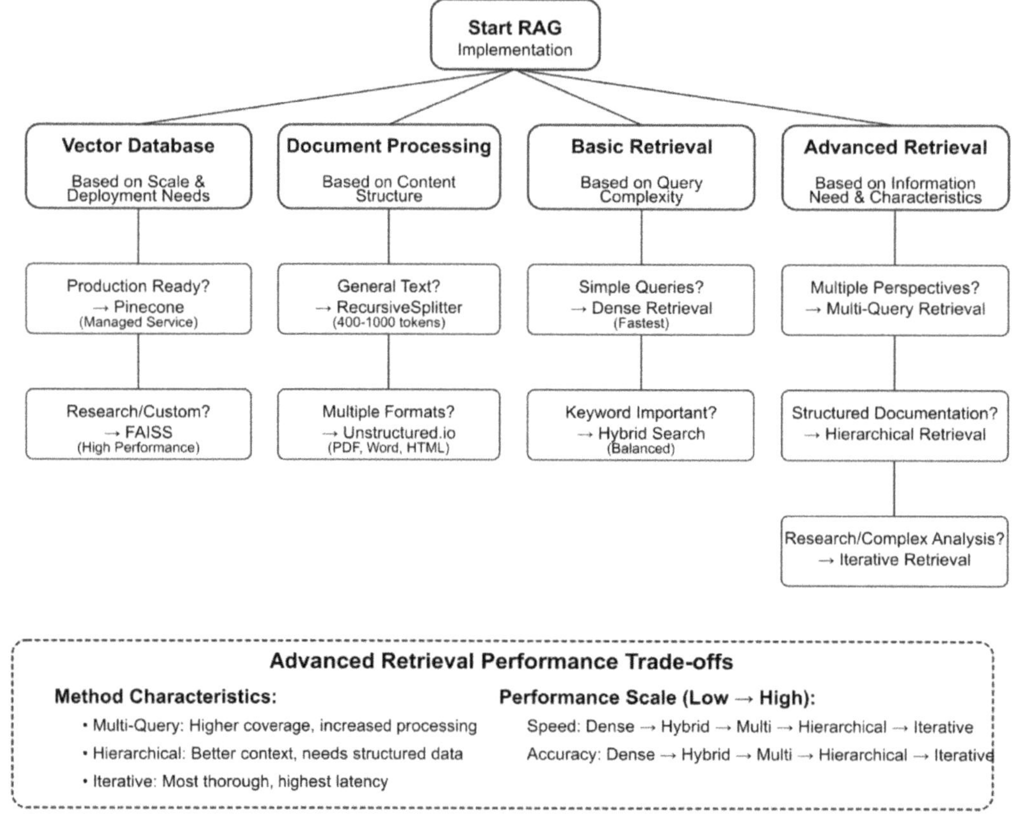

Fig. 13.7: A comprehensive decision tree guide for RAG system implementation, showing component selection based on specific needs and use cases, with detailed performance trade-offs for different retrieval strategies, Performance Optimization, and Best Practices.

The future of retrieval systems lies in making these advanced techniques more efficient and accessible. As models become more sophisticated, we'll likely see even more intelligent approaches to understanding and fulfilling complex information needs.

Summing it up the decision tree for building a RAG system

Building a RAG system that performs well in production requires careful attention to both retrieval quality and system efficiency. Fig.13.7 explains the RAG System component selection. Let's explore key optimization strategies that make the difference between a prototype and a production-ready system.

CACHING STRATEGIES

Think of caching in RAG systems like a librarian's memory. Just as a librarian remembers frequently requested books, a well-designed caching system remembers common queries and their results. This is particularly powerful for enterprise systems where similar questions often arise.

```
1.   class CachedRetriever:
2.      def __init__(self, base_retriever):
3.         self.retriever = base_retriever
4.         self.cache = {}
5.         self.cache_ttl = 3600  # 1 hour default
6.
7.      def retrieve(self, query: str) -> List[Document]:
8.         cache_key = self.normalize_query(query)
9.
10.        if cache_key in self.cache:
11.           if not self.is_cache_stale(cache_key):
12.              return self.cache[cache_key]
13.
14.        results = self.retriever.get_relevant_documents(query)
15.        self.cache[cache_key] = results
16.        return results
```

Code Exhibit 13.10: Implements caching wrapper around base retriever to store and reuse query results, improving response time for repeated queries while managing cache staleness.

QUERY OPTIMIZATION

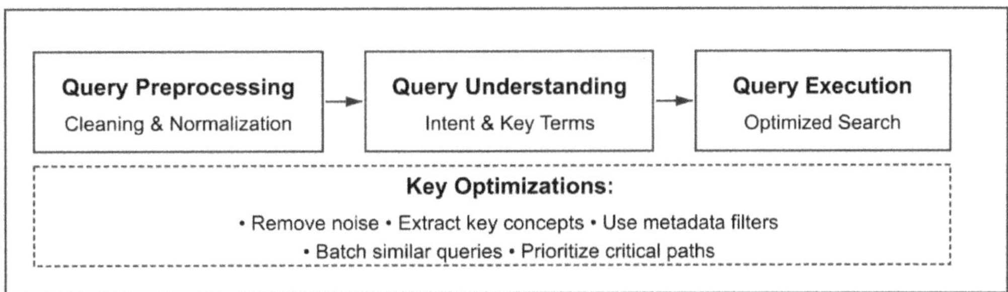

Fig. 13.8: The diagram illustrates the complete query optimization flow in RAG systems: starting with query preprocessing (cleaning & normalization), moving through query understanding (intent & key terms), and culminating in optimized execution. The bottom section highlights key optimization strategies including noise removal, concept extraction, metadata filtering, and query batching for improved performance.

Query optimisation is about working smarter, not harder (fig.13.8). Before rushing to search the vector database, we can significantly improve performance through intelligent query processing:

1. **Query Preprocessing**: Clean and normalise queries to remove noise that could mislead the retrieval system.
2. **Key Term Extraction**: Identify the most important concepts in the query to focus the search.
3. **Query Routing**: Direct different types of queries to appropriate search strategies.

Batch Processing and Vectorization

When dealing with multiple queries or documents, batch processing can dramatically improve throughput. Consider this optimized approach:

```
1.   class BatchOptimizedRetriever:
2.     def __init__(self, embedding_model, vector_store, batch_size=32):
3.       self.embedding_model = embedding_model
4.       self.vector_store = vector_store
5.       self.batch_size = batch_size
6.
7.     async def batch_retrieve(self, queries: List[str]) -> List[List[Document]]:
8.       # Process queries in batches
9.       embeddings = []
10.      for i in range(0, len(queries), self.batch_size):
11.        batch = queries[i:i + self.batch_size]
12.        batch_embeddings = await self.embedding_model.encode_batch(batch)
13.        embeddings.extend(batch_embeddings)
14.
15.      # Parallel search in vector store
16.      results = await self.vector_store.batch_search(embeddings)
17.      return results
```

Code Exhibit 13.11: Implements batch processing and parallel search for multiple queries, optimizing throughput by encoding queries and searching vector store in batches.

RESOURCE MANAGEMENT

Managing computational resources effectively is crucial for production systems. This includes:

1. **Connection Pooling**: Maintain a pool of connections to your vector store to handle concurrent requests efficiently.
2. **Load Balancing**: Distribute queries across multiple retrieval instances for higher throughput.
3. **Resource Monitoring**: Track system performance and adjust parameters dynamically.

Quality Monitoring

A production RAG system needs continuous monitoring to maintain high performance:

```
1.   class MonitoredRetriever:
2.     def retrieve(self, query: str) -> Tuple[List[Document], Dict]:
3.       start_time = time.time()
4.       results = self.base_retriever.get_relevant_documents(query)
5.
6.       metrics = {
7.         'latency': time.time() - start_time,
8.         'num_results': len(results),
```

```
9.         'query_complexity': self.assess_complexity(query),
10.        'result_diversity': self.calculate_diversity(results)
11.      }
12.
13.      self.log_metrics(metrics)
14.      return results, metrics  # Removed duplicate return statement
```

Code Exhibit 13.12: Wraps a base retriever to track and log key performance metrics like latency, result count, query complexity, and result diversity for monitoring and optimization.

The key to successful optimisation is finding the right balance for your specific use case. Start with the basics, measure everything, and iterate based on real usage patterns.

As we've explored various retrieval techniques and their implementations, a new frontier emerges in the form of GraphRAG - an approach that addresses the limitations of traditional RAG systems by incorporating structured knowledge relationships. This evolution represents a significant step forward in how we can represent and retrieve complex, interconnected information.

GRAPHRAG: WEAVING KNOWLEDGE STRUCTURES INTO RETRIEVAL

While traditional RAG systems excel at retrieving relevant chunks of text, they often struggle with tasks requiring complex reasoning across interconnected information. Imagine trying to answer questions about a company's organisational structure, understanding the plot of a complex novel with multiple character relationships, or analysing the cascading effects in a supply chain. These scenarios demand more than just text retrieval – they require understanding the relationships between different pieces of information. This is where GraphRAG comes into play.

Why Traditional RAG Falls Short

Consider a seemingly simple query: "Who reports to the head of engineering who previously worked in the marketing department?" A traditional RAG system might struggle here because the answer requires connecting multiple pieces of information: current reporting relationships, historical role changes, and departmental structures. The relevant information might be scattered across different documents, making it difficult to piece together through simple text retrieval alone.

The GraphRAG Solution

GraphRAG enhances traditional retrieval-augmented generation by incorporating a knowledge graph structure into the retrieval process. Instead of treating documents as independent chunks, GraphRAG maintains a graph where nodes represent entities (people, departments, concepts) and edges represent relationships between them. This structured representation allows for more nuanced and context-aware retrieval.

```
1.  class GraphRAGSystem:
2.    def __init__(self):
3.      self.graph_db = NetworkStorage()   # Graph database (e.g., Neo4j)
4.      self.vector_store = VectorDB()     # Vector store for embeddings
5.      self.llm = LanguageModel()         # Base language model
6.
```

```
7.      def process_query(self, query: str):
8.          # Extract relevant entities from query
9.          entities = self.entity_extractor(query)
10.
11.         # Graph-based retrieval
12.         graph_context = self.retrieve_graph_context(entities)
13.
14.         # Traditional vector retrieval
15.         vector_context = self.vector_store.retrieve(query)
16.
17.         # Combine both contexts
18.         enriched_context = self.context_merger(
19.            graph_context,
20.            vector_context
21.         )
22.
23.         # Generate response using combined context
24.         return self.llm.generate(query, enriched_context)
25.
26.     def retrieve_graph_context(self, entities):
27.         # Example Cypher query for Neo4j
28.         query = """
29.         MATCH (start)-[r*1..3]-(connected)
30.         WHERE start.name IN $entities
31.         RETURN DISTINCT r, connected
32.         """
33.         return self.graph_db.execute(query, {'entities': entities})
```

Code exhibit 13.13: Implementation of GraphRAG's core system, combining a knowledge graph database with vector store retrieval to enable relationship-aware query processing and context enrichment.

Real-World Applications and Benefits

GraphRAG shows particular strength in scenarios requiring:

1. **Complex Relationship Understanding** For example, in legal document analysis, understanding the relationships between cases, statutes, and precedents is crucial. GraphRAG can map these connections and retrieve relevant information along relationship chains.
2. **Temporal Reasoning:** When dealing with evolving situations like project management or historical analysis, GraphRAG can track changes over time and understand how different events relate to each other.
3. **Multi-hop Reasoning** In technical documentation, finding answers might require following a chain of related concepts. GraphRAG excels at traversing these conceptual relationships to find relevant information.

EVALUATING RAG SYSTEMS: BEYOND SIMPLE METRICS

RAG system evaluation requires a comprehensive approach examining three critical components: context retrieval quality, answer generation accuracy, and user experience metrics. Let's explore the technical implementation of each component and how they combine to provide a holistic evaluation framework.

The effectiveness of RAG systems depends not just on individual components but on how well they work together to enhance LLM capabilities. A comprehensive evaluation framework must consider multiple dimensions - from retrieval accuracy to final response quality - to ensure optimal system performance.

Core Evaluation Components

1. Context Retrieval Quality
The foundation of RAG effectiveness lies in retrieving relevant context. We measure this through:
- **Semantic Relevance**: Using embedding similarity between query and retrieved passages
- **Context Diversity**: Analysing embedding-based distances between retrieved chunks
- **Coverage**: Comparing retrieved information against ground truth when available

2. Answer Generation Quality
Beyond basic accuracy, we evaluate:
- **Factual Consistency**: Using BERTScore to verify alignment with source context
- **Coherence**: Measuring inter-sentence semantic similarity
- **Query Relevance**: Computing semantic similarity between query and response

3. User Experience Metrics
Practical deployment requires monitoring:
- **Response Time**: Latency measurements
- **Readability**: Linguistic complexity analysis
- **User Satisfaction**: Direct feedback metrics

Here is the one example implementation using NLP libraries.

```
1.   from sentence_transformers import SentenceTransformer
2.   from bert_score import score as bert_score
3.   import numpy as np
4.   from typing import List, Dict
5.
6.   class RAGEvaluator:
7.     def __init__(self):
8.       self.embedding_model = SentenceTransformer('all-mpnet-base-v2')
9.
10.    def evaluate_full_pipeline(
11.      self,
12.      query: str,
13.      response: str,
14.      contexts: List[str],
15.      response_time: float
16.    ) -> Dict[str, float]:
17.      """Comprehensive RAG evaluation across all dimensions"""
18.      # Context quality
19.      context_scores = self._evaluate_contexts(query, contexts)
20.
21.      #Answer quality
22.      answer_scores = self._evaluate_answer(response, contexts, query)
```

```
23.
24.       # User experience
25.       ux_scores = self._evaluate_ux(response, response_time)
26.
27.       # Combine all metrics
28.       all_metrics = {
29.          **context_scores,
30.          **answer_scores,
31.          **ux_scores
32.       }
33.
34.       return {
35.          'detailed_scores': all_metrics,
36.          'overall_score': np.mean(list(all_metrics.values()))
37.       }
38.
39.   def _evaluate_contexts(
40.       self,
41.       query: str,
42.       contexts: List[str]
43.   ) -> Dict[str, float]:
44.       """Evaluate context retrieval quality"""
45.       # Calculate embeddings
46.       query_emb = self.embedding_model.encode([query])[0]
47.       context_embs = self.embedding_model.encode(contexts)
48.
49.       # Calculate relevance scores
50.       relevance = np.mean([
51.          np.dot(query_emb, ctx_emb)
52.          for ctx_emb in context_embs
53.       ])
54.
55.       # Calculate diversity
56.       diversity = 1 - np.mean([
57.          np.dot(emb1, emb2)
58.          for i, emb1 in enumerate(context_embs)
59.          for j, emb2 in enumerate(context_embs)
60.          if i < j
61.       ])
62.
63.       return {
64.          'context_relevance': float(relevance),
65.          'context_diversity': float(diversity)
66.       }
67.
68.   def _evaluate_answer(
69.       self,
70.       response: str,
71.       contexts: str,
72.       query: str
73.   ) -> Dict[str, float]:
74.       """Evaluate answer generation quality"""
75.       # Calculate factual consistency
76.       precision, recall, f1 = bert_score(
77.          [response],
78.          [' '.join(contexts)],
79.          lang='en'
80.       )
81.
```

```
82.        # Calculate query relevance
83.        query_emb = self.embedding_model.encode([query])[0]
84.        response_emb = self.embedding_model.encode([response])[0]
85.        query_relevance = np.dot(query_emb, response_emb)
86.
87.        return {
88.          'factual_accuracy': float(f1.mean()),
89.          'query_relevance': float(query_relevance)
90.        }
```

Code Exhibit 13.14: The code implementation leverages state-of-the-art NLP libraries for comprehensive RAG evaluation. SentenceTransformer provides efficient semantic embeddings for relevance and diversity calculations, while BERTScore enables robust factual consistency checking. The RAGEvaluator class encapsulates methods for assessing context quality, answer accuracy, and generates normalized scores across all evaluation dimensions.

EMERGING FRONTIERS IN RAG SYSTEMS

As RAG systems evolve, we're witnessing a transformation from pure text-based approaches to more sophisticated architectures that promise to reshape how we interact with information. This evolution is driven by two key trends: the emergence of multi-modal capabilities and the development of adaptive retrieval mechanisms.

Multi-Modal RAG: Beyond Text

The integration of multiple modalities represents perhaps the most exciting frontier in RAG development. Unlike traditional text-based systems, multi-modal RAG can process and synthesize information from diverse data types. In healthcare, for instance, these systems can analyse both radiological images and medical literature to provide more comprehensive diagnostic insights. They can compare visual patterns against extensive databases of medical imaging while retrieving relevant research papers and clinical guidelines.

Consider a medical diagnosis scenario:

```
query = "What does this chest X-ray suggest about the patient's condition?"
context = {
"images": ["chest_xray.png"],
"text": ["recent_radiological_reports.txt", "medical_literature.pdf"]
}
```

The system would need to:

1. Extract features from the X-ray image
2. Match these features with relevant medical knowledge
3. Synthesize a response that integrates both visual and textual insights

Adaptive Systems: Learning and Evolution

Perhaps even more transformative is the emergence of adaptive RAG systems. These systems dynamically modify their behaviour based on:

- **Query Patterns**: Learning to recognize query types and adjusting retrieval strategies accordingly
- **User Interaction**: Incorporating feedback to refine response generation
- **Context Management**: Dynamically adjusting context window sizes based on query complexity

Here's an example of how an adaptive system might optimize its retrieval strategy:

```python
1.    class AdaptiveRAG:
2.      def __init__(self):
3.        self.query_analyzer = QueryPatternAnalyzer()
4.        self.retrieval_strategies = {
5.          'technical': TechnicalRetriever(chunk_size=1000),
6.          'conceptual': ConceptualRetriever(chunk_size=2000),
7.          'summary': SummaryRetriever(chunk_size=3000)
8.        }
9.
10.     def process_query(self, query: str) -> Dict[str, Any]:
11.       # Analyze query pattern
12.       query_type = self.query_analyzer.classify(query)
13.
14.       # Select appropriate retrieval strategy
15.       retriever = self.retrieval_strategies[query_type]
16.
17.       # Adjust parameters based on complexity
18.       complexity = self.query_analyzer.assess_complexity(query)
19.       retriever.adjust_parameters(complexity)
20.
21.       # Retrieve and generate response
22.       contexts = retriever.get_relevant_contexts(query)
23.       response = self.generate_response(query, contexts)
24.
25.       # Learn from interaction
26.       self.update_patterns(query, response, user_feedback)
27.
28.       return response
```

Code Exhibit 13.15: This adaptive RAG implementation demonstrates a flexible architecture that can dynamically select and adjust retrieval strategies based on query patterns. The system learns from each interaction, optimizing parameters like chunk size and retrieval depth while maintaining a modular design that can accommodate new retrieval strategies as requirements evolve.

Future Challenges and Opportunities

As these systems evolve, several critical challenges emerge:

1. **Computational Efficiency**: Multi-modal processing significantly increases computational demands
2. **Cross-Modal Understanding**: Ensuring coherent integration of information across different modalities
3. **Privacy and Security**: Managing sensitive data across multiple modalities while maintaining security
4. **Quality Assurance**: Developing evaluation metrics that work across different modes of information

The future of RAG lies in systems that can seamlessly integrate multiple data types while adapting to user needs and query patterns. As we tackle these challenges, we're moving towards more sophisticated, context-aware systems that can handle increasingly complex information needs while maintaining efficiency, accuracy, and privacy.

This frontier represents not just a technical evolution but a fundamental shift in how we interact with and process information. The successful implementation of these advances will require continued innovation in areas ranging from neural architectures to evaluation metrics, promising an exciting future for RAG technology.

DISCUSSION

Retrieval-Augmented Generation represents more than just an extension of Large Language Models - it embodies a fundamental shift in how we approach AI systems' knowledge utilization. Throughout our exploration of RAG components, retrieval mechanisms, and evaluation frameworks, we've seen how combining dynamic knowledge retrieval with LLM capabilities creates systems that are both more powerful and more reliable. This synthesis mirrors the broader pattern we've observed throughout this book: the most effective advances often come not from increasing model size or complexity, but from thoughtfully combining existing capabilities in ways that enhance their individual strengths.

What makes RAG particularly fascinating is its position at the intersection of information retrieval and language generation. While previous chapters focused on model architectures and serving strategies, RAG demonstrates how external knowledge integration can fundamentally enhance model capabilities. Expert practitioners consistently emphasise starting with robust retrieval foundations before adding complexity, highlighting that success often comes from understanding the interplay between components rather than implementing every possible feature. The careful balance between retrieval accuracy, processing efficiency, and response quality has become increasingly crucial as these systems scale to real-world applications.

Looking ahead to prompt engineering in Chapter 14 and LLM agents in Chapter 15, the insights gained from RAG systems become increasingly valuable. The ability to ground model responses in specific information while maintaining the flexibility and power of LLMs opens new possibilities for more reliable and capable AI systems. Current developments in multi-modal RAG and graph-based approaches show promise in extending these capabilities further, but they also remind us that the future lies not just in more sophisticated retrieval mechanisms, but in finding fundamentally more effective ways to combine knowledge sources while maintaining practicality and reliability. Success in this domain will ultimately depend on developing systems that can seamlessly integrate external knowledge while preserving the remarkable capabilities that make LLMs so powerful.

KEY TAKEAWAYS:

1. Retrieval-Augmented Generation (RAG) systems combine LLMs with external knowledge retrieval to overcome the limitations of static model knowledge.
2. The key components of a RAG system, including vector databases, embedding models, and efficient retrieval mechanisms, work together to provide relevant context for improved model responses.

3. Advanced retrieval techniques, such as multi-query, hierarchical, and iterative approaches, can significantly enhance the quality and comprehensiveness of information retrieved for RAG systems.

REFLECTIVE PROMPTS:

1. The integration of external knowledge retrieval with LLMs, as explored in this chapter, demonstrates the importance of grounding AI systems in real-world information and context. How might this approach influence the development of more robust and trustworthy AI assistants that can reliably handle complex, open-ended queries?

2. The architectural choices and design trade-offs in RAG systems, particularly regarding the balance between retrieval accuracy, processing efficiency, and response quality, highlight the nuanced challenges in building effective knowledge-augmented AI. What are the implications of these trade-offs for the future of knowledge representation and reasoning in artificial intelligence?

3. As RAG systems become more sophisticated, incorporating techniques like multi-modal integration and adaptive learning, what new frontiers might emerge in the field of AI-human collaboration? How can these advancements shape the way we interact with and leverage intelligent systems to enhance our own cognitive capabilities?

As we've explored the technical foundations of LLMs, the next frontier is understanding how to effectively interact with and guide these powerful systems through prompt engineering, the focus of Chapter 14.

THE ART AND SCIENCE OF PROMPT ENGINEERING: A DEEP DIVE

Reflective Prompt: The team wants to optimize the LLM's interactions with users. Discuss how the knowledge of how LLMs "think," as explored through prompt engineering techniques, might influence the design of more natural and intuitive human-AI interfaces.

INTRODUCTION: UNDERSTANDING THE DANCE OF LANGUAGE AND LOGIC

Imagine having a conversation with the world's most knowledgeable librarian – one who has read every book ever written, but who interprets your requests with perfect literalness and thinks in patterns of attention and context. This is essentially what we're doing when we engage with Large Language Models (LLMs). Prompt engineering is the art and science of speaking this librarian's language, understanding how they think, and guiding them to give us the insights we need.

But to master this art, we need to understand what happens behind the scenes when we interact with these models. It's not just about crafting clever instructions – it's about understanding how the model processes information, maintains context, and generates responses.

UNDERSTANDING THE FOUNDATIONS

The Neural Canvas: Hidden States

Think of hidden states as the model's active thoughts – a vast neural canvas where information is painted, refined, and connected. Just as our thoughts evolve as we read a sentence, the model's hidden states transform with each word it processes.

When you input the simple phrase "The quick brown fox," here's what happens in the model's mind:
1. First Token ("The"):
    a.   Initial context is minimal
    b.   Basic language patterns activate
    c.   Anticipation of a noun phrase begins
2. Second Token ("quick"):
    a.   Adjective meaning is processed
    b.   Relationship with "The" is established
    c.   Expectations for what follows are refined

3. Third Token ("brown"):
   a. Multiple adjectives are balanced
   b. Colour information is integrated
   c. Pattern of descriptive sequence is recognised
4. Fourth Token ("fox"):
   a. Complete noun phrase is formed
   b. All descriptors are connected to the subject
   c. Full contextual understanding emerges

This evolution of understanding happens through hidden states, which act as the model's working memory. Each transformer layer maintains its own set of hidden states, creating a hierarchy of understanding:

- Lower Layers (1-4): Low-level feature extraction carries out operations like Morphological analysis, Part-of-speech tagging, Local syntactic patterns, and it focuses more on token-level representations.
- Middle Layers (5-8): Semantic composition; carry out operations like phrase structure composition, word sense disambiguation, semantic role labelling, and it focuses on capturing phrase-level semantics.
- Higher Layers (9-12): Abstract reasoning, carry out operations like long-range dependencies, logical relationship extraction, task-specific transformations, and it focuses on task-oriented representations.

The evolution of hidden states can be expressed as:
$h\_t = LayerNorm(FFN(LayerNorm(MultiHead(Q,K,V) + h\_\{t-1\})))$

Where:
- h_t: Hidden state at position t
- MultiHead: Multi-head attention mechanism
- FNN: Feed-forward neural network
- Q, K, V: Query, Key, Value matrices

The Three Pillars of Memory

LLMs operate with three distinct types of memory, each serving a crucial role in understanding and generating text. These three types of memory are Working Memory, which handles immediate context; Parametric Memory, which stores learned knowledge; and Attention Memory, which creates dynamic connections between information pieces.

1. **Working Memory: Hidden State Implementation**

Think of working memory as a sophisticated neural workspace, implemented through hidden states, where the model actively processes and manipulates information in high-dimensional vector space. Like a well-organized workbench with finite space, it's constrained by the context window (typically 4K to 32K tokens), yet within these bounds, it dynamically maintains conversations, tracks calculations, holds immediate context, and forges connections between related concepts through continuous vector transformations. The effectiveness of this working memory depends directly on how information is represented and updated in the hidden states, with newer information either enriching or replacing older content as it reaches its capacity limits.

2. Parametric Memory: The model weight

Parametric memory represents the model's learned knowledge base, encoded within its neural network weights and biases. This static memory system, crystallised during training, holds encoded patterns, linguistic structures, and world knowledge across its weight matrices, much like a vast neural library. While it can't be modified during inference, it serves as the foundational knowledge repository that guides the model's understanding and generation capabilities, functioning through precise mathematical transformations as information flows through the network layers.

3. Attention Memory: Dynamic learning

Attention memory functions as a dynamic neural routing system, computing real-time connections between information pieces through learned attention mechanisms. While the computation rules are encoded in parametric memory (weights and biases), the actual attention patterns are generated dynamically during inference, creating context-specific relationships between tokens. This system enables the model to weigh the relevance of different pieces of information, establishing connections and temporal relationships on the fly, essentially serving as the model's dynamic reasoning mechanism that determines how information should be integrated and processed based on the current context.

Here is how they work together.

Input: "The quick brown fox jumps"

1. Working Memory (Hidden States):
- Maintains the current representation of "quick brown fox"
- Updated with each new token
- Limited by context window

2. Parametric Memory (Weights):
- Knows what "fox" means
- Understands grammar patterns
- Stores word relationships

3. Attention Memory (Dynamic):
- Connects "fox" with "jumps"
- Weights relevance of previous words
- Creates context-specific links

Process Flow:
Token → Embedding → Attention Computation → Hidden State Update
↑ ↑
Parametric Memory Attention Patterns

The Flow of Information

To understand how these components work together, let's visualise the journey of a single prompt through the system, as illustrated in Fig.14.1:

Large Language Model Processing Pipeline

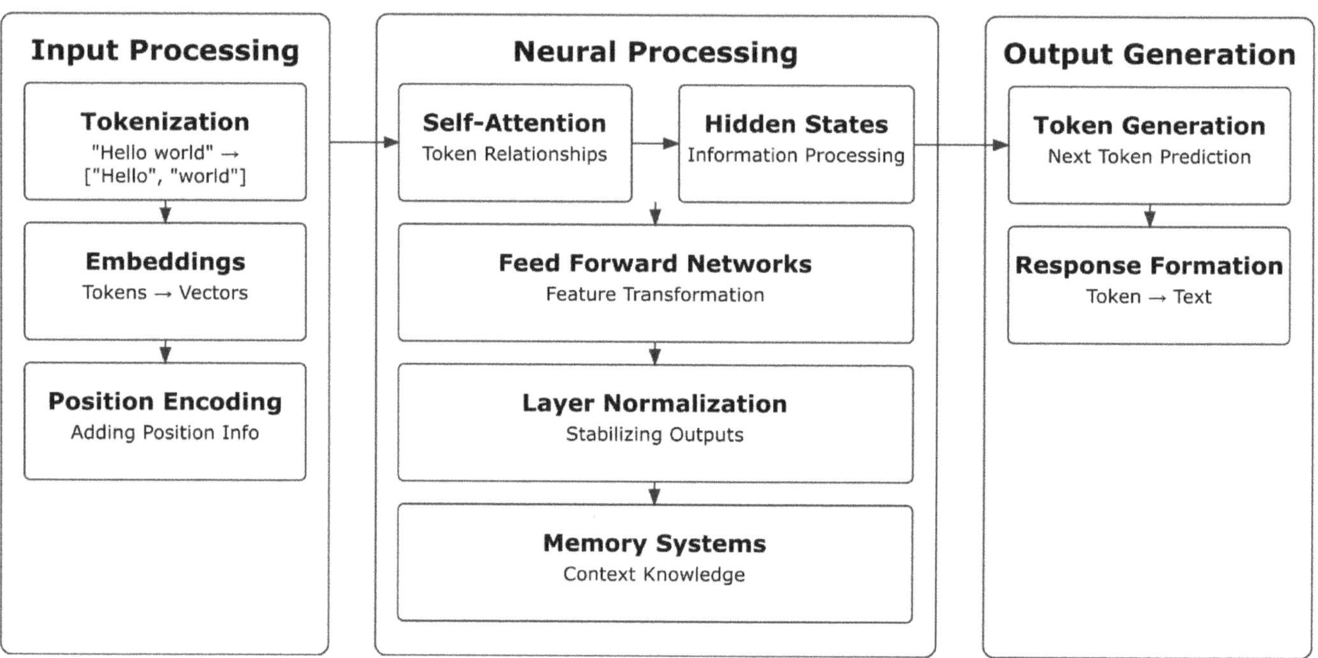

Fig. 14.1: This figure illustrates the complete processing pipeline of a Large Language Model (LLM), showing how input text flows through three main stages: Input Processing (tokenization, embedding, position encoding), Neural Processing (self-attention, hidden states, feed-forward networks), and Output Generation (token prediction and response formation). The arrows indicate the flow of information between different components, demonstrating how text is transformed and processed at each step to generate meaningful responses.

When you input a prompt, it flows through several stages:
1. **Input Processing**
   a. Text is broken into tokens
   b. Tokens are converted to embeddings
   c. Positional information is added
2. **Neural Processing.**
   a. Multiple transformer layers process information
   b. Hidden states evolve and refine
   c. Attention mechanisms connect relevant information
3. **Response Generation.**
   a. Knowledge is integrated
   b. Context is considered
   c. Coherent output is formed

This process is continuous and dynamic, with each component influencing the others in a complex dance of information processing.

PRACTICAL PROMPT ENGINEERING TECHNIQUES

Armed with a deep understanding of how LLMs process information through their memory systems, we can now explore practical prompt engineering techniques that leverage this knowledge to elicit more accurate and insightful responses and understand how different prompting techniques work with memory systems

Few-Shot Prompting: The Art of Teaching by Example

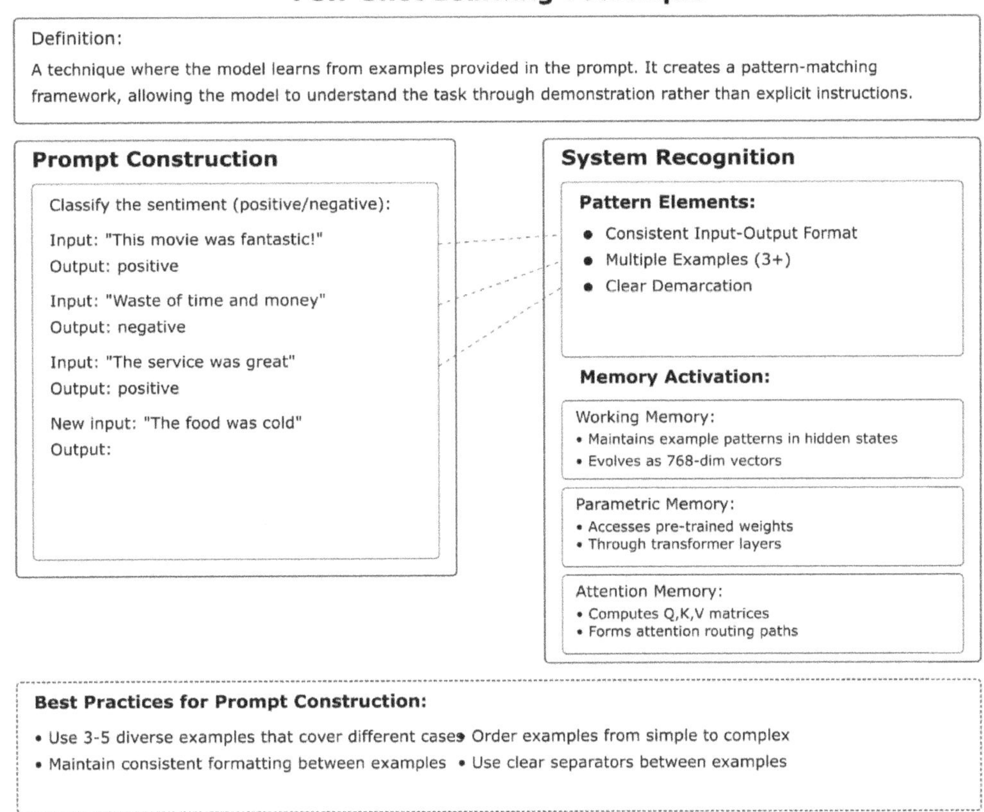

Fig. 14.2: This diagram illustrates how Few-Shot prompting works, mapping the relationship between prompt construction and how the system processes it. The left side shows the prompt structure, while the right side reveals how the system recognises and processes the pattern, with memory activation shown at different levels.

Few-Shot prompting, explained in Fig.14.2, is like teaching someone through examples rather than explaining rules. Just as a teacher might show several solved math problems before asking a student to solve one, Few-Shot prompting demonstrates the pattern we want the model to follow. The power of Few-Shot prompting lies in its ability to create temporary "teaching moments" within the model's working memory. By providing multiple examples, we're essentially creating a mini-training session within the context window. The model's attention mechanism can then draw direct parallels between the examples and the new query, leading to more accurate and consistent responses.

When using this technique, think of yourself as a teacher providing examples. The key is to:

- Start with clear, representative examples
- Maintain consistent formatting

- Progress from simple to complex cases
- End with your actual query in the same format

Chain-of-thought prompting: Step-by-step reasoning

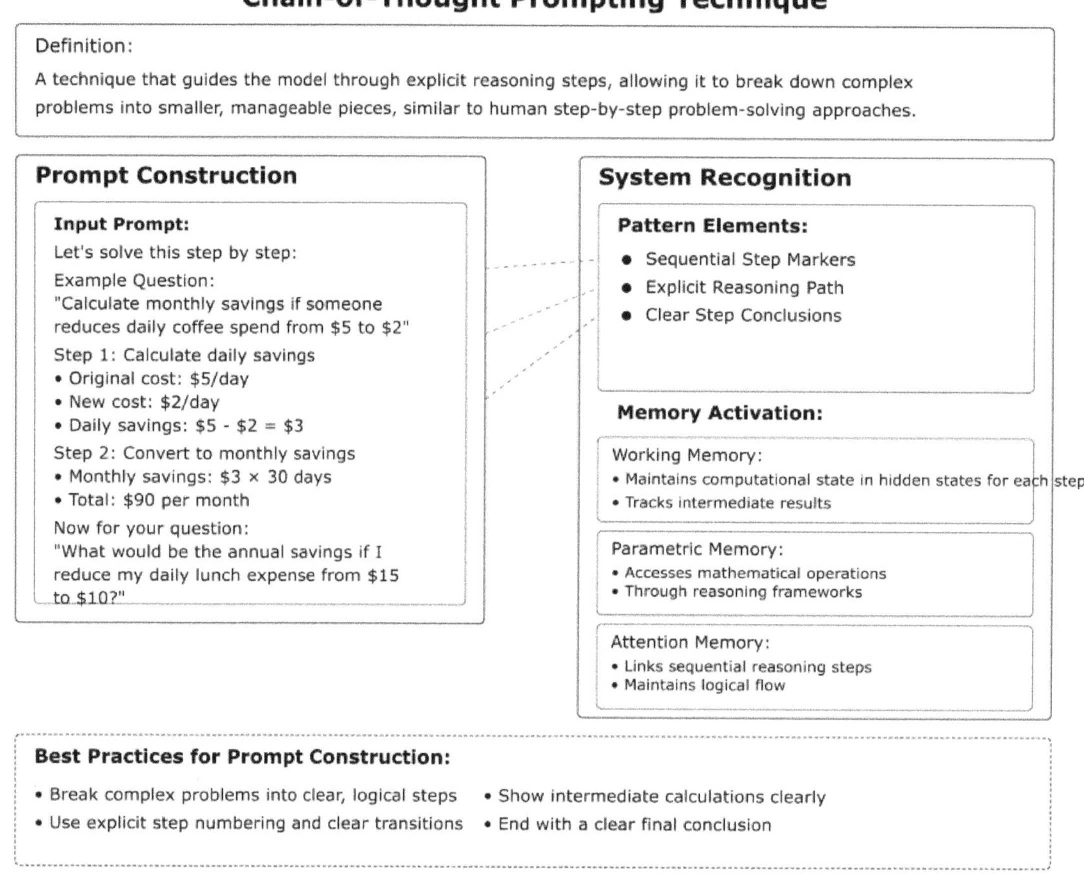

Fig.14.3: This image is a detailed infographic explaining the "Chain-of-Thought Prompting Technique" - a method used in AI interactions that breaks down complex problems into step-by-step reasoning processes. It shows how to construct prompts on the left (with an example about calculating coffee savings) and how AI systems process these prompts on the right, along with best practices at the bottom.

Chain-of-Thought prompting, exaplined in Fig.14.3, harnesses the model's architecture by breaking down complex problems into sequential steps. The model's attention mechanisms create strong links between each reasoning stage, while its working memory maintains the computational state. This process allows the model to better track intermediate results and leverage its understanding of mathematical and logical operations.

When using this technique, imagine yourself as a tutor who shows his work:

- Start with a clear "Let's solve this step-by-step" signal
- Break down complex problems into numbered steps
- Show all intermediate calculations and reasoning
- Conclude with a clear final answer

Think of it as creating a clear path of logical connections, where each step naturally flows into the next for more reliable problem-solving.

Context Engineering: The Art of Setting the Stage

Context Engineering Prompting Technique

Definition:
A technique that strategically provides background information and situational context to guide the model towards more informed and nuanced responses, similar to briefing an expert before seeking their opinion.

Prompt Construction

Input Example:
Let's consider the context:
Example Scenario:
"Recommend investment strategy for a 25-year-old with $10,000 savings"
Context:
• First-time investor
• Monthly income: $4,000
• Risk tolerance: Moderate
• Goal: House down payment in 5 years
Your Question:
"What investment mix would you recommend for this scenario?"

System Recognition

Pattern Elements:
- Context Identification
- Parameter Recognition
- Constraint Analysis

Memory Activation:

Working Memory:
• Maintains active context in hidden states
• Tracks key parameters

Parametric Memory:
• Accesses domain knowledge
• Applies contextual rules

Attention Memory:
• Focuses on relevant context
• Weighs important factors

Best Practices for Context Engineering:

• Provide relevant, concise background information
• Structure context from general to specific
• Include key constraints and parameters
• Frame query within provided context

Fig. 14.4: This diagram illustrates how Context Engineering prompting works by showing how background information and situational parameters are structured and processed by the model. The left side demonstrates prompt construction with relevant context layers, while the right side reveals how the system integrates this context through different memory systems to generate informed responses.

Context Engineering prompting, illustrated in Fig.14.4, harnesses the model's contextual understanding by strategically providing relevant background information and situational parameters. Just as a doctor makes better decisions when given a patient's full medical history, this technique enables more informed and nuanced responses by activating relevant knowledge within the model's architecture. The power lies in how provided context helps the model filter and weight its knowledge base, creating a focused lens through which to process queries and generate responses.

When using this technique, think of yourself as preparing a thorough briefing:

- Provide relevant historical or background context
- Set clear situational parameters
- Define specific constraints or requirements
- Frame the core query within this context

Role/Persona Prompting: Shaping Expertise Through Identity

Role Prompting Technique

Definition:

A technique that assigns specific roles or personas to guide the model's perspective and expertise, similar to how different experts would approach and respond to the same question differently.

Prompt Construction

Input Example:

Let's assume this role:

Example Role:
"You are an experienced Data Scientist with ML expertise"

Role Parameters:
- 10 years experience
- ML/AI specialization
- Technical communication
- Focus on practical solutions

Your Question:
"How would you approach this classification problem?"

System Recognition

Pattern Elements:
- Role Understanding
- Expertise Filtering
- Style Adaptation

Memory Activation:

Working Memory:
- Maintains role perspective
- Tracks response alignment

Parametric Memory:
- Accesses role expertise
- Applies domain knowledge

Attention Memory:
- Links expertise to query
- Maintains role consistency

Best Practices for Role Prompting:
- Define clear role characteristics and expertise
- Specify communication style and tone
- Match role to task requirements
- Maintain role consistency throughout

Fig. 14.5: This diagram maps out the Role Prompting technique, showing how specific personas and expertise levels are defined and processed by the model. The left side details role construction with clear expertise parameters, while the right side illustrates how the system maintains role consistency and expertise filtering through its memory systems for specialised responses.

Role Prompting leverages the model's ability to adapt its knowledge retrieval and response patterns based on assigned personas (see Fig.14.5). Like how actors embody different characters, this technique helps the model maintain a consistent perspective and domain expertise throughout interactions. The technique works by creating a temporary expert framework in the model's working memory, influencing how it filters and presents information through that specific lens.

When using this technique, approach it as a director giving character notes:
- Define the role's expertise level and background
- Specify behavioural characteristics
- Set communication style and tone
- Maintain consistency with the role's perspective

Each technique activates different aspects of the model's architecture:
- Context Engineering primarily engages with knowledge integration and relevance filtering
- Role Prompting focuses on perspective maintenance and expertise filtering

Task Decomposition Prompting: Breaking Down Complex Problems

Task Decomposition Prompting Technique

Definition:

A technique that breaks down complex tasks into hierarchical subtasks, allowing the model to tackle problems systematically, similar to how project managers break large projects into manageable components.

Prompt Construction

Input Example:
Let's break this down:
Main Task:
"Create a content strategy for a new product launch"
Subtasks:
1. Market Analysis
• Target audience research
• Competitor content review
2. Content Planning
• Channel selection
• Content types
3. Timeline Development
• Pre-launch phase
• Launch sequence

System Recognition

Pattern Elements:
- Hierarchical Structure
- Task Dependencies
- Subtask Organization

Memory Activation:

Working Memory:
• Maintains task hierarchy
• Tracks progress state

Parametric Memory:
• Accesses domain knowledge
• Applies task patterns

Best Practices for Task Decomposition:
- Break complex tasks into logical subtasks
- Maintain clear hierarchy and dependencies
- Define scope for each subtask
- Ensure subtasks are self-contained

Fig. 14.6: This diagram illustrates how the Task Decomposition technique breaks down complex tasks into manageable subtasks, showing how the model processes hierarchical structures. The left side demonstrates a multi-level task breakdown example, while the right side reveals how the system maintains task relationships and progress tracking through its memory systems.

Task Decomposition prompting, illustrated in Fig.14.6, leverages the model's ability to handle hierarchical problem-solving by breaking complex tasks into manageable components. Like how a project manager breaks down a large project into smaller deliverables, this technique enables systematic problem-solving through organized subtasks. The power lies in how it helps the model maintain focus on specific components while understanding their relationships to the larger goal.

When using this technique, think of yourself as a project planner:

- Start with a clear main objective
- Break down into logical subtasks
- Define dependencies between components
- Address each subtask systematically

The technique uniquely engages the model's memory systems:

- Working Memory tracks the hierarchy and progress
- Parametric Memory accesses relevant domain expertise for each subtask
- Attention Memory maintains relationships between components

This approach particularly shines when dealing with complex, multi-step problems that could overwhelm other prompting techniques. By managing cognitive load through structured decomposition, it enables more reliable and comprehensive solutions.

System Message Engineering: Setting the Foundation

System Message Engineering Technique

Definition:

A technique that establishes foundational behavioral guidelines and operating parameters for the model, similar to setting rules of engagement before a strategic discussion or consultation.

Prompt Construction

Input Example:

System Parameters:

1. Role Definition:
• Technical documentation expert
• Focus on clarity and precision

2. Response Format:
• Use markdown formatting
• Include code examples
• Structure with headers

3. Constraints:
• Beginner-friendly language
• Step-by-step explanations
• Include error handling

System Recognition

Pattern Elements:
- Global Parameters
- Behavioral Rules
- Format Controls

Memory Activation:

Working Memory:
• Maintains active rules
• Tracks format compliance

Parametric Memory:
• Applies format rules
• Enforces constraints

Best Practices for System Message Engineering:
• Define clear behavioral parameters
• Specify format requirements
• Set appropriate constraints
• Maintain consistent guidelines

Fig. 14.7: This diagram shows how System Message Engineering establishes behavioural and formatting guidelines for model interactions. The left side demonstrates the structured setup of system parameters and constraints, while the right side illustrates how these rules are processed and maintained across the model's memory systems for consistent responses.

System Message Engineering (see Fig.14.7) establishes the core behavioural framework for model interactions. Like setting ground rules before a strategic meeting, this technique creates a consistent foundation for all subsequent interactions. The power lies in its ability to shape how the model processes and responds to all queries within a session, ensuring alignment with desired parameters and constraints.

When using this technique, think of yourself as setting up operating protocols:
- Define clear behavioural guidelines
- Establish response formats
- Set specific constraints
- Create consistent interaction patterns

The technique uniquely engages the model's memory systems:
- Working Memory actively maintains rules and guidelines
- Parametric Memory applies format restrictions and constraints
- Attention Memory ensures consistent rule application

This foundational technique is particularly effective when combined with other prompting methods, as it establishes the base operating parameters that guide all subsequent interactions. It's essential for maintaining consistency across complex interactions and ensuring outputs meet specific requirements.

Combining Prompting Techniques: The Art of Integration

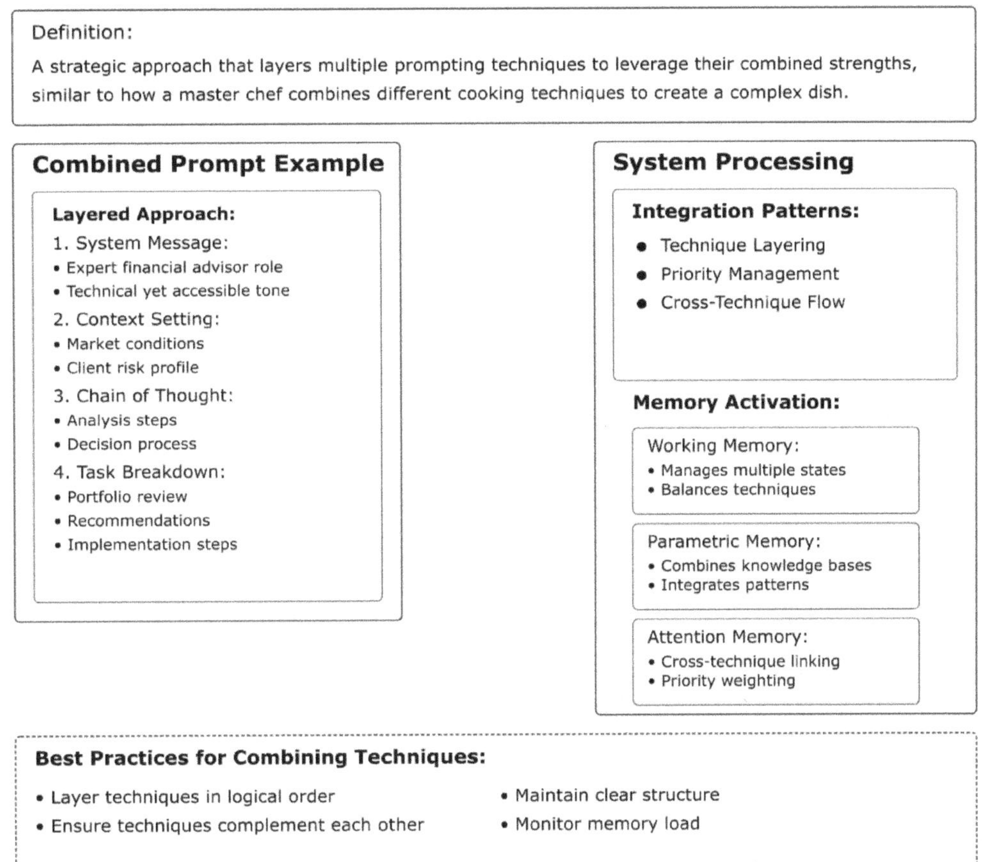

Fig. 14.8: This diagram illustrates how multiple prompting techniques can be layered and combined effectively. The left side shows an example of integrated techniques in a single prompt, while the right side demonstrates how the model's memory systems manage and process these combined approaches for enhanced results.

Combining prompting techniques is like orchestrating a complex symphony where different instruments (techniques) work together to create a more powerful and nuanced performance (see Fig.14.8). This advanced approach leverages the strengths of multiple techniques while managing their interactions to solve complex problems more effectively.

Key Combinations and Their Applications:

1. Role + Chain-of-Thought
   o Expert persona providing step-by-step reasoning
   o Enhanced credibility and clarity in complex explanations
2. Context + Task Decomposition
   o Rich background information with structured problem-solving
   o Comprehensive solution development

3. System Message + Few-Shot
   o Consistent behaviour with learning by example
   o Reliable pattern recognition and application

The technique uniquely challenges the model's memory systems:

- Working Memory must juggle multiple task states
- Parametric Memory integrates different knowledge patterns
- Attention Memory manages cross-technique relationships

Common Synergies:

- System Messages provide the foundation for all other techniques
- Context Engineering enhances Role Prompting's effectiveness
- Chain-of-Thought complements Task Decomposition
- Few-shot examples can reinforce any other technique

COMMON PITFALLS AND TROUBLESHOOTING

Just as understanding effective prompting techniques is crucial, recognising common pitfalls and knowing how to troubleshoot them is equally important for successful prompt engineering. Common Failure Modes:

1. Memory Overload
   - Symptoms: Incomplete responses, lost context, and confused reasoning
   - Cause: Exceeding working memory capacity with too much information
   - Solution: Chunk information, prioritise crucial context
2. Context Collapse
   - Symptoms: Mixing roles, losing perspective, inconsistent tone
   - Cause: Competing contexts overwhelming attention and memory
   - Solution: Maintain clear role boundaries, refresh context periodically
3. Pattern Interference
   - Symptoms: Mixed formats, inconsistent reasoning, blended styles
   - Cause: Conflicting patterns in parametric memory activation
   - Solution: Use clear, non-competing instruction sets

SYSTEMATIC TROUBLESHOOTING APPROACH

When encountering issues with prompt responses, a systematic approach to troubleshooting can help quickly identify and resolve problems. The following decision tree provides a structured method for diagnosing and addressing common issues, as illustrated in Fig.14.9.

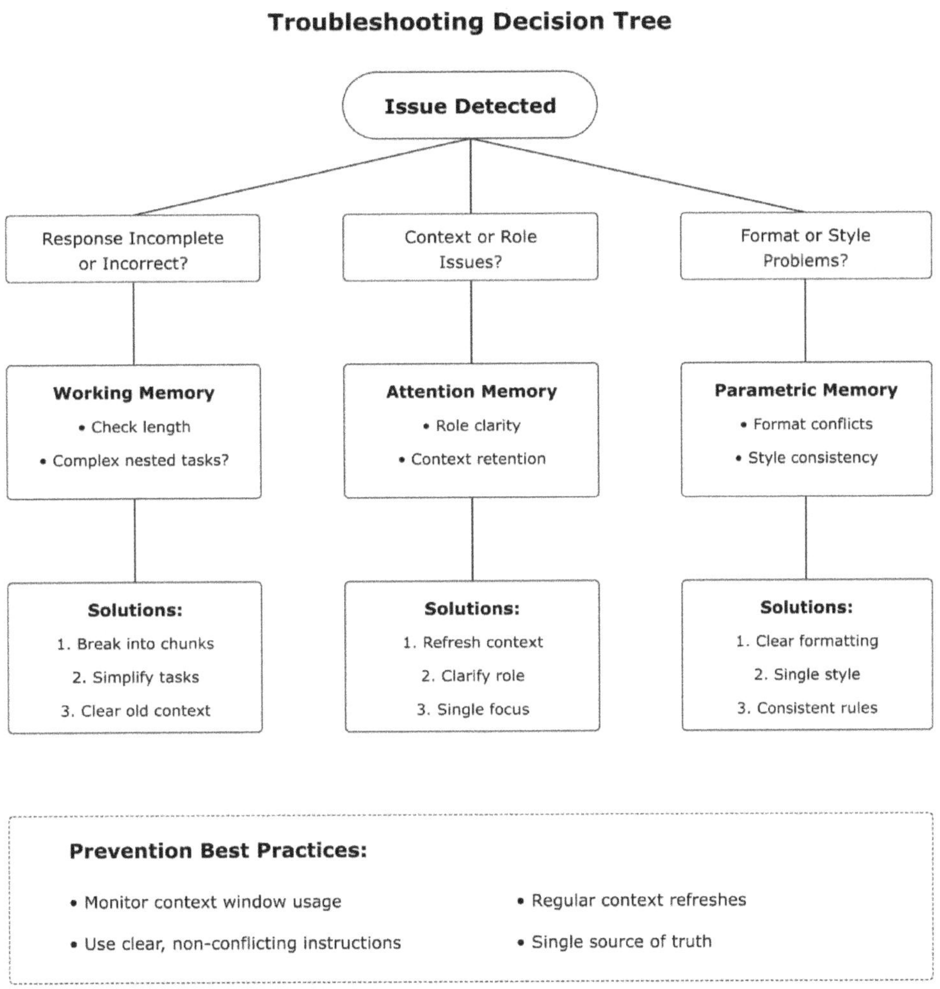

Troubleshooting Decision Tree

Fig. 14.9: This decision tree provides a systematic approach to diagnosing and resolving common prompt engineering issues, mapping out specific solutions for each type of memory-related problem. Each path leads from symptom identification through diagnosis to targeted solutions, with a focus on maintaining optimal model performance.

This decision tree guides you through three main diagnostic paths:

1. Response Quality Issues
   - o Identify when the model struggles with output completion or accuracy
   - o Check for working memory overload
   - o Implement chunking and simplification strategies
2. Context and Role Problems
   - o Diagnose issues with perspective maintenance
   - o Address context retention problems
   - o Restore clear role boundaries
3. Format and Style Concerns
   - o Resolve inconsistencies in output format
   - o Fix style conflicts
   - o Maintain consistent parameters

PRACTICAL GUIDE TO PROMPT ENGINEERING TECHNIQUES

While understanding the theoretical foundations of prompt engineering is crucial, practitioners need clear guidelines on when and how to apply different techniques. Like a master craftsman selecting the right tool for each task, effective prompt engineering requires knowing which technique to use in different situations.

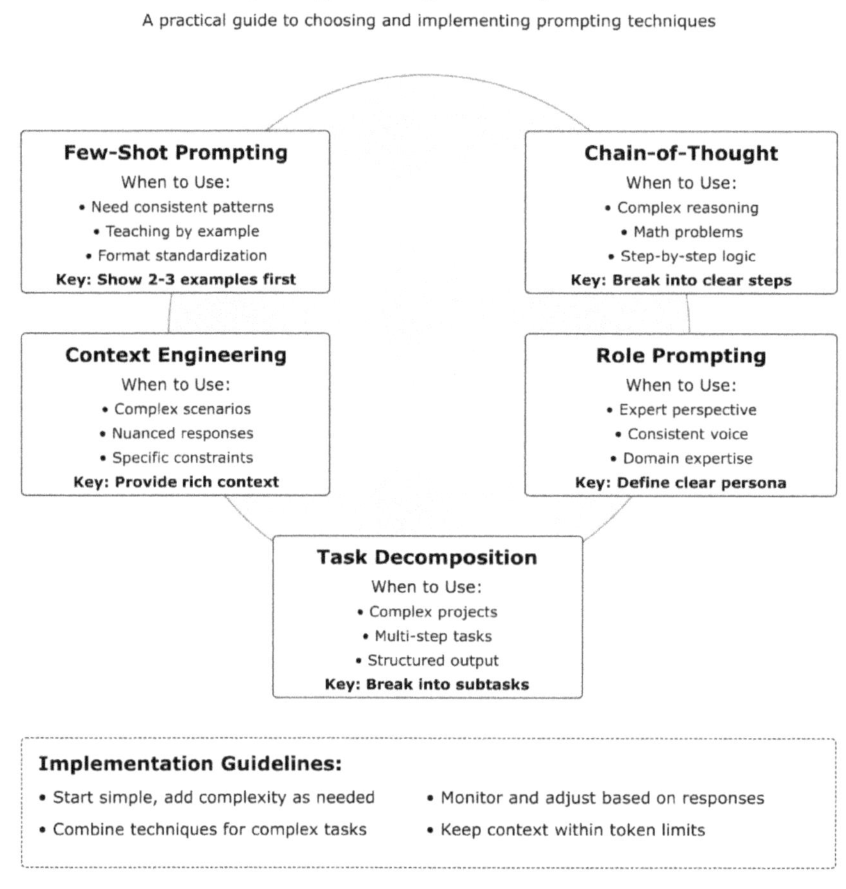

Fig. 14.10: This comprehensive map outlines five core prompting techniques, showing when each is most effective and how to implement them. The circular arrangement illustrates how these techniques can be combined, while the implementation guidelines at the bottom provide practical tips for optimal usage in real-world applications.

This guide, illustrated in Fig.14.10, maps out the core prompting techniques and their optimal use cases. Each technique serves specific purposes:

- Few-Shot Prompting excels when you need to establish clear patterns through examples.
- Chain-of-Thought is invaluable for complex reasoning and multi-step problem solving.
- Context Engineering helps when nuanced understanding of situation is crucial.
- Role Prompting shines when consistent expertise and perspective are needed.
- Task Decomposition works best for breaking down complex projects into manageable pieces.

These techniques aren't mutually exclusive; they can be combined and layered for more sophisticated applications. The key is starting with the simplest approach that might work and adding complexity only as needed.

DISCUSSION

The art and science of prompt engineering represents a remarkable synthesis of linguistic creativity and technical precision. Building upon the mathematical foundations explored in earlier chapters, these prompting techniques demonstrate how carefully crafted language can guide LLMs to perform complex tasks and exhibit nuanced understanding. The progression from simple instruction following to sophisticated role-playing and task decomposition showcases not just the power of prompts, but deeper insights into how language shapes machine intelligence.

What makes prompt engineering particularly intriguing is its position at the intersection of human expression and computational structure. While previous chapters focused on the internal workings of LLMs, this chapter illuminates how those architectures respond to external guidance. Expert practitioners consistently emphasise the importance of understanding the interplay between prompts and the model's memory systems, underscoring that effectiveness depends not just on surface-level phrasing but on aligning instructions with the model's learned patterns and processing mechanisms. This alignment becomes increasingly crucial as prompts grow more complex, guiding the model through multi-step reasoning and perspective shifts.

Looking ahead, the insights gained from prompt engineering will likely prove instrumental in shaping the future of human-AI interaction. The ability to elicit reliable, context-appropriate responses through strategic prompting hints at the potential for more naturalistic and intuitive interfaces. Yet, it also highlights the need for caution and responsibility in prompt design, ensuring that the model's outputs align with intended goals and values. As we continue to explore the art and science of prompting, the key challenge will be striking a balance between unleashing the full potential of these language models and ensuring that potential is channelled towards beneficial ends. Success in this domain will require not just technical mastery but a deep appreciation for the power of language to shape understanding and behaviour, in machines and humans alike.

KEY TAKEAWAYS:

1. Prompt engineering is the art of speaking the "language" of Large Language Models, understanding how they process information, and guiding them to provide desired outputs.
2. Techniques like Few-Shot Prompting, Chain-of-Thought, and Role Prompting leverage the model's memory systems to elicit more accurate and insightful responses.
3. Combining multiple prompting techniques in a strategic manner can lead to more sophisticated and effective interactions with LLMs, enabling the development of powerful AI agents.

REFLECTIVE PROMPTS:

1. The prompt engineering techniques discussed in this chapter highlight the importance of understanding the underlying architecture and information processing mechanisms of LLMs. How might this knowledge of how LLMs "think" influence the way we design more natural and intuitive human-AI interfaces in the future?
2. The strategic combination of prompting techniques, as explored in this chapter, demonstrates the potential for LLMs to serve as collaborative partners in complex problem-solving and decision-making. What are the ethical considerations that must be addressed to ensure these powerful AI agents are developed and deployed responsibly?

3. The prompt engineering approach, with its emphasis on guiding LLMs through structured language, raises questions about the boundaries between human and machine intelligence. How might the continued advancements in this field impact our understanding of cognition and the nature of intelligence, both artificial and natural?

Building on the prompt engineering concepts, Chapter 15 will explore the next evolution of LLMs: the creation of autonomous AI systems or agents, that can plan, reason, and take actions to achieve specific goals.

LLM AGENTS - BUILDING AUTONOMOUS AI SYSTEMS

Reflective Prompt: You are building an autonomous LLM Agent. Explain how the emergence of these systems raises fascinating questions about the nature of intelligence and the future of human-AI collaboration.

INTRODUCTION AND CORE CONCEPTS

The evolution of Large Language Models has opened a new frontier: LLM Agents. These aren't just models that respond to prompts; they're autonomous systems that can plan, reason, and take actions to achieve specific goals. Think of an LLM Agent as a skilled assistant who not only understands your requests but can break them down into steps, use tools, remember context, and adapt its approach based on outcomes. At their core, LLM Agents are autonomous systems that combine advanced language understanding and generation with goal-oriented reasoning and action, as shown in Fig.15.1.

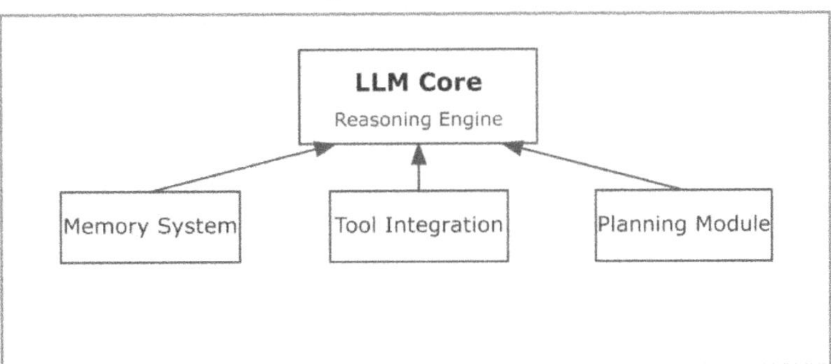

Fig. 15.1: The diagram illustrates the fundamental architecture of an LLM Agent, with the LLM Core (reasoning engine) at its centre connected to three key capabilities: memory systems for information retention, tool integration for external interactions, and planning modules for strategic decision-making.

CORE CAPABILITIES: THE BUILDING BLOCKS OF LLM AGENTS

At the heart of every effective LLM Agent lies a sophisticated interplay of capabilities that transform a simple language model into an autonomous system. These core capabilities include:
1. Memory Systems: Enabling agents to store, retrieve, and learn from information
2. Planning and Reasoning: Allowing agents to break down tasks, set goals, and adapt strategies
3. Tool Integration: Empowering agents to interact with external systems and perform actions
4. Adaptive Learning: Facilitating continuous improvement and learning from experience

Let's dive deep into each of these building blocks and understand how they work together.

Memory Systems: Beyond Simple Context

Memory in LLM Agents mirrors how humans process and retain information, but with the precision of digital systems. Think of it as building a brain that can not only remember conversations but also learn from experiences and accumulate knowledge.

Memory is a critical component of LLM Agents, enabling them to store and retrieve information across conversations, learn from past experiences, and build up knowledge over time, much like humans do.

How Memory Works in Agents

An agent's memory architecture consists of three interconnected systems:

1. **Working Memory (Short-term)** This is where immediate context lives - the ongoing conversation, recent actions, and current task state. Like a human's working memory, it has limited capacity but provides quick access to relevant information. In practice, this is often implemented as a sliding window over recent interactions.
2. **Episodic Memory (Experience-based)** This system stores complete interactions and experiences. When an agent faces a new situation, it can recall similar past experiences to inform its decisions. The implementation typically uses vector embeddings to enable semantic search across past experiences.
3. **Semantic Memory (Knowledge based)** Think of this as the agent's accumulated knowledge base. It stores facts, relationships, and learned patterns in a structured way, often using knowledge graphs or other structured formats.

Practical Implementation

In the real-world, building this memory architecture leverages several key technologies. LangChain, one of the most popular frameworks, provides built-in memory classes:

```
from langchain.memory import ConversationBufferMemory
memory = ConversationBufferMemory(return_messages=True)
```

For more sophisticated needs, vector databases become essential. Common choices include:
- Chroma for development and small-scale deployments
- Pinecone for production systems needing managed infrastructure
- Weaviate when you need complex semantic search capabilities

The choice depends on your scale and requirements. For instance, a customer service agent might use Pinecone to store thousands of past interactions, while a personal assistant might work fine with Chroma running locally.

Best Practices and Considerations

When implementing memory systems, consider:
1. Memory Persistence: How long should different types of information be retained?
2. Privacy Requirements: What information should be stored, and how should it be protected?
3. Retrieval Strategy: How do you ensure the most relevant information is recalled?

Here's a common pattern for managing different memory types:

```
1.   class AgentMemory:
2.     def __init__(self):
3.        # Choose storage based on your needs
4.        self.working_memory = ConversationBufferMemory()
5.        self.episodic_store = ChromaDB()  # For development
6.        # self.episodic_store = Pinecone()  # For production
7.
8.     async def store_interaction(self, interaction):
9.        # Store in working memory
10.       self.working_memory.save_context(interaction)
11.
12.       # Determine if interaction should be stored long term
13.       if self.is_significant(interaction):
14.          await self.episodic_store.add(interaction)
```

Code Exhibit 15.1: The AgentMemory class implements a dual-memory architecture combining short-term working memory for immediate context and long-term episodic storage for persistent knowledge. This design mirrors human memory systems, allowing agents to maintain both immediate conversation context and learn from significant past interactions.

When building your own agent's memory system, start simple and scale up as needed. Begin with basic conversation memory, then add long-term storage as your use case demands it. Popular frameworks like LangChain make this incremental approach practical.

Planning and Reasoning: The Strategic Mind of Agents

Planning and reasoning are the cognitive capabilities that allow LLM Agents to break down complex tasks, set goals, formulate strategies, and adapt their approach based on ongoing results and challenges. Planning and reasoning transform a reactive chatbot into a strategic agent. This capability enables agents to break down complex tasks, formulate strategies, and adapt their approach based on progress and obstacles.

How Planning Works in Agents

The planning system typically operates in three key phases:

1. **Task Decomposition** Agents break complex goals into manageable subtasks. For instance, when asked to "analyse market trends and prepare a report," an agent might decompose this into: gathering data, identifying patterns, analysing competitors, and synthesising findings.

2. **Strategy Formation** For each subtask, the agent determines the best approach, including:

Which tools to use-
   o What information to gather
   o How to sequence actions
   o What success looks like

3. **Execution and Adaptation** As the agent executes its plan, it continuously monitors progress and adjusts its strategy based on intermediate results.

Practical Implementation

Modern frameworks offer different approaches to implementing planning. LangChain's ReAct (Reasoning and Acting) framework is particularly popular:

```
1.    from langchain.agents import create_react_agent
2.    from langchain.tools import Tool
3.
4.    # Define available tools
5.    tools = [
6.      Tool(
7.         name="search",
8.         func=search_engine.search,
9.         description="Useful for searching current information"
10.     ),
11.     Tool(
12.        name="calculator",
13.        func=calculator.calculate,
14.        description="Useful for mathematical calculations"
15.     )
16.  ]
17.
18.  # Create a ReAct agent
19.  agent = create_react_agent(
20.     llm=llm,
21.     tools=tools,
22.     verbose=True
23.  )
```

Code Exhibit 15.2: This implementation creates a ReAct (Reasoning and Acting) agent equipped with search and calculation capabilities. The agent uses LangChain's framework to systematically reason about tasks and select appropriate tools, following the ReAct paradigm of breaking down complex queries into actionable steps.

This process of decomposition, strategy formation, and adaptation allows LLM agents to tackle complex, multi-step problems in a structured and flexible manner.

For more sophisticated planning needs, you might consider:

o   AutoGPT for autonomous long-running tasks

o   BabyAGI for task prioritization and management

o   Chain-of-Thought prompting for complex reasoning

Tool Integration: Extending Agent Capabilities

Tool integration is what transforms an LLM from a conversational partner into a capable actor in the digital world. Like giving hands to a brain, tools allow agents to interact with external systems, access real-time information, and perform concrete actions.

Understanding Tool Integration

Think of tool integration as building a skilled worker's toolbox. Each tool serves a specific purpose, and the agent must know not just what each tool does, but when and how to use it effectively.

In the context of LLM Agents, tools refer to the specific capabilities or APIs that an agent can access and utilise to perform actions or retrieve information, while skills refer to the higher-level abilities that emerge from the combination of these tools.

The tool integration system handles three critical functions:

1. **Tool Discovery and Selection**
   o Understanding tool capabilities
   o Matching tools to tasks
   o Managing tool permissions and access
2. **Tool Execution**
   o Preparing inputs
   o Handling execution
   o Managing errors and retries
3. **Result Integration**
   o Processing tool outputs
   o Combining multiple tool results
   o Incorporating results into the agent's reasoning

Modern Tool Integration Approaches

LangChain Tools Framework

```
1.    from langchain.agents import Tool, initialize_agent
2.    from langchain.tools import BaseTool
3.
4.
5.    class CustomDatabaseTool(BaseTool):
6.      name = "database_search"
7.      description = "Search the database for specific records"
8.
9.      def _run(self, query: str) -> str:
10.        # Implement actual database search
11.        return database.search(query)
```

Code Exhibit 15.3: This implementation extends LangChain's tool framework to create a custom database search capability, enabling agents to directly query databases through a standardized tool interface.

You can see in the code database search tool is created with a description of what it does. An agent based on the description decides when to call this tool to access data.

Common Tool Categories and Examples

1. **Information Access**
   o Web search (DuckDuckGo, Google Custom Search)
   o Database queries (SQL, MongoDB)
   o API calls (REST, GraphQL)
2. **Data Processing**
   o Calculators
   o Data analysis (Pandas)
   o Text processing

3. **External Actions**
   o Email sending
   o File operations
   o API interactions

Adaptive Learning: Building Self-Improving Agents

Adaptive learning refers to the ability of LLM agents to continuously improve their performance and acquire new knowledge based on their interactions and experiences, without the need for explicit retraining.

Understanding Adaptive Learning

Adaptive learning in agents operates across three key dimensions:

1. **Performance Learning**
   o Tracking success and failure patterns
   o Understanding which strategies work best
   o Optimising tool selection and usage

2. **Context Learning**
   o Building user preference models
   o Understanding domain-specific patterns
   o Improving context interpretation

3. **Strategy Refinement**
   o Optimising task decomposition
   o Refining prompt strategies
   o Enhancing tool combinations

Adaptive Learning: Framework Support and Implementation

While adaptive learning is still an evolving field, several frameworks provide building blocks for implementing learning capabilities in agents. Let's explore the practical approaches using current tools.

LangChain's Approach

LangChain provides several components that can be used for adaptive learning:

```python
1.   from langchain.callbacks import BaseCallbackHandler
2.   from langchain.memory import VectorStoreRetrieverMemory
3.   from langchain.chat_models import ChatOpenAI
4.   from langchain.agents import AgentExecutor, create_react_agent
5.
6.
7.   class LearningCallback(BaseCallbackHandler):
8.     def __init__(self):
9.       self.feedback_store = VectorStore()
10.
11.    def on_chain_end(self, outputs, **kwargs):
12.      # Store successful chains
13.      self.feedback_store.add(
14.        outputs,
15.        metadata={"success": True}
16.      )
```

```
17.
18.    def on_chain_error(self, error, **kwargs):
19.        # Learn from failures
20.        self.feedback_store.add(
21.            error,
22.            metadata={"success": False}
23.        )
24.
25.
26.  class AdaptiveLangChainAgent:
27.    def __init__(self):
28.        # Initialize memory with vector store
29.        self.memory = VectorStoreRetrieverMemory(
30.            vectorstore=Chroma(
31.                collection_name="agent_experiences"
32.            )
33.        )
34.
35.        # Create agent with learning callbacks
36.        self.agent = AgentExecutor.from_agent_and_tools(
37.            agent=create_react_agent(llm, tools),
38.            tools=tools,
39.            memory=self.memory,
40.            callbacks=[LearningCallback()],
41.            verbose=True
42.        )
43.
44.        # Track performance metrics
45.        self.metrics = AgentMetrics()
```

Code Exhibit 15.4: This implementation creates an adaptive agent that learns from both successes and failures, storing experiences in a vector database for future reference. The LearningCallback system enables continuous improvement by capturing interaction outcomes, while the AgentExecutor integrates memory, tools, and performance tracking for enhanced decision-making.

However, adaptive learning also poses challenges, such as the potential for agents to learn undesirable behaviours or to overfit to specific situations, requiring careful monitoring and adjustment of learning parameters.

ADVANCED TOPICS: MULTI-AGENT SYSTEMS AND COLLABORATION

The future of LLM Agents lies not just in individual capabilities, but in their ability to work together. Multi-agent systems enable complex problem-solving through specialised agents working in concert.

Much like how a team of experts with diverse skills can tackle complex projects more effectively than any individual, a well-coordinated multi-agent system has the potential to break down large, multifaceted problems into specialised subtasks that can be handled by purpose-built agents. This is illustrated in Fig.15.2.

Multi-Agent System Architecture

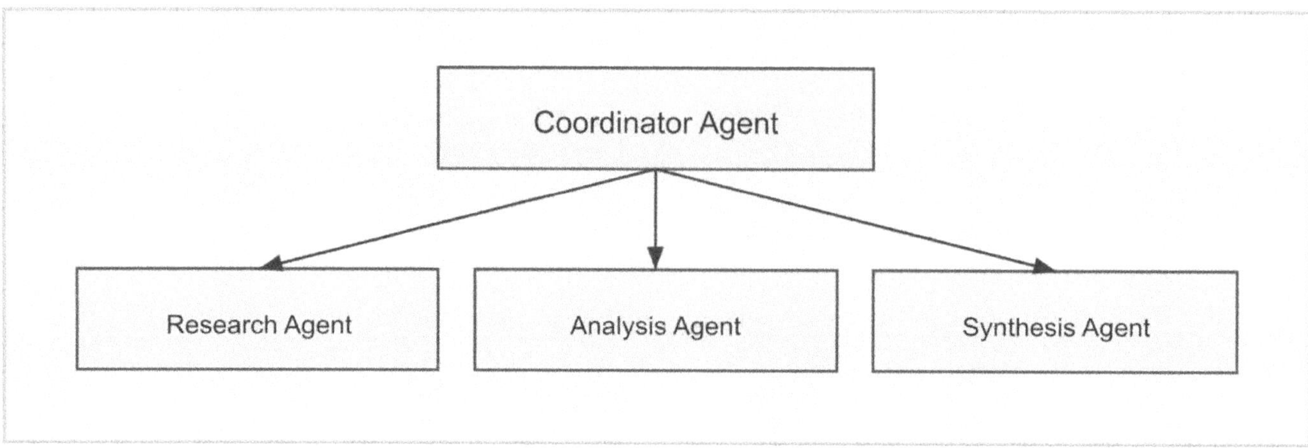

Fig15.2: A visualization of a multi-agent system's architecture, featuring a Coordinator Agent at the top level that manages and delegates tasks to specialised agents below. The connecting arrows demonstrate the communication flow and hierarchical relationship between the coordinator and the specialised agents (Research, Analysis, and Synthesis) that perform specific aspects of complex tasks.

Implementation with Modern Frameworks

LangChain provides building blocks for multi-agent systems:

```
1.    class MultiAgentSystem:
2.      def __init__(self):
3.        self.coordinator = CoordinatorAgent()
4.        self.agents = {
5.          'research': ResearchAgent(),
6.          'analysis': AnalysisAgent(),
7.          'synthesis': SynthesisAgent()
8.        }
9.        self.message_bus = MessageBus()
10.
11.     async def execute_task(self, task: ComplexTask):
12.        # Coordinator breaks down task
13.        subtasks = await self.coordinator.decompose_task(task)
14.
15.        # Assign subtasks to specialized agents
16.        results = []
17.        for subtask in subtasks:
18.          agent = self.agents[subtask.agent_type]
19.          result = await agent.execute(subtask)
20.          results.append(result)
21.
22.        # Synthesize results
23.        return await self.coordinator.synthesize_results(results)
```

Code Exhibit 15.5: This implementation orchestrates a multi-agent system where a coordinator agent decomposes complex tasks, delegates to specialised agents through a message bus, and synthesises their results into a cohesive output.

Key challenges in designing effective multi-agent systems include coordination mechanisms, communication protocols, and ensuring alignment of individual agent goals with the overall system objectives.

Best Practices for Multi-Agent Systems

1. **Design Principles**
   o Clear agent responsibilities
   o Well-defined communication protocols
   o Robust error handling
   o Efficient resource management

2. **Implementation Guidelines**
   o Start with simple agent interactions
   o Add complexity gradually
   o Monitor and optimise performance
   o Maintain system stability

When implementing multi-agent systems, developers have several powerful frameworks to choose from, each serving different needs in the ecosystem. LangChain remains the most mature solution with extensive tool integration and documentation, making it ideal for building initial multi-agent systems or when extensive tool integration is needed. Microsoft's AutoGen excels in scenarios requiring complex agent-to-agent conversations and autonomous interactions, providing sophisticated group chat capabilities that feel more natural. Semantic Kernel, another Microsoft offering, stands out in enterprise settings with its structured approach to skills and Azure integration. The newer CrewAI framework takes an intuitive role-based approach that's particularly effective for task-oriented systems. AWS Bedrock's agent capabilities, while newer to the space, offer strong enterprise-grade features with seamless AWS service integration, built-in knowledge bases, and robust security - making it particularly attractive for organizations heavily invested in the AWS ecosystem or requiring strict enterprise controls. For most developers starting with multi-agent systems, LangChain provides the gentlest learning curve and broadest community support. However, if your project requires sophisticated inter-agent dialogue, AutoGen might be the better choice. Enterprise projects with AWS infrastructure would benefit from Bedrock's native integration capabilities, Azure-centric projects would find Semantic Kernel valuable, while teams looking for intuitive task-based agent collaboration should consider CrewAI.

FUTURE DIRECTIONS AND CHALLENGES

The rapid evolution of LLM Agents has showcased their potential to revolutionize how we interact with AI systems and tackle complex, open-ended problems across various domains. The landscape of LLM Agents is rapidly evolving, presenting both exciting opportunities and significant challenges. As we look toward the future, several key trends and challenges are shaping the development of these systems.

Emerging Capabilities

1. Multi-Modal Agents: Integrating vision, speech, and other modalities will enable richer, more natural interactions and expand the range of tasks LLM Agents can handle.
2. Autonomous Learning: As LLM agents become more autonomous in their learning, key challenges will include ensuring the quality and safety of learned behaviours and mitigating potential negative feedback loops.
3. Ethical Considerations: Ensuring LLM agents respect privacy, avoid biases, and remain transparent in their reasoning and decision-making will be critical for building trust and acceptance of these systems.
4. Resource Optimization: Advanced techniques like model compression, efficient inference, and hardware acceleration will be essential for deploying LLM Agents at scale while minimising computational costs and environmental impact.

SOCIETAL IMPACT OF LLM AGENTS

As LLM agents become more sophisticated and widely adopted, their impact on society will be significant. In healthcare, LLM agents could assist in diagnosis, treatment planning, and patient support, potentially improving outcomes and reducing healthcare costs. In education, these agents could enable personalised learning, intelligent tutoring systems, and increased accessibility for students with diverse needs.

In the business world, LLM agents have the potential to enhance customer service, automate tasks, and improve decision-making processes. They could also collaborate with humans in creative industries, such as design, writing, and content creation, leading to new forms of expression and innovation.

However, the widespread adoption of LLM agents also raises concerns about job displacement, privacy, and the need for responsible development. As these technologies advance, it will be crucial to address these challenges and ensure that the benefits of LLM agents are distributed equitably across society.

DISCUSSION

The journey of LLM Agents showcases a remarkable evolution from simple prompt-response systems to sophisticated autonomous collaborators. Through our exploration of memory systems, planning capabilities, and tool integration, we've seen how modern agents have transcended basic chatbot functionality to become powerful problem-solving entities. The emergence of multi-agent systems, supported by frameworks like LangChain, AutoGPT, and BabyAGI, marks a significant milestone in this evolution. Expert practitioners consistently emphasise starting with focused, single-agent implementations before scaling to multi-agent architectures, prioritizing efficient memory management, and carefully selecting tools based on core functionalities rather than maximizing integrations.

Looking forward, the field stands at an exciting intersection of capability and complexity. While current implementations demonstrate impressive abilities in task decomposition, memory management, and tool utilization, the future points toward more sophisticated multi-modal interactions and truly adaptive learning systems. The key challenge lies not in building more powerful individual agents, but in creating effective collaborative ecosystems that maintain reliability while pushing the boundaries of what's possible. As we continue to develop these systems, the focus shifts from individual agent capabilities to orchestrating seamless collaboration while addressing crucial considerations of efficiency, ethics, and practical utility.

The future of LLM Agents is not just about technological advancement, but about redefining how we interact with and leverage AI systems. As these agents become more integrated into various domains, from personal assistants to research aids and beyond, they have the potential to transform how we learn, create, and solve problems. However, realising this potential requires a thoughtful balance of innovation and responsibility. By developing agents that are not only capable but also aligned with human values, transparent in their reasoning, and robust in their performance, we can harness their power to drive positive change. The path forward lies in embracing the challenges and opportunities of this exciting frontier, guided by a commitment to creating LLM Agents that augment and empower human intelligence while remaining grounded in the principles of ethical and responsible AI development.

KEY TAKEAWAYS:

1. LLM Agents combine advanced language understanding and generation with goal-oriented reasoning and action, transforming them from simple response systems into autonomous collaborators.
2. Key capabilities of LLM Agents include sophisticated memory systems, planning and reasoning abilities, integration with external tools, and adaptive learning.
3. The development of multi-agent systems, where specialised agents work together to tackle complex problems, represents an exciting frontier in the field of LLM-powered AI.

REFLECTIVE PROMPTS:

1. The emergence of LLM Agents, as described in this chapter, raises fascinating questions about the nature of intelligence and the future of human-AI collaboration. How might these advancements in autonomous systems influence our understanding of cognition and the potential for artificial general intelligence?
2. The integration of LLM Agents with external tools and their ability to learn and adapt based on experience suggest a paradigm shift in how we interact with and leverage intelligent systems. What are the potential societal implications of these autonomous AI collaborators being deployed in various domains, from healthcare to education to creative industries?
3. The development of multi-agent systems, where specialised agents work together to solve complex problems, highlights the importance of coordinated intelligence and the challenges in aligning the goals and behaviours of artificial agents. What ethical considerations and governance frameworks might be necessary to ensure these multi-agent systems operate in a manner that benefits humanity as a whole?

As we reach the conclusion of our exploration, Chapter 16 will look ahead to the future of Large Language Models, examining the emerging trends and innovations that promise to reshape the landscape of artificial intelligence.

THE FUTURE OF LARGE LANGUAGE MODELS - BREAKING NEW FRONTIERS

Reflective Prompt: The LLM architecture is evolving. Describe how the revolutionary architectural innovations, such as sparse transformers and multimodal integration, demonstrate the continued pursuit of more efficient and versatile AI systems.

INTRODUCTION: STANDING AT THE EDGE OF INNOVATION

The field of Large Language Models stands at a fascinating crossroads. Like the early days of the internet, we're witnessing the emergence of technologies that will fundamentally reshape how we interact with artificial intelligence. This chapter explores the exciting frontiers that lie ahead. Fig.16.1. illustrates the timeline from the past to a possible future.

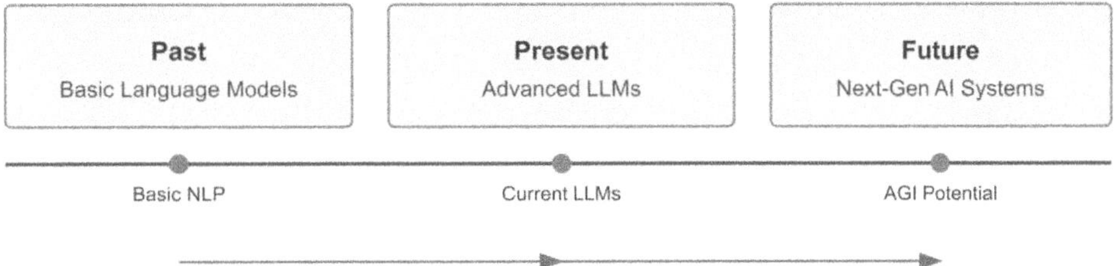

Fig. 16.1: This timeline visualization shows the progression of language models from basic NLP through current LLMs to potential Artificial General Intelligence (AGI), highlighting key milestones and transitions in the field's development.

The future of Large Language Models is being shaped by four interconnected trends: revolutionary architectures that enable more efficient processing, multimodal capabilities that break down barriers between different types of data, new learning paradigms that make models more adaptable, and progress toward artificial general intelligence. Each of these developments builds upon and enables the others, creating a virtuous cycle of innovation that pushes the boundaries of what's possible with AI technology.

REVOLUTIONARY ARCHITECTURES

The need for new architectures stems from the increasing demands placed on language models. As we push towards more complex tasks and larger datasets, traditional transformer architectures face challenges in computational efficiency, memory usage, and specialised processing capabilities. These challenges have sparked innovations that are reshaping how we build and deploy LLMs.

The Evolution Beyond Transformers

The familiar Transformer architecture that revolutionised NLP in 2017 is evolving into more sophisticated forms. Three key innovations are reshaping how we build LLMs (see Fig.16.2):

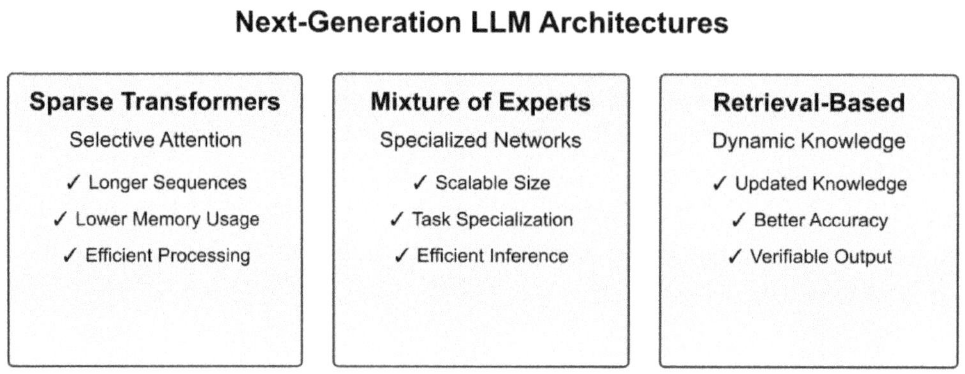

Next-Generation LLM Architectures

Fig. 16.2: This comparative diagram illustrates the three major architectural innovations in LLMs: Sparse Transformers for efficient attention, Mixture of Experts for specialised processing, and Retrieval-Based models for dynamic knowledge access. Each approach is shown with its key advantages and characteristics.

These architectural innovations represent more than just technical improvements; they are enabling fundamentally new capabilities in language models. Sparse Transformers make it possible to process longer sequences efficiently, enabling better understanding of complex documents and conversations. Mixture of Experts allows models to develop specialised knowledge across different domains, while Retrieval-Based approaches provide access to vast amounts of knowledge without increasing model size. Together, these advances create the foundation for more sophisticated AI systems.

BREAKING DOWN MODAL BARRIERS

The architectural innovations discussed above have made it possible to break free from the constraints of text-only processing. Efficient attention mechanisms and specialised expert networks are particularly crucial for handling the complex interactions between different types of data, enabling the next evolution in AI: true multimodal understanding.

The Rise of Multimodal AI

As we move beyond pure text processing, LLMs are evolving to understand and generate multiple types of content simultaneously. This represents a fundamental shift in how AI systems process and interact with information.

This convergence of modalities represents a fundamental shift in how AI systems understand and interact with the world. Just as humans naturally integrate visual, auditory, and textual information to make sense of their environment, modern LLMs are developing the ability to process and synthesize information across multiple channels simultaneously, as illustrated in Fig.16.3.

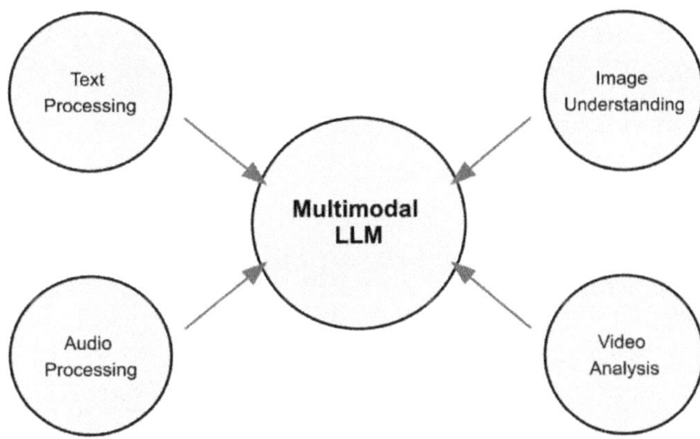

Fig. 16.3: This diagram shows how modern LLMs are integrating different types of data (text, images, audio, video) through unified processing architectures, illustrating the convergence of previously separate AI domains.

The field of multimodal integration has witnessed remarkable advancements, revolutionizing how AI systems perceive and interact with the world. Vision-language models have made significant strides in understanding and generating visual content from natural language descriptions, with potential applications in healthcare, robotics, and education. Simultaneously, audio-language integration has enabled more natural and intuitive conversational interfaces, enhancing accessibility features for individuals with hearing or speech impairments.

At the core of these developments is cross-modal learning, which allows AI systems to develop a unified understanding across different modalities. By leveraging the commonalities and complementary information present in various data types, these models can learn more comprehensive representations of the world, enabling seamless transfer learning between modalities. As research in multimodal integration continues to progress, we can expect AI systems that not only understand the world more deeply but also interact with it in increasingly sophisticated and intuitive ways, transforming industries and unlocking new frontiers in artificial intelligence.

NEW LEARNING PARADIGMS

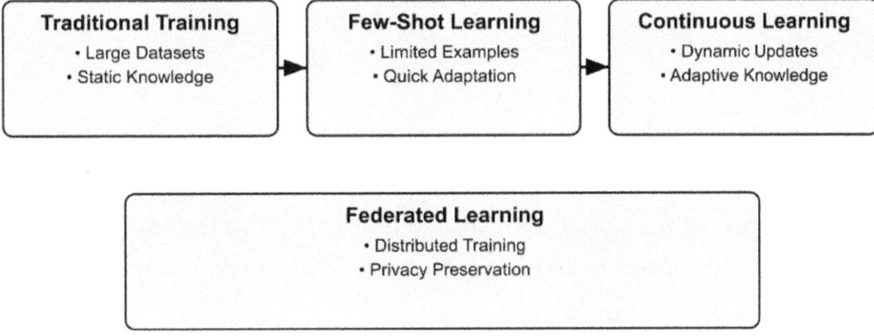

Fig. 16.4: This visualization shows the progression from traditional training methods to advanced learning paradigms, highlighting how modern LLMs are becoming more adaptable and efficient in their learning processes.

The landscape of artificial intelligence is witnessing the emergence of innovative learning approaches that are set to redefine how AI systems acquire and apply knowledge (see Fig. 16.4). Few-shot and zero-shot learning enable AI models to rapidly adapt to new tasks with minimal or no example data, opening up a world of possibilities for tackling a broader range of challenges without extensive retraining. Simultaneously, continuous learning systems are pushing the boundaries of adaptability by allowing AI models to update their knowledge in real-time, eliminating the need for periodic retraining and ensuring their relevance and effectiveness in rapidly changing environments.

As AI becomes increasingly integrated into various aspects of our lives, federated learning emerges as a promising solution to address data privacy and security concerns. By enabling collaborative training of AI models on distributed data sources without centralised data collection, federated learning preserves the privacy of individual data contributors while democratising access to AI technology. This decentralised approach to knowledge acquisition not only enhances data security but also unlocks new opportunities for secure and privacy-preserving AI applications across industries, from healthcare to finance and beyond, paving the way for a more inclusive and responsible AI ecosystem.

These learning paradigms work synergistically with the architectural innovations discussed earlier. Sparse attention mechanisms make few-shot learning more efficient, while Mixture of Experts architectures naturally complement continuous learning approaches by allowing different components to specialize and adapt independently. This integration of advanced architectures and learning methods is creating AI systems that are more adaptable and capable than ever before.

THE PATH TOWARD ARTIFICIAL GENERAL INTELLIGENCE

The Path to AGI: Key Milestones

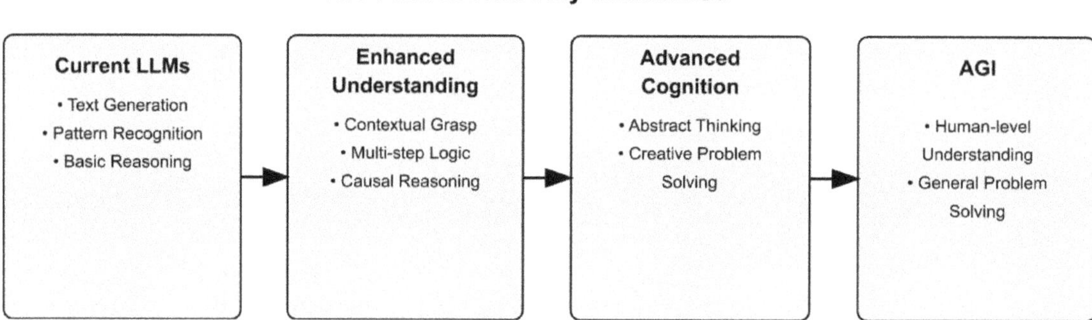

Fig. 16.5: This visualization maps the progression from current LLMs towards AGI, highlighting key capabilities and milestones along the path.

The convergence of revolutionary architectures, multimodal capabilities, and new learning paradigms brings us closer to artificial general intelligence (AGI) than ever before, see Fig.16.5. Each development contributes essential pieces to the AGI puzzle: efficient processing enables complex reasoning, multimodal understanding provides rich world knowledge, and adaptive learning allows for continuous improvement and generalisation.

As artificial intelligence systems continue to evolve and scale, there are emerging signs that suggest the potential for the development of general intelligence. One of the most compelling indicators is the observation of scaling effects, where AI models exhibit unexpected and emergent abilities as their size and complexity increase. These models, when trained on vast amounts of data and with advanced architectures, have shown the capacity for complex reasoning and problem-solving that goes beyond their initial training objectives. This emergence of unforeseen capabilities hints at the possibility of a more general form of intelligence that can adapt and apply knowledge across a wide range of domains.

Another crucial aspect of the journey towards general intelligence is the development of grounded understanding in AI systems. By integrating real-world context and modelling physical world dynamics, these systems are beginning to demonstrate practical reasoning abilities that extend beyond mere pattern recognition. This grounded understanding enables AI to make more informed decisions and navigate complex, real-world scenarios with greater flexibility and adaptability. Moreover, the emergence of advanced reasoning capabilities, such as multi-step problem-solving, abstract concept manipulation, and logical deduction, further underscores the potential for AI to achieve human-like cognitive abilities. As these systems continue to evolve and incorporate more sophisticated reasoning mechanisms, they move closer to exhibiting the hallmarks of general intelligence, opening up new frontiers in AI research and application.

While true AGI remains a future goal, the foundations being laid today through architectural innovations, multimodal integration, and advanced learning approaches are creating clear stepping stones toward more general artificial intelligence. Each advancement in these areas brings us closer to systems that can understand, reason, and learn in ways that increasingly resemble human cognitive capabilities.

ETHICAL CONSIDERATIONS AND CHALLENGES

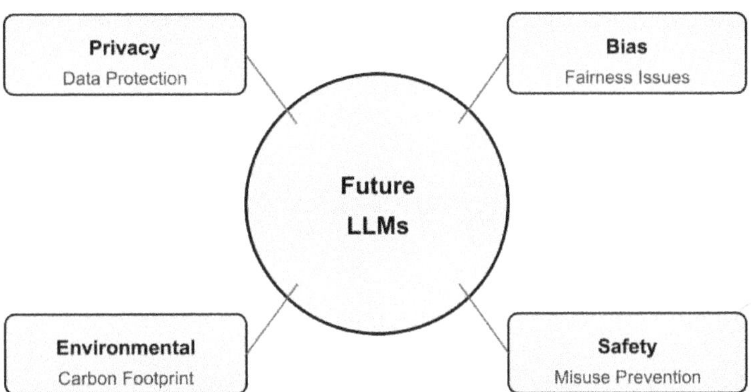

Fig. 16.6: This diagram illustrates the interconnected ethical considerations and technical challenges facing future LLM development.

As AI systems become more advanced and integrated into various aspects of our lives, it is crucial to address the key ethical considerations that arise from their development and deployment (see Fig.16.6). One of the most pressing concerns is the issue of privacy and data protection. With AI models relying on vast amounts of user data for training and operation, ensuring the security and confidentiality of this information is of utmost importance. Robust data protection measures, such as encryption, anonymisation, and strict access controls, must be implemented to safeguard user privacy. Additionally, obtaining informed consent from individuals whose data is used for AI training is essential to maintain trust and transparency in the development process.

Another critical ethical consideration in the realm of AI is bias and fairness. AI systems are only as unbiased as the data they are trained on, and ensuring fair representation in training datasets is crucial to prevent the perpetuation of societal biases. Developers must actively work to identify and mitigate biases in both the input data and the resulting outputs, striving for equitable treatment of all individuals regardless of their demographics. Moreover, the environmental impact of AI cannot be overlooked. The energy-intensive nature of AI training and inference processes contributes to a significant carbon footprint, necessitating the development of more sustainable and energy-efficient approaches. Researchers and industry leaders must prioritise the creation of AI systems that minimise energy consumption and promote environmental sustainability. Lastly, the safety and security of AI systems are of paramount importance. Stringent measures must be put in place to prevent the misuse of AI technologies for malicious purposes, such as content filtering to identify and block harmful or illegal material. Robust security protocols and continuous monitoring are essential to protect AI systems from cyber threats and ensure their responsible deployment in society.

INDUSTRY-SPECIFIC TRANSFORMATIONS:

The future of LLMs holds immense promise for transforming various industries. In healthcare, LLMs could advance biomedical research, accelerate drug discovery, and enable more personalised medicine. They could also revolutionise the finance industry by enhancing risk assessment, detecting fraud, and improving customer service.

In the legal domain, LLMs could assist in legal research, contract analysis, and case preparation, making legal services more efficient and accessible. LLMs also have the potential to transform transportation by improving autonomous vehicles, optimizing traffic management, and streamlining logistics.

While these industry-specific applications offer significant benefits, such as increased efficiency and innovation, they also present challenges. Adapting LLMs to specific domains may require extensive fine-tuning and domain-specific data, raising concerns about data privacy and regulatory compliance. As LLMs are integrated into various industries, it will be essential to address these challenges and develop best practices for their responsible deployment.

FUTURE DIRECTIONS OF LLMS

The essential points of the future directions of LLMs is depicted in Fig.16.7.

Essential Points for the Future:

1. Technical Innovation:
- Architectural advances will continue to improve efficiency and scalability
- Multimodal capabilities will become standard features
- Enhanced reasoning abilities will emerge from the integration of various architectural and learning innovations

2. Ethical Development:
- Privacy-first approaches will be built into architecture design
- Bias mitigation will be integrated into training processes
- Environmental impact will guide architectural choices and deployment strategies

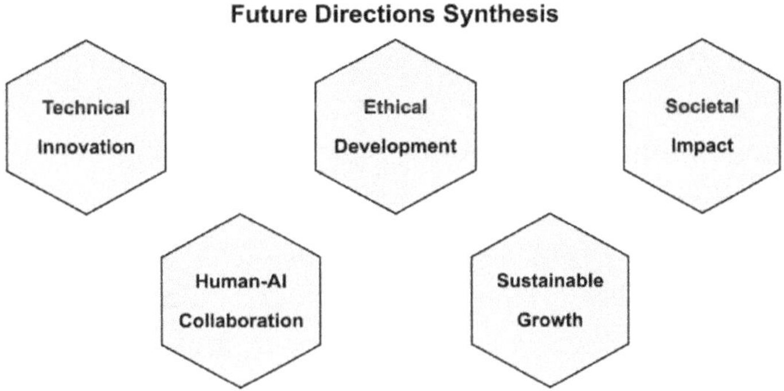

Fig. 16.7: This final visualization summarises the key developments and considerations for the future of LLMs.

3. Practical Impact:
- Democratised access through more efficient architectures
- Personalized learning enabled by multimodal understanding
- Scientific discovery accelerated by improved reasoning capabilities

4. Path Forward:
- Balanced approach combining architectural innovation with ethical considerations
- Collaborative development frameworks supporting responsible advancement
- Integration of technical capabilities with societal needs and constraints

The future of Large Language Models holds immense promise, but realising this potential requires careful navigation of technical, ethical, and societal considerations. As we move forward, the focus must remain on developing these powerful technologies in ways that benefit humanity while mitigating potential risks.

DISCUSSION

The exploration of future frontiers in Large Language Models reveals a fascinating convergence of multiple technological streams. From the mathematical foundations explored in Chapter 1 through the architectural innovations detailed in Chapters 7 and 8, to the sophisticated deployment strategies discussed in Chapter 12, we're witnessing not just technological progress, but a fundamental reimagining of what's possible in artificial intelligence. The evolution from current transformer architectures to more sophisticated forms like sparse transformers and mixture of experts demonstrates not just architectural innovation, but deeper insights into how we can structure AI systems to process information more efficiently and effectively.

What makes the future of LLMs particularly intriguing is its position at the intersection of multiple transformative technologies. While previous chapters focused on current capabilities and implementations, this forward-looking chapter shows how different advances - from multimodal integration to new learning paradigms - could combine to create systems of unprecedented capability. Expert practitioners consistently emphasise the importance of balancing innovation with responsibility, suggesting that future developments should focus not just on raw capabilities but on creating systems that are efficient, ethical, and aligned with human values. The careful consideration of both technical advancement and ethical implications becomes increasingly crucial as these models grow in sophistication and societal impact.

Looking ahead to how these future developments might interact with the autonomous agents discussed in Chapter 15 and building upon the responsible AI principles explored in Chapter 11, the path forward becomes both exciting and sobering. The convergence of multimodal capabilities, advanced architectures, and new learning paradigms suggests possibilities far beyond current applications, but also raises important questions about safety, ethics, and societal impact. Current developments in areas like sparse attention mechanisms and adaptive learning show promise in addressing scaling challenges, but they also remind us that the future of LLMs lies not just in more powerful models, but in finding fundamentally more efficient and responsible ways to advance artificial intelligence. Success in this domain will ultimately depend not just on technological innovation, but on our ability to develop these systems in ways that benefit humanity while carefully managing potential risks.

KEY TAKEAWAYS:

1. Revolutionary architectures, such as sparse transformers, mixture of experts, and retrieval-based models, are driving the evolution of LLMs beyond standard transformer designs.
2. Multimodal AI, integrating text, images, audio, and video, is breaking down barriers between data types and enabling a richer understanding and generation.
3. New learning paradigms, including few-shot learning, meta-learning, and continual learning, are crucial for creating more adaptable and efficient LLMs.

REFLECTIVE PROMPTS:

1. The architectural innovations discussed in this chapter, such as sparse transformers and mixture of experts, demonstrate the continued pursuit of more efficient and scalable AI systems. How might these advancements shape the future of hardware-software co-design and the interplay between model development and deployment considerations?
2. The integration of multimodal capabilities in LLMs, as explored in this chapter, suggests a more holistic approach to language understanding and generation. What are the potential implications of this shift for human-AI interaction, and how might it influence the way we conceptualise and design intelligent systems?
3. The new learning paradigms, including few-shot and continual learning, point to the ongoing quest for AI systems that can adapt and generalise more effectively. What are the ethical implications of these advancements, particularly in terms of safety, robustness, and the reliable deployment of LLMs in real-world applications?

As we close this journey, Chapter 17 will reflect on the transformative potential of Large Language Models and the path forward for realising their benefits while navigating the challenges and responsibilities they bring.

CONCLUSION AND FUTURE OUTLOOK - EMBRACING THE LLM ERA

Reflective Prompt: As we stand at the precipice of the LLM era, what are the most pressing challenges and opportunities that must be addressed to ensure these transformative technologies benefit all of humanity?

BACKGROUND

As we reach the end of our exploration of Large Language Models, it's clear that we are not at a conclusion, but at the precipice of a new beginning. The LLM era is upon us, and it promises to reshape the very fabric of how we interact with technology, knowledge, and each other.

Having journeyed through the technical depths of LLMs - from their mathematical foundations to advanced architectures, from optimization strategies to ethical considerations - we now stand equipped to both harness their extraordinary potential and navigate the profound responsibilities they bring. Our deep understanding of these systems' inner workings reveals not just their capabilities, but the crucial role we must play in shaping their development.

THE TRANSFORMATIVE POWER OF LLMS

Throughout this book, we've witnessed the extraordinary capabilities of Large Language Models. From their intricate neural architectures to their vast knowledge spanning countless domains, LLMs are not merely tools; they are intellectual partners that can understand, generate, and reason with human language in ways that were once the stuff of science fiction.

The implications are profound. LLMs are breaking down the barriers between humans and machines, enabling interactions that are more natural, intuitive, and empowering than ever before. They are democratising access to knowledge and creativity, putting the power of sophisticated language AI into the hands of individuals and organizations across the globe.

Yet, as we've seen, LLMs are not without their challenges. Questions of bias, ethics, safety, environmental, and societal impact loom large. As these models become more integrated into the decision-making processes that shape our lives, we must confront these challenges head-on. We must ensure that the development and deployment of LLMs are guided by principles of fairness, transparency, and accountability.

These transformative capabilities, while extraordinary, come with profound implications for society. As we stand at this technological crossroads, the time for thoughtful action is now.

LOOKING BACK

Our exposition in the previous chapters about the Large Language Models and Generative AI can be summarised in the following points:

Technical Evolution:
1. Paradigm Shift: LLMs represent a significant leap in AI, enabling more general-purpose, human-like language understanding and generation.
2. Rapid Advancement: The field of LLMs is progressing at an unprecedented pace, with continuous improvements in model size, capability, and efficiency.
3. Multimodal Integration: The future of LLMs lies in seamless integration of multiple data types, such as text, images, and audio.

Societal Impact:
1. Transformative Impact: LLMs have the potential to revolutionize various domains, including healthcare, education, research, and creative industries.
2. Human-AI Collaboration: The most promising applications of LLMs involve enhancing human capabilities and fostering new forms of human-AI collaboration.
3. Democratisation and Accessibility: Advances in LLMs may lead to more widespread access to sophisticated language technologies.

Responsibility and Governance:
1. Ethical Imperatives: As LLMs grow more powerful, addressing ethical concerns around bias, privacy, transparency, and responsible deployment becomes critical.
2. Regulatory Landscape: The increasing societal integration of LLMs will necessitate the development of robust regulatory frameworks and governance models.
3. Environmental Considerations: Addressing the environmental impact of training and deploying large-scale models will be a critical focus for the AI community.

Future Preparedness:
1. Societal Readiness: As LLMs continue to advance, there is a growing need for public discourse and preparation for their potential impact on various aspects of society, such as employment and education.

The journey through understanding LLMs - from their mathematical foundations to their ethical implications - has prepared us for the responsibility of guiding their development. This deep understanding equips us with not just knowledge, but wisdom about how to harness these powerful tools for humanity's benefit.

These points underscore the transformative potential of Large Language Models and the complex landscape of opportunities and challenges they present. LLMs will undoubtedly play a pivotal role in shaping the trajectory of AI and its impact on society. The responsibility falls on researchers, developers, policymakers, and society at large to guide their development and application in ways that maximise benefits while mitigating potential risks.

As we close this exploration, we stand at the beginning of what promises to be the most exciting chapter in the story of artificial intelligence. Our path forward requires balancing technological enthusiasm with ethical responsibility, ensuring that the evolution of LLMs serves to enhance human knowledge, creativity, and well-being. The future beckons not with an ending, but with an invitation to shape the next era of human-AI collaboration.

THE CALL TO ACTION: SHAPING OUR AI FUTURE

The future of LLMs is not predetermined. It is a future that we, as researchers, developers, business leaders, policymakers, and citizens, have the power and the responsibility to shape. We stand at a pivotal moment in the history of artificial intelligence, and the choices we make today will reverberate for generations to come.

To the AI community, I say this: Let us approach the development of LLMs with a sense of purpose and a commitment to the greater good. Let us push the boundaries of what's possible, but always with an eye towards the ethical implications of our work. Let us strive to create models that are not only powerful but also fair, transparent, and accountable.

To business leaders and policymakers: Embrace the transformative potential of LLMs, but do so responsibly. Develop frameworks for ethical AI governance, create incentives for responsible innovation, and ensure that the benefits of these technologies are distributed equitably.

And to society at large: Engage with LLMs thoughtfully and critically. Embrace the opportunities they present for personal and societal growth, but also remain vigilant against potential misuse. Foster a culture of digital literacy and lifelong learning, so that we may all navigate this new era with wisdom and resilience.

This collective responsibility sets the stage for envisioning and creating a future where the potential of LLMs is realised in service of human flourishing.

A FUTURE UNBOUNDED: THE DAWN OF THE LLM ERA

As we step into the era of Large Language Models, a world of unprecedented possibilities emerges. LLMs have the potential to revolutionize how we learn, create, and tackle complex challenges. They could serve as tireless intellectual companions, accelerating scientific breakthroughs, enhancing education, and democratising access to knowledge.

However, with great power comes great responsibility. As we shape the future of LLMs, we must prioritise the development of AI systems that align with human values, promote ethical principles, and benefit society as a whole. This requires transparent, accountable, and responsible practices in the development and deployment of these technologies.

The path ahead is one we must navigate with wisdom and courage. The LLM era presents an opportunity to reimagine the relationship between humans and machines, exploring new frontiers of intelligence and creativity. It is up to us – researchers, developers, policymakers, and society – to seize this moment and shape a future where the power of language AI is harnessed for the greater good.

As we embark on this extraordinary journey, let us do so with open minds, bold visions, and a steadfast commitment to the responsible development and deployment of LLMs. Together, we can forge a path towards a brighter, more intelligent, and more interconnected world, where the synergy between human and artificial intelligence propels us to new heights of understanding, innovation, and progress.

The dawn of the LLM era is upon us, and the transformative potential is vast. Let us embrace the challenges and opportunities that lie ahead, ready to learn, grow, and shape a future in which the power of language AI benefits all of humanity.

DISCUSSION

The journey through Large Language Models we've undertaken in this book - from mathematical foundations to future possibilities - shows us something remarkable: we're not just building more powerful AI systems; we're reshaping how humans and machines will interact for generations to come. The pieces we've examined, from the intricacies of model architecture to the challenges of deployment, from ethical considerations to future innovations, all point to a crucial understanding: technical excellence alone isn't enough. The true power of LLMs lies in how we guide their development to benefit humanity.

What makes this moment in AI history particularly exciting is that we now have both the technical knowledge and the growing wisdom to shape these technologies thoughtfully. As we've seen throughout this book, the most successful approaches to LLM development combine deep technical understanding with careful consideration of real-world impact. The future ahead is not just about building bigger or faster models - it's about building the right ones, in the right ways, for the right reasons. As we stand at this threshold of a new era in artificial intelligence, we have an unprecedented opportunity to harness these remarkable technologies to expand human knowledge, unleash creativity, and open new frontiers of discovery and innovation.

KEY TAKEAWAYS:

1. The LLM era is upon us, and it promises to reshape the very fabric of how we interact with technology, knowledge, and each other.
2. Harnessing the power of LLMs requires a balanced approach, combining technological innovation with a deep commitment to ethical and responsible development.
3. The future of LLMs lies not just in advancing their capabilities, but in ensuring that these powerful tools serve to enhance human knowledge, creativity, and well-being.

REFLECTIVE PROMPTS:

1. As we stand at the precipice of the LLM era, what are the most pressing challenges and opportunities that researchers, developers, and policymakers must collectively address to ensure these transformative technologies are developed and deployed in a way that benefits all of humanity?
2. The transformative potential of LLMs, as outlined in this chapter, raises important questions about the future of work, education, and human-machine collaboration. How might the integration of these powerful AI systems into various facets of society shape the way we learn, create, and solve problems in the decades to come?
3. The call to action presented in this chapter emphasises the profound responsibility that comes with the development of advanced AI systems like LLMs. What are the specific actions that individuals,

communities, and institutions can take to foster a future where the synergy between human and artificial intelligence propels us towards greater understanding, innovation, and progress?

As we conclude this exploration, the path forward for Large Language Models is clear: to embrace the extraordinary potential of these technologies while navigating the profound responsibilities they bring, shaping a future where the synergy between human and artificial intelligence propels us to new heights of understanding, innovation, and progress.

APPENDICES

These appendices serve as practical companions to the concepts explored throughout this book. From the mathematical foundations discussed in Chapter 1 to the future directions outlined in Chapter 16, these resources provide concrete tools, frameworks, and references for implementing and extending your understanding of Large Language Models. Each appendix is designed to bridge theoretical knowledge with practical application, helping readers transition from understanding to implementation.

APPENDIX A: GLOSSARY OF KEY TERMS

Architectural Terms

Attention Mechanism [Ch. 5, 7]: A neural network component that allows models to dynamically focus on different parts of the input when generating output, crucial for understanding context in language processing.

Transformer [Ch. 5, 7, 16]: A neural network architecture introduced in 2017 that revolutionized NLP through self-attention mechanisms, forming the foundation for modern LLMs.

Embedding [Ch. 3, 5]: Vector representation of words or tokens in a continuous high-dimensional space, fundamental to how LLMs understand language.

Parameter [Ch. 6, 8]: Adjustable values in neural networks that are learned during training, determining the model's ability to process and generate language.

Model Types and Frameworks

Large Language Model (LLM) [Ch. 6]: Advanced AI systems trained on massive text datasets to understand and generate human-like text, typically containing billions of parameters.

Foundation Model [Ch. 6]: Pre-trained AI models that can be adapted to various downstream tasks through fine-tuning or prompting.

BERT (Bidirectional Encoder Representations from Transformers) [Ch. 6, 8]: A transformer-based model that learns bidirectional context, specialised for understanding tasks.

GPT (Generative Pre-trained Transformer) [Ch. 6, 8]: A series of autoregressive language models focused on text generation.

Mixture of Experts (MoE) [Ch. 7, 16]: An architecture where multiple specialised neural networks (experts) handle different aspects of input processing.

Training Concepts

Pre-training [Ch. 8]: Initial training phase where models learn general language understanding from large datasets.

Fine-tuning [Ch. 8]: Process of adapting a pre-trained model to specific tasks or domains through additional training.

Transfer Learning [Ch. 8]: A technique where knowledge from one task is applied to another, fundamental to modern LLM development.

Few-shot Learning [Ch. 6, 14]: Ability to learn new tasks from just a few examples.

Zero-shot Learning [Ch. 6, 14]: Capability to perform tasks without any specific training examples.

Prompt Engineering [Ch. 14]: Practice of designing effective inputs to elicit desired outputs from language models.

Technical Components

Tokenization [Ch. 6]: Process of converting text into smaller units (tokens) that models can process.

Embedding [Ch. 3, 5]: Vector representation of words or tokens in a continuous high-dimensional space.

Parameter [Ch. 6, 8]: Adjustable values in neural networks that are learned during training.

Hidden State [Ch. 5, 14]: Internal representation of information in neural networks between input and output.

Attention Head [Ch. 7]: Individual component in multi-head attention that learns to focus on specific aspects of the input.

Model Behaviours and Features

Hallucination [Ch. 6]: When models generate plausible but factually incorrect information.

Emergence [Ch. 6, 16]: Appearance of capabilities in larger models that weren't explicitly trained for.

Chain-of-Thought [Ch. 14]: Technique where models break down reasoning into step-by-step thinking.

Context Window [Ch. 6]: Maximum length of text a model can process at one time.

Temperature [Ch. 6]: Parameter controlling randomness in model outputs.

Optimization and Performance

Quantization [Ch. 9]: Technique to reduce model precision for improved efficiency.

Pruning [Ch. 9]: Removing unnecessary connections in neural networks to reduce size.

Knowledge Distillation [Ch. 9]: Process of transferring knowledge from larger to smaller models.

Gradient Descent [Ch. 5]Optimization algorithm used to train neural networks.

Loss Function [Ch. 5]: Measure of how well a model is performing during training.

Advanced Concepts

Retrieval-Augmented Generation (RAG) [Ch. 13]: Techni combining language models with external knowledge retrieval.

Neural Architecture Search (NAS) [Ch. 16]: Automated process of finding optimal neural network architectures.

Continuous Learning [Ch. 15, 16]: Ability to update model knowledge without full retraining.

Multimodal Learning [Ch. 16]: Processing multiple types of input (text, images, audio, video) simultaneously.

Prompt Tuning [Ch. 14]: Technique of adjusting continuous prompt embeddings rather than model weights.

Infrastructure and Deployment

Model Parallelism [Ch. 9, 12]: Distributing model components across multiple computing devices.

Pipeline Parallelism [Ch. 12]: Processing different stages of model computation in parallel.

KV Cache [Ch. 12]: Memory optimization technique for storing key-value pairs during generation.

Tensor Parallelism [Ch. 12]: Splitting individual tensors across devices for parallel processing.

Inference Optimization [Ch. 12]: Techniques to improve model performance during deployment.

Evaluation and Safety

Perplexity [Ch. 10]: Measure of how well a model predicts text sequences.

ROUGE Score [Ch. 10]: Metric for evaluating generated text quality.

BLEU Score [Ch. 10]: Metric primarily used for evaluating machine translation.

Alignment [Ch. 11]: Ensuring model outputs match human values and intentions.

Bias [Ch. 11]: Systematic errors in model outputs reflecting training data biases.

APPENDIX B: LLM DOWNSTREAM TASKS AND EVALUATION MATRIC

LLM Evaluation Task Categories and Types

The following task categories and metrics directly relate to the evaluation frameworks discussed in Chapter 10 and the deployment considerations from Chapter 12. They provide practical benchmarks for assessing model performance across different applications and use cases.

Category	Task Type	Description	Key Benchmarks	Primary Metrics
Understanding Tasks	These tasks form the foundation of model evaluation discussed in Chapter 10. When implementing these benchmarks, consider the trade-offs between different metrics based on your specific use case and deployment requirements (Chapter 12).			
	Natural Language Inference	Determine logical relationships between sentences	- SNLI - MultiNLI - XNLI	- Accuracy - F1 Score
	Reading Comprehension	Extract information from passages	- SQuAD - RACE - CoQA	- Exact Match - F1 Score
	Commonsense Reasoning	Make common-sense inferences	- SWAG - CommonsenseQA - Winograd	- Accuracy - Multiple Choice Score
	Semantic Similarity	Assess meaning similarity between texts	- STS-B - SICK - MRPC	-Pearson/ Spearman Correlation - Accuracy
Classification Tasks	These metrics connect directly to the generation capabilities explored in Chapters 8 and 9. Consider combining multiple metrics for a more comprehensive evaluation of generative performance.			
	Sentiment Analysis	Determine text sentiment	- SST-2/3 - IMDB - Yelp	- Accuracy - F1 Score
	Topic Classification	Categorise text by topic	- AG News - DBPedia - Yahoo Answers	- Accuracy - Macro F1
	Intent Classification	Identify user intentions	- CLINC150 - SNIPS - TOP	- Accuracy - Intent F1

	Fact Verification	Verify factual claims	- FEVER - VITAMINC - HoVer	- FEVER Score - Accuracy
Generation Tasks	These tasks evaluate the model's ability to generate human-like text, a key capability discussed in Chapters 8 and 9.			
	Text Summarization	Generate concise summaries	- CNN/DailyMail - XSum - SAMSum	- ROUGE Scores - BERTScore
	Machine Translation	Translate between languages	- WMT - IWSLT - OPUS	- BLEU - METEOR - chrF
	Dialogue Generation	Generate conversational responses	- PersonaChat - MultiWOZ - DailyDialog	- Response Quality - Engagement
	Story Generation	Create narrative content	- WritingPrompts - ROCStories - STORGE	- Narrative Quality - Coherence
Information Extraction	These tasks assess the model's ability to extract structured information from unstructured text, a crucial skill for many applications discussed in Chapter 12.			
	Named Entity Recognition	Identify and classify entities	- CoNLL-2003 - OntoNotes - ACE	- Precision/Recall - F1 Score
	Relation Extraction	Identify relationships between entities	- TACRED - SemEval - FewRel	- Precision/Recall - F1 Score
	Event Extraction	Detect and classify events	- ACE - ERE - MAVEN	- Event F1 - Trigger F1
	Coreference Resolution	Link mentions of the same entity	- OntoNotes - GAP - PreCo	- CoNLL F1 - MUC Score
Specialised Tasks	These tasks evaluate model performance on domain-specific applications, connecting to the specialised deployment scenarios discussed in Chapter 12.			
	Code Understanding	Comprehend programming code	- CodeXGLUE - APPS - HumanEval	- Pass@k - BLEU
	Mathematical Reasoning	Solve math problems	- MATH - GSM8K - MATHQA	- Solution Accuracy - Reasoning Steps
	Visual Language Tasks	Process text with images	- VQA - NLVR2 - Visual7W	- Accuracy - CLIP Score
	Multimodal Generation	Generate text from multiple modalities	- MS-COCO - Visual Storytelling - Image Chat	- BLEU - Human Evaluation
Meta-Learning Tasks	These tasks assess the model's ability to learn and adapt, key capabilities for future LLM development discussed in Chapter 16.			
	Few-shot Learning	Learn from limited examples	- FewGLUE - CrossFit - FLEX	- Adaptation Score - Few-shot Accuracy
	Zero-shot Learning	Perform without task-specific training	- GPT-3 Evaluation - BLOOM Bench - CrossFit	- Zero-shot Accuracy - Transfer Score
	Instruction Following	Follow natural language instructions	- FLAN - Natural Instructions - Super-Natural Instructions	- Instruction Score - Completion Quality

The hierarchy of LLM evaluation tasks reflects the progression from fundamental language understanding to complex reasoning and generation capabilities. Tasks are organised into categories that build upon each other: Understanding Tasks form the foundation, followed by Classification Tasks that demonstrate discrimination ability, Generation Tasks that test creative and constructive capabilities, Information Extraction Tasks that assess detailed comprehension, and finally Specialised and Meta-Learning Tasks that evaluate advanced cognitive abilities. This organisation helps practitioners systematically evaluate LLM capabilities across different complexity levels and use cases.

APPENDIX C: IMPLEMENTING LLM ARCHITECTURES: TOOLS AND LIBRARIES

For those interested in implementing their own LLM architectures or experimenting with existing ones, several powerful libraries and frameworks are available. This section will provide an overview of some popular tools and offer implementation insights for aspiring LLM architects.

Popular open-source Libraries for LLM Implementation

The following tools and libraries support the architectural patterns introduced in Chapter 7 and the optimization strategies from Chapter 9. Each tool offers different advantages for specific deployment scenarios (Chapter 12) and supports various aspects of responsible AI development (Chapter 11).

Library	Supplier	Category	Key Strengths	When & Why to Use
Transformers	Hugging Face	Model Hub & Implementation	• Extensive pre-trained model collection • Easy model fine-tuning • Strong community support	• When you need quick access to pre-trained models • For NLP tasks with minimal setup • When community support is crucial
JAX	Google	ML Framework	• Hardware acceleration • Automatic differentiation • Function transformations	• For research implementations • When performance is critical • For complex mathematical computations
PyTorch	Meta	Deep Learning Framework	• Dynamic computational graphs • Pythonic interface • Rich ecosystem	• For research and prototyping • When flexibility is needed • For academic projects
TensorFlow	Google	Deep Learning Framework	• Production deployment • Enterprise support • TensorBoard visualisation	• For production deployment • When enterprise support is needed • For large-scale applications
DeepSpeed	Microsoft	Training Optimization	• Model parallelism • Memory optimisation • Training acceleration	• For training very large models • When memory optimization is crucial • For distributed training setups
Megatron	NVIDIA	Large-scale Training	• Model parallelism • Multi-GPU optimization • Training efficiency	• For training billion+ parameter models • When using multiple GPUs • For scalable model training
ONNX	Microsoft, Meta	Model Interoperability	• Cross-platform compatibility. • Model optimisation • Runtime efficiency.	• For deploying across different platforms • When model portability is needed • For production optimisation
Triton	OpenAI	GPU Programming	• Custom CUDA kernels • Performance optimisation • Hardware flexibility	• For custom GPU operations. • When maximum performance is needed • For specialised hardware optimizations

Keras	Google	High-level API	• User-friendly interface • Quick prototyping • Multi-backend support	• For beginners in deep learning. • Quick prototyping • When simplicity is a priority
FastAI	Fast.ai	High-level Framework	• Best practices built in • Quick experimentation • Teaching focus	• For rapid prototyping • Learning deep learning • When following best practices is crucial

Implementation Considerations

Practice Category	Key Components	Tools/Libraries	Implementation Benefits
Modular Design	• Attention mechanisms. • Feed-forward layers • Component separation.	N/A	• Easy experimentation • Flexible configuration • Better maintainability
Efficient Data Loading	• Lazy loading • Caching mechanisms	• WebDataset • Data loaders	• Reduced memory usage • Faster data processing • Better scalability
Distributed Training.	• Multi-GPU support • Parallel processing	• PyTorch DistributedDataParallel • Horovod	• Faster training time • Better resource utilisation • Scalable training
Mixed Precision Training	• FP16/FP32 mix • Automatic precision handling	• NVIDIA Apex • PyTorch AMP	• Reduced memory usage. • Increased training speed. • Hardware optimisation
Checkpointing	• Model state saving • Gradient checkpointing	• Built-in framework tools • Custom implementations	• Training resumption • Memory optimisation • Progress preservation
Monitoring and Visualization	• Training metrics • Performance tracking	• TensorBoard • Weights & Biases	• Real-time monitoring • Better debugging • Progress tracking

APPENDIX D: RESPONSES TO THE REFLECTIVE PROMPTS

CHAPTER 1

Initial Reflective Prompt: "The quick brown fox jumps over the lazy dog. What mathematical concept allows computers to process and understand human language in ways that traditional rule-based systems cannot?"

Response: You know, this question points to vector embeddings and high-dimensional spaces. Think of it like giving each word a unique location in a vast mathematical space - much more flexible than strict rules. When we convert words into these mathematical representations (vectors), we can capture relationships between words by measuring distances and directions between them. For instance, "king" minus "man" plus "woman" could point to "queen" in this space. Pretty neat, right?

End-of-Chapter Reflective Prompts:

1. "How do the mathematical representations explored in this chapter enable LLMs to process and understand human language in ways that traditional rule-based systems cannot?"

Response: Imagine going from having a strict cookbook (rule-based systems) to understanding cooking by recognizing patterns and relationships between ingredients (mathematical representations). These vector spaces allow models to capture subtle meanings, contextual relationships, and even analogies in ways that simple if-then rules never could. It's like giving the computer a rich, multidimensional understanding of language rather than a rigid set of instructions.

2. "What are the potential limitations of modelling language purely through statistical patterns and probability distributions? How might these limitations be addressed in future developments?"

Response: Think of it like learning a language just by watching movies without ever interacting with native speakers. You might pick up patterns and correlations, but miss deeper understanding. Statistical patterns can't always capture causation, common sense, or real-world knowledge. Future systems might need to combine these statistical approaches with structured knowledge bases or better reasoning mechanisms - kind of like complementing movie-watching with actual conversation practice.

3. "What ethical considerations arise from the heavy reliance on optimization techniques like gradient descent when training large-scale AI systems?"

Response: This is like teaching a child by exposing them to certain books and media - they'll absorb whatever patterns and biases exist in that material. When we use gradient descent to optimize these massive models, they might learn and amplify societal biases present in the training data. We need to be mindful about data selection, evaluation metrics, and how we define "optimal" behaviour. It's crucial to consider not just what the models can learn, but what they should learn.

CHAPTER 2

Initial Reflective Prompt: "A human brain analyses language using billions of neurons yet consumes less power than a light bulb, while Large Language Models require massive computing resources to achieve similar capabilities. What can the elegant design of biological neural networks teach us about building more efficient and capable artificial intelligence systems?"

Response: Think about this - our brain is like a super-efficient smartphone that runs for decades on a tiny battery, while current AI systems are like massive supercomputers needing enormous power plants! The brain achieves this through clever parallel processing, selective activation (not all neurons fire at once), and a brilliant chemical signalling system. These biological design principles could inspire more energy-efficient AI architectures.

End-of-Chapter Reflective Prompts:

1. "The brain processes language with remarkable efficiency using mechanisms fundamentally different from those in LLMs. How might understanding these differences influence the development of more efficient AI architectures?"

Response: You see, the brain uses a fascinating mix of electrical and chemical signals, with neurons that can strengthen or weaken their connections over time. It's like having a network that rewires itself constantly for maximum efficiency. Understanding these mechanisms could help us design AI systems that use more localized, adaptive processing instead of brute-force computation. Imagine AI chips that mimic the brain's sparse activation patterns - only using energy when absolutely necessary!

2. "As LLMs continue to scale, what lessons from biological neural networks might become increasingly relevant for addressing challenges of efficiency and adaptability?"

Response: Consider how your brain doesn't need to process everything at maximum power all the time. It uses different regions for different tasks, adapts to new information, and balances energy use beautifully. As our AI models get bigger, we could learn from this biological approach - maybe implementing more specialized subsystems, dynamic resource allocation, and better energy management. It's like learning to run a marathon instead of just using more powerful muscles!

3. "The brain's ability to learn continuously and adapt from limited examples stands in stark contrast to current LLM training approaches. How might these biological insights inform the development of more flexible and efficient learning systems?"

Response: This is fascinating - your brain learns from every conversation, every experience, without needing massive retraining sessions. It's like the difference between learning a language by living in a country versus memorizing an entire dictionary at once! Understanding how biological networks achieve this continuous, efficient learning could help us develop AI systems that learn more naturally and adaptively, perhaps with incremental updates and better memory consolidation mechanisms.

CHAPTER 3

Initial Reflective Prompt: "Imagine a book with pages of geometric shapes. How do the properties of these shapes reflect the way humans understand and reason about language?"

Response: Think of it like this - just as shapes can be close or far apart, similar or different, overlap or be completely separate, our understanding of words works the same way! When we think of "dog" and "cat," they're like shapes that are close together (both pets) but not identical. Meanwhile, "coffee" and "skyscraper" are like shapes far apart because they're quite unrelated. This geometric way of thinking about meaning is exactly how modern AI systems represent language!

End-of-Chapter Reflective Prompts:

1. "How do the geometric properties of embedding spaces, such as similarity and analogy, reflect the way humans understand and reason about language? What are the implications of this connection for developing more human-like AI systems?"

Response: You know how we naturally understand that "king" is to "man" as "queen" is to "woman"? In embedding spaces, these relationships become actual geometric operations - like walking the same path from "king" to "queen" as from "man" to "woman". This mirrors how our brains make connections and analogies! This suggests that by making AI systems that can represent relationships geometrically, we might be getting closer to how human minds process language.

2. "As LLMs become more sophisticated in their ability to capture nuanced meaning through contextual embeddings, what new challenges might arise in terms of interpretability and transparency?"

Response: Think about how the word "bank" can mean different things - a financial institution or a river bank. Just as it might be hard for us to explain exactly how we know which meaning is correct from context, it's becoming harder to understand exactly how AI systems make these distinctions. As these systems get better at understanding context, we face the challenge of keeping their decision-making process transparent and explainable.

3. "How might the continued evolution of embedding techniques impact the field of knowledge representation and reasoning in artificial intelligence?"

Response: This is like wondering how improving our maps might change how we navigate! As embedding techniques get better at capturing the subtle relationships between concepts, we might see AI systems that can reason more flexibly and creatively, similar to human thinking. Instead of just matching patterns, they might develop deeper understanding of relationships and even abstract concepts.

CHAPTER 4

Initial Reflective Prompt: "The model requires over 700 GB of memory to store its parameters. Explain how the immense scale of Large Language Models highlights the computational challenges in deploying these AI systems."

Response: Think of it like trying to fit an entire library into your backpack! When we're dealing with models that need 700 GB of memory, it's like trying to carry thousands of books at once. This creates huge challenges - not just in terms of storage space, but also in how quickly we can access and use this information. It's similar to how having too many books would make it hard to quickly find the one you need!

End-of-Chapter Reflective Prompts:
1. "What are the trade-offs between memory efficiency and computational complexity when it comes to the design of data structures for LLMs? How might these trade-offs evolve as hardware capabilities continue to improve?"

Response: Imagine you're organizing a massive library. You could either organize books by exact location (using more space but making them faster to find) or use a more compact system that takes longer to locate books. In LLMs, we face similar choices - we can store data in ways that use less memory but require more computation time, or use more memory for faster access. As computers get better, these trade-offs will shift, kind of like how digital libraries changed how we store and access books!

2. "How can the principles of data structure optimization explored in this chapter be applied to other domains of artificial intelligence beyond language processing?"

Response: You know how the techniques we use to efficiently store and process language can also help with other types of data? Think about how compression techniques used for text could also help with storing image features in computer vision, or how efficient memory management could benefit game-playing AI. It's like learning to pack a suitcase efficiently - those skills help whether you're packing clothes, books, or sports equipment!

3. "What are the potential societal implications of developing highly efficient and compact LLM architectures? How might these advancements impact the accessibility and democratisation of advanced AI capabilities?"

Response: This is fascinating to think about! Just as smartphones brought computing power to billions of people, more efficient AI models could make powerful language technology accessible to more people and organizations. Instead of needing a massive data center, maybe future AI could run on personal devices. However, this also raises questions about responsible use and equal access to these technologies - kind of like ensuring everyone has access to education, not just those with the most resources.

CHAPTER 5

Initial Reflective Prompt: "Consider a neural network with three hidden layers. Describe how the architectural choices, such as activation functions and optimization algorithms, reflect the fundamental principles of information processing in the human brain."

Response: Think about how your brain processes information in layers - from basic sensory input to complex thoughts. Similarly, neural networks use multiple layers that transform data from simple features to complex understanding. Just as your brain uses chemical signals to activate neurons, artificial neural networks use activation functions to determine when neurons should "fire." The optimization process is like your brain learning from experience, adjusting neural connections to get better at tasks over time!

End-of-Chapter Reflective Prompts:

1. "How do the architectural choices in neural networks, such as the selection of activation functions and optimization algorithms, reflect the fundamental principles of information processing in the human brain? What insights can be gained from this connection?"

Response: You know how your brain might get overwhelmed if every neuron fired at once? That's why we have activation functions like ReLU that help neural networks be selective about what information to pass forward. The way we train these networks through optimization algorithms mirrors how our brains learn through repeated exposure and feedback. This parallel helps us design better AI systems by understanding what makes biological learning so effective!

2. "As neural network architectures become increasingly complex, what are the potential challenges in maintaining interpretability and transparency? How might future developments address these concerns?"

Response: This is like trying to understand how a brain makes decisions - as networks get more complex, it becomes harder to trace exactly why they make certain choices. Just as we can't easily explain how we recognize a friend's face, deep neural networks often can't "explain" their decisions in human terms. Future developments might focus on building more interpretable architectures or better visualization tools, like having a window into the network's "thought process."

3. "The evolution of sequential processing approaches, from RNNs to Transformers and Mamba, demonstrates a shift in how AI systems handle temporal and contextual information. What are the broader implications of these advancements for AI's ability to mimic human-like reasoning?"

Response: Imagine how you process a conversation - you don't just focus on the current word but understand context from the entire discussion. The evolution from RNNs to Transformers and now Mamba shows how we're getting better at mimicking this natural ability to process information in context. It's fascinating because each new approach brings us closer to how humans naturally handle sequential information, suggesting we might be on the path to more human-like AI reasoning capabilities!

CHAPTER 6

Initial Reflective Prompt: "The LLM has been trained and is ready for deployment. Discuss how the computational and memory demands of these models shape the ethical considerations around their development and deployment, with potential societal implications."

Response: Think about this like building and running a massive power plant. Just as a power plant requires enormous resources to build and operate, LLMs need vast computational power and energy. This raises important ethical questions - who gets access to these powerful tools? What about the environmental impact of running these models? It's like deciding whether to build a power plant that could benefit many but might only be accessible to those with significant resources.

End-of-Chapter Reflective Prompts:
1. "How do the computational and memory demands of LLMs shape the ethical considerations around their development and deployment? What are the potential societal implications of these resource-intensive AI systems?"

Response: You know how only large tech companies can typically afford to build and run these massive models? This creates a kind of 'AI divide' - think of it like having cutting-edge hospitals only in wealthy areas. The high resource demands mean smaller organizations or developing nations might be left behind. We need to consider how to make this technology more accessible while balancing environmental concerns and fair access.

2. "The historical progression of language models demonstrates a shift from rule-based to data-driven approaches. What are the advantages and limitations of each paradigm, and how might future LLMs balance these perspectives?"

Response: This is like comparing learning a language through grammar books (rule-based) versus learning through immersion (data-driven). Rule-based systems are precise but rigid, like following a cookbook exactly. Data-driven approaches are more flexible and natural but can pick up biases from their training data. Future models might combine both - perhaps using data-driven learning while incorporating explicit rules for things like logical reasoning or fact-checking.

3. "As LLMs become more prominent in our daily lives, what are the potential risks and benefits of these systems being integrated into various industries and applications? How can we ensure responsible use?"

Response: Imagine introducing a powerful new tool into society - like when smartphones became ubiquitous. LLMs could revolutionize education, healthcare, and creative work, but they also raise concerns about job displacement, misinformation, and privacy. We need to think carefully about guidelines and safeguards, similar to how we developed regulations for other transformative technologies. It's about maximizing benefits while protecting against potential misuse.

CHAPTER 7

Initial Reflective Prompt: "You are tasked with deploying an LLM in a production environment. Explain the trade-offs between model performance, computational efficiency, and resource requirements, and how they highlight the fundamental challenges in scaling these systems."

Response: Think of deploying an LLM like setting up a restaurant kitchen - you need to balance the quality of food (model performance), cooking speed (computational efficiency), and kitchen resources (hardware requirements). Just as a bigger kitchen with more chefs might cook better food but cost more to run, larger LLMs might perform better but require more computational resources. It's about finding the sweet spot between these factors for your specific needs!

End-of-Chapter Reflective Prompts:

1. "The architectural choices in LLMs, such as the use of attention mechanisms and feed-forward networks, reflect a deeper understanding of how language is processed in the human brain. What insights can be drawn from this connection and how might it inform future developments in artificial general intelligence?"

Response: Just as our brain can focus on different parts of a conversation while maintaining context, attention mechanisms in LLMs allow them to weigh the importance of different words in understanding meaning. This parallel is fascinating because it suggests that mimicking certain aspects of human cognition - like our ability to process information in parallel and maintain context - can lead to more effective AI systems. This might guide us toward building AI that thinks more like humans do!

2. "As LLMs continue to scale in size and complexity, what are the potential implications for their environmental impact in terms of energy consumption and carbon footprint? How can the field of AI address these concerns proactively?"

Response: This is like considering the environmental impact of increasingly larger factories. As LLMs grow bigger, they consume more energy - sometimes as much as a small town! We need to think about more efficient architectures, like how solar panels and wind turbines made energy production greener. Maybe through techniques like sparse attention or more efficient training methods, we can build powerful models that don't require massive energy consumption.

3. "The trade-offs between model performance, computational efficiency, and resource requirements highlight the challenges in deploying LLMs at scale. What creative solutions or alternative approaches might emerge to overcome these fundamental constraints?"

Response: Imagine trying to make a sports car both faster and more fuel-efficient - it requires creative engineering solutions. Similarly, we're seeing innovative approaches in LLM architecture like sparse models (using only necessary parts of the model) or retrieval-augmented models (combining smaller models with external knowledge). The future might bring even more creative solutions, like specialized models for specific tasks or new ways to compress knowledge without losing performance.

CHAPTER 8

Initial Reflective Prompt: "You are training a Large Language Model. Explain how the training techniques, such as self-supervised learning and efficient optimization strategies, enable the development of sophisticated language understanding capabilities in the model."

Response: Think of training an LLM like teaching a child language - but instead of learning from conversations and corrections, the model learns by predicting missing words in billions of sentences. Self-supervised learning allows the model to discover patterns and relationships in language naturally, like how a child learns grammar through exposure rather than explicit rules. The optimization strategies are like finding the most efficient teaching methods - using techniques like distributed learning (multiple teachers working together) and mixed precision (focusing on key details while being more general with others) to help the model learn faster and better.

End-of-Chapter Reflective Prompts:

1. "The training process for LLMs relies heavily on unsupervised learning from large text corpora. What are the potential biases and limitations that could arise from this data-driven approach, and how might they impact real-world applications?"

Response: This is like learning about the world only through books - if those books contain biases or represent limited viewpoints, that's what you'll learn. LLMs trained on internet data might pick up societal biases, outdated information, or miss perspectives from communities with less online presence. Just as a person who learns about the world only through specific sources might develop biased views, an LLM's understanding is limited by its training data.

2. "How might advancements in training efficiency enable the democratization of access to powerful AI systems, and what are the implications for the future of AI research and innovation?"

Response: Think about how the development of smaller, more efficient engines made cars accessible to more people. Similarly, more efficient training techniques could make AI development possible for smaller organizations and researchers, not just tech giants. This could lead to more diverse applications and innovations, like how personal computers sparked a revolution in software development. However, we need to balance this accessibility with responsible development practices and consider the broader societal impacts.

3. "The multi-staged training process, involving pretraining, fine-tuning, and reinforcement learning from human feedback, highlights the complexity of developing LLMs that can reliably and safely interact with humans. What further research and ethical considerations might be necessary to ensure the responsible deployment of these models in sensitive domains, such as healthcare or finance?"

Response: Think of it like training a doctor - first they learn general medicine, then specialize in a specific field, and finally learn through hands-on practice under supervision. When we use LLMs in sensitive areas like healthcare or finance, we need similar careful steps.

We need:

- Strong safety checks to prevent mistakes and catch errors
- Specific training for each field (like healthcare or banking)
- Clear ethical rules about what the AI can and can't do
- Regular testing to make sure the AI stays reliable
- Input from experts in each field to guide the training
- Clear communication about what the AI can and can't handle

It's like having multiple experienced doctors check a new doctor's work - we need multiple layers of verification to ensure these AI systems are safe and reliable in critical situations.

CHAPTER 9

Initial Reflective Prompt: "The LLM you are developing faces constraints in terms of performance, efficiency, and resource requirements. Describe the 'scaling trilemma' faced by the development team and how these trade-offs might evolve in the future."

Response: Think of building an LLM like designing a car - you want it to be fast (performance), fuel-efficient (computational efficiency), and affordable (resource requirements). Just as improving the car's speed often means using more fuel or expensive parts, making an LLM better at tasks usually requires more computing power and resources. With current technology, you typically have to sacrifice one of these aspects to improve the others. However, just as electric cars are changing these traditional car design trade-offs, new AI hardware and smarter algorithms might help us better balance these competing needs in the future.

End-of-Chapter Reflective Prompts:

1. "How might the continued evolution of hardware capabilities, such as specialized AI accelerators, impact the way these trade-offs are navigated in the future?"

Response: Just as the invention of specialized sports car engines revolutionized performance without massive fuel consumption, new AI chips might help us run larger models more efficiently. We're seeing promising developments in AI-specific hardware that could make these massive models run faster and use less energy, potentially easing the current trade-offs between power and efficiency.

2. "What are the potential avenues for addressing challenges in parallelization strategies, and how might they influence the overall reliability of large-scale AI systems?"

Response: It's like coordinating a team of chefs in a kitchen - when you add more chefs (parallel processing), you need systems to ensure they work together smoothly without crashes or mistakes.

Better communication tools between processors, smarter ways to split up tasks, and more robust error recovery systems could make these distributed systems more reliable. This could make large AI models more stable and trustworthy.

3. "How can optimization techniques be applied to other domains of AI beyond language processing, and what are the broader implications for sustainable AI development?"

Response: These techniques are like efficiency tricks that could help any complex system - from image recognition to robotics. For instance, the same methods we use to compress language models could help make computer vision systems more efficient. This could lead to more sustainable AI development across all fields, using less energy and resources while maintaining performance.

CHAPTER 10

Initial Reflective Prompt: "Your team has deployed the LLM, but you need to evaluate its capabilities. Discuss how emerging evaluation approaches, such as adversarial testing and ethical assessments, are crucial for gaining a comprehensive understanding of the model's strengths and limitations."

Response: Think of it like testing a new car - you wouldn't just check its speed on a straight road. You'd want to test it in different weather conditions (adversarial testing), ensure it's safe for all passengers (ethical assessment), and verify it performs well in real-world situations. Similarly, modern LLM evaluation needs to go beyond basic performance metrics to understand how the model behaves in challenging situations, whether it shows biases, and if it's safe and reliable for real-world use.

End-of-Chapter Reflective Prompts:
1. "How might the development of more holistic evaluation frameworks, incorporating aspects like common sense reasoning and real-world application performance, shape the future of LLM assessment?"

Response: Just as we judge human intelligence not just by test scores but by problem-solving ability, creativity, and practical skills, we need broader ways to evaluate AI. Future frameworks might test how well models understand common sense, apply knowledge in practical situations, and adapt to new challenges. This could help us build AI systems that are truly useful and reliable in real-world applications.

2. "What new evaluation paradigms or techniques might emerge to better assess the capabilities and limitations of these advanced AI systems?"

Response: As LLMs get more sophisticated, we'll need smarter ways to test them. We might develop tests that check for deeper understanding rather than just pattern matching, similar to how we evaluate human expertise through complex problem-solving rather than simple memorization. This could include testing for logical reasoning, consistency across different tasks, and ability to explain their thinking.

3. "How can the integration of bias detection, safety testing, and transparency measures into the evaluation process help ensure that LLMs are deployed in a manner that benefits society?"

Response: Think of it like safety testing for new medicines - thorough evaluation before public release helps prevent problems. By building comprehensive testing for biases, safety issues, and transparency into our evaluation process, we can better understand potential risks and benefits before deployment. This helps ensure AI systems are beneficial and trustworthy for everyone, not just technically capable.

CHAPTER 11

Initial Reflective Prompt: "The LLM is ready for deployment, but you need to ensure it operates in an ethical and responsible manner. Outline the key aspects of bias identification and mitigation, privacy and security, and transparency and explainability that must be addressed."

Response: Think of launching an LLM like releasing a powerful medicine - before it goes public, we need thorough safety checks. We must examine if it shows any biases (like favoring certain groups), ensure it protects user privacy (like medical privacy laws), and make its decision-making process clear (like a doctor explaining treatment choices). These checks help ensure the AI system is both powerful and responsible.

End-of-Chapter Reflective Prompts:

1. "How might the principles of responsible AI development shape the future trajectory of LLM research and deployment?"

Response: Just as environmental concerns have shaped car development toward electric vehicles, responsible AI principles are steering LLM development toward more ethical and fair systems. We're seeing researchers focus not just on making models more powerful, but on making them more fair, transparent, and accountable. This could lead to new techniques that balance performance with ethical considerations.

2. "What innovative approaches might emerge to balance the benefits of LLMs with privacy and security concerns?"

Response: Think of it like developing secure banking systems - we need ways to use powerful AI while protecting sensitive information. New techniques like federated learning (where models learn without directly accessing private data) and better encryption methods are emerging. The challenge is making these systems both powerful and secure, like having a bank that's both convenient and safe.

3. "How might the trend toward more transparent AI systems influence public acceptance and adoption of LLM technologies?"

Response: Just as food labels helped build trust in processed foods, making AI systems more explainable could increase public trust. If people can understand how and why AI makes decisions, they might be more willing to adopt these technologies in important areas like healthcare or education. This transparency could shift AI from being seen as a mysterious black box to a trustworthy tool.

CHAPTER 12

Initial Reflective Prompt: "You are tasked with designing the serving architecture for your LLM. Explain how the deployment strategies and architectural patterns highlight the challenges in transitioning powerful AI models from research to production-ready systems."

Response: Think of it like moving from a laboratory experiment to a full-scale factory production. In the lab, you might focus on getting the model to work correctly, but in production, you need to worry about efficiency, reliability, and scale. Just as a factory needs assembly lines and quality control systems, LLM deployment requires careful architecture planning to handle multiple users, maintain performance, and manage resources efficiently.

End-of-Chapter Reflective Prompts:

1. "What are the implications of practical deployment considerations for the pace of innovation and democratization of access to advanced AI capabilities?"

Response: It's like the early days of computers - while research labs had powerful machines, practical limitations made it hard to get them to everyday users. Today's challenge is making powerful AI models accessible despite their huge resource needs. Smart deployment strategies, like model compression and distributed systems, could help make these technologies more widely available, similar to how cloud computing made powerful computing accessible to everyone.

2. "How might advancements in model compression and edge deployment impact environmental sustainability of AI systems?"

Response: This is like developing more fuel-efficient engines - by making models run more efficiently through techniques like quantization and pruning, we can reduce their energy consumption and environmental impact. However, we need to balance this optimization against maintaining model performance, just as car manufacturers balance fuel efficiency with performance.

3. "What are the potential benefits and risks of distributed and modular serving architectures?"

Response: Think of it like building with LEGO blocks versus carving from a single stone. Modular systems are more flexible and easier to fix when something goes wrong, but they also have more potential points of failure. While distributed architectures can make AI systems more reliable and scalable, we need to carefully manage the increased complexity and ensure all parts work together smoothly.

CHAPTER 13

Initial Reflective Prompt: "The LLM is capable, but you want to enhance its knowledge and accuracy. Describe how the integration of external knowledge retrieval with the LLM demonstrates the importance of grounding AI systems in real-world information and context."

Response: Think of it like giving a smart person access to a library. Even the most knowledgeable person can benefit from having reliable reference materials. Similarly, RAG systems allow LLMs to combine their general understanding with specific, up-to-date information from external sources.

This makes responses more accurate and trustworthy, just like how a doctor makes better decisions by consulting both their medical knowledge and a patient's specific records.

End-of-Chapter Reflective Prompts:
1. "How might this approach influence the development of more robust and trustworthy AI assistants?"

Response: Just as a good advisor combines expertise with research, RAG systems allow AI to blend its capabilities with reliable external information. This could lead to AI assistants that not only give answers but can explain where their information comes from, making them more trustworthy and useful for complex tasks.

2. "What are the implications of these trade-offs for the future of knowledge representation in AI?"
Response: It's like balancing speed and accuracy - do you want quick answers or thoroughly researched ones? RAG systems must balance how much information to retrieve, how to process it efficiently, and how to maintain response quality. These decisions will shape how future AI systems handle and use knowledge.

3. "How can these advancements shape the way we interact with and leverage intelligent systems?"
Response: Think of it as evolving from having a smart calculator to having a knowledgeable research assistant. As RAG systems get better at combining AI capabilities with real-world information, they could become powerful tools for enhancing human thinking and decision-making, helping us access and understand complex information more effectively.

CHAPTER 14

Initial Reflective Prompt: "The team wants to optimize the LLM's interactions with users. Discuss how the knowledge of how LLMs 'think' might influence the design of more natural and intuitive human-AI interfaces."
Response: Think of it like learning to communicate with someone from a different culture - understanding how they process information helps us communicate more effectively. By understanding how LLMs handle memory, process context, and generate responses, we can design interfaces that work with their strengths rather than against them. Just as we might adjust our communication style when speaking with someone learning our language, understanding LLM "thinking" helps us create more natural interactions.

End-of-Chapter Reflective Prompts:
1. "How might understanding how LLMs 'think' influence the design of more natural human-AI interfaces?"
Response: Just as knowing how people process information helps us design better user interfaces, understanding LLM behavior helps create more intuitive AI interactions. Instead of forcing users to learn special commands, we can design interfaces that match how LLMs naturally process information, making interactions feel more like natural conversations.

2. "What ethical considerations must be addressed when developing AI agents through prompting techniques?"

Response: When we make AI systems more powerful through better prompting, we need to ensure they're used responsibly. Like giving someone a powerful tool, we need to think about safety, fairness, and potential misuse. This includes ensuring AI responses are truthful, unbiased, and aligned with human values.

3. "How might advances in prompt engineering impact our understanding of human and machine intelligence?"

Response: As we get better at communicating with AI through prompts, we learn more about both machine and human thinking. It's like studying how people learn languages helps us understand human cognition. This might change how we think about intelligence itself and the similarities and differences between human and machine thinking.

CHAPTER 15

Initial Reflective Prompt: "You are building an autonomous LLM Agent. Explain how the emergence of these systems raises fascinating questions about the nature of intelligence and the future of human-AI collaboration."

Response: Think of it like creating a digital assistant that can not only understand and respond, but also plan, learn, and take action on its own. This raises interesting questions about intelligence - when an AI system can plan tasks, use tools, and learn from experience, how does that compare to human intelligence? It's like watching a child grow into a capable collaborator, making us think about what makes intelligence unique and how humans and AI might work together in the future.

End-of-Chapter Reflective Prompts:

1. "How might these advancements influence our understanding of cognition and artificial general intelligence?"

Response: As we build AI systems that can remember, plan, and learn like humans do, it helps us better understand how intelligence works. It's like studying how birds fly helped us understand aerodynamics - by building systems that mimic aspects of human cognition, we learn more about both artificial and natural intelligence.

2. "What are the potential societal implications of autonomous AI collaborators in various domains?"

Response: Just as the introduction of computers transformed many fields, autonomous AI agents could revolutionize areas like healthcare, education, and creative work. Imagine having AI collaborators that can help doctors analyze medical data, provide personalized tutoring, or assist in creative projects. However, we need to carefully consider how this might affect jobs, privacy, and human relationships.

3. "What ethical considerations are necessary for multi-agent systems that benefit humanity?"

Response: When we have multiple AI agents working together, it's like creating a new kind of organization. We need to ensure these systems work towards beneficial goals, respect human values, and operate transparently. Think of it like creating laws and guidelines for a new type of workforce - we need frameworks to ensure these systems help rather than harm society.

CHAPTER 16

Initial Reflective Prompt: "The LLM architecture is evolving. Describe how the revolutionary architectural innovations demonstrate the continued pursuit of more efficient and versatile AI systems."

Response: Think of it like how computers evolved from room-sized machines to powerful smartphones. LLMs are going through similar transformations with innovations like sparse transformers (making them more efficient) and multimodal integration (allowing them to understand different types of information like text, images, and audio). These changes show how we're constantly finding smarter ways to build AI systems that can do more while using fewer resources.

End-of-Chapter Reflective Prompts:

1. "How might these architectural advancements shape the future of hardware-software co-design?"
Response: Just as mobile apps and smartphone hardware evolved together to create better user experiences, new LLM architectures will influence how we design both AI software and hardware. Innovations like sparse transformers might lead to specialized chips that make AI systems faster and more energy-efficient.

2. "What are the potential implications of multimodal capabilities for human-AI interaction?"
Response: Imagine going from text-only chat to having a conversation with an AI that can see, hear, and understand context like humans do. As LLMs become able to process multiple types of information (text, images, audio), they could interact with us more naturally and handle more complex tasks, similar to how smartphones became more useful when they added cameras and voice recognition.

3. "What are the ethical implications of new learning paradigms for real-world applications?"
Response: As AI systems become better at learning and adapting, like humans learning from few examples or continuously updating their knowledge, we need to ensure they do so safely and reliably. It's like developing a new medicine - the ability to adapt and improve is powerful, but we need careful testing and monitoring to prevent unintended consequences.

CHAPTER 17

Initial Reflective Prompt: "As we stand at the precipice of the LLM era, what are the most pressing challenges and opportunities that must be addressed to ensure these transformative technologies benefit all of humanity?"

Response: Think of it like standing at the dawn of the internet age - we can see enormous potential but also significant challenges ahead. Just as the internet transformed society, LLMs could revolutionize how we learn, work, and solve problems. The key is ensuring these benefits reach everyone while addressing concerns about bias, privacy, and responsible use - like creating safety standards for a powerful new tool that everyone will use.

End-of-Chapter Reflective Prompts:

1. "What pressing challenges and opportunities must researchers, developers, and policymakers address to ensure LLMs benefit all of humanity?"

Response: We need to balance rapid technological progress with careful consideration of its impacts. Like developing a new medicine, we need to ensure these powerful tools are both effective and safe. This means addressing technical challenges (like efficiency and reliability) while also tackling social challenges (like fairness and accessibility) to make sure everyone can benefit, not just a privileged few.

2. "How might the integration of LLMs shape learning, creating, and problem-solving in the decades to come?"

Response: Think of how smartphones changed how we communicate and access information. LLMs could similarly transform education (with personalized tutoring), work (with AI collaborators), and creativity (with enhanced tools for expression). But we need to shape this integration thoughtfully to enhance rather than replace human capabilities.

3. "What specific actions can individuals, communities, and institutions take to foster positive human-AI synergy?"

Response: Just as we developed frameworks for responsible internet use, we need to create guidelines and practices for working with AI. This could include education programs to help people understand and use LLMs effectively, policies to ensure responsible development, and community initiatives to share the benefits widely. Everyone has a role in shaping this future.